THE REMAINING TASK OF THE GREAT COMMISSION

& The Spirit-Empowered Movement

Explore These Other Empowered21 Titles

Global Renewal Christianity: Spirit-Empowered Movements Past, Present, and Future. Vinson Synan, Amos Yong, general editors.
   Volume 1: Asia and Oceania.
      ISBN:978–1–62998–688–3
   Volume 2: Latin America with Miguel Álvarez, editor
      ISBN: 978–1–62998–767–5
   Volume 3: Africa, with J. Kwabena Asamoah-Gyadu, editor
      ISBN: 978–1–62998–768–2
   Volume 4: Europe and North America.
      ISBN: 978–1–62998–943–3

The Truth About Grace: Spirit-Empowered Perspectives. Vinson Synan, editor.
   ISBN: 978–1–62999–504–5, softcover; ISBN: 978–62999–505–2, ebook

Human Sexuality & The Holy Spirit: Spirit-Empowered Perspectives.
Wonsuk Ma, Kathaleen Reid-Martinez, Annamarie Hamilton, editors.
   ISBN: 978–1–950971–00–8, softcover; ISBN: 918–1–95071–01–5, ebook

Proclaiming Christ in the Power of the Holy Spirit: Opportunities & Challenges.
Wonsuk Ma, Emmanuel Anim, Rebekah Bled, editors.
   ISBN: 978–1–950971–03–9, softcover; ISBN: 978–950971–05–3, ebook

Good News to the Poor: Spirit-Empowered Responses to Poverty. Wonsuk Ma, Opoku Onyinah, Rebekah Bled, editors.
   ISBN: 978-1-950971-11-4, softcover; ISBN: 978-1-950971-12-1, ebook

THE REMAINING TASK OF THE GREAT COMMISSION
& The Spirit-Empowered Movement

Edited by
Wonsuk Ma *and* **Opoku Onyinah**
Rebekah Bled, *Associate Editor*

ORU
PRESS
Tulsa, Oklahoma USA

The Remaining Task of the Great Commission & the Spirit-Empowered Movement
Copyright © 2023 Oral Roberts University

Published by ORU Press
7777 S. Lewis Ave., Tulsa, OK 74171 USA

ORU.edu/ORUPress

ORU Press is the book-and-journal-publishing division of Oral Roberts University.

All rights reserved. No part of this publication may be reproduced, stored in a retrieval system, or transmitted in any form or by any means without the prior permission of the publisher. Brief quotation in book reviews and in scholarly publications is excepted.

Published in the United States of America with permission from Empowered21, Tulsa, Oklahoma

Empowered21 aims to help shape the future of the global Spirit-empowered movement throughout the world. This kingdom initiative is served by Oral Roberts University, www.oru.edu.

Cover Designer, Jiwon Kim
Project & Copy Editor, Rebekah Bled
Consulting Editor, Mark E. Roberts
Interior Designer & Compositor, Sandra Kimbell

ISBN: 978-1-950971-20-6 (softcover)
ISBN: 978-1-950971-21-3 (ebook)

Printed in the United States of America

Contents

Foreword ix

Acknowledgements xi

Introduction 1
Opoku Onyinah and Wonsuk Ma

Part I: Foundational

1. The Value of Biblical Pneumatology to a Post COVID-19 World 11
   Glenn Balfour

2. For Outsiders and Unbelievers: Paul and the 27
   Spirit-Empowered Witness of the Corinthian Community
   Christopher G. Foster

3. Theology of Spirit-Empowered Witness 45
   Julie C. Ma

4. I and Thou: Rethinking Spirit-Empowered Missions 61
   in South Asia
   Brainerd Prince

Part II: Geographical

5. The Great Commission and Pentecostalism in Southern Africa 79
   Harvey Kwiyani

6. Asian Pentecostal Mission and Spirituality: 97
   The Dual Quests in the Globalized World
   Connie Au

7. Resurrecting Europe's Christian Heritage: 121
   Opportunity for the Spirit-Empowered
   Arto Hämäläinen

8. Focusing on the People of the Margins in Latin America: 141
   A New Approach to Social Concern
   Miguel Alvarez

9. The Unfinished Task in North America 155
   and Its Impact on Spirit-Empowered Christianity
   Daniel D. Isgrigg

Part III: Strategic

10. Home and World Evangelism: Nigerian Church with Islam and Internationalization
    Samson A. Fatokun — 179

11. Low-Income People Discipling the Poor: Low-Fee Christian Schools Fulfilling the Great Commission
    Makonen Getu — 193

12. The Spirit Empowered Mission of Chinese House Churches
    Evan J. Liu — 207

13. God's Mighty Work in the Graveyard of Missions: Transformation Breaking Forth Among the Bhojpuri People of North India
    Victor John, with Dave Coles — 221

14. Extroversion of Worship: Spirit, Worship, and Witnessing
    Thang San Mung — 237

15. The Role of the Holy Spirit in the Great Commission through the Lens of Migration in the Middle East
    Stavros Ignatiou — 251

16. Saturation Church Planting: Towards a New DAWN?
    Raphaël Anzenberger — 265

17. Spirit-Empowered Youth Evangelism with Christians Together: Lessons from *An Tobar Nua*, Ireland
    Tomasz Białokurec — 281

18. Mass Healing Evangelism: The Unique Contribution of the Spirit-Empowered Movement to Evangelism
    Daniel C. King — 301

19. The Impact of Evangelism and Prayer: Pentecostals in Central America, with Emphasis on Guatemala and Honduras
    Mireya Alvarez — 315

20. Missional Spirituality of the Global G12 Network
    Richard Harding and Manuela Castellanos Harding — 331

21. The Stubbornness of the Spirit: A Reflection on the Mission of God in Brazil
    Elizabeth Salazar-Sanzana — 345

22. Let the River Flow: A Study on the Cross-Cultural Church Planting Ministry of a Chinese Spirit-Empowered Church in the United States *Stephen Yeem*	357
23. Spirit-Empowered Internet Evangelism in an Age of Global Individuality *Mark Flattery*	373
Almost, Not Yet, Already: Postscript *Rebekah Bled*	387
Contributors	399
Select Bibliography	405
Name and Subject Index	411
Scripture Index	431

Foreword

Empowered21 has adopted an ambitious goal: "That every person on earth would have an authentic encounter with Jesus Christ through the power and presence of the Holy Spirit…by Pentecost 2033." With about ten years remaining, this book, *The Remaining Task of the Great Commission*, is a substantial contribution to this concerted global effort toward the evangelization of the world. Through its publications of the annual academic gatherings, the Scholars Consultation has strengthened not only the global Spirit-empowered churches, mission organizations, and networks, but also world Christianity. It has taken up a pertinent issue in each consultation: hyper grace (2016), human sexuality (2017), mega cultural forces (2018), poverty (2019), evangelization (2020), and COVID-19 (2021). The books resulting from these consultations are distinct resources offering unique views and experiences from Spirit-empowered perspectives.

Pentecostal-Charismatic churches or the Spirit-empowered movement in the world have a distinct role to play in fulfilling the Great Commission. The third edition of the *World Christian Encyclopedia* (2019) reveals that these churches are growing fastest among the mega-Christian blocks. Thus, the continuing growth of Christianity is largely owed to the evangelistic mission work and church growth among the Spirit-empowered churches. The charismatic segment of several historical denominations is also responsible for slowing or even reversing the dreadful loss of members through the renewal work of the Holy Spirit.

However, the splendid growth of Spirit-empowered Christianity is not without challenges. First of all, the continental pictures are uneven: Africa has been leading the growth, followed by Asia. However, the Western continents lag below the population growth rate. Part 2 of this book reflects on these realities, challenging global networks such as Empowerd21 and the Pentecostal World Fellowship to chart the path toward overall growth. This book represents such coordinated efforts. Secondly, a Spirit-empowered community, which once experienced celebrated strength and dynamism, may go through a life cycle, eventually losing its effectiveness. This is what we observe not only in the West, but also in several urban congregations in the global South. This again requires both North-South, South-South, and North-North interactions. Similarly, the books out of the annual Consultations foster such dialogues and mutual learning. Thirdly, on the global level, we need to test the comfortable observation of Andrew Walls: Christianity moves serially while Islam progressively. Islam's faster and more sustained growth than global Christianity may prove the thesis plausible. While accepting this challenge, global Spirit-empowered communities need to assess their experiences and contest Walls' observation. In my view, Africa holds a promise as Sub-Saharan Christianity has preached the gospel both to Muslims and African religionists.

The Lord of the harvest will return only when everyone has had a chance to hear the good news. Therefore, the people of audacious faith in God through the power of the Holy Spirit should also move in the firm faith that the ultimate purpose of the Spirit's presence is for all the believers to be empowered witnesses (Act 1:8). Thus, I congratulate the editors of the book for their vision and hard work. I am sure that this book is offered to the global Spirit-empowered churches, mission organizations, and countless frontline workers as a valuable resource.

Younghoon Lee, Ph.D.
Senior Pastor, Yoido Full Gospel Church, Seoul, Korea
Member, Global Council of Empowered21

Acknowledgements

The 2020 Scholars Consultation, initially planned as part of Empowered21's global celebration in Jerusalem, turned into an entirely virtual meeting. The efficient IT team of Oral Roberts University, led by Michael Mathews, brilliantly facilitated the Consultation, for which we are deeply grateful. Our special appreciation goes to the presenters to the Consultation and the contributors who joined the book project. The Empowered21 leaders provided exceptional support to make the Consultation and the book a unique "gift" to the global Spirit-empowered communities.

Editors
Easter, 2022

Introduction

Opoku Onyinah and Wonsuk Ma

Biblical Mandate

As God called Abraham and made a covenant with him, the mission of God becomes central in the entire Bible. The content of the covenant announces the redemptive plan of God for all peoples on earth (Gen 12:1–3). This is the beginning of the gospel for all nations (Gal 3:8). The mission of God becomes clear through the life and ministry of our Lord Jesus Christ, especially during the last forty days of his ministry on earth, that is, between his resurrection and ascension. Jesus commands his disciples to "go and make disciples of all of nations"—a command which is referred to as the "Great Commission" (Matt 28:18; see also Mark 16:15; Luke 24:46–49; John 20:21–22). Jesus had earlier told his disciples that he would build his church and the gates of hades would not prevail against it (Matt 16:18). This Great Commission implied that the Church was the extension of God's mission through Jesus to the world; the Church was to be the visible manifestation of God's kingdom on earth. This enormous task would be realized through the empowerment of the Holy Spirit (Acts 1:8).

Over the years, the Church has approached this task of mission from many perspectives. For some, it was getting people saved from eternal damnation, expanding the Church, or getting the world transformed into God's kingdom.[1] Others considered this mission as the activities carried outside the Church's life, seen more in reaching out to geographical regions or a particular group of people, such as Africa, Asia, and Latin America, or the Roma ("gypsies"), the vagrants, or the people in the margins.[2] Still others consider the Church as inclusive in Jesus' commission and thus consider its ministry in threefold dimension — "the Church ministers to God in worship, to the saints in nurture, and to the world in witness."[3]

Against this backdrop, early mission activities have been carried out by both mission agencies and the local church. Much was accomplished through social interventions, such as education, healthcare, and agriculture. However, at the beginning of the twentieth century, the Western church felt that much needed to be done to accomplish world evangelization. At the same time, the church realized that it was entering many challenges in the missionary lands.[4]

This condition provided a good background to the historic World Missionary Conference in Edinburgh in 1910. The spirit of the conference as driven by the Protestant Missionary community, was "The Evangelization of the World in this Generation."[5] A common desire which was also expressed at the meeting was a call to unity among Protestant missionaries. In addition, especially considering the work that the Catholic and the Orthodox churches had done, there was the concern to adopt strategies to deal with the problems in relation to the non-Christian world. This was reflected in the title of the conference, which was "A Consideration of the Problems facing Missionary Societies in the Non-Christian World."[6]

There were about 1,200 delegates in 1910 Edinburgh Conference, of which only eighteen came from non-Western continents.[7] The greatest achievement of the conference was the creation of a Continuation Committee which gave birth to the International Review of Missions and led to the formation of the International Missionary Council in 1921.[8] The 1910 Edinburgh Conference can be considered as having achieved its aim, since it is considered the beginning of the Ecumenical Movement, which created the training platform for future ecumenical leaders. It also began a sense of fellowship for all Christians, including races, nations, and various traditions. Following the 1910 Edinburgh Conference, Africa, Asia, and the Pacific Islands experienced the greatest presence of missionaries. Thus, over 110 years after Edinburgh, we experience in this generation what some scholars consider as a shift in the center of gravity of Christianity from the global North to the global South. The church in Africa, Asia, and Latin America vigorously engage in mission today. Meanwhile there has been a decline of Christianity in the West to the point that now Asia, Africa, Latin America have begun sending missionaries to the West. The Two-Thirds World that was at the receiving end of missionaries and mission's resources from the West are now the "sending agents;" the "mission fields" have become the "mission bases." The face of mission has changed.[9] It is against this backdrop that Empowered21 seeks to find out the remaining task and address it.

2020 Scholars Consultation

The Global Council of Empowered21 prayerfully considered inviting scholars in the movement to reflect on the current state of world evangelization, to identify the remaining task, and to strategize ways to reach the ambitious goal set by the movement. Based on this, Empowered21 Scholars Consultation took place in Tulsa, Oklahoma, from June 1–2, 2020. The Consultation centered on regional studies that reflect on the current state of world evangelization, to identify the remaining task, and to examine new ways to accomplish the audacious goals set by the movement. Regionally based studies covered issues of evangelism, the Great Commission, and discipleship. All studies were conducted by Zoom in two regional sessions: Africa and Europe, and Asia and the Americas. Times were adjusted to accommodate maximum participation.

The four Asian Region studies focused on house churches, church planting among Chinese Americans, and evangelism in South Asia. The three African Region studies focused on Spirit-empowered evangelism strategies among Africans, immigrant populations, and through education. The two Europe Region studies focused on evangelism strategies for post-Christian Europe and opportunities for evangelism of migrant communities. The four Americas Region studies focused on discipleship, mass healing evangelism, and prayer as strategies for reaching North, South, and Central American communities.

The Theme

The organizers prepared the following theme description to aid the presenters at the Consultation and contributors to the book:

> Prayerfully determined by the Global Council of the Empowered21, this theme invites scholars in the movement (and others wishing to help) to reflect on the current state of world evangelization, to identify the remaining task, and to strategize ways to reach the ambitious goal set by the Movement. Recognizing the sovereign work of the Holy Spirit, this Consultation intends to identify the gifts endowed upon the Spirit-Empowered Movement and its faithful stewardship of the unique call for witnessing and the giftedness. Due to the wide scope of the theme and multiple layers of reflections, the process may involve other groups within the Empowered21 movement, such as Evangelism Group, Youth Group, and pastors. The following description of the theme aims to inform

and guide the participants and presenters in their preparation for the consultation and the ensuing book project.

The Empowered21 Movement has set an ambitious goal for world evangelization:

> "Our vision within the Empowered21 network is to unite the global Spirit-empowered movement, connecting nations and generations in the 21st century, so that every individual in the world would have an authentic encounter with Jesus Christ through the power and presence of the Holy Spirit by Pentecost 2033."

The Consultation, which coincides with the Global Congress of Empowered21, recognizes the crucial role which Spirit-Empowered Christianity has played and will be playing toward the realization of the vision as the fastest growing religious movement today.

During the Global Congress, the state of the global church will explore answers to the question, "What is God doing in the Spirit-empowered church around the world?" For the past three years, Empowered21 has partnered with the Center for the Study of Global Christianity at Gordon-Conwell Theological Seminary and Dr. Todd Johnson to conduct a study of Spirit-empowered Christianity around the world. We will be releasing that study at the Global Congress, and Dr. Johnson will be sharing the highlights of the study in the Tuesday afternoon session.

The Consultation envisions various studies to contribute to the theme, but the scope of most studies may be either global, regional (e.g., a continental), areal (e.g., West African), national, or local. The Consultation plans to give its priority attention to the regional and area studies, while the book and the author's presentation will provide a helpful global picture of the movement. With the book made available in advance as a pre-publication form, each study is expected to engage with at least the following questions:

a) What has been the growth trajectory (or lack thereof) in the last quarter or half a century? What were the major contributing factors to the experience, both contextual and theological? Hence, the study may like to investigate the way how the movement with its unique spiritual distinctives engaged with the social challenges to distinguish itself from other Christian families or other religions, giving an evangelistic edge to reach the current level;

b) What is the current state of the Spirit-empowered movement, particularly in the fulfilment of the Great Commission? This assessment is rooted in the previous experience (no. 1) as to how successfully (or disappointingly) the movement negotiated the challenges. The author is also to identify any new challenges, e.g., rapid social changes; and

c) What is the desirable role which the Spirit-empowered sector of the region or area can play towards the vision of 2033? What is the basis for such a possibility, assessing the resources, strength, and opportunities, but also challenges and measures to overcome them? The prospect is for the next quarter or half a century. The author may introduce various initiatives or recommended efforts.

Also, there may be studies dealing with key transversal themes related to the consultation theme. They may include "Women in Evangelism," "Witnessing in Hostile Environment," "Healing and Evangelism," "Reaching the Next Generation," "Technology and Evangelism," "Spirit-empowered Missionary Movement," "Migration and Evangelism," and others.

This intellectual exercise rooted in the reality and state of the Spirit-empowered movement of the area. The crux of each study will be the unique role that the SE Movement can play germinating out of its own distinct theological, spiritual, and missional identity. The study may provide an opportunity to identify the unique (spiritual as well as contextual) gifts. Hence, there may be "foundational" studies covering biblical, theological, missiological, and philosophical layers of the Spirit Empowered Movement's identity. As in all the Consultations, this gathering and the ensuring book project are also intended to be a space for mutual learning. There may be "friends" of the SEM offering their ecclesial or geographical reflection on the fellow Spirit-Empowered communities. The Consultation, therefore, desires to be a space and process through which the participants learn how various Spirit-Empowered communities are working towards world evangelization, and even non-SE participants could provide helpful insights to the movement to fulfil its evangelistic call.

The Book

After the consultation, we commissioned some people to write on specific additional topics. The final outcome of the consultation is what is published in this book, *The Remaining Task of the Great Commission & The Spirit-Empowered Movement*.

The book is divided into three parts, with twenty-three chapters. The authors come from across the globe, with six female authors.

The first section, which consists of three chapters, provides a biblical, theological, and missiological foundation. The first presenter uses 1 Corinthians as a case study to demonstrate how Paul's preaching might have been characterized as Spirit-empowered and how the church in

Corinth might have been a Spirit-empowered witness to unbelievers and outsiders. Using the great effect of the Azusa Street's experience of the Spirit baptism as an example, the presenter shows the importance, need and necessity for the Spirit-empowerment in evangelization. From missiological perspective, the last presenter in this section argues that unless there is an authentic Spirit-empowered relationship between the missionaries and the missionized, the mission work will not bear fruit. These three presentations form the foundation for our reflections.

The second section brings together five regional geographical studies covering Africa, Asia, Europe, Latin America, and North America. Here, the presenters give a general overview of evangelism in the region with special emphasis on the significant contributions that the Spirit-filled and empowered communities have made towards evangelization. They also bring about unique accomplishment as well as strategies that will propel the church to accomplish its mission ahead. This section introduces the reader to the third section which deals with strategies.

The third section, which comprises fifteen chapters, deals with various strategies used to accomplish the success so far and how these can be rejuvenated in the postmodern world for the church to accomplish its unfinished task. The scope of study here includes both local and global levels. The chapters are organized by region, though readers will note that some of the studies encompass more than one geographic locale. In these cases, the editors have placed the study in the region that provides the primary context for the study. For example, one of the studies on Chinese churches is placed with the North American chapters because it examines the church planting strategies of the largest Chinese Christian church in the United States, located in Silicon Valley, in California. In most of these studies, the case study method is used. The presenters covered vital topics including house churches, church planting movements, migration and evangelism, evangelism to Islam-dominated nations, saturation church planting, mass healing evangelism, and Christian School educational evangelism. Other interesting themes dealt with are passionate and prayer evangelism, the Global G12 Network, the new missionary movement in Brazil, youth evangelism, worship and evangelism, and internet evangelism.

Every chapter shows how the Spirit-empowered community is working towards the unfinished task through its own adopted strategy and provides insight into how the Spirit-empowered community can together fulfill the command of the Great Commission. The book is a wake-up call for the Spirit-empowered community to meet the challenges of the unfinished task.

Notes

1 David Bosch, *Transforming Mission: Paradigm Shifts in Theology of Mission* (Maryknoll, NY: Orbis Books, 2001), 389.
2 Leslie Newbigin, *The Open Secret: An Introduction to Theology of Mission*, rev. ed. (Grand Rapids: Eerdmans, 1995), 1.
3 D. A. Carso, ed., *The Church in the Bible and the World* (Exeter: Paternoster, 1987), 15.
4 Brian Stanley, *The World Missionary* Conference, *Edinburgh 1910* (Grand Rapids: Eerdmans, 2009), 16.
5 B. M. Thomas, "Edinburgh 1910 and the International Missionary Council (IMC), with Special Reference to the IMC as Means of Involving Asian and African Christians in Ecumenical Movement up till 1961," in *Federated Faculty for Research in Religion and Culture, Kottayam: The Ecumenical Movement HC* 3a (2015), 3.
6 Thomas, "Edinburgh 1910 and the International Missionary Council," 3.
7 Stanley, *The World Missionary Conference*, 16.
8 Thomas, "Edinburgh 1910 and the International Missionary Council," 9.
9 Stefan Paas, "Mission from Anywhere to Europe: Americans, Africans, and Australians Coming to Amsterdam," *Mission Studies* 32 (2015), 5.

I
Foundational

1 The Value of Biblical Pneumatology to a Post-COVID-19 World

Glenn Balfour

Abstract

Pentecostal theology has a range of distinct features, all of which are expressions of its fundamental pneumatological emphases. These emphases focus especially on the empowering characteristics of the Holy Spirit – the Holy Spirit brings supernatural, positive, and tangible transformation to any and every situation. Pentecostal pneumatology finds its biblical epicenter within the Lukan corpus. Nonetheless, it finds support throughout scripture – the Spirit brings about creation, produces life, causes restoration, gives wisdom, anoints leaders, enables prophecy, and is the source of genuine holiness. Even without recourse to the Lukan corpus, the transforming and empowering work of the Holy Spirit is replete in biblical texts. This has vital relevance for the post-COVID-19 world. What is also apparent repeatedly in scripture is the adaptability of the Holy Spirit to operate in new and unexpected situations. This is evident at Creation, at the Flood, at the Exile, in the Temple destructions, in the advent of the Christ, in salvation, and in the life of the believer. This too has vital relevance for a post-COVID-19 world.

Introduction: Methodology and Terminology

In this chapter we explore the transforming and empowering qualities of the Holy Spirit without recourse to the Lukan corpus.[1] Let me say something about our methodology. We use explicit references to the Spirit of God/Holy Spirit to highlight the activity of the Holy Spirit in the Bible. We do this from the Christian confessional position that the Old Testament (not including the deutero-canonical writings) and the New Testament comprise our scriptures, and that the references to God's Spirit throughout are references to one and the same third member of the Godhead, the Holy Spirit. We also presume the primacy of scripture in our approach to the texts. We are conscious that by focusing on explicit references to the Spirit of God/Holy Spirit, we do not generally take into account implicit references. (The avoidance of explicit references to the Spirit of God in Jeremiah is a particular case in point.) We are also conscious that limiting our scope to explicit references still requires a judgement call about those times the explicit terminology (*ruach/pneuma*) is in fact a reference to the Spirit of God/Holy Spirit. Nonetheless, this gives us more than enough primary source material to draw on.

Let me also say something about our terminology. First, we occasionally use the masculine pronoun for the Holy Spirit. This, however, is not intended to suggest the Spirit is male. Indeed, the use in the Bible of three nouns for the Holy Spirit, each with a different grammatical gender, helps demonstrate that grammatical gender should not be confused for biological gender.[2] Second, we use specifically Christian terminology. In particular, we refer to the "Old Testament" and the "New Testament." We also treat biblical texts through a specifically Christian lens. For example, we refer at times to the "Holy Spirit" in both Testaments and understand this terminology in light of subsequent Christian Trinitarian formulations.[3] This is to acknowledge that our treatment of biblical texts is, I trust, critically aware, but also hermeneutically confessional.

The Role of the Holy Spirit in Creation

The very opening words of the Bible make reference to "the Spirit of God." Just before the activity of creation begins, the Spirit of God is "hovering" over the face of the waters (Gen 1:2).[4] Gerhard von Rad dismisses this single reference to the Spirit's role in creation, arguing instead that Genesis 1:1–2 speaks simply of the "primal chaos" before the activity of creation begins.[5] It is apparent, however, that the rest of the Hebrew Bible does not agree with him. In Job 26:13 we read that God made the heavens fair "by his Spirit;" in Psalm 33:6 the Lord made the hosts of heaven "by the breath of his mouth;" in Psalm 104:30 people are created and the face of the earth is renewed when the Lord sends forth his Spirit; in Isaiah 42:5 the presence of people in creation is the result of the Lord giving them "breath" (*n^{e}shamah*) and "spirit" (*rûach*); and in Jeremiah 10:12–13 God creates all things by his own elemental forces – by his power and by his wisdom (cf. Jer 51:15–16).[6] Moltmann puts it well, "The whole of creation is a fabric woven by the Spirit and is therefore a reality to which the Spirit gives form."[7] So let us take note of this. The Holy Spirit is integrally involved in a pivotal, changing moment in history. The Spirit is involved in the very act of creation!

It is possible to see the Spirit involved in further acts of creation. We see a reversal of creation in the Flood narrative (Gen 6–8), when God's Spirit is removed from everything outside the Ark. The Lord states that his Spirit will not remain in mortals forever – rather, it will be removed in 120 years (6:3).[8] And indeed, after this time the "breath (*rûach*) of life" is removed from everything except for what goes into the Ark (6:17; 7:15, 22). At this point the whole earth returns to the primordial state of "uncreation" as described in Genesis 1:1–2. A "re-creation" is only enacted, moreover, when once again God makes a "wind" (*rûach*) blow over the earth, and the waters subside (8:1; cf. Gen 1:2). It is possible to see the role of God's "breath"/"spirit" again triumphing over the primal watery chaos when it creates an "exodus" through the waters for the Israelites; and for those waters to return when the wind/spirit again moves (Exod 15:8, 10; cf. 10:13, 19; 14:21).

In Isaiah, a "spirit from on high" will be poured out on God's people, and the wilderness will become a fruitful field and forest (32:15). Again, when the Lord restores his people, his Spirit will be poured out on them (44:3). In Ezekiel, God will put his Spirit into his people, and the land that was laid waste will again become like the garden of Eden (36:27, 35). The associated theme of restoration is repeated by the two prophets that return with Zerubbabel and Jeshua to build a second temple. They remind God's people that his Spirit is still with them (Hag 2:5; Zech 6:8). Indeed, the Lord will pour out "a spirit of compassion and supplication" on his people (Zech 12:10). In Jeremiah, conversely, God's removal of his saving presence results in the earth returning to its primal state of being "formless and void" (4:23).[9]

This role of the Holy Spirit in (re-)creation is given further expression in the New Testament. In Paul's letters, the Spirit is again the agent of physical (re-)creation, that is to say, bodily resurrection. The Spirit of God raised Jesus from the dead; he will also give life to our mortal bodies; and our own "bodily redemption" will lead to the freedom from decay for the whole of creation (Rom 8:11, 19, 23). Indeed, this is what makes the Spirit "a deposit, guaranteeing what is to come" (2 Cor 5:5; cf. 1:22). Furthermore, the present pneumatological reality – that we are "in Christ" – means that the "new creation" has already come (2 Cor 5:17).

In John's Gospel the role of the Word of God in creation is understandably given emphasis (1:1–4). Yet the role of the Spirit too in those "born of the Spirit" (3:6–8) is still apparent to see. Both the Father and the Son will make their "home" (*monē*)[10] in the disciples when the disciples receive the Paraclete, the Holy Spirit (14:23, 25–26; cf. 7:37–39). The permanent indwelling of the "other Paraclete" (14:16) – the Holy Spirit, whom one Johannine scholar describes as the "alter-ego of Jesus"[11] – is the source of "[eternal] life" for those who believe (3:16; 20:31). At the moment of Johannine Spirit-reception we see the perfect creation motif, when Jesus "breathes into"[12] his disciples and gives the command, "Receive [the] Holy Spirit" (20:22).[13]

What does all this mean for a Pentecostal response to a post-COVID-19 world? It surely means that we need to replicate the creative role of the Holy Spirit. This has a specific application for those who function in an apostolic role. The barrier-breaking, horizon-defying, unimaginably innovative drives in the apostolic gift make it the foundational gift it is for the church (Eph 2:19). But more than that, the "creative" characteristics of the Holy Spirit need to be seen in all of us. This is not to take on ourselves the divine prerogative of the One who creates *ex nihilo*; but it is to take on ourselves the creativity of the Spirit. Our spiritual DNA, our spiritual identity has creativity, innovation, even inventiveness, already built into it. We need to offer this creativity in the way we serve a post-COVID-19 world.

The Role of the Holy Spirit in Producing Life

Another related activity and function of the Holy Spirit throughout the Bible is to produce life. The first instance of this is when the Lord God breathes the breath of life into the man's nostrils, and he becomes a living being (Gen 2:7).[14] This association between "spirit"/"breath" and "life" appears elsewhere in the Hebrew Bible. (Cf. Gen 6:17; 7:15, 22; Num 16:22; 27:16; Job 12:10; 27:3; 33:4; 34:14; Psalm 104:29; 135:17; 146:4; Eccles 11:5; 12:7; Isa 38:16.) Equally significantly, the point is especially drawn out in the Latter Prophets that "the Spirit of God" also brings back to life. In the truest sense of the word, he brings revival. We see this especially in Ezekiel's vision of the breath of God breathing life into the valley of dry bones (37:5–10). The point is clear: "I will put my Spirit within you, and you shall live" (37:14). Conversely, again, the "un-creation" narrated in Jeremiah 4:19–26 when God's people are removed into exile is as much about the removing of all life, including human life, bird life, and plant life (vv. 25–26).

This language also changes from merely physical revival to metaphysical or spiritual revival. The Lord promises his people, "I will pour water on the thirsty land, and streams on the dry ground; I will pour my Spirit upon your offspring, and my blessing on your descendants" (Isaiah 44:3; cf. 59:21). The Lord will put "a new spirit" within his people (Ezek 11:19; 18:31; 36:26–27; 39:21–29). God's promise to his people is clear: "I will not hide my face any more from them, when I pour out my Spirit upon the house of Israel, declares the LORD God" (39:29). Indeed, a centerpiece of the "chariot mysticism" in Ezekiel is that the Spirit is not geographically bound – God has wheels (!), and his Spirit can go with his people into the land of their exile (See Ezek 1:12, 20, 21; 2:2; 3:12, 14, 24; 8:3; 10:17; 11:1, 5, 24; cf. 37:1; 43:5.) The same sentiment appears in Jeremiah: ". . . I will make a new covenant with the house of Israel and the house of Judah . . . I will put my law within them, and I will write it on their hearts" (31:31, 33; cf. Heb 10:15).

In Psalm 51, David's prayer of repentance, the writer's desperate plea for a revived spirit, a "new and right spirit," is a repeated theme (vv. 10, 11, 12, 17). "Heightened" uses of the Hebrew word for "spirit"/"breath" are, in fact, quite rare in the Psalms. So, its repeated use here is all the more noticeable. The psalmist's plea for God not to take his "Holy Spirit" (v. 11) from him takes on new emphasis when we appreciate how much in the Hebrew Bible the presence of God's Spirit is tantamount to the presence of life. The psalmist will later, and in a way that would sooth the post-exilic people of God, sing a rhetorical note of praise that he can never leave the Lord's Spirit, that is to say, his presence (Psalm 139:7).

This unique quality of the Holy Spirit to bring life, and new life, is continued in the New Testament. The Holy Spirit is central, of course, to the raising of Christ from the dead (Rom 8:11; 1 Tim 3:16). We have already made note of the Holy Spirit as the giver of (eternal) life, but this fits into a wider narrative of the Holy Spirit as the agent of God's salvation. This is a key feature of the Pauline corpus. Our new life in Christ began with the Spirit (Gal 3:2–3, 14; cf. 1 Thess 4:8; Rom 8:10; 2 Cor 3:3). The love of God has been poured into us "by the Holy Spirit" (Rom 5:5; cf. 1 Thess 1:5–6). Indeed, integral to us being God's children is that God sent "the Spirit of his

Son" into our hearts (Gal 4:6; cf. Rom 8:15–16). This is so much the case that we can join in with Son's heart-felt cry, "Abba, Father" (cf. Mark 14:36). Our very identity "in Christ" is that we have "the Spirit," that is to say, "the Spirit of God," that is to say, "the Spirit of Christ" (Rom 8:9; cf. vv. 2, 4–6).[15] The very thing that distinguishes the last Adam from the first Adam, moreover, is that the last Adam is "a life-giving Spirit" (1 Cor 15:45).

Similarly in 1 Corinthians 2:12–15, the reality that we have received "the Spirit who is from God" is what makes us "spiritual" (*pneumatikoi*) rather than "natural" (*psuchikoi*). We see a similar stark contrast in Jude 1:18–19: "natural people" (*psuchikoi*) simply "do not have (the) Spirit." We, on the other hand, should build ourselves up in our most holy faith, "praying in the Holy Spirit" (v. 20). In 1 Peter 4:14 the readers are told that they are blessed even when they are being insulted due to the name of Christ, because "the Spirit of glory and of God" rests on them.[16]

Paul can tell the Corinthian believers that they have been washed, sanctified, and justified in the name of the Lord Jesus Christ and "by the Spirit of our God" (1 Cor 6:11; cf. 12:3). Indeed, Paul's understanding of the believer, "in Christ," as someone that has received the Holy Spirit, is so strong it has practical applications for his own ministry. It means that even when he is physically absent from the Corinthian believers, he is present "in spirit" – "I am with you in spirit, and the power of our Lord Jesus is present" (1 Cor 5:3–5; cf. 6:17; Col 2:5). This is not just a "turn of phrase." Paul's presence "in the Spirit" has dramatic "real time" ramifications.

Similarly in the Johannine corpus, "the Spirit gives life" (John 6:63). So, in typical fulfillment of eschatological hopes regarding the temple, those who believe in Jesus will receive the Spirit (John 7:39). The famous "Paraclete passages" (John 14:15–17, 25–26; 15:26–27; 16:5–16) make it abundantly clear that the Father and the Son will both "abide" (*menō*) in the believer when "the Holy Spirit," "the other Paraclete," comes (cf. 1 John 3:24; 4:4, 13). We have already noted the moment the recently risen Jesus breathes into his disciples and says, "Receive [the] Holy Spirit" (John 20:22).

We should also note the powerful proto-Trinitarian language in the Great Commission in Matthew 28:19. The risen Jesus commands his eleven disciples to make disciples of all nations, "baptizing them in the name of the Father and of the Son and of the Holy Spirit." In other words, all three members of the Godhead are explicitly involved in the life of the disciple from the very outset (1 Cor 12:4–6; 2 Cor 13:14). We could go on, but the point is made. The Holy Spirit produces life! Again, then, the Holy Spirit is integrally involved in pivotal, changing moments: the Spirit is involved in the moment of new life! This post-COVID, potentially "new Iron Curtain" world, is just such a changed context and so, it is one in which we should be both believing for and giving expression to the life-giving qualities of the Spirit, dispensed through a "Spirit-filled" community.

The Role of the Holy Spirit in Empowering

A third role of the Holy Spirit repeated throughout scripture might be described as "empowering." This is evidenced not just in the presence of healings and miracles (a Pentecostal–charismatic emphasis, of course), but in anointing for wisdom and for leadership, and in the process of "sanctification," of a "holy," "set-apart-for-God's-purposes" life.

Pharaoh correlates the leadership skills of Joseph with someone in whom is "the spirit of God" (Gen 41:38). Many years later, another Gentile ruler makes much the same correlation regarding Daniel (Dan 4:8, 9 18; 5:11, 12, 14). The writer, moreover, is sure to back up this correlation (Dan 6:3).[17] The Lord directs Moses to utilize for the constructing of the tabernacle everyone who has ability, that is to say, everyone whom he has filled with "a spirit of wisdom" (Exod 28:3). About Bezalel specifically the Lord says, "I have filled him with divine spirit, with ability, intelligence, and knowledge in every kind of craft" (Exod 31:3; 35:31). Again, many years later, the Lord encourages Zerubbabel with the building of the Second Temple – "Not by might, not by power, but by my Spirit, says the Lord of Hosts" (Zech 4:6).

The association of the Holy Spirit with the presence of wisdom and leadership skills is evident when the Lord tells Moses regarding those who will bear the burden of the people along with him, "I will take some of the spirit that is on you and put it on them" (Num 11:17). Similarly, Joshua is full of "the spirit of wisdom," because Moses had laid his hands on him (Deut 34:9; cf. Num 27:18).[18] Caleb too, the other of the two good spies, is also distinguished because he has "a different spirit" then the ten bad spies (Num 14:24; Job 32:8).

The association of the Spirit with anointing for leadership comes out especially in the book of Judges. The "Spirit of the Lord" is explicitly cited as "coming upon" or "stirring" or even "rushing on" four of the judges/leaders (Othniel: 3:10; Gideon: 6:34; Jephthah: 11:29; Samson: 13:25, 14:6, 19, 15:14). Since these comprise the first named judge and the four given the most space and attention in Judges, this is often seen as paradigmatic (1 Chron 12:18; 2 Chron 15:1; 20:14; 24:20). Much later, the Lord will be "a spirit of justice" to the one who sits in judgement (Isa 28:6). In the opening line about the unnamed figure referred to by Bernhard Duhm as the "Suffering Servant," the Lord declares that he will bring justice to the nations because he has "my spirit" on him (Isa 42:1).

This anointing by the Spirit for leadership comes out too in the anointing of Israel and Judah's kings. David is a particular case in point; and when he is anointed, "the Spirit of the Lord" comes on him mightily (1 Sam 16:13). King David, of course, becomes paradigmatic of the Messiah, God's ultimate earthly ruler. Note the significance of the term "anointed one."[19]

The association of the Spirit with this ultimate ruler on God's behalf is perhaps epitomized in Isaiah 11:2. The recurring theme in this passage is self-evident: "The spirit of the Lord shall rest on him, the spirit of wisdom and understanding, the spirit of counsel and might, the spirit of knowledge and of the fear of the Lord."[20] This theme of anointing by the Spirit in order to dispense God's justice and mercy is picked up again in Isaiah 61:1: "The spirit of the Lord God is upon me, because the Lord has anointed me . . ."[21]

This empowering work of the Holy Spirit takes on many facets in the New Testament. Paul writes that the Holy Spirit intercedes on our behalf "with sighs too deep for words" (Rom 8:26–27; 15:30).[22] He prays for the Roman believers to abound in hope "by the power of the Holy Spirit" (Rom 15:13), and goes on to say that he has won obedience to God from the Gentiles "by the power of signs and wonders, by the power of the Spirit of God" (15:19; cf. v. 16). Similarly in 1 Corinthians 2:4–5, he writes that his words and proclamation were effective because of "a demonstration of the Spirit and of power . . . the power of God" (Heb 2:4; 1 Pet 1:12). In the "deutero-Pauline" letters too, the writer draws on the empowering work of the Holy Spirit (see especially Eph 3:16; 5:18; 6:17–18; cf. 4:3–4; Phil 3:3).

In all three Synoptic Gospels, Jesus tells his disciples they should not worry about what to say when they stand of trial, because it will not be them speaking; rather, the Holy Spirit will direct them (Mark 13:11; Matt 10:20; Luke 12:12).[23] In the fourth Gospel, having told the disciples that they will suffer persecution (16:1–4), Jesus similarly tells them that the Holy Spirit, "the Spirit of Truth,"[24] will continue his work by leading them into all truth (16:12–15).

We should also note that, even though Implicit Logos Christology is a major theme in John's Gospel – i.e., Jesus consistently behaves in the way one would expect the Word of God to behave if he were here, "in flesh" (cf. John 1:14) – the Holy Spirit still plays a vital role in the preparing of Jesus for ministry (see John 1:32–34; 3:34). After all, the most fundamental identity of Jesus remains that he is "the anointed one" (1:17, 41; 20:31). Within the Johannine corpus, the writer's realized eschatological agenda and Temple Replacement language make "abiding presence" a more significant pneumatological theme than "empowerment." Indeed, to that end it is significant that, during the ministry of Jesus the disciples are not "sent" and perform no miracles. This would not fit the writer's pneumatological schema. The disciples do not receive the "other Paraclete" until after Jesus is glorified. This schema makes perfect sense when one thinks of the Holy Spirit as the on-going, "abiding" presence of Jesus (and the Father) in the believer (John 7:39; 14:15–23). After all, how many Jesus-es do you need at once?

There is, however, a remarkable addendum to this. Within the Johannine narrative, when the risen Jesus commands the disciples to receive the Spirit, he does send them, and he send them to do the "greater work" mentioned in John 14:12; he sends them to release people from their sins! (See John 20:22–23.) Now that's what I call empowerment! Here is not the place to get into the myriad of "Pentecostal questions" related to the "Johannine Pentecost." (Going as far back as Theodore of Mopsuestia [c. 350 – 428], these are more often than not concerned with fitting the Johannine corpus into our understanding of the Lukan corpus.) Rather, it is to highlight that the Holy Spirit empowers the believer in the Johannine corpus too![25]

We could leave this here and cut to our paraenesis. Namely, in the twenty-first century, we too need the empowering work of the Holy Spirit to impact our world with the good news of Christ and the kingdom of

God. The biblical text is so rich with this motif, however, it warrants further attention.

Empowerment and Prophecy

The Spirit of God is especially associated with prophecy in the Hebrew Bible. Indeed, some scholars note that the fundamental hallmark of the Spirit's activity is that of "the spirit of prophecy." We see this when the Lord takes some of the power of the Spirit on Moses and puts it on the seventy elders. They prophesy, including the two remaining in the camp. Moses' response to the objections is clear: "Would that all the Lord's people were prophets and that the Lord would put his spirit on them!" (Num 11:25–29).

Balaam too, while an enemy of God's people, prophesies when "the spirit of God" comes on him (Num 24:2). Incidentally, much later Caiaphas, another individual who is not on the side of truth, also brings genuine prophecy (John 11:49–53; cf. 18:14). There is an important lesson to learn from this. We must not assess character by gift. And we must be careful to distinguish the empowering work of the Holy Spirit from the salvific work of the Holy Spirit.[26] Our need for and dependency on the empowering work of the Holy Spirit today make these cautions crucial.

King Saul provides another instance of this. The prophet Samuel says to him, "Then the spirit of the Lord will possess you, and you will prophesy along with [the prophets]; and you will be turned into a different person." And so it proves to be (1 Sam 10:5–12). Much the same thing happens later in Saul's life, while he is seeking to kill David, and to three groups of his men. The Spirit of God comes upon them, and they all prophesy (1 Sam 19:20–24).

In a beautiful poetic moment, King David, the "sweet singer of Israel," opens his final song with the words, "The spirit of the Lord speaks through me; his word is upon my tongue" (2 Sam 23:2).

The Spirit of the Lord is well known for carrying the prophet Elijah away to other locations (1 Kings 18:12). His time on earth, moreover, comes to a dramatic, death-defying end, when the Lord carries him up to heaven in a whirlwind; and for a while the company of prophets searches for where the Spirit of the Lord might have put him down (2 Kings 2:1–16). Much later, the Spirit of the Lord similarly transports the evangelist

Philip to another location (Acts 8:29, 39). The prophet Elisha asks for, and receives, a double share of "the spirit of Elijah" (2 Kings 2:9, 15). Again, much later, this language is alluded to in Luke's Gospel when an angel tells Zechariah that his son, the prophet John the Baptist, will "go on before the Lord, in the spirit and power of Elijah" (Luke 1:17; cf. 16:16).

Right at the start of Ezekiel's call to be a prophet, "[the] Spirit" enters him and raises him to his feet (Ezek 2:2). In Hosea 9:7 the prophet is "the man of the Spirit." In Micah 3:8, the prophet is "filled with power, with the Spirit of the Lord" in order to make his declaration (cf. Neh 9:30; Job 32:18). In Joel 2:28–29, of course, the Lord promises, "Afterwards I will pour out my Spirit on all flesh." The first cited result of this is noteworthy: "Your sons and daughters will prophesy."[27] This same result is cited first (and then repeated) in Peter's speech in Acts 2:17–18. So, prophecy is integral to the fulfilment of the Lord's promise when the disciples are filled with the Holy Spirit and speak in tongues on the Day of Pentecost![28]

Let's move on to the New Testament. The writers of scripture are especially seen as having their prophetic words inspired by the Holy Spirit in the New Testament. We could turn to many passages, but a handful will illustrate our point. Perhaps the most well-known verse is 2 Timothy 3:16: "All scripture is God-breathed. . ."[29] Equally explicit is 2 Peter 1:19–21: "We have the more sure and firm prophetic word," the writer begins. And they continue: "Above all, you must understand that no prophecy of scripture came about by the prophet's own interpretation of things. For. . . prophets, though human, spoke from God as they were carried along by the Holy Spirit" (cf. Matt 22:43; Mark 12:36; Acts 1:16; 4:25; 28:25; Heb 3:7; 9:8; 10:15.)

The writer's phrasing of a similar sentiment in 1 Peter 1:11 is fascinating. They note that the prophets diligently wrote the scriptures, "trying to find out the times and circumstances to which the Spirit of Christ in them was pointing, when he predicted the sufferings of Christ and the glories that would follow." Let us be clear what they are saying. The Spirit of Christ (aka the Holy Spirit: 2 Pet 1:21) was in the Old Testament prophets, empowering them to write about Christ![30]

One particular facet of empowerment in Paul's letters relates to "spiritual gifts." While he mentions spiritual gifts elsewhere (e.g., Rom 1:11), it is not surprising he gives them greatest attention in 1 Corinthians. The

Corinthians (gentile) believers would have brought their experience of the ecstatic and supernatural, especially via the Mystery Religions, etc., into their new faith in Christ (1 Cor 12:2). Here is not the place to study spiritual gifts in depth. All we need note is the necessary involvement of the Holy Spirit in these explicitly supernatural activities in the believing community. It should come as no surprise that the gift of prophecy is singled out for special attention (see 1 Cor 12:4, 7–11, 13; 14:1–3, 12–17; cf. Eph 3:5).

The association of the Holy Spirit with prophecy comes out strongly again in Revelation. John receives his prophecy while his is "in [the] Spirit" (1:10; cf. 4:2; 17:3; 21:10). The message to each of the seven churches is "what the Spirit says to the churches" (2:7: 2:7, 11, 17, 29; 3:6, 13, 22).[31] An angel utters an amazing statement near the end of the revelation: "For the testimony of Jesus is the Spirit of prophecy" (19:10). Right at the end, both the Spirit and the bride cry in unison to Jesus, the Root and the Offspring of David, and the bright Morning Star, "Come!" (22:17).

The point is clear. Prophecy is fundamental hallmark of the empowering work of the Holy Spirit and is core to the role of the church today (Eph 2:20). It reveals the hidden things of the heart, and brings the response, "God is truly among you!" (1 Cor 14:25).[32]

Empowerment and Holiness

There is some development of the Spirit of God in the Hebrew Bible as a source of holiness. Three times reference is made to the "Holy Spirit," or, "spirit of holiness" (Psalm 51:11; Isa 63:10–11),[33] and twice reference is made to God's "Good Spirit" (Neh 9:20; Psalm 143:10).[34] Beyond this, however, it is in the New Testament writings that an explicit link between the Holy Spirit and holiness is most apparent.

In Paul's letters particularly, the indwelling Holy Spirit in the believer creates both the demand and the internal ability for us to lead holy lives. This forms the bulk of his *paraenesis* in Galatians. (See especially 5:16–18, 22–25.) By walking/living/being led[35] "by [the] Spirit," we produce "the fruit of the Spirit" rather than "the works of the flesh." How we choose to live in this respect has stark consequences (6:8; cf. Rom 8:13).

Paul calls us "the spiritual ones" (Gal 6:1); and as such we should, "by [the] Spirit," restore others who are involved in a sin. In a later letter (1 Cor 2:10–16) Paul expounds further on our identity as "spiritual ones" – "we received not the spirit of the world but the Spirit who comes from God" (v. 12).[36] He bemoans, however, the pastoral reality that the Corinthian believers are still "fleshly" (1 Cor 3:1); a stark reminder that as Christians (and as charismatic Christians, to boot!), we can have the Spirit and yet still choose to do the things that please our (old) selves. We can still choose to live fractured, internally contradictory, unholy lives! Take note. We need to "keep in step with the Spirit" in order to have something authentic to offer the contemporary world!

Paul goes on to note that both individually and together, since God's Spirit, the Holy Spirit, is in us, believers are God's "most holy place" (1 Cor 3:16–17; 6:19).[37] This means both that we are holy, separated for God's work, and that we should live holy lives. In 2 Corinthians 3:17–18 we read that "the Spirit of the Lord" brings freedom, and that "we are being transformed"[38] into the Lord's image with ever-increasing glory, which comes from the Lord, who is the Spirit.

In 1 Peter 1:2 the writer refers to their readers as those who have been "sanctified by the Spirit." In the virgin birth narrative in the two later Synoptic Gospels, the effect of the work of the Holy Spirit on Mary is that the one she conceives is holy (Luke 1:35) and will save his people from their sins (Matt 1:21). The point is clear: for our world to be truly impacted by a Spirit-empowered people, it needs to encounter a genuinely holy people of God. This is integral to our mission.

Closing Words

All the above must both form and inform our mission to a post-COVID-19 world. The empowering characteristics of the Spirit, associated especially with new and daunting situations, are far from the exclusive domain of the Lukan corpus. They are embedded in Christian scripture, and so are fundamental to Christian faith and praxis. Nonetheless, the distinct emphasis on the third member of the Godhead among Pentecostal and charismatics means that we of all people should champion them. We of all people, as "people of the Spirit," need to see the moral and missional imperative embedded in biblical pneumatology. This is as relevant today, in an ever-changing world, emerging from a global pandemic, as it has ever been. All this, moreover, is without us turning our attention especially to the single biggest corpus in the New Testament – the Lukan corpus.³⁹ That would require a chapter all of its own!

Notes

1 Recourse to the Lukan corpus would require a chapter of its own.

2 In the Hebrew Bible, the Noun for "spirit"/"wind" is *ruach* (רוּחַ). It is Feminine.
 In the Greek Bible, the Noun for "spirit"/"wind" is *pneuma* (πνεῦμα). It is Neuter.
 Specifically in John's Gospel, a new term for the Holy Spirit is *paraklētos* (παράκλητος). It is Masculine.

3 Some writers prefer the term "Spirit of God" to refer to the Spirit in the Jewish scriptures. This is appropriate. For our purposes, however, we do not wish to suggest any distinction between the Spirit of God in the First Testament and the Holy Spirit in the Second Testament.

4 The NRSV translates this as, "a wind from God swept over the face of the waters." We prefer the more traditional reading. This is partly because the only other time the root of the verb translated here as "hover" appears in the Hebrew Bible is in Deuteronomy 32:11; and there it is used of an eagle hovering over its young.

5 Gerhard von Rad, *Genesis: A Commentary* (Louisville, KY: Westminster John Knox Press, 1972), 49–50.

6 It is noticeable that there is no reference to "the Spirit of God" anywhere in Jeremiah. The scholarly consensus is that the prophet wishes to distance his own message from the messages of the other (false) prophets in the royal court, who are invoking the Spirit to promote their own message (cf. Jer 5:13; 14:13–15; 23:9–40; 1 Kings 22:22–23).

7 Jürgen Moltmann, *God in Creation* (London: SCM Press, 1985), 99.

8 This is one scholarly reading of the reference to 120 years here.

9 This is the only other use in the Hebrew Bible of the term used in Genesis 1:2 – *tōhû vāvōhû* (וְהֹבוּ וְהֹת).

10 The noun appears only here and in John 14:2 in the New Testament. This is realized eschatology!

11 Raymond E. Brown, *The Gospel According to John: Chapters XIII–XXI* (Garden City, NY; Doubleday, 1970), 639.

12 The Greek verb used here for "I breathe in(to)" (*emphusaō*; ἐμφυσάω) is also used in Genesis 2:7 LXX.

13 Some writers see a difference between the anarthrous and non-anarthrous uses of *pneuma* (πνεῦμα) in the New Testament. This is, frankly, difficult to maintain. Either way, we will stick with the NRSV/NIV translations (unless otherwise indicated).

14 The Hebrew word used here is *neshāmāh* (הַנְּשָׁמָה). This word is often used interchangeably with the more frequent word for "breath"/"spirit" in the Hebrew Bible – *rûach* (רוּחַ). Cf. Genesis 7:22; 2 Samuel 22:16; Job 4:9; 27:3–4; 32:8; 33:4; 34:14–15; Psalm 18:15; Isaiah 42:5; 57:16.

15 This theme of the Holy Spirit as the agent of (spiritual) life continues beyond the "uncontested" Pauline letters, e.g., Ephesians 1:13; 2:18, 22; 4:30; 2 Timothy 1:14; Titus 3:5–6.

16 The writer is alluding to Isaiah 11:2 here.

17 This all occurs in the Aramaic section of Daniel (2:4b – 7:28). The Spirit of God is not limited by exile!

18 This is one of only two appearances of the term *rûach* in the whole of Deuteronomy (Deut 2:30).

19 The Hebrew term *māshîaḥ* (מָשִׁיחַ) appears thirty-nine times in the Hebrew Bible. The Greek Septuagint (LXX) renders all these instances as *christos* (χριστός). The sense remains the same – "anointed one."

20 It is possible to count as many as seven spirits here. Some scholars have suggested that this passage is alluded to in the references to "the seven Spirits" in Revelation (see Rev 1:4; 3:1; 4:5; 5:6).

21 It is, perhaps, impossible for any Christian not to recall Jesus invoking this very passage as the mandate for his own ministry in Luke 4:16–21. Of course, this happens following his own anointing (Luke 3:22).

22 Contrary to popular Pentecostal readings, the language here suggests that Paul is not referring to "speaking in tongues." The same probably applies to Ephesians 6:18 and Jude 1:20. What is clear, however, is that the Spirit works with us in our prayers. We are not on our own!

23 In Matthew's Gospel Jesus refers to "the Spirit of your Father" rather than to "the Holy Spirit." As often, the variety of terms used by the (Greek-speaking) writers are noteworthy.

24 In the New Testament this is a uniquely Johannine term (John 14:17; 15:26; 16:13; 1 John 4:6). Interestingly, it also appears in the Dead Sea Scrolls (1QS 3.18 – 4.26).

25 One should also note the poignant statement made by Jesus in John 4:23–24 that the time is coming – surely a reference to the Temple destruction in 70 CE – when the true worshippers will no longer worship the Father in the Temple but "in spirit and truth."

26 One could also use these biblical passages to suggest that an "empowering" by the Holy Spirit is not necessarily concomitant on a "soteriological" reception (Luke 1:15; Acts 10:44).

27 In the Hebrew Bible, the versification is 3:1–2.

28 I have made a few references to the Lukan corpus in the last few paragraphs since they are especially relevant.

29 The Greek adjective *theopneustos* (θεόπνευστος) appears only here in the New Testament. It is easy to see how it is formed from the Greek nouns for "God" (*theos*; θεός) and "Spirit" (*pneuma*; πνεῦμα).

30 Of course, we know that the Holy Spirit is the Spirit of Christ. This is a fundamental part of Christian Systematics. But to see it in "black and white" in scripture is quite breath-taking! (Cf. Rom 8:9; 2 Cor 3:17–18.)

31 The unique reference to "the seven Spirits" (Revelation 1:4; 3:1; 4:5; 5:6) may well have connection with Isaiah 11:2. Either way, it certainly has a connection to "the seven churches" in Revelation 1–3. It is almost as if the "whole" Holy Spirit is given to each of the seven churches!

32 Paul appears to be alluding here to Isaiah 45:14 (and perhaps Zech 8:23).

33 The Hebrew is *rûach qōdesh* (רוּחַ קֹדֶשׁ).

34 Compare the reference to "a new and right spirit" in Psalm 51:10 (12). Perhaps contrast the reference to "a lying spirit" in 1 Kings 22:22–23; 2 Chronicles 18:21–22.

35 The semantic link with the halakhic language of Second Temple Judaism is clear to see.

36 Every New Testament writer uses the verb *lambanō* (λαμβάνω) for when someone "receives" the Holy Spirit.

37 The Greek noun for "temple" here refers to the "inner shrine" – *naos* (ναός).

38 This verb, *metamorphomai* (μεταμορφόμαι), appears elsewhere in the New Testament only in Romans 12:2 and in the transfiguration accounts (Mark 9:2; Matt 17:2).

39 Luke's Gospel and Acts comprise just over 28 percent of the New Testament word-count.

2 For Outsiders and Unbelievers: Paul and the Spirit-Empowered Witness of the Corinthian Community

Christopher G. Foster

Abstract

This study examines, first, how Paul's preaching might be characterized as Spirit-empowered[1] and, second, how the Corinthian *ekklēsia*[2] might have a Spirit-empowered witness to unbelievers and outsiders. Paul established the Corinthian church and recalled that his gospel proclamation of Christ-crucified came "with a demonstration of the Spirit and of power" (1 Cor 2:4).[3] A re-examination of the Spirit's power in the context will help determine its meaning and to what extent this includes preaching, conversion, and the miraculous. Some, as will be noted, have overly restricted the meaning of "power" due to the rhetorical context. Literary and historical context will help show the viability of including miraculous activity in the interpretation. The second part will explore the various ways Corinthian believers might interact with unbelievers and outsiders. In general, Paul advocates for holy, countercultural behavior to bolster the community's reputation and witness. Paul evangelistically targets unbelieving family members of mixed marriages (ch 7) and then unbelievers and outsiders within the worship gatherings (ch 14). The latter highlights the role of Spirit-inspired revelation and the importance of intelligibility when speaking in tongues so that it will not be a negative sign to unbelievers. Instead, intelligible, Spirit-inspired revelation within the community has an evangelistic purpose. These findings have implications for contemporary practice.

Introduction

In pursuit of a biblical concept of Spirit-empowered evangelism, First Corinthians is a fruitful place to begin. In 1 Corinthians 2:4, Paul qualifies that his preaching of the cross comes "with a demonstration of the Spirit and of power" (1 Cor 2:4). In light of commentators restricting the meaning of this phrase to powerful preaching and conversion, a re-exploration of the broader context (e.g., 2 Cor 12:12) will help ascertain if miraculous activity might be included in the interpretation. After this determination, how does Paul instruct the Corinthian *ekklēsia* to witness with the same

Spirit and power to unbelievers and outsiders? The community can offer a Spirit-empowered witness to the mystery of God through communal unity and transformation as well as through intelligible, Spirit-inspired revelation and other demonstrable gifts in corporate worship gatherings. Paul's corrective concerning spiritual utterances, like tongues-speaking, may highlight an evangelistic purpose to them. When gifts of the Spirit are exercised properly and communally, unbelievers and outsiders will declare, "God is really among you" (1 Cor 14:25).

"A Demonstration of the Spirit and of Power"

In 1 Corinthians, Paul addresses a variety of issues that pertain to the unity, sanctification, and witness of the community. He confronts the factionalism within the church by reminding the Corinthian believers of his own call "to proclaim the gospel, not with eloquent wisdom so that the cross of Christ might not be emptied of its power" (1 Cor 1:17b). He reminds them that he proclaimed the mystery[4] of God concerning Christ crucified. He came in weakness (2:3), and he kept to the message of the cross, which he identifies as the power of God (1:18). He states, "My speech (*logos*) and my proclamation (*kērygma*) were not with plausible words of wisdom, but with a demonstration of the Spirit and of power so that your faith might rest not on human wisdom but on the power of God" (2:4–5).

Paul's phrase "a demonstration of the Spirit and power" (*en apodeixei pneumatos kai dynameōs*) is of particular interest to Pentecostals and charismatics (v. 4). Part of this examination is to determine its meaning to see how this might inform the concept of Spirit-empowered evangelism. The context of 1 Corinthians must guide the interpretation. Through his *theologia crucis*, Paul takes an "anti-sophistic" approach to counter the Corinthians' over-esteem of skilled oratory.[5] In the passage, he alludes to Graeco-Roman rhetoric, especially with *apodeixis* (demonstration) and *dynamis* (power) in v. 4.[6] Paul claims a lack of oratorical skill either in plausible words of wisdom or persuasiveness of wisdom.[7] The *apodeixis*, instead of being rhetorical arguments and deductive proofs, has to do with the Spirit and power. The New Testament *hapax legomenon*, *apodeixis*, has a range of meaning from "showing forth" to "arguments in proof" by words.[8] The "proof" contextually poses the opposite of *peithoi sophias* (plausible wisdom): "proof consisting in possession of the Spirit and miracle-working power."[9] Anthony Thiselton clarifies, "The reference to the Holy Spirit contrasts not only with persuasive linguistic styles but more especially with the self-presentation and self-prominence associated with the 'presence' of the sophist."[10] However, a question remains: what does this "proof" or "demonstration" mean?

A look at a prominent early church father will help set up the interpretive challenge. Chrysostom argues for the demonstration to be "signs," such as "dead mean rising to life and devils cast out," rather than words; he further identifies these as "miracles."[11] Interestingly, he then adds the question of why are miracles withheld now with evangelism? Perhaps, other authors will explore this question. Finally, note the decline in miraculous activity by the fourth century.

Is Chrysostom's interpretation of the proof as "miracles" legitimate? Before providing an answer, two issues must be examined.[12] First, Paul directly criticizes that "Jews demand signs (*sēmeia*)" (1:22). Does it logically follow for Paul to turn around and base the demonstration solely on a miraculous sign, a.k.a. power? Paul does not explain the meaning of "signs" in v. 22. In the scriptural background, "signs" refer to "mighty acts of God"[13]—such as cosmological incidents, like the darkening of the sun (cf. Joel 2:30–31) and God's acts in delivering his people from Egypt.[14] The "demand" seemingly errs by putting God to the test (cf. Isa 7:11). Paul presents corroborating proof from the Spirit's powerful action as a natural outgrowth to his preaching of Christ crucified. Christ and the Spirit confirm the gospel through divine demonstration. In no way does this put God to the test. Paul, moreover, has no problem mentioning "signs and wonders" in 2 Corinthians 12:12 as substantiation of his apostolic ministry. If this is the case, then interpreting "power" as miraculous activity would not contradict the passage's argument. Instead, it would complement that his preaching is not by persuasive rhetoric alone.

Second, does Paul's use of the singular, *dynameōs* (power) restrict its meaning? The word *dynamis* has multiple meanings, which could include the rhetorical "capacity to convey thought" or "power that works wonders."[15] Clinton Arnold notes that the plural form of *dynamis* in the New Testament frequently refers to "supernatural acts such as healings of exorcisms, and is normally translated as "miracle;" if Paul intended miracles, then, according to Arnold, he would likely have used the plural.[16] Consequently, some, like Roy Ciampa and Brian Rosner, conclude that the passage does not refer to miracles, signs, and wonders.[17] Gordon Fee appears to concur with this interpretation, but he also contends that miraculous phenomena are commonplace with Paul's evangelism as evident in other Pauline passages (2 Cor 12:12; Rom 15:18–19; Gal 3:1–5).[18] Arnold, however, may have unnecessarily delimited the meaning of the singular. Graham Twelftree makes a convincing case that *dynamis* "on its own could mean miracle" and combined with Holy Spirit could "refer to miracles."[19] Moreover, Paul may have intended a broader range of meaning by "Spirit's power" that might include the miraculous as well as anointed proclamation and converting power.

In this discussion, three further interpretive matters must be acknowledged. First, while Graeco-Roman rhetoric has helped shed light on Paul's argument, one must be careful not to allow a rhetorical lens to become an overly restrictive interpretive scheme that needlessly truncates the meaning of "power" in the passage.[20] Likewise, one must carefully weigh anti-supernatural presuppositions of a Western worldview so as not to interpret away the potential meaning of power. Third, Paul's Jewish worldview as a Pharisee steeped in Second Temple Judaism would affirm an "expectation of the miraculous."[21] With the eschatological fulfillment arriving in Christ and the pouring out of the Holy Spirit, Paul would have anticipated an increase in the miraculous. Additionally, Paul asserts that signs, wonders, and "powers" are part of his prophetic and apostolic calling like the other apostles and early church traditions about Jesus' ministry (2 Cor 12:12).[22]

Now, coming back to the text, what does the passage mean grammatically from the context? The genitives *pneumatos* (Spirit) and *dynameōs* (power) can be variously interpreted. If an objective genitive, the phrase would mean that "God's Spirit and power provide such proof" (NRSV, NASB).[23] A genitive of apposition (epexegetical) would mean "a demonstration consisting in Spirit and power."[24] Since Spirit and power for Paul are almost interchangeable, Paul may have intended a hendiadys "one concept expressed by two words,"[25] which could be "a demonstration of spiritual power" or "of the Spirit's power."[26] A combination of the latter two is more probable. The demonstration or proof consists "of the Spirit's power"—a broad concept in Paul that would incorporate miraculous activity, proclamation, edification, and conversion.[27]

From the context, Paul argues that in the face of his human weakness and lack of sophistry, the power in his preaching comes not through employing oratorical tools but through a *theologia crucis* and the enlivening work of the Holy Spirit, who affects conviction and conversion among his hearers (cf. 1 Cor 4:20).[28] He counters the eloquent Corinthian preachers' *theologia gloria*. Skillful rhetoric and reason alone cannot generate faith; a clear message of Christ crucified along with the power of the Spirit are necessary to affect conversion. This mirrors 1 Thessalonians where he states, "because our message of the gospel came to you not in word only, but also in power and in the Holy Spirit and with full conviction" (1:5). "Full conviction" (*plērophoria*) could also be translated as "assurance," "full certainty," or simply as "fullness."[29] Paul may mean the gospel came in the fullness of the power of God's Spirit—a message and an experience of God's miraculous power.[30] Reception of the gospel was made evident in the transformed lives of the Corinthians, who responded to Paul's preaching of the gospel and experience of the Spirit's power. In Second Corinthians, Paul explains, "you are a letter of Christ, prepared by us, written not with ink but with the Spirit of the living God, not on tablets of stone but on tablets of human hearts" (3:3). Thus, the Corinthian community itself evinces "the manifest action of the Holy Spirit in both preacher and hearer, which resulted in the abundant conversions that followed his [Paul's] preaching, and also to the charisms with which the Spirit-filled the community."[31] The Spirit's power, here, comprises more than conviction and conversion. For example, the following chapter adds Spirit-inspired and anointed words—"taught by the Spirit" (1 Cor 2:13) and charisms (v. 12).

A brief survey of early Pentecostal publications corresponds to this interpretation; the demonstration consists of the tangible presence and power of the Spirit in preaching of God's word that affects conversion and transformation among the hearers.[32] One testimony by Eschel Owens, Y. P. E. president, relays:

> The building was filled with the mighty power and presence of the Holy Ghost. Old-time conviction seized the hearts of people, and they came weeping their way through to God. Several were saved, sanctified, and six filled with the Holy Ghost. Rev. Marks preached Bible holiness with a demonstration of Spirit and power.[33]

Sometimes writers, like Chrysostom, include miracles, healings, and exorcisms in their descriptions of these demonstrations; nonetheless, most see the latter as supplemental to the former.[34]

The context of 1 Corinthians 2:4–5 primarily concerns the Spirit's power in the preaching and conversion with the possibility of some visible miraculous demonstration. Do signs and wonders have a more pronounced role in Paul's evangelistic practice elsewhere in his correspondence, whereby Spirit-empowered witness regularly involves the miraculous? A key passage to the investigation is 2 Corinthians 12:12. In Paul's apostolic defense against the super-apostles, Paul feels driven to boast in a heavenly ascent that ironically only discloses the audible revelation that the Lord's "power is made perfect in weakness" (2 Cor 12:9). In repeating this concomitant theme that goes all the back to 1 Corinthians 1, Paul reinforces his *theologia crucis*. Paul humbly offsets foolish autobiographical boasting or *"Die Narrenrede"*[35] (the fool's speech) of his "visions and revelations of the Lord" (v. 1) with "weaknesses, insults, hardships, persecutions, and calamities for the sake of Christ" (v. 10). At the end of this section, Paul's statement in v. 12 can be examined in two segments. First, he recalls, "The signs of a true apostle were performed among you with utmost patience" (v. 12). These apostolic signs (*ta men sēmeia*) are not exclusively "signs and wonders and mighty works." The required "with utmost patience" (*en pasē hypomonē*) speaks more to Paul's apostolic preaching, life, and suffering. For Paul, Christ crucified has become a paradigmatic example for his own life. Jesus' "access to divine power did not circumvent his need to suffer and die."[36] Paul, likewise, saw divine empowerment in suffering (*pathēmata Christou*, cf. 2 Cor 1:5–7) as central to his apostolic calling and witness: a key apostolic sign. "For whenever I am weak, then I am strong" (v. 10). This extraordinary power does not come from Paul but "belongs to God" (4:7). Additional signs are the "converted and transformed lives of the Corinthian community itself."[37] They are the seal of his apostleship—a living letter (1 Cor 9:2; 2 Cor 3:1–3). In his ministry, Paul also prioritizes the upbuilding of the community (1 Cor 14) and self-deferential love (1 Cor 12–14). Thus, Paul maintains that a Christ-crucified ministry and life are central to true apostleship.[38]

The "signs and wonders and mighty works" in v. 12b appear to be secondary to the apostolic signs. He does not downgrade their importance, nor does he exclude them as some interpreters might on "existential" grounds.[39] Indeed, these form part of his apostolic legitimacy, just not exclusively so. By this, Paul avoids the triumphalism (self-exaltation) promoted by the super-apostles and maintains proper Christlike balance in his ministry. Paul narrates the whole heavenly ascent account to reveal the paradoxical nature of his embodied, Christlike ministry (power in weakness) and to encourage the Corinthian community to do likewise.[40] The "signs and wonders and mighty works" (*sēmeiois te kai terasin kai dynamesin*) performed among them speak to the miraculous. Note this comes after his foolish boasting. The phrase "signs and wonders" (*sēmeiois te kai terasin*) alludes to references in the LXX to the "liberation of the people of Israel during the Exodus,"[41] and the miraculous (cf. Dan 6:28; 2 Thess 2:9).[42] Paul's addition of the plural *dynamesin*, as noted earlier, means "mighty works" or "miracles," which "intensifies the importance of the expression."[43] Jan Lambrecht notes that these three point to the witness of "God's transcendent power" (miracle), "call for attention" due to its "exceptional nature" (wonder), and "refers to a deeper reality" (sign).[44] The dative construction may indicate that the endurance and apostolic signs were accompanied by the miraculous[45] and the passive *kateirgasthē* ("were performed") implies divine action.

Other passages corroborate an ongoing experience of the miraculous (signs, wonders, healings, and exorcisms) in Paul's ministry. In Romans 15:18–19, Paul clarifies that his evangelization of the Gentiles comes "by word and deed, by the power of signs and wonders, by the power of the Spirit of God." Note that Paul acknowledges that signs and wonders and "miracles have been wrought through him" by the power of God's Spirit.[46] These signs and wonders accompany Paul's preaching of the gospel so that it is not by words alone. In another epistle, he contends that God gives his Spirit and works miracles (*energōn dynameis*) among the Galatians by their hearing of faith, not by works of the law (Gal 3:5).[47] Paul was at least present to witness these miracles, if not the person by whom they were enacted. In Acts, numerous signs and wonders, healings, and exorcisms are attributed to Paul and his companions as they spread the gospel from city to city (see Acts 13:4–12; 14:3, 8–10; 15:12; 16:16–18; 19:6, 11–12; 20:7–12 and 28:3–8).[48] As a result of this evidence, one can deduce that the miraculous frequently occurred with Paul's proclamation and demonstration of the gospel.[49]

Spirit-Empowered Witness of the Community

Since Spirit-empowered evangelism for Paul has been laid out from the Corinthian correspondence, the second part of this investigation can proceed. How did evangelism through the Spirit's power function within the Corinthian *ekklēsia*? Proclamation of the gospel for Paul predominantly took place in synagogues, houses, and marketplaces rather than in public platforms designed for the skilled orator. Corinth is no exception (Acts 18). In the Corinthian correspondence, Paul indirectly discloses his perspective of personal evangelism by addressing contingent issues within the community. These center around the reputation and the interaction of the Corinthian community with the immoral of this world. Paul advocates a Christian ethic centered on holy behavior (1 Cor 7:19) within the community, chiefly characterized by self-deferential love for others. He warns against arrogant boasting (3:21; 5:6), carnal actions, factionalism (3:1–23; 11), and participation in immoral activities. Along with vice lists (6:9), Paul specifically addresses members who are fornicating (5:1–13; 10:8), visiting prostitutes (6:13–20), taking other believers to court before unbelievers (6:1–6), eating food sacrificed to idols (8:1–13; 10), and worshipping idols (v. 10). Paul reminds the believers that they are to become who they already are in Christ—washed, sanctified, and justified (6:11). They are no longer to live like the immoral of this world, but "do everything for the glory of God" (10:31). Paul's goal appears to be an evangelistic one. He exhorts them to avoid giving unnecessary offense and instead seek the advantage of others "so that they may be saved" (v. 32). Paul qualifies that they are to be "imitators" of himself, as he imitates Christ (11:1). In other words, the gospel proclamation should be supported by Christlikeness and holy, countercultural behavior.

Paul identifies the potential target audience as Jews, Greeks (10:32), those outside (5:12), unbelievers (6:6; 7:12), and "an unbeliever or outsider" (14:24, cf. 16). Paul does not advocate disassociation from the immoral of the world, "since you would then need to go out of the world" (5:10). Paul identifies them as ones who are "outside" (v. 12). Consequently, behavioral concerns are directed solely at believers within the church; a believer's behavior directly impacts the reputation and witness of the community.

Paul becomes most explicit about evangelism when speaking of unbelievers and outsiders who come within the sphere of the *ekklēsia*.

He does this in two places: mixed marriages (ch. 7) and observers in corporate gatherings (ch. 14). In 1 Corinthians 7:12, Paul addresses the Corinthians' question about mixed marriages: should a believer remain married to an unbelieving spouse? Paul favors staying married as long as the unbelieving spouse consents—Paul hopes for eventual conversion and forbids "mandatory divorce."[50] Some Corinthians saw mixed marriage as problematic and recommended divorce. Some perceived the unbeliever to be a defiling force of uncleanness. The believing spouse, the children, and the *ekklēsia* could become unclean or defiled by the unbeliever. This stance likely comes from traditional Jewish purity concerns and prohibitions against exogamy (Exod 24:15–16; Deut 7:3–4; 31:16; Lev 18). Second Temple Jewish literature exhibits a similar sentiment. For example, the author of *Jubilees* identifies intermarriage as a moral impurity that defiles the sanctuary of the Lord, profanes his holy name, defiles the land, and brings judgment on the whole nation (cf. 41:26).[51] Paul differs in respect to traditional Jewish purity concerns other than the defiling nature of immorality and idolatry by believers within the community (1 Cor 5 and 6). As already noted, Paul does not see contact with unbelievers as bringing contagion into the community (1 Cor 5:9). By his approach, he alleviates the fears of those who may see unbelievers as a potential source of defilement to the community/body of believers (1 Cor 3:16; 6:19; 5:11–13). For Paul, the intermarriage, which happened prior to one spouse converting, is a legal union, whereby the unbelieving spouse and children are sanctified in the believer. This follows Jesus's new paradigm of "contagious holiness."[52] Paul has two concerns: first, a familial concern—for the sake of "unclean" children being made holy and the family's ongoing participation in the community of faith, and second, the potential salvation of the unbelieving spouse and children. These unbelievers for Paul would not necessarily be seen as outsiders, but rather unbelieving insiders who are participants in the community though not full-fledged members.

It must be mentioned that the make-up of the Corinthian community and their family relationships would be quite complex. Margaret MacDonald and Leif Vaage helpfully elucidate the complexities of the social context for "legally licit marriages" in a Greco-Roman city like Corinth. Many different forms of cohabitation existed, from concubinage, slaves, children of slaves, slaves of nonbelievers, and more. No legal capacity for marriage between slaves further complicated the situation. In the house churches, there may be slave families, free, and freed parents.[53] Moreover, masters had the power to separate slave families or use slaves and children for sexual gratification. A person in a slave state could be separated from a spouse, children, or parents at any point. With *paterfamilias*, the male authority figure of a family would have some say in slaves being a believer or not.[54] The realities of these social dynamics with ancient families as well as divorce, widowhood, and remarriage presents a more complex, non-middle class non-Western picture of the nuclear family. Imaginably, this is even a bit closer to some blended-family social dynamics today. With the complexities of family life and the mixture of social groups, children in the Corinthian congregation could have half-siblings and stepsiblings as well as potentially live in a home other than with their mother. Consequently, when the Corinthian believers assembled for communal worship in a possible two-room dwelling or even a craft shop that could fit around forty people,[55] there would likely be unbelieving family relations in their midst and unrelated outsiders (servants, slaves, co-workers).

Paul seems to maintain a distinction in 1 Corinthians 14 between an outsider (*idiōtai*)[56] and unbelievers (*apistoi*). The outsiders, whom Paul gives a particular place in the assembly (14:16), are not insiders.[57] In verse 23, he writes, "If, therefore, the whole church comes together and all speak in tongues, and outsiders and unbelievers enter, will they not say that you are out of your mind?" Perhaps, unbelievers are relatives (ch 7); outsiders may be unrelated unbelievers who are not sanctified to be familial participants of the faith community. Paul has an evangelistic concern for these unbelievers and outsiders as they witness corporate worship and experience various manifestations of the Holy Spirit.

In 1 Corinthians 12–14, Paul gives corrective and instructive guidance concerning the function of *pneumatika* ("spiritual utterances")[58] (1 Cor 12:1; 14:1) and charismata (gifts) (12:4, 9, 28, 30, 31) within the *ekklēsia*. Through a deliberative rhetorical argument,[59] he contends for "articulate intelligible speech" with Spirit-inspired utterances and godly order (14:26–40) for the dual purpose of evangelism and communal edification (vs. 12, 25–26).[60] If a participant speaks in a tongue without putting it into comprehensible words (interpreting), then the tongue will be a sign to unbelievers. Paul's usage of Isaiah 28:11–12 indicates that uninterpreted tongues are a sign of judgment to unbelievers because they are kept ignorant by a lack of intelligibility. His point seems to be that other tongues[61] did not lead the Israelites to obedience. Neither will tongues-speaking in Corinth lead sinners to obedience;[62] thus, he considers the "missionary effect" of tongues (*glōssai*).[63] Unbelievers and outsiders cannot understand, nor can they interpret tongues speaking. Subsequently, the believing community will be deemed out of their minds (14:23). Uninterpreted tongues will "serve to harden and thus condemn the unbeliever."[64] Paul calls this childish (v. 20). He argues, instead, for the priority of prophesy (intelligible revelation) over uninterpreted tongues-speaking so that the community of faith may be edified, and unbelievers and outsiders will be convicted. Conversely, interpreted tongues and prophecy reverse the precarious effect of the "sign" of tongues to unbelievers and instead brings the redemptive and convicting judgment of God, which leads to repentance.[65] Paul further clarifies how intelligible, Spirit-inspired revelation can affect conversion; "But if all prophesy, an unbeliever or outsider who enters is reproved by all and called to account by all. After the secrets of the unbeliever's heart are disclosed [judged[66]], that person will bow down before God and worship him, declaring, 'God is really among [in] you[67]'" (1 Cor 14:24–25). Paul's hope is for the individual to turn to the Lord (Christ), so that "the veil is removed" (2 Cor 3:16). This way, unbelievers and the uninstructed can see the "glorious light of the gospel of the glory of Christ" (4:4).

It is noteworthy that Paul encourages communal participation in the Spirit[68] rather than an authoritative group or a leader solely operating in the gifts. He democratizes Spirit-inspired revelation, which could come through various participants ("all" v. 23) in a diversity of ways. He instructs, "When you [plural] come together, each one has a hymn, a lesson, a revelation, a tongue, or an interpretation. Let all things be done for building up" (1 Cor 14:26). Like a healthy functioning body (ch 12), a gathering of believers ought to allow room for the Holy Spirit to move through others out of self-deferential love (ch 13). He goes on, "For you can all prophesy one by one, so that all may learn and all be encouraged" (v. 31). Perhaps, evangelism and conversion might blossom in gatherings of believers that allow for communal participation in the Spirit whereby all believers can share Spirit-inspired revelation. The result will be the conversion of unbelievers and outsiders in their midst who recognize God's presence.

In this way, Paul advocates for Spirit-empowered evangelism of unbelievers and outsiders associated with the community of faith. Paul seeks for the Corinthian believers to imitate his proclamation of Christ crucified (2 Cor 4:5). The demonstration of the Spirit's power for the community predominately comes through Spirit-inspired revelation, whether this is "a hymn, a lesson, a revelation, a tongue or an interpretation" (v. 26). Paul's expectation of miraculous activity among the Corinthians remains unabated. His description of various *charismata*, services, workings, and manifestations of the Spirit in chapter 12 include Spirit-inspired speech (vv. 8–11) and miraculous activity. He lists "deeds of power" (*dynameis*) and "gifts of healing" (*charismata iamatōn*), indicating this was common to the community's experience (vv. 28–29). Paul qualifies that for these gifts to be most effective, they must be practiced in self-deferential love for the purpose of edifying others and maintaining godly order within the community of faith—not for spiritual self-interest. This furthers his evangelistic purpose to demonstrate to unbelievers and outsiders the oneness of the community as a reflection of the image of Christ (2 Cor 3:18) and individually as ambassadors of reconciliation (2 Cor 5:18–20). The display of the Spirit's power confirms the power of the gospel and signals that God is with his people.

A Reflection on Contemporary Practice

This two-part investigation presents several challenges to contemporary witness and practice. First, has the proclamation of the gospel retained both the *theologia crucis* of Paul's gospel and tangible demonstrations of the Spirit's power? If not, how can both be restored? Second, churches would do well to reconsider the "missionary effect" of intelligible, Spirit-inspired revelation for the unbelievers and outsiders in their midst. Interpreted tongues-speaking has an important evangelistic role if Paul's admonition for comprehensibility is followed. Third, a necessary shift to communal participation in the Spirit, whereby all believers are encouraged and trained to hear and share Spirit-inspired revelation, will help fulfill the dual purpose of mutual edification and evangelism within worship gatherings. The democratization of charisms may prove challenging at first, but spiritual manifestations practiced with godly order evince God's presence in and among gathered believers and help foster a healthier and more loving body of Christ—another vital witness to the world.

Notes

1. Spirit-empowered here refers to the power and work of the Holy Spirit through people.
2. The Greek word *ekklēsia*, like in 1 Corinthians 14:19, means gathered assembly or church.
3. Unless otherwise noted, all English scripture references are from the New Revised Standard Version.
4. In 1 Corinthians 2:1, the preferred *mystērion*, "mystery" (𝔓⁴⁶ A C), has a textual variant of martyrion, "witness" (ℵ² B D F G).
5. Bruce W. Winter, *Philo and Paul Among the Sophists: Alexandrian and Corinthians Responses to Julio-Claudian Movement* (Grand Rapids: Eerdmans, 2002), 147–48.
6. Winter, *Philo and Paul*, 148 and 151. See also Dio, Orations 47:22; Philo, De Vita Mosis, 1.16 §95.
7. Two prominent variants allow for either *peithoi sophias*, "plausible wisdom" (𝔓⁴⁶ F G) or *peithois sophias logois*, "persuasive words of wisdom" (ℵ B D).
8. "ἀπόδειξις," LSJ 196.
9. "ἀπόδειξις," Frederick W. Danker, ed., *Greek-English Lexicon of the New Testament and Other Early Christian Literature*, 3rd ed. (Chicago: University of Chicago Press, 2000), 109. This translation, unlike the second edition, seems to argue for something tangible related to miracle-working power.
10. Anthony C. Thiselton, *The First Epistle to the Corinthians: A Commentary on the Greek Text* (Grand Rapids: Eerdmans, 2000), 209.
11. Chrysostom, *Homilies on the First Epistle of St. Paul the Apostle to the Corinthians* 6.3–4 (NPNF1 12:30–31).
12. Frederic Louis Godet, *Commentary on First Corinthians* (Grand Rapids: Kregel Publications, 1977), 129–130.
13. Joseph A. Fitzmyer, *First Corinthians: A New Translation with Introduction and Commentary* (New Haven: Yale University Press, 2008), 158. Scribes and Pharisees demand signs in Mark 8:11; Matt 12:38; Luke 11:16; 29. Signs appears in Exod 7:3; Deut 4:34; 28:46; 34:11; Ps 135:9; Isa 8:18. See also, Karl Rengstorf, "σημεῖον," *Theological Dictionary of the New Testament* 7:200–268, who notes that the signs demanded of Jesus are not miracles (*dynameis*) in the synoptics (235).
14. Graham H. Twelftree, "Paul's Ministry and the Miraculous," *Evangelical Quarterly* 88:3 (2016/17), 230.

15 "δύναμις," Bauer, Danker, Arndt, and Gingrich, *Greek-English Lexicon of the New Testament*, 262.

16 Clinton E. Arnold, "Power, NT Concept of," David N. Freedman et al., eds., *Anchor Bible Dictionary* (New York City: Doubleday, 1992), 5:444–46.

17 Roy E. Ciampa and Brian S. Rosner, *The First Letter to the Corinthians* (Grand Rapids: Eerdmans, 2010), 112.

18 Gordon Fee, *God's Empowering Presence: The Holy Spirit in the Letters of Paul* (Grand Rapids: Baker Academic, 2012), 92; Gordon Fee, *The First Epistle to the Corinthians* (Grand Rapids: Eerdmans, 1987), 95, n. 28.

19 Twelftree, "Paul's Ministry," 225. See also n. 34 and 35 for biblical references in support. From Paul, see Rom 1:4; 15:19; 1 Cor 4:20; 1 Thess 1:5; and 2 Thess 2:9.

20 In this respect, Godet stridently critiques Chrysostom's interpretation of power as miracles: "Such an interpretation, allowable in the infancy of exegesis, should now be no longer possible," *First Corinthians*, 130.

21 Twelftree, "Paul's Ministry," 225.

22 Twelftree, "Paul's Ministry," 223–226.

23 Fitzmyer, *First Corinthians*, 173. Hans Conzelmann argues against the objective genitive and claims this is contrary to Paul's argument concerning the signs Jews demand. He is correct that for Paul, ecstatic phenomena and miracles are "subject to the criterion of the cross." However, the objective genitive does not preclude other demonstrations of the Spirit besides miracles. Instead, Conzelmann argues for a possessive genitive. George W. MacRae, ed., trans. James W. Leitch, *I Corinthians: A Commentary on the First Epistle to the Corinthians* (Philadelphia: Fortress, 1975), 55.

24 David E. Garland, *1 Corinthians* (Grand Rapids: Baker Academic, 2003), 87.

25 C. K. Barrett argues for a plenary objective and hendiadys, *A Commentary on the First Epistle to the Corinthians* (New York: Harper & Row, 1968), 65–66.

26 Garland, *1 Corinthians*, 87.

27 Grundmann, "δύναμαι/δύναμις," 311.

28 Timothy H. Lim, "'Not in Persuasive Words of Wisdom, But in the Demonstration of the Spirit and Power'" *Novum Testamentum* 29:2 (1987), 137–149

29 "πληροφορία" Danker, *Greek-English Lexicon*, 827 means fullness in Col 2:2; Heb 6:11; 10:22; Rom 15:29; and 1 Clement 42:3.

30 Twelftree, "Paul's Ministry," 228.

31 George Montague, *First Corinthians* (Grand Rapids: Baker Academic, 2011), 58.

32 *Consortium of Pentecostal Archives* (Springfield, MO: The General Council of the Assemblies of God, 2018) https://pentecostalarchives.org/, accessed May 7, 2021.

33 Eschel Owens, "Revivals and Their Results," *Church of God Evangel* 32:25 (August 16, 1941), 5.

34 Miracles do not necessarily prove the rightness of the content.

35 Hans Windisch, *Der zweite Korintherbrief* (Göttingen: Vandenhoeck & Ruprecht, 1924), 349.

36 Arnold, "Power, NT Concept of," 445.

37 Ralph P. Martin, *2 Corinthians*, 2nd ed. (Grand Rapids, MI: Zondervan, 2014), 633.

38 Martin, *2 Corinthians*, 633.

39 Fee, *God's Empowering Presence*, 389.

40 James B. Wallace, *Snatched into Paradise* (2 Cor 12:1–10): *Paul's Heavenly Journey in the Context of Early Christian Experience* (Berlin: de Gruyter, 2011), 235.

41 Jan Lambrecht, *Second Corinthians* (Collegeville, MN: Liturgical Press, 1999), 212.

42 See Rengstorf, "σημεῖον," 7:200–268.

43 Lambrecht, *Second Corinthians*, 212.

44 Lambrecht, *Second Corinthians*, 212.

45 Martin, *2 Corinthians*, 633.

46 Joseph A. Fitzmyer, *Romans: A New Translation with Introduction and Commentary* (New Haven: Yale University Press, 2008), 713.

47 Miracles cannot be earned but rather come through faith.

48 This study approaches Acts with a hermeneutic that trusts it is a fair representation of Paul's mission activity from Luke's perspective. Jacob Jervell argues that the contingent nature of Paul's letters explains why Acts has more accounts of the miraculous than Paul's letters, "The Signs of an Apostles: Paul's Miracles," in Jacob Jervell, *The Unknown Paul: Essays on Luke-Acts and Early Christian History* (Minneapolis: Augsburg, 1984), 77–95.

49 From these passages, Fee makes a similar case that Paul's converts normally experienced miraculous phenomena, *God's Empowering Presence*, 92. Peter Head agrees that "Paul conceived of his ministry as customarily associated with the miraculous activity of the Holy Spirit," 70. He, however, contends Fee overplays his hand that miracles always occurred with evangelism for Paul. Instead, he concludes that one can only assert that Paul's "preaching was sometimes associated with dramatic miraculous activity." See, "God's Empowering Presence by G. D. Fee: An Extended Review," *Churchman* 111 (1997), 70. It may be best to say that miraculous activity frequently accompanied Paul's evangelism and other Spirit-activity, such as charismata, regularly followed conversion.

50 Stanley E. Porter, "Holiness, Sanctification," Gerald F. Hawthorne, Ralph P. Martin, and Daniel G. Reid, eds., *Dictionary of Paul and His Letters* (Westmont, IL: Intervarsity), 1993, 400. Paul likely does this first due to the Lord's prohibition against divorce (Matt 19:3–12; Mark 10:2–12; Luke 16:18).

51 Yonder M. Gillihan, "Jewish Laws on Illicit Marriage, the Defilement of Offspring, and the Holiness of the Temple: A New Halakic Interpretation of 1 Corinthians 7:14," *Journal of Biblical Literature* 121:4 (2002): 724–44. See also *T. Levi* 9:9–10; Spec 3.5.29; *Jub.* 25:1; 4QMMT; CD 4:12–18; Deut 23:3.

52 Craig L. Blomberg, *Contagious Holiness: Jesus' Meals with Sinners* (Downers Grove: IVP, 2005). Jesus, in like manner, shifts the dynamics of the purity system in his interaction with unclean people. He cleanses the leper rather than being defiled. He cleanses/heals the unclean woman with an issue of blood. The unclean spirits flee before him. In their place, one finds healing, wholeness, soundness of mind, and holiness (cf. Mark 1:40–44; Matt 8:2–3; Luke 5:12–14; Mark 5:25–34, 39–42).

53 David G. Horrell, "Domestic Space and Christian Meetings at Corinth: Imaging New Contexts and the Buildings East of the Theatre," *New Testament Studies* 50 (2004), 349–369. He proposes two-room dwellings for most church meetings rather than large Roman villas, as Murphy-O'Connor supposed.

54 Margaret Y. MacDonald and Leif E. Vaage, "Unclean but Holy Children: Paul's Everyday Quandary in 1 Corinthians 7:14c," *Catholic Biblical Quarterly* 73:3 (2011): 538. See also, Carolyn Osiek and Margaret Y. MacDonald, *Woman's Place: House Churches in Earliest Christianity* (Minneapolis: Fortress Press, 2006), Dale B. Martin, *Slavery as Salvation: The Metaphor of Slavery in Pauline Christianity* (New Haven: Yale University Press, 1990), and Dale B. Martin, "Slave Families and Slaves

in Families," in David L. Balch and Carolyn Osiek, eds., *Early Christian Families in Context: An Interdisciplinary Dialogue* (Grand Rapids: Eerdmans, 2003), 207–30.

55 Peter Oakes, *Reading Romans in Pompeii: Paul's Letter at the Ground Level* (Minneapolis: Fortress Press, 2009).

56 Outsiders will be used, but it could also mean the uninstructed.

57 Thiselton, *Corinthians*, 1115. See also n. 29 and n. 30.

58 Thiselton, *Corinthians*, 1083. This is a more viable translation than "spiritual manifestations" proposed by Howard M. Ervin, *Spirit Baptism: A Biblical Investigation* (Peabody, MA.: Hendrickson, 1987), 85–96.

59 Ben Witherington III, *Conflict & Community in Corinth: A Socio-Rhetorical Commentary on 1 and 2 Corinthians* (Grand Rapids: Eerdmans, 1995), 253; Fee, First Epistle, 570.

60 Thiselton, *Corinthians*, 1098; Anthony C. Thiselton, "The 'Interpretation' of Tongues? A New Suggestion in Light of the Greek Usage in Philo and Josephus," *Journal of Theological Studies* 30:1 (1979): 15–36.

61 As an aside, Isa 28:10 in the Masoretic Text is untranslatable and appears to be gibberish; one wonders how this Hebraic imitation of *glossolalia* relates to the nature of speaking in tongues at Corinth.

62 Fee, *First Epistle*, 680.

63 Conzelmann, *Corinthians*, 242.

64 Barrett, *First Epistle*, 324.

65 Thiselton justifiably reasons for both a positive and negative use of tongues depending on the way an individual appropriates the gift, *Corinthians*, 1095.

66 *Anakrinō* can also mean judgment.

67 In this quote from Isa 45:14 (Zech 8:23), Paul changed the "you" to plural, reinforcing his communal emphasis.

68 See Christopher G. Foster, "Communal Participation in the Spirit: The Corinthian Correspondence in Light of Early Jewish Mysticism in the Dead Sea Scrolls" (Ph.D. diss., University of Manchester, 2013).

3 Theology of Spirit-Empowered Witness

Julie C. Ma

Abstract

The Azusa Street revival movement took place from 1906–1909 under the African American preacher William J. Seymour's leadership. The most prominent Pentecostalism began through the revival movement in Azusa Street. Attendees who experience the Holy Spirit's baptism and are empowered by the Spirit are inspired and urged to go to the nations to witness Christ. Through supernatural occurrences, particularly healing, numerous people came to Christ globally.

Introduction

Spirit empowerment is Pentecostalism's treasured experience, which underscores being a witness of Christ after being empowered. In the Azusa Street revival (1906–1909), people gathered to seek the baptism of the Holy Spirit. As anticipated, they experienced the outpouring of the Holy Spirit. Their interpretation of being baptized was going to the world to bring souls to Christ, not only within the nation but also overseas. Hence, people went to China, India, Japan, Egypt, Liberia, Angola, and other parts of the world. There was also the influence of healing on the spread of the gospel worldwide through the work of prominent evangelists. For example, Oral Roberts conducted approximately 300 healing revival meetings in different countries. Many other evangelists spread the gospel through divine healing manifestation. Historical records display that some Pentecostal women dedicated their lives to missions both local and foreign. Their lives for God's mission were a prime example of empowerment for witness. This study will focus on Pentecostal's Spirit-empowered mission and evangelism through the baptism of the Holy Spirit.

Why Empowered?

Jesus' command to his disciples as recorded in Luke 24:47–49 is put in the larger setting of his exposition of scripture (24:44–49). After an initial account regarding the essential establishment of total "scriptural prophecies about himself" (44), Jesus explicates to the disciples that his death and resurrection were predicted in scripture and were therefore vital rudiments of the heavenly plan (46). In v. 47, Jesus specifies that the order of "scriptural prophecy" incudes the future mission of the church: "and repentance of forgiveness of sins will be preached in his name to all nations, beginning at Jerusalem." The scriptural foundation for this claim is perhaps Isaiah 49:6, which is quoted in Paul's preaching in Pisidian Antioch (Acts 13:47) and indicated in Luke and Acts (Luke 2:32; Acts 1:8; 26:23).[1] By receiving the calling of Israel to be a servant commanded to carry "light to the nations" and "salvation to the ends of the earth" (Isa 49:6), the disciples vigorously take part in the actualization of Old Testament scriptures.

The theoretical backdrop of Isaiah 49:6 is also eminent in the equivalent version of the commission recorded in Acts 1:4–8. Jesus' command is again placed in the setting of teaching (Acts 1:2–3), though the teaching is not knotted to scripture as in Luke 24:44–45. His commission to wait in "Jerusalem to receive power when the Holy Spirit comes on you" comes after a query from the disciples: "Lord, are you at this time going to restore the kingdom to Israel" (Acts 1:6). This query is a "literary device which anticipates possible misconceptions and thus calls for further clarification."[2] It further delineates:

> Jesus' response is intended to challenge the disciples' narrow expectation of a restoration limited to the faithful of Israel: "you will be my witnesses ... to the ends of the earth" (Acts 1:8; cf. Isa 49:6). Echoing the words and concepts of Isa 49:6, Jesus declares that God's promises are indeed being fulfilled; however, 'the promise of God's reign is not simply the restoration of the preserved of Israel, but the renewal of the vocation of Israel to be a light to the nations to the ends of the earth.[3]

Leonard Allen discusses being "filled with the Spirit," which is an image of continuing receptiveness to the Spirit. Just as the Spirit has been "poured out," so the Church and individual Christians can be filled with the Spirit. "To be filled with the Spirit is to come under the progressively more intense and intimate influence of the Spirit." The fact is that the Spirit's filling can be reduced and later experienced again a multitude of times through a spiritual journey. Paul speaks about "God's provision of the Spirit" (Phil 1:19) in encountering adversity. Through the suffering inherent in mission, disciples can experience "God's love and empowering presence in a fuller, more intense way," as Ephesians 3:16 notes, "strengthened [. . .] with power through his Spirit in your inner being."[4]

Because the Spirit is present and dynamic in the Christian community as well as in individual Christian life, believers can experience new fillings of the Spirit, sometimes experiencing unfathomable healing in believers' lives, other times inspiring a freshness of joy and peace, some other times illuminating the "fire of mission" within the church community. Additionally, there is a biblical commission for the Church's experience of the Spirit for the witnessing and fulfilling of mission. We, as his disciples, are "filled with the Spirit" to fulfill a distinctive commission-mission.[5]

Baptism of the Holy Spirit

Acts 1:8 says, "But you will receive power when the Holy Spirit comes on you, and you will be my witnesses in Jerusalem, and all Judea and Samaria, and to the ends of the earth" (NIV). This statement is both a "command and a promise." The disciples were to wait to receive power so that they could undertake their calling as witnesses to the "risen Messiah."[6] The Father assured that the calling of Christ and the calling of the disciples become integral to each other by the channel of the Holy Spirit, as the "anointing upon Christ is to be transferred to the disciples and the *ecclesia*" (1:4).[7] This verse further designates witnesses in mission as the goal of empowerment.

Pentecostals are well-known for their unique experience called "baptism in the Holy Spirit," while others, without advocating this certain doctrinal statement, are open to the supernatural work of the Holy Spirit. When mainline churches began to experience what was called the "fullness of the Spirit," the earlier doctrinal template no longer applied to these new Charismatics. Many Christians maintained the beliefs and doctrines of their mother churches, and the Pentecostal spiritual experiences were a supplement to their existing theology and spirituality.[8]

Acts 2:4 notes, "All of them were filled with the Holy Spirit and began to speak in other tongues as the Spirit enabled them." Filling with the Holy Spirit refers to the indwelling of the Spirit. The verb is an "aorist passive of *pinplemi*: they were filled," but it appears as if Luke uses a diversity of watery kind of analogy to delineate the Spirit coming upon people — filling, baptizing, and pouring, and uses them correspondently, although he does not use the verb "to baptize of subsequent infilling."[9]

When the Holy Spirit came upon the assembly place, God would supernaturally empower the people gathered there to speak other languages without necessitating these languages be learned first. Hence, the Pentecostals were understood as missionary tongues (*xenolalia*).[10] The linking between tongues and mission was frequently forgotten, but the Pentecostal's awareness of power for mission persevered. Because Luke observed the Spirit's power for the mission, he stressed the most apparent connection between the "prophetic dimension of the Spirit's activity and the cross-cultural element."[11] The more significant fact is that the baptism with the Holy Spirit is neither the final aim nor the pinnacle of the believer's Christian life. Rather, it is a starting to a "fuller and richer spiritual life."[12]

Azusa Street Revival Movement

The modern Pentecostal movement is close to one hundred years old, and its role in Christianity, and in mission in specifically, has been extremely important. The vibrant "growth of churches in this movement"[13] supports it. The movement began in North America at the beginning of the "twentieth century, mainly at the Azusa Street Mission (1906–1909) under the leadership of the African preacher William J. Seymour." However, the astounding "discoveries" of the so-called "indigenous Pentecostals" from Africa and Asia advocate the idea of "multiple fountainheads for the start of Pentecostal Christianity."[14] On the night of April 9, 1906, Seymour and seven men were anticipating God on Bonnie Brae Street. For three days and nights, the house was filled wall-to-wall with people praying and praising, unceasingly and loudly. Anderson further describes the scene:

> A few whites joined this group, and the house became too small. Within a week they had rented and moved into an old building used for storage at 321 Azusa Street, a former African Methodist Episcopal church, where the Apostolic Faith Mission was born. With sawdust-sprinkled floors and rough planks as benches, daily meetings commenced at about ten in the morning and usually lasted until late at night. They were completely spontaneous and

usually emotional, without planned programs or speakers. Singing in tongues and people falling to the ground "under the power" or "slain in the Spirit" were common phenomena. The racial integration in these meetings was unique at that time, and people from ethnic minorities discovered "the sense of dignity and community denied them in the larger urban culture."[15]

Seymour's central leadership group was entirely combined with black and white men and women accountable for diverse ways of the ministry (more than half were women), but Seymour remained in top responsibility. Seymour was the symbol of a "spiritual father to thousands of early Pentecostals in North America."[16] For the next three years, the revival in Azusa Street was the utmost propounding "center of Pentecostalism, further promoted by Seymour's periodical, *The Apostolic Faith*, which reached an international circulation of 50,000 at its peak in 1908." People influenced by the revival began a few new Pentecostal places in the Los Angeles area, thus by 1912, there were at the minimum twelve in the city. From Los Angeles, news of the "outpouring of the Holy Spirit" outspread through the nation and around the world by "word of mouth and the printed page." Soon, Pentecostal revivals could be discovered in Canada, England, Scandinavia, Germany, India, China, Africa, and South America.[17] Anderson continues:

> The guaranteeing revival at the Azusa Street Mission signified an abnormality on the American religious sight. Diverse age groups of people congregated to Los Angeles with both uncertainty and a yearning to take part. Blacks, whites, and Hispanics worshiped together. Female and male mutually took up leadership task. The mixture of races and the members cheering of women in leadership was extraordinary. The obstacle between priesthood and lay people disappeared from the time when members believed that the giving "spiritual power for ministry was intended to be received by all."[18]

From its inception, North American Pentecostalism laid stress on soul-winning and missions. People who came from distant countries went back to their homes with the baptism experience and became witnesses of Christ. Many people committed to the mission, going from Azusa Street all over the world, reaching more than twenty-five nations within two years, including far-flung nations such as China, India, Japan, Egypt, Liberia, Angola, and South Africa.[19] This was a huge accomplishment and the launching of the noteworthy development in Christianity history.

Going to Nations with the Gospel

It was supposed that since the assembled people were experienced a foreign language (*xenolalia*) through Spirit baptism, they had to go to diverse nations to share the gospel. The initial North American missionaries that left for mission "only five months after the Azusa Street revival had begun" were self-financing, and most of them were women. Caucasian pastors Alfred and Lillian Garr, after being baptized in the Holy Spirit at Azusa Street, trusted that they had spoken in "Bengali and left Los Angeles for India, arriving in Calcutta in 1907." Though their language skills were not up to the level, they were invited to lead services in a Baptist church and conduct a Pentecostal revival.[20] Other numerous missionaries went to diverse mission fields:

> African American evangelist Lucy Farrow was also one of the first missionaries from Azusa Street, arriving in Liberia in 1907. Also from Azusa Street, Canadian evangelist and former elder in Dowie's Zion City, John G. Lake, travelled to South Africa in 1908 with Thomas Hezmalhalch and established the Apostolic Faith Mission there. Others left for the Bahamas in 1910 and for British East Africa in 1911. Kathleen Miller and Lucy James left for India from Britain under the Pentecostal Missionary Union in 1909, followed by four others a year later, one of whom, John Beruldsen, spent thirty-five years in North China. Pentecostal phenomena broke out in a missionary convention in Taochow, China in 1912 when William Simpson (1869–1961), missionary in China and Tibet from 1892–1949, became a Pentecostal.[21]

Anderson further delineates that Simpson journeyed through China, on many occasions by foot, helped in the "training of Chinese ministers, and became one of the best-known missionaries in Pentecostalism." Other renowned innovators "Pentecostal missionary was H. A. Baker (1881–1971), missionary to Tibet and China from 1912–1950 and in Taiwan for sixteen years until he died in 1971." He ministered to tribal peoples and created a children's home in Yunnan. In 1909, the Pentecostal message was brought by Gunnar Vingren and Daniel Berg in Chicago, started the the Assemblies of God (AG) denomination in Brazil, currently the major "non-Catholic denomination in Latin America and the largest AG in any nation."[22]

Women in Mission

Though women have played a very important role in the growth and development of Pentecostal denominations, particularly in the field of mission and church ministry, Pentecostal groups have distinguished the responsibilities that women should undertake. In this section, I will present and acknowledge prominent women out of countless women as an illustration of those who were involved in and dedicated to both overseas mission and local ministry and made a marvelous impact.

Jasil Choi

Yoido Full Gospel Church was pioneered in the tent church outskirt of the city by David Yonggi Cho in 1958 together with Jasil Choi, who was Cho's mother-in-law. The church rapidly grew and, several years later, moved township to house the growing members. As the church constantly grew in number, they decided to move to Yoido Island. One day, when she prayed for the future of the church, the idea of setting up a prayer mountain popped up in Choi's mind. As Choi continually prayed for this crucial matter, she mentioned it to senior pastor Yonggi Cho, and he gladly accepted her idea. He knew and acknowledged that prayer opens doors for access to the gospel.[23]

Despite the financial challenge, the prayer mountain was established in 1973. People who came to pray there had to fast. It became a rule of this prayer mountain following the name of the prayer mountain, Osanri Choi-Jasil Fasting Prayer Mountain. Shortly, the place began to draw people from Japan, Taiwan, and other parts of the world, and people discovered a new spiritual dimension through prayer with fasting. This Prayer Mountain turned into the first international facility for prayer and fasting. A growing amount of the sick experienced divine healing. It wasn't long before numerous people had an experience of healing from hopeless sicknesses through rigorous and passionate prayer accompanied by fasting. Such news soon traveled within the nation and overseas and more people who were in desperate circumstances came to pray. Even after Choi's death, the prayer mountain hosts people from other denominations within the country and church people from diverse nations.

Choi's spiritual ministry soon crossed national boundaries and expanded to other countries. God opened a door for her to reach the Japanese, as church leaders repeatedly invited her to come. Before her preaching, it was Choi's custom to spend the whole night in prayer for the next day's service. The effects of her prayer were so evident that many people in the service were filled with the Holy Spirit. Many in the United States were called into the ministry through Choi's influence. Her ministry in America, Thailand, Hong Kong, Germany, and other places produced identical outcomes. Choi's international ministry was also her commitment to the call to mission found in Acts 1:8, "But you will receive power when the Holy Spirit comes on you, and you will be my witnesses in Jerusalem, and in all Judea and Samaria, and to the ends of the earth."[24] Prior to her expeditions, Choi spent two or three weeks in prayer and fasting. She was not only preparing for an approaching ministry but was also making herself a living message of God's power through prayer and fasting.

Elva Vanderbout

On December 15, 1946, Elva Vanderbout left her land to take up residence in the Philippines. She traveled by ship, which went to the Philippines via different countries. After twenty-three days of a long and tedious journey, the Islands of the Philippines began to loom near. On January 7, 1947, Vanderbout finally trod the soil of the Philippine Islands to begin mission work.[25] Vanderbout had a God-given burden for the mountain people. She reached Baguio City, which had access to tribal people in the mountain. Vanderbout soon found that each time she preached the gospel, more and more people were coming to hear the message of God. Vanderbout finally decided to hold open-air services to house the crowds. As she often met these people, she observed numerous attendees were stricken by disease. She learned that during the war most of the mountain people lost their entire properties, and this left them poverty-stricken and devastated. Lives of deprivation caused them to lose bodily fighting to disease.[26]

In 1948, Vanderbout and local ministers held revival meetings in Tuding week after week, in addition to having regular services on Sunday nights. The Holy Spirit moved among and touched the gathered people. Many non-believers were saved, and surprisingly more than 150 were baptized in water. The gathered people: old, young adults, and children shared delightful testimonies of the power of God, which saved their lives from darkness and the bondage of sin.[27]

God's miracles of healing are demonstrated in different services. One girl, eighteen years of age, who agonized as a deaf-mute for twelve years, was instantaneously healed. During each morning and night service, the sick lined up for healing.[28] God healed people by the scores. The blind became able to see. Paralytics were healed. People in anguish from tuberculosis and countless other illnesses were cured. One well-known woman in the city was healed of a very big goiter.[29] The miracles that occurred through the mission of Vanderbout could be continued.

Pandita Ramabai

Pandita Ramabai was an Indian female Christian[30] "reformer, Bible translator and social activist, particularly revival movement in her mission." Ramabai became a Christian from the Brahmin caste by rejecting the Hindu social "propriety" and marriage system. She became a widow with her daughter within two years after her marriage. She returned to India in 1889, after her studies and established a ministry for widows close to Bombay (now Mumbai), which was relocated to Pune after a year. In 1895, she began a mission on a farm she had bought at Kedgaon, near Pune. Ramabai and her working team named this mission "Mukti," which means salvation. Its chief goal was to provide shelter for underprivileged girls and young women including numerous women who were child brides and then became widows. Others were released from starvation of a shortage of food. There were forty-eight girls and young women in 1896, but throughout that year, 300 girls were freed from hunger. By 1900, nearly 2,000 people were cared for.[31]

Ramabai ascertained Hindu women could experience absolute freedom by converting to Christ. At the same time, her mission trained them in income-generating skills.[32] Ramabai's strong mission vision and passion developed thusly:

> By 1907, the Mission had expanded to include a rescue mission, a hospital, an oil-press, a blacksmith forge, a printing press, a complete school that provided college entrance training, a school for the blind, and training departments in teaching, nursing, weaving, tailoring, bread and butter making, tinning, laundering, masonry, carpentry, and farming.[33]

Ramabai had a robust belief in and experience with the work of the Holy Spirit. She once expressed, "I found it a great blessing to realize the personal presence of the Holy Spirit in me and to be guided and taught by Him."[34] Later, she began to obtain a strong desire to be filled with the Holy Spirit to "enter into a new experience of God's power to save, bless and use."[35]

She came to realize that prayer was the key to the crucial elements for revival.[36] Ramabai started a "special early-morning daily prayer meeting, where seventy women would meet and pray." She expressed her commitment "for the true conversion of all the Indian Christians including ourselves and for a special outpouring of the Holy Spirit on all Christians of every land."[37] The many people who attended this daily prayer meeting progressively went up to 500. The revival was sustained for a year and a half and resulted in "1,100 baptisms at the school, confessions of sins and repentances, prolonged prayer meetings and the witnessing of 700 of these young women going out in teams into the surrounding areas."[38] Ramabai also began a Bible school of 200 young women to form "Praying Bands" to pray and "to be trained in witnessing to their faith."[39] According to Ramabai's knowledge, no revival such as this took place prior to 1905.

Impact of Healing on Global Growth through Evangelists

Healing evangelists have continually been a part of the Pentecostal movement, and healing creates an effective environment for the growth of mission in the Holy Spirit. Some eminent healing evangelists in earlier years are Maria Woodworth-Etter, John G. Lake, Aimee Semple McPherson. Some others in the 1960s–1990s are Kathryn Kuhlman, Benny Hinn, and German evangelist Reinhard Bonnke. Leading independent healing evangelists at this time were William Branham (1909–1965), T. L. Osborn (1923–2013), Oral Roberts (1918–2009), Tommy Hicks (1909–1973), and amazing healings and miraculous phenomena were stated in their movement. Branham and Roberts were perhaps the most recognized and most extensively journeyed. Branham's astonishing healing services that started in 1946 were accurately recorded, and he was the pacemaker for people who "followed before he became involved in doctrinal controversies."[40] Hicks conducted a revival in Argentina in 1954 and contributed to the faster growth among Pentecostal churches there. Osborn had big crowds at his crusades in "Central America and the Caribbean, Indonesia and East Africa."[41]

By 1960, Oral Roberts had become the leading healing evangelist, increasingly accepted by "mainline" denominations, and one of the most influential Pentecostals in the emergence of the Charismatic movements."[42] He led roughly 300 healing crusades, preached thousands of sermons, prayed for the healing of the sick by laying his hand in forty-six states in the U. S. and seventy nations on all continents, praying for more than 1.5

million sick people individually by the laying on of hands. Roberts stated, "I can testify that every person is sick, in one way or another, and that person won't be made whole without good medical science plus a miracle from God's healing streams flowing together.[43]

Roberts describes his healing ministry in East Africa:

> In 1969, as I stood on the soil of East Africa and preached to as many as 100,000 people a day, God began to give me a burden and vision for sending healing teams back there someday. Teams of young doctors, dentists, nurses, lawyers, business people, singers, and others could take God's healing power to the world in an even greater way than I, being one, could ever do. Since that time, my soul has been on fire to do what God has called me to do. And, in faith, we at Oral Roberts University have been preparing in every way we know for the time when God would open the doors for the Healing Teams to go into all the nations of the world.[44]

Theological Incentive for Pentecostal Witnessing

Five theological features convey the external nature of mission in the Spirit. The first impetus is a sense of "eschatological urgency" that originated amongst initial Pentecostals. The experience of the baptism in the Holy Spirit emphasized a premillennial orientation, commonly created in the self-claimed of Pentecostal revival as the "latter rain" (Joel 2:23), which motioned that the church was present-day in the last days before the "imminent return of Christ." Being a witness of Christ became a crucial primacy, and numerous young men and women went instantaneously overseas for the mission.[45] By 1910, nearly 200 Pentecostal missionaries, later dubbed "one-way missionaries," left different places of the world, regularly with no mission training[46] and with no intent to return home.

The second, the baptism in the Holy Spirit, was found as empowering element to "witness-mirroring" Acts 1:8, the exceptional scripture for the mission movement. The theological connection between Spirit baptism and mission as a witness for the non-believers had pivotal suggestions for mission practices, main amongst them the acceptance of speaking with tongues. Numerous Pentecostal forerunners thought to have received the "gift of known languages (*xenolalia*) to preternaturally authorize them to be a gospel bearer to the nations. This euphoric anticipation was often disappointed, but the sense of Spirit empowerment carried on," and missionaries did not return home even when they had not experienced the real spoken languages.[47]

Third, the belief that baptism of the Holy Spirit was for "all believers" (see Acts 2:17–18) rearranging the acceptance of divine calling: the call to mission was most commonly seen as not only given to the priesthood but was extended to entire Christians. Obscuring the "clergy-laity demarcation" and using women and children, Pentecostalism developed a lower grassroots missionary movement.[48] Mission was a means of life rather than an inaccessible feature of church ministry.

Fourth, countless initial Pentecostal followers derived from poorer social levels and discovered their "spiritual experience uplifting, liberating, and empowering." Pentecostalism developed a religion of the low strata, embracing the socially disregarded into their group and increasing mission to entire social groups of people. In turn, the Pentecostal mission extended out to the verges of the world by reaching through all societal levels with the clear purpose of "holistic transformation."[49]

The last incentive is the vibrant part of "spiritual experience in the missional orientation of Pentecostals." Their theology emphasizes the meeting with God, with assertions of "healing" from God experiencing his "touch" and experiencing the presence of God. The Pentecostal perception displays a strong awareness of the spiritual realm, anticipating the lively presence of both "the Holy Spirit and evil spirits in the world around them." Further:

> Following the example of the early church, spiritual gifts have become part of the Pentecostal mission strategy to serve as "signs and wonders" of the authenticity of the Christian message. Hence, missiology is also a dynamic expression of spiritual warfare. The dynamic of these different motivations carries Pentecostal missions along three dominant waves.[50]

Concluding Remarks

This study discussed a way of being a witness: empowering by the Spirit as Jesus said in Acts 1: 8, "But you will receive power when the Holy Spirit comes on you, and you will be my witnesses in Jerusalem, and in all Judea and Samaria, and to the ends of the earth." Pentecostals truly practice obedience following this command. As delineated in this study, Pentecostals became a witness of Christ in distinctive ways: going to naions for the mission as being the Spirit-empowered, through healing, and many other ways. Following people's needs, it is necessary to practice a holistic mission. In fact, many Pentecostal churches and missionaries have already been involved in holistic mission works. My desire is that ministry in the social concern should be accompanied by being the Spirit-empowered witness. I hope Pentecostals will continue to be marvelous eschatological witnesses until Christ's return.

Notes

1 D. L. Tiede, "The Exaltation o Jesus and the Restoration of Israel in Acts 1," *Harvard Theological Review* 79 (1986), 285–286.

2 Robert Menzies, *Empowered for Witness: The Spirit in Luke-Acts* (Sheffield: Sheffield Academic Press, 1994), 169.

3 Menzies, *Empowered for Witness*, 169.

4 Leonard Allen, *Poured Out: The Spirit of God Empowering the Mission of God* (Abilene, TX: Abilene Christian University Press, 2018), 110.

5 Allen, *Poured Out*, 110.

6 Craig S. Keener, *Acts: An Exegetical Commentary*, vol. 1 (Grand Rapids: Baker Academic, 2012), 675.

7 Clark H. Pinnock, *Flame of Love: A Theology of the Holy Spirit* (Downers Grove, IL: IVP, 1966), 113.

8 Hwa Yung, "Endued with Power: The Pentecostal-Charismatic Renewal and the Asian Church in the Twenty-First Century," *Asian Journal of Pentecostal Studies* 6:1 (2003), 65–82.

9 Ben Witherington, III, *The Acts of the Apostles: A Socio-Rhetorical Commentary* (Grand Rapids: Eerdmans, 1998), 131.

10 Allan H. Anderson, *An Introduction to Pentecostalism* (Cambridge: Cambridge University Press, 2004), 33–34.

11 Craig S. Keener, *Spirit Hermeneutics: Reading Scripture in Light of Pentecost* (Grand Rapids: Eerdmans, 2016), 22–23.

12 Verna M. Linzey, *The Baptism with the Holy Spirit: The Reception of the Holy Spirit as Confirmed by Speaking in Tongues* (Grand Rapids: Zondervan, 1978), 45.

13 Anderson, *An Introduction to Pentecostalism*, 39.

14 Anderson, *An Introduction to Pentecostalism*, 40.

15 Anderson, *An Introduction to Pentecostalism*, 39–40.

16 Anderson, *An Introduction to Pentecostalism*, 39–40.

17 Anderson, *An Introduction to Pentecostalism*, 39–40.

18 Stanley Burgess and Eduard Maas, eds., *The New International Dictionary of Pentecostal and Charismatic Movements* (Grand Rapids: Zondervan, 2003), xviii.

19 D. William Faupel, T*he Everlasting Gospel: The Significance of Eschatology in the Development of Pentecostal Thought* (Sheffield: Sheffield Academic Press, 1996), 182–186, 212–216.

20 Anderson, *An Introduction to Pentecostalism*, 57.

21 Anderson, *An Introduction to Pentecostalism*, 58.

22 Anderson, *An Introduction to Pentecostalism*, 58.

23 Roberta C. Bondi, *To Pray and to Love* (Minneapolis: Fortress Press, 1991), 163.

24 Jasil Choi, *I Was Mrs. Hallelujah* (Seoul: Seoul Logos, 1978), 437–460.

25 Inez Sturgeon, *Give Me This Mountain* (Oakland, CA: Hunter Advertising Co., 1960), 76–80.

26 Sturgeon, *Give Me This Mountain*, 93.

27 Juan B. Soriano, "Pentecost in the Philippines," *Pentecostal Evangel* (August 7, 1948), 1.

28 Elva Vanderbout, "Salvation-Healing Revival in Baguio City, Philippines," *Pentecostal Evangel* (June 1955), 4.

29 Vanderbout, "Salvation-Healing Revival," 4.

30 Allan H. Anderson, *Spreading Fires: The Missionary Nature of Early Pentecostalism*, (London: SCM Press, 2007), 77: "Ramabai is both significant in the origins of Pentecostalism and in the acceptance of its phenomena among some in the wider Christian community. The importance of her revival movement is borne out by the prominence given to it in reports in the emerging Pentecostal press, both in India and especially in Britain and North America."

31 Jessie H. Mair, *Bungalows in Heaven: The Story of Pandita Ramabai* (Kedgaon, India: Pandita Ramabai Mukti Mission, 2003), 87–88.

32 Anderson, *Spreading Fires*, 77. See also S. M. Adhav, *Pandita Ramabai*, 114–115. Ramabai became nationalistic by stimulation of "British rulers" repression and arrogance towards Indian social structures . . . She was

a dedicated ecumenist before the word was coined in the twentieth century, deploring the divisions within Christianity and pleading for a united Indian church." See also R. E. Hedlund, *Quest for Identity: India's Churches of Indigenous Origin: The 'Little Tradition' in Indian Christianity* (Delhi: ISPCK, 2000), 160: "Gauri interprets Ramabai's conversion as a quest for intellectual and spiritual freedom...Ramabai set about refashioning Christianity to her own requirements, says Gauri. If so, it is not surprising that in Ramabai one finds an incipient Indian Christian nationalism expressed in a critique of missionary paternalism and rejection of colonial control."

33 Rambai Mukti Mission, *Mukti Prayer-Bell* 3:4 (September 1907), 21–22.

34 Rajas Krishnarao Dongre and Josephine E. Patterson, *Pandita Ramabai: A Life of Faith and Prayer* (Chennai: Christian Literature Society, 1963), 18, 24.

35 Anderson, *Spreading Fires*, 79.

36 Gary McGee, "Minnie F. Abrams: Another Context, Another Founder," in James R. Goff Jr. and Grant Wacker eds., *Portraits of a Generation* (Fayetteville: University of Arkansas Press, 2002), 87–104.

37 Anderson, *Spreading Fires*, 78.

38 Anderson, *Spreading Fires*, 78.

39 Anderson, *Spreading Fires*, 79.

40 Anderson, *An Introduction to Pentecostalism*, 59.

41 Anderson, *An Introduction to Pentecostalism*, 58.

42 Anderson, *An Introduction to Pentecostalism*, 58–59. See also, Vinson Synan, "Pentecostal Roots of Oral Roberts' Healing Ministry," *Spiritus* 3:2 (2018), 287–302.

43 Oral Roberts, *Expect a Miracle: My Life and Ministry, an Autobiography* (Nashville: Thomas Nelson, 1995), vi.

44 James Winslow, "Kenya: A Nation Crying Out for Healing Teams," *Abundant Life* (August 1981), 13.

45 Anderson, *An Introduction to Pentecostalism*, 40.

46 Wonsuk Ma and Julie C. Ma, "Missiology: Evangelization, Holistic Ministry, and Social Justice," in Wolfgang Vondey, ed., *The Routledge Handbook of Pentecostal Theology* (Abingdon: Routledge, 2020), 280.

47 Ma and Ma, "Missiology," 280.

48 Ma and Ma, "Missiology," 280.

49 Wonsuk Ma, "When the Poor are Fired Up: The Role of Pneumatology in Pentecostal-Charismatic Mission," *Transformation* 24:1 (2007), 28–34.

50 Julie C. Ma and Wonsuk Ma, *Mission in the Spirit: Towards a Pentecostal/ Charismatic Missiology* (Oxford: Regnum Books, 2010), 59–71.

4 I and Thou: Rethinking Spirit-Empowered Missions in South Asia

Brainerd Prince

Abstract

This study problematizes the relationship between missionaries and the missionized in order to broadly argue that unless there is an authentic Spirit-empowered relationship between them, the mission work done will not bear fruit. I begin this study by reviewing how the postcolonial discourse inspired by the works of Frantz Fanon problematizes the self-other relationship. I will then present briefly findings I have from my fieldwork amongst the Bhakti community in Maharashtra to explore what relational mission could look like on the field. Finally, we will end with a meditation on Martin Buber's central work *I and Thou* in order to glean insights for our understanding of the relationship between missionaries and the missionized others.

Introduction

While all would agree that there is a category difference between the researcher and those researched upon, or the missionized and the missionary, I wonder if the relationship between these two groups has been sufficiently problematized. There is a lot of mission research done on the unreached groups in our world and also on those groups that have been reached with the Christian message. Equally, much research has been done on missionaries both in the field as well as when they come back 'home' after their mission assignments. However, my claim is that not sufficient research or critical reflection has been done on the relationship between these two groups. The underlying assumption is that it is in the interstitial space between the self and the other, the space that is in-between the persons, that the Spirit is able to move and work. While the Spirit is able to enable deep reflexivity, understanding, and insight, it is also able to regulate this space so that the engagement between the one who witnesses and the one which is witnessed to is able to overcome the barriers of miscommunications and misinterpretations, which are hugely prevalent in the context of dominant world religions.

In the world of mission or mission research, there is a clear distinction between the missionary or mission researcher on the one hand and the others who are being missionized or researched upon. Even this book represents those who are involved in collecting and analyzing "mission information," and of course, the authors are not the ones getting missionized. One does mission while the other receives mission. The issue I am raising is that while there is ample research on missionaries or the mission fields, there is not sufficient research and critical thinking on the relationship between the missionaries and the missionized. It is this 'mission relationship' that needs to be problematized.

What should be the relationship between missionaries, mission researchers, and the communities and individuals they work with? In the relationship they share, how should the 'other' be understood? Perhaps, more importantly, how should they, as missionaries and mission researchers, understand themselves in the relationship they share with the communities? I would like to argue that a deep reflection on mission relationship will not only give us a better understanding of the 'missionary self' and the 'missionized other' but also on the nature of mission itself.

This is not to say that there has been no reflection on mission in light of the missionized other. As a matter of fact, in the twentieth century, new models of mission have emerged that have taken the missionized others seriously. Within mission studies, different models have emerged that embody these changing understandings of the self's relationship with the other. We have come a long way, from a colonial model of mission to indigenous mission to what Jenkins has called 'reverse mission' in his *The Next Christendom*. Two models that come to mind are inculturation and contextualization. The term 'inculturation' was used for the first time in 1962 and then officially by Pope John Paul II in 1979.[1] The term 'contextualization' had its historic first appearance in 1972 in the ecumenical publication of the *Theological Education Fund, Ministry in Context*. These two models came out of the larger change in the philosophical climate in academia, which has been termed as the postmodern turn. While contextualization is very similar to inculturation, Darrell L. Whiteman notes that contextualization seeks to make the gospel/text relevant to the context of the culture.[2] It is the model of contextualization that necessitated the rise of contextual theology, giving importance not only to the scripture but also to the context in which it surfaces.³ However, in both these models, the relationship between the missionary and the missionized community remains invisible and unaddressed.

I therefore begin this study by demonstrating how in broader academia, the self-other relationship has been problematized, particularly in the postcolonial discourse inspired by the works of Frantz Fanon. While Fanon's critique is important and acceptable, how should we move forward? I will briefly present findings I have from my fieldwork amongst the Bhakti community in Maharashtra to explore what relational mission could look like on the field. Finally, we will end by briefly meditating on the Austrian Jewish philosopher Martin Buber's central work *I and Thou* in order to further augment our understanding of the relationship between missionaries and the missionized others.

The Postcolonial Critique

The terms 'difference,' 'diversity,' and 'plurality,' with a realization of the presence of an 'other' who is different from the self has gained huge currency in the past few decades and have been problematized not only in the public space but also have a history of discourse within academia. Subaltern studies, postcolonial studies, and even what has come to be known as postmodern philosophy are, to name but a few discourses that have focused on problematizing these terms. If in mission studies the discourse focusing on context arose in light of the missionary doing mission in other communities, then in the broader academia, this discourse arose in response to colonial subjugation and control. The goal for looking at the postcolonial discourse is for us to identify the critical issues at stake in this debate. For example, as early as 1952, Frantz Fanon, the famed author of *Black Skin White Masks* from the Caribbean island of Martinique, talks about the relationship between the colonizers and the colonized, particularly in the context of French colonialism. His words are very telling, even as he explicitly shares his displeasure as well as his aspiration:

> On that day, completely dislocated, unable to be abroad to the other, the white man, who unmercifully imprisoned me, I took myself far off from my own presence, far indeed, and made myself an object. What else could it be for me but an amputation, an excision, a hemorrhage that spattered my whole body

with black blood? But I did not want this revision, this thematization. All I wanted was to be a man among other men. I wanted to come lithe and young into a world that was ours and to help to build it together.[4]

The above quote clearly critiques the relationship the colonizer and the colonized shared. John McLeod, in a commentary on this text, says that here:

> Fanon's identity is defined in negative terms by those in a position of power. He is forced to see himself not as a human subject, with his own wants and needs as indicated at the end of the quotation, but an object, a peculiarity at the mercy of a group that identifies him as inferior, less than fully human, placed at the mercy of their definitions and representations.[5]

Anindita Mondal argues that Fanon's book, *Black Skin, White Masks* sets forth the relationship between the colonizer and the colonized. She explains that the explains that:

> The colonized subject who is forced into the internalization of the self as an "other" is seen in stark contrast to the colonizers who are civilized, rational, intelligent: the "Negro" remains "other" to all these qualities against which colonizing peoples derive their sense of superiority and normality.[6]

The tragedy of this was that even after the colonized responded to the colonizer and did everything as required, he was never accepted as an equal. So Mondal says, "however hard the colonized try to accept the education, values, and language of France—to don the White mask of civilization that will cover up the 'uncivilized' nature indexed by their black skins—they are never accepted on equal terms."[7] "The white world," writes Fanon, "the only honorable one, barred me from all participation. A man was expected to behave like a man. I was expected to behave like a black man."[8] Although Fanon's book captures some of the darkest moments of human history, if we replace the colonizer-colonized binary with the missionary-missionized, it would, perhaps reveal insights that make visible the critical issues that govern the relationships prevalent in the mission field.

The first insight is that there is a significant power difference between the two parties in the modern missionary movement. Mission was done from a position of power amongst people who were less powerful and less resourceful. There is a huge difference between the missionary self and the missionized other. This difference continues today. There is a conceptualization of this unequal binary, namely, missionary-missionized. Using Afaf Al-Saidi's work, I am going to replace the colonizer or imperialist with missionary and the colonized with missionized in order to tease out the binary at play. Al-Saidi argues that "to maintain authority over the Other in a [mission] situation [the missionary] must see the Other as different from the self...Politically as well as culturally, the self and the other are represented as the [missionary] and the [missionized]."[9] Explicating the difference between the self and other, Al-Saidi writes:

> The Other by definition lacks identity, propriety, purity, literality. In this sense, he can be described as the foreign: the one who does not belong to a group, does not speak a given language, does not have the same customs; he is the unfamiliar, uncanny, unauthorized, inappropriate, and the improper."[10]

The creation of this binary opposition contrasts for us the difference between the world of the missionary and the world of the missionized community. Although these worlds intersect, they do so with all the power differentiation that exists between them, and one wonders how this relationship can be characterized.

Secondly, within this binary, there is an objectification of the colonized or the missionized. Here, if I may come directly to the point, mission research in particular needs to be careful not to objectify those they seek to represent. It is a reduction of a human to characteristics and numbers "placed at the mercy of [our] definitions and representations."[11] Homi Bhabha adds in his book *The Location of Culture* that "the objective of colonial discourse is to construe the colonized as a population of degenerate types on the basis of racial origin, in order to justify conquest and to establish systems of administration and instruction."[12] This could be said as true of mission research that feeds into mission strategy. I am going to rewrite a paragraph Mondal wrote but replace the colonized-colonizing binary with missionized-missionary language and the colonial discourse with mission studies:

> [. . .] the "[missionized] subject" is a radically strange creature whose bizarre and eccentric nature is the cause for both curiosity and concern. The [missionized] are considered the "other" of the Westerner or the "[missionary] subject," essentially outside of Western culture and civilization. Yet, on the other hand, the discourse of [mission studies] attempts to domesticate [missionized] subject and abolish their radical "otherness," bringing them inside Western understanding through the Orientalist project of constructing

knowledge about them. The construction of "otherness" is thus split by the contradictory positioning of the [missionized] simultaneously inside and outside of Western knowledge.[13]

In Bhabha's words, "[mission] discourse produces the [missionized] as a social reality which is at once an 'other' and yet entirely knowable and visible."[14]

Finally, there is no authentic relationship between these two parties – at least not a relationship of equals. The relationship is always lopsided as it is one-sided. If the other is objectified and is at the other end of the power equation, then how is it even possible to have a relationship? More so, if the missionary has an agenda for the missionized, whom he or she wants to transform, then how is the missionized able to be equal with the missionary? Apart from the economic and even political inequality, there is an understanding of the other as incomplete, needing care, like a child to a parent, or a student to a teacher, or a novice to an expert. It is Frantz Fanon who develops the idea of the Other. To him, the other is the "not me; he is the other."[15] The missionized other is one with whom the missionary self can never truly relate.

While the application of the postcolonial critique on missions and mission studies can tease out the critical issues involved in mission work and mission research, can we find in the postcolonial discourse resources to move past these challenges so that we have a healthier relationship between the missionary and the missionized? In the work of Homi Bhabha, particularly in his ideas of "hybridity" and "third space," we find a way forward in terms of reassigning meanings to the old binary of colonizer and colonized, and in our case, the missionary and the missionized.[16] Applying Bhabha to our mission discourse would mean that in the encounter between the missionary and the missionized, there is a new hybrid identity that interweaves both these worlds, and thus the identity of both parties escapes essentialist cultural identities. Hybridity is positioned as an antidote to essentialism, or "the belief in invariable and fixed properties which define the 'whatness' of a given entity"[17] as Bhabha would himself argue that "all forms of culture are continually in the process of hybridity."[18] According to Bhabha, this third hybrid space is an ambivalent site where cultural meaning and representation have no "primordial unity or fixity"[19] and opens up the space for new forms of cultural meaning that call into question established categories of identity and culture.

The concept of the third space is useful for analyzing the "enunciation, transgression, and subversion of dualistic categories, going beyond colonial binary thinking and oppositional positioning."[20] Despite the exposure of the third space to contradictions and ambiguities, it provides a spatial politics of inclusion rather than exclusion that "initiates new signs of identity, and innovative sites of collaboration and contestation."[21] Once again, revisiting our principle presupposition, it is in this third space where the Spirit is able to move and have its being and influence both the missionary and the missionized.

While Bhabha's analysis opens up a new space for us to rethink the relationship between the missionary and the missionized, he is primarily concerned about identity and cultural representations. While we are interested in these themes, we are more so interested in the existential or real-life relationships between the missionary and the missionized other. It appears that neither the postcolonial critique nor the newer models of mission have rigorously interrogated the fundamental "I-Thou" relationship, using Martin Buber's language, that underlies mission practice and mission studies. Let's summarize the three critical issues we have raised so far: First, the binary representation of the missionary and the missionized. How should we understand the relation between the missionary self and the missionized other? Second, how do we overcome the objectification of the missionized other, especially in mission research? Finally, what is the nature of the existential relationship between the missionary and the missionized community? With these questions, let us go to the works of Martin Buber with a view to draw insights for mission studies. However, before that, let us briefly look at some ground research done on the mission work done on the Bhakti community of Maharashtra, India.

Mission Research on the Bhakti Community

This research draws on the experience and data collected by a research team that went to research the Bhakti community in Maharashtra. As the name suggests, the Bhatkis, translated as wanderers, are travelers. They are an astrologer community. Presently only the men practicing astrology travel while the women and children stay in the villages and take care of their daily business. The two astrologer brothers we met travel for almost eight months of the year. Astrology has been their occupation for generations. The brothers used to accompany their father and have learned the trade from him.

We visited their village and got into one of their huts to speak with them. The living conditions were poor, and the brothers were unimpressive to the sight. Immediately the team, ready with their questionnaires, became disillusioned wondering if any information could be obtained or was if this another wasted trip. The brothers were immediately dismissed. However, one of the brothers started to speak and address us. He asked us our names and where we lived in a slightly provocative manner. He was trying to guess where we were from on the basis of the information we provided. The team felt frustrated and even irritated with the questions. We had less time and a long questionnaire to complete, and of course, we were not going to entertain these "irrelevant" questions. One team member, coming from a remote part of Northeast India, for fun (as she said) gave the name of her village. Immediately, the astrologer's brother started to mention street names and landmarks in her village, which completely bewildered her, and all of us suddenly turned to look, for the first time, towards these brothers. We knew that we were being addressed and spoken to and that we had to listen. Pencils down, interview sheets set aside, we leaned forward to listen. It would not be inappropriate to attribute this transformation in the researchers' attitude to the work of the Spirit in the third interstitial space that both separated as well as enjoined the mission researchers from the missionized. The barriers and the annoyance that inhibited fruitful engagement came crashing down, and there was a transformation in attitudes. Perhaps, this is the evidence of the role of the Spirit in inter-religious and inter-faith engagement.

The astrologers said that they have a lot of followers across different cities. They have a process of establishing connections. They stay in the popular hotels in the cities and then publish advertisements about their services in the leading newspapers. They connect with the politicians and leading businessmen, and through them their network expands. They visit the cities at least once a year to keep the connections fresh. Travels give them a chance to exchange knowledge, and they learn a lot in the process. In their words, they usually travel with a mindset of learning something from everyone they meet. When they are open to learning, in turn, the other person will learn too, they claimed. This is their philosophy of engagement. One of the brothers believes that this mindset will reduce a lot of differences amongst people and bring peace between diverse communities. In their own way, the astrologer brothers expressed the need for and importance of inter-faith approaches through dialogue. When they visit any village, they make stops in the *paan*-shops and local markets, etc. From these places, they get to learn a lot about the local people. They grasp as much as they can about the new village and community. When they visit one household, they also do similar research to find out more about the others. This is how they increase their knowledge base. When asked about what they feel about conversion, the elder brother replied, *"Karne do na bhai! Parivartan kaun nahi karta?"* (Let them! Who doesn't change?) He said it is important to question, criticize, and change traditions. Society will not change directly all of a sudden. People have to change.

Martin Buber for Mission Studies

Martin Buber was a Jewish philosopher who was born in Vienna in 1878. He studied philosophy and the history of art at the University of Vienna and the University of Berlin, received his Ph.D. at the age of twenty-six, and taught in the University of Frankfurt for ten years (1923–1933).[22] However, Buber does not write from a position of power. He was one of the survivors of the Nazi holocaust and was a leader of the German Jews' battle against Nazism. Although he was an interpreter of the Hebrew Bible and a spokesman for Judaism, from his youth he had been deeply concerned with Jesus and the New Testament and had many significant dialogues with Christian theologians. The German Catholic thinkers Eugene Kogon and Karl Thieme speak of Buber in this way: "In everything that he writes the undertone reveals that here speaks a man of faith, and, indeed, a man of active faith."[23] Although he was a leader of the Jews, he has worked for "Jewish-Arab cooperation and friendship."[24] Karl Wilker, the German educator, writes about Buber that he must have "experienced life's deepest essence . . . He must have lived and suffered . . . and he must have shared with us all our life and suffering.'[25] Even a quick reflection on his biography shows that Buber's insights on the relationship between different kinds of people arose from his deep engagement with "others." He was a Jew who was engaged with Germans, Christians, and Arabs, and sought to work out human friendship in each encounter. In 1923, his magnum opus *I and Thou* appeared, and it is from this book that we will seek insights into the missionary self's relationship with the missionized other.

The first insight we get from Buber is about understanding the relationship between the self and the other. He argues that even before there is an "I" or a "You," there is a primary or even primal word "I-You" or "I-It" that determines how we understand the "I" and the "You." He writes, "There is no I taken in itself, but only the I of the primary word I-Thou and the I of the primary word I-It."[26] In other words, according to Buber, our understanding of ourselves and others depends on how we understand the relationship between ourselves and the other. So, we do not begin with how I view myself in isolation or who others are in isolation, both these insights on how we understand ourselves and how we understand others are informed by how we understand the primary relationship between ourselves and others. This is counter-intuitive, as normally if we have to think about our relationship with someone, we begin by thinking about ourselves and then the other, and then about the relationship. That seems to be the logical thing to do. However, Buber's argument is that there is a fundamental posture or attitude to a relationship with others that predetermines who we are and who the others are for us. In my view, this is extremely important, particularly for those of us involved in mission research.

What is our fundamental understanding of the relationship we share with those to whom we minister or research? First, when we stand in a relationship with another, we do not experience parts of them; rather, we know them in their wholeness, in their unboundedness. It is the meeting of another like oneself, with infinite possibilities. Buber asks, "What, then, do we know of Thou?" and answers, "Just everything. For we know nothing isolated about it anymore."[27] Second, "The Thou meets me through grace – it is not found by seeking."[28] But what does this mean? For Buber, it meant that we were chosen and met with, all of which is the action of grace. In this gracious meeting, there is suffering and action. He writes, "The Thou meets me. But I step into direct relation with it. Hence, the relation means being chosen and choosing, suffering and action in one."[29] Third, this relation is direct, face to face, and not mediated by a system of ideas or foreknowledge. There are no ulterior motives or aims. Buber writes, "No aim, no lust, and no anticipation intervene between I and Thou . . .Every means is an obstacle. Only when every means has collapsed does the meeting come about."[30] Fourth, "Relation is mutual. My Thou affects me, as I affect it. We are molded by our pupils and built by our works."[31] Both the self and the other are actors and sufferers. It is a relationship that moves both ways, in a sense, equally. Finally, this relation is best characterized by love. This love is not to be confused with feelings:

> Feelings dwell in man, but man dwells in his love. . . Love does not cling to the I in such a way as to have the Thou only for its 'content,' its object, but love is between I and Thou . . .In the eyes of him who takes his stand in love and gazes out of it, men are cut free from their entanglement to bustling activity. Good people and evil, wise and foolish, beautiful and ugly, become successively real to him; that is, set free, they step forth in their singleness and confront him as Thou.[32]

The implications for mission practice and mission research are enormous.

The second insight we get from Buber is about how we should or should not view the other. He postulates that there are two ways of viewing the other, each dependent on what we hold on to as our primary word. Buber gives us two primary words. He says it is either an "I-Thou" or an "I-It." We have already seen how the other could be considered out of the "I-Thou" primary word. This insight is about how the other should not be looked upon; the other should not be seen as an "It." For Buber, for a person to become an "It" is to reduce the person to an object that can be experienced. He writes: "I perceive something. I am sensible of something. I imagine something. I will something. I feel something. I think something." He then concludes that "this and the like together establish the realm of 'It.'" Buber is strongly against experiencing others because of the superficiality resulting from the use of our senses. He writes: "Man travels over the surface of things and experiences them. He extracts knowledge about their constitution from them. . . He experiences what belongs to the things." His argument is that in this attitude of treating others like objects that can be experienced and known, all one gets is an "accumulation of information."[33]

The human is not a thing amongst other things. The human is not a "he" or a "she" but a "thou" that is unbounded and hence cannot be objectified.

A person can be set in a particular time and space, as well as one can describe "the color of his hair, or of his speech, or of his goodness," but each time this is done, the person ceases to be a "Thou." Buber is quick to add melancholically that in our world, however, every "Thou" eventually becomes an "It" – an object among objects, one that can "be described, taken to pieces, and classified... But so long as I can do this, he is no more my Thou and cannot yet be my Thou again."[34] There is a strong critique against treating those we missionize or research upon as objects for whom we have an agenda.

The final insight from Buber is on how the "I" should be in relation to the "Thou." If the other is treated as a "Thou" and not an "It," then what does that do to the "I"? Buber replies: "Through the 'Thou' a man becomes 'I.'"[35] Each time a person treats another as a person, the unchanging consciousness of the person that reaches out to the "Thou" emerges clearly and breaks out into an "I" that is reflectively like a "Thou" and takes possession of oneself. In other words, when I treat another as a person, then only I am able to reflectively know the kind of person I am. Prior to this, the "I" in treating the other as an "It" was itself an "It" without any real connection. And now that he is able to know himself as a "Thou," he is able to observe and analyze the other but from the perspective of a "Thou" so that the other appears as a whole, a sum of qualities.

Buber is describing a fundamental posture that one needs to have with regard to the other. Also, this is a journey of discovering oneself and learning to relate with others. His inspiration is that the other is an echo of the "eternal Thou" and is therefore as unbounded as his maker. Hence, there is no other way to meet with the other but as a person, in friendship, without agenda. As we cultivate this I-Thou relationship, the other addresses and speaks to us, and we respond to them. In these responses, we discover perhaps for the first time that we are authentically ourselves. Once we have found ourselves in our fullness as a person, not someone who has been machinated or mechanized, but as a person, then each time we meet with the other, we know how to treat them as a person. We do not reduce them to their parts but treat them as persons created in the image of God. In our journey with others, once we have reached this level, we can then indeed do mission work and mission research, but how we do it will be very different.

Conclusion

I have tried to problematize the relationship between missionaries and mission workers with the communities they serve. The inspiration for this study was primarily from the Evangelical Lutheran Church in Finland. One day unintentionally, I stumbled upon their website and was intrigued by their statement of their mission philosophy. Their header read "Mission is Collaboration."[36] They seem to understand the Buberian model for mission well. So, in conclusion, following Buber closely and the examples shared above, I will end by listing three characteristics of how one could do mission and mission research.

A missionary or a mission researcher would meet with the community as a person meeting a friend on holiday. There is no need to exercise power, or have condescension, or even any agenda. The meeting is premised on the enjoyment of friendship. All that differentiates me from my friend, be it money, education, etc., all of that becomes meaningless in the participation and enjoyment of friendship. It echoes John 15:15: "I no longer call you servants, because a servant does not know his master's business. Instead, I have called you friends, for everything that I learned from my Father I have made known to you." It also resonates with Aristotle's discrimination of three kinds of friendship. For Aristotle, friendships are based on utility or pleasure, or they are not true friendships. In *Nicomachean Ethics*, he writes:

> Complete friendship is that of good people, those who are alike in their virtue: they each alike wish good things to each other in so far as they are good, and they are good in themselves. Those who wish good things to a friend for his own sake are friends most of all since they are disposed of in this way towards each other because of what they are, not for any incidental reason.[37]

In such a friendship, often, one is not in control of the conversation or action. The friend has the power to speak and address, and we are called to respond. Buber says that in responses, we find ourselves. I have deeply reflected on this to get a sense of what is being said here.

With regard to the missionary and the missionized, it is precisely in their relationship that not only the missionized but also the missionary finds nurture and is ministered. In other words, God has placed the missionized in the missionary's life for his spiritual growth and discipleship. So, we look at those we do mission with as those who are ordained to minister to us. Amos Yong claims that emergent churches are already participating in these forms of engagement in that they "Emphasize genuine dialogue, encourage visiting other sacred sites and even participating in their liturgies, and insist on learning about the lives and religious commitments of others."[38] On the basis of Gibbs and Bolger's *Emerging Churches*, Yong argues that "These activities are informed by the conviction that there is much to be learned from other cultures, even to the point of being evangelized by those of other faiths in ways that transform Christian self-understandings."[39]

Once the missionary or mission researcher has participated in this friendship and in that participation has discovered herself, then Buber suggests that the missionary is able to do all the research and mission work she wants to do. One is able now to avoid cheap reductionism and is able to appreciate the person as a whole – as a friend. So, it appears that Buber is not against research or doing acts of good but looks at it as a later event only to be done by those who have journeyed to personhood through their friendships. Without the work of the Spirit, this journeying is impossible; it is the Spirit that provides both the impetus and the resources to undertake the journey so that in His hands, we are instruments to bring wholesome life to the missionized.

Notes

1 Timothy J. Gorringe, *Furthering Humanity: A Theology of Culture* (Burlington, VT: Ashgate, 2004), 199.
2 Darrell L. Whiteman, "Contextualisation: The Theory, the Gap, the Challenge," *International Bulletin of Missionary Research* 21:1 (1997), 2–6.
3 Stephen B. Bevans and Katalina Tahaafe-Williams, eds., *Contextual Theology for the Twenty-First Century* (Cambridge: James Clarke, 2012), 9.
4 Frantz Fanon, *Black Skin White Masks*, Charles Lam Markmann, trans. (London: Pluto Press, 1986), 112–113.
5 John McLeod, *Beginning Postcolonialism* (Manchester: Manchester University Press, 2000), 20.
6 Anindita Mondal, "Postcolonial Theory: Bhabha and Fanon," *International Journal of Science and Research* 3:11 (2013), 2966.
7 Mondal, "Postcolonial Theory," 2966.

8 Fanon, *Black Skin White Masks*, 114.
9 Afaf Ahmed Hasan Al-Saidi, "Post-Colonialism Literature the Concept of Self and the Other in Coetzee's Waiting for the Barbarians: An Analytical Approach," *Journal of Language Teaching and Research* 5:1 (2014), 95.
10 Al-Saidi, "Post-Colonialism Literature," 95.
11 Mondal, "Postcolonial Theory," 2966.
12 Homi Bhabha, *The Location of Culture* (London: Routledge, 1994), 70.
13 Mondal, "Postcolonial Theory," 2967.
14 Bhabha, *The Location of Culture*, 70–71.
15 Frantz Fanon, *The Wretched of the Earth*, trans. Constance Farrington (New York: Grove, 1963).
16 Bhabha, *The Location of Culture*; Homi Bhabha, "Frontlines/Borderposts," in Angelika Bammer, ed., *Displacements: Cultural Identities in Question* (Bloomington: Indiana University Press, 1994), 269–272; Homi Bhabha, "Cultures in Between" in Stuart Hall and Paul Du Gay, eds., *Questions of Cultural Identity* (London: Sage Publications, 1996), 54.
17 Diana Fuss, *Essentially Speaking: Feminism, Nature & Difference* (New York: Routledge, 1991), xi.
18 Jonathan Rutherford, "The Third Space: Interview with Homi Bhabha," in Jonathan Rutherford, ed., *Identity, Community, Culture, Difference* (London: Lawrence and Wishart, 1990), 207–221.
19 Bhabha, *The Location of Culture*, 55.
20 Lisa Law, "Dancing On The Bar: Sex, Money and the Uneasy Politics of Third Space," in Steven Pile and Michael Keith, eds., *Geographies of Resistance* (London: Routledge, 1997), 107–123.
21 Bhabha, *The Location of Culture*, 1.
22 Maurice S. Friedman, *Martin Buber: The Life of Dialogue* (Chicago: University of Chicago Press, 1955), 8.
23 Eugene Kogon and Karl Thieme, "Martin Buber," *Frankfurter Hefte* 3 (March 1951), 195–199.
24 Friedman, *Martin Buber*, 8–9.
25 Friedman, *Martin Buber*, 8–9.
26 Martin Buber, *I and Thou*, trans. Ronald Gregor Smith (New York: Scribner Classics, 2000), 20.
27 Buber, *I and Thou*, 25.

28 Buber, *I and Thou*, 25.

29 Buber, *I and Thou*, 26.

30 Buber, *I and Thou*, 26.

31 Buber, *I and Thou*, 29.

32 Buber, *I and Thou*, 28–29.

33 Buber, *I and Thou*, 4–5.

34 Buber, *I and Thou*, 13.

35 Buber, *I and Thou*, 20.

36 Evangelical Lutheran Church of Finland, "Mission is Collaboration," https://evl.fi/our-work/international-dimension/mission/mission-is-collaboration, accessed March 29, 2022.

37 Aristotle, *Nicomachean Ethics*, translated and edited by Roger Crisp (Cambridge: Cambridge University Press, 2004), 147.

38 Amos Yong, *Hospitality and the Other: Pentecost, Christian Practices and the Neighbor* (NY: New York University, 2008), 36.

39 Yong, *Hospitality and the Other*, 36.

II
Geographical

5 The Great Commission and Pentecostal Evangelism in Southern Africa

Harvey Kwiyani

Abstract

In the decades following 1970, Pentecostal and Charismatic Christianity has gone through explosive growth in sub-Saharan Africa. All countries in the southern part of the continent now identify as more than 80 percent Christian, increasing from less than 10 percent one hundred years ago. African Pentecostals and Charismatics have made good use of mass evangelism to saturate the religious market of Southern Africa. They have also put a great deal of emphasis on mission, both local and international, to spread their expression of Christianity. Since the late 1990s, they have also been very keen to engage in politics, some for a higher platform of power and others for true community and national transformation. This essay makes a historical survey of the development of Pentecostal and Charismatic Christianity in Southern Africa, exploring the rise and impact of African Independent Churches, the growth of Pentecostal and Charismatic Christianity, and how they have adapted to the need to engage in politics in postcolonial Africa. It uses the story of Zambian Pentecostalism to discuss the growing influence of Pentecostals and Charismatics in Southern Africa.

Introduction

In this essay, I explore the development of Spirit-empowered Christianity in Southern Africa in the fifty years between 1970 and 2020.[1] I seek, on the one hand, to connect the explosion of Pentecostalism in Africa with the phenomenon of African Independent Churches (AICs) that have existed in sub-Saharan Africa since the 1870s[2] and, on the other hand, to explain some factors behind the explosion that has happened in Spirit-empowered churches in Southern Africa since the 1970s. These factors include their strong emphasis on evangelism, prayer, mission, and, oddly, their engagement in the social arena of politics. The explosion of Spirit-empowered Christianity in Southern Africa is partly attributed to the religious heritage of African cultures, which makes Pentecostalism relatable to many Africans due to the path-breaking work of the AICs of old. Evangelism is one of the hallmarks of African Christianity but, until the 1990s, a great deal of this evangelism was haphazard, with its sole focus being to "plunder hell and populate heaven,"[3] Paying little attention to the issues of the converts' day-to-day life. After the turn of the century, like the early church in the New Testament, Spirit-empowered Christians in Southern Africa began to consider the implications of the delayed *parousia*[4] and to engage in other sectors of social life such as politics, economics, education, and health. This has led to a further increase in the growth of the movement in Africa.

AICs and Pentecostalism

The current religious landscape of Southern Africa is, to a great extent, a result of the "Pentecostalization" of Christianity in Africa. Or, dare I say, it is the outcome of the "Africanization of Christianity."[5] Studies suggest that today almost 60 percent of sub-Saharan Africa's population identifies as Christian.[6] One hundred years ago, that percentage was much less than ten.[7] Each of the countries in Southern Africa has Christianity as its strongest religion; many of them have between 80 and 90 percent of their populations identify as Christians. Some, like the Democratic Republic of Congo, Namibia, and Lesotho, have over 90 percent of their populations following Christianity.[8] While a greater part of that growth has taken after the 1970s when Europe's political colonization of Africa came to an end, the explosion of Christianity in Africa started in AICs during the colonial era, away from the suspicious gaze of European colonizers and missionaries.[9] Many of these AICs came into existence to create space to translate the gospel and transform Christianity into a religion that makes sense to the African mind, using the Bible itself, bypassing European interpretations of Christianity. Of course, this should not surprise us. The spirit-centered cosmology of most African cultures demands a type of Christianity that is able to engage the spirits (just like the Africa religion does). Scholars like Allan H. Anderson suggest that many AICs, through their spirit-centered ecclesiology and independent reading of the scriptures, were able to meet the demand for a Spirit-empowered (charismatic-led) Christianity where the missionaries and their followers could not.[10] To a great extent, it is for this reason that many Western missionaries and European colonizers found AICs difficult to comprehend and made every effort to suppress them. It was not until the collapse of European colonialism in Africa that Pentecostalism exploded on the back of the many AICs that had existed for almost a century, giving fresh and modernized expressions to AIC ecclesiologies, enabling some of them to join the global Pentecostal movement. Of course, many chose to reject modernization and have remained AICs until today. However, many more have modernized themselves to join the global movement of Spirit-empowered Christians. In many ways, AICs prepared the way for the Pentecostal explosion that we celebrate today in Southern Africa.[11]

Pentecostalism, the movement that caught fire in 1906 at the Azusa Street Mission in Los Angeles, spread to South Africa in 1908 through the work of John G. Lake and others and immediately formed the Apostolic Faith Mission, one of the most significant Pentecostal denominations in Southern Africa.[12] Before long, several breakaway churches came into existence. What later became the Assemblies of God was established in 1909. The Catholic Apostolic Holy Spirit Church in Zion was formed in 1910, and the Zion Apostolic Faith Mission came into existence in 1920. Later, in 1925, Engenas Lekganyane formed the Zion Christian Church that grew to become South Africa's largest church by the end of the twentieth century. Anderson suggests that by 1990, South Africa has more than 6,000 independent African Pentecostal churches.[13] A PEW survey of 2006 established that 10 percent of urban South Africans were Pentecostal, while 20 percent were charismatic. In total, Spirit-empowered Christians comprised 25 percent of South Africa's urban population. Overall, one third of all Protestants surveyed in South Africa said that they were Pentecostal or charismatic, and one third of all South African AIC members said they were charismatic.[14] This Pentecostal explosion in South Africa has, over the past century, precipitated a similarly explosive growth of spirit-empowered Christianity in Southern Africa, mainly in Zimbabwe, Zambia, and Malawi, due to labor migration.[15]

From Todd Johnson's and Gina Zurlo's *Introducing Spirit-Empowered Christianity*, we learn that, overall, across Africa, Pentecostal/Charismatic Christianity has exploded from 900 thousand adherents in 1900 to 230 million in 2020.[16] South Africa, which had 805,000 Pentecostal/Charismatic Christians in 1900, now has more than 27 million.[17] The Democratic Republic of Congo, which had unregistered numbers of Spirit-empowered Christians in 1900 (because the numbers were too small), now boasts 28 million.[18] In 2020, 52 percent of Zimbabwe's Christians identified as Spirit-empowered. For South Africa, that figure is at 47 percent, while it is at 41 percent for Eswatini.[19] In addition, several countries in Southern Africa are among the countries experiencing the fastest growth in Spirit-empowered Christianity. For instance, Zimbabwe's Pentecostal/Charismatic movements are growing at a rate of 14 percent per year.[20]

Enthusiastic and Independent

There is a direct line connecting AICs to the many Pentecostal, Charismatic, Neo-Pentecostal, and Prophetic movements thriving in Africa today. We cannot rightly celebrate current Pentecostal leaders in Southern Africa without acknowledging people like Isaiah Shembe,[21] Simon Kimbangu,[22] and, of course, the Western Pentecostal missionaries like John G. Lake[23] who also contributed to Pentecostalism in Southern African during the colonial era. All these men and their movements made it possible for Africans to imagine a Christianity faithfully contextualized to the African world—one that can fill up all of life and answer all life's questions. For most Africans, it is now, as it was back then, impossible to tell religion from culture as the two are generally inseparable sides of the same coin of life. Africans generally understand religion to be entirely about staying connected with the spirit world of ancestors and other spirits, including that of the Supreme Being or the Creator God, and their cultures tend to facilitate this use of religion. This is what they need from Christianity, and it becomes possible only in its enthusiastic expressions. This is exactly what they get from Pentecostalism and, to a great extent, shapes the ways in which Africans respond to evangelism.

Today, 200 years after the arrival of the missionaries, when a great majority of sub-Saharan populations are Christian, the belief in a spirit world is unaffected. In some areas, it has intensified. I cannot count how many times I heard as a young African growing up in Malawi that "the spirit-world is more real than the physical world" and that "human beings are essentially spirits that have (and live in) human bodies." It seems plausible to me that it is this belief in an active spirit world that has enabled Pentecostal Christianity to catch fire in postcolonial Africa. *The gap between AICs, Pentecostals, and Charismatics has narrowed significantly in postcolonial sub-Saharan Africa.*

Another aspect of AICs that shapes contemporary Pentecostalism in Africa is their independence. African Independent Churches were independent of both the missionaries and the colonial governments. They were not just self-financing, self-governing, and self-propagating as had been the wish of the missionaries.[24] Most important, they were self-theologizing. They had to self-theologize if they were to make sense of the miraculous ministries of their charismatic leaders. Free theological thought was needed if they were to keep their Christianity independent. Most missionaries could not articulate a theology that made sense of the people's understanding of spiritual powers and how they affect human life, for instance, how people used spiritual power to bless or curse others. Therefore, it was needful for Africans to self-theologize, but this is also why self-theologizing was risky. There was always the danger of syncretism, and this was used as a threat to discourage people from independent theological thought and to discredit those who dared to do this. It is in connection to this that the 1990s were a very significant decade in the development of Pentecostal and Charismatic Christianity in Southern Africa. It was the decade when Pentecostalism reached the tipping point and passed the critical barrier to become the most popular expression of Christianity in Southern Africa. With this came the confidence in African Pentecostalism to let go of Western identities and to become truly African in its expression and thought. African Pentecostals and Charismatics gained the courage to theologize for themselves on a large scale, being suspicious that Western theological education only quenches the fire of the Spirit.

Pentecostal Mission and Evangelism in Southern Africa

The Pentecostal movement in Southern Africa is marked by three major characteristics: evangelism (and this includes their sense of church multiplication and discipleship), prayer (which includes fasting, deliverance, and spiritual warfare), and a growing awareness of the need to participate in the mission of God both locally and globally. These three factors have led to the massive growth that we have experienced since the 1970s. It has often been suggested that Africa has been evangelized by Africans. While this is partly true, it is necessary to acknowledge that Western Pentecostal evangelists have also played a significant part. Certainly, most of the work has been done by Africans, but Western evangelistic organizations like Reinhardt Bonnke's Christ for All Nations (CfAN) have contributed significantly to the evangelization of the continent.[25] For forty years, evangelists such as Reinhardt Bonnke, Ernest Angley, and Morris Cerullo have crisscrossed the continent, filling stadiums with hundreds of thousands of people, performing numerous miracles, and leading millions to Jesus. Let us now return to the key factors.

Evangelism

Evangelism is the bedrock of African Pentecostalism first because of its theology. Pentecostals in Southern Africa anticipate the manifestation of the power of the Holy Spirit in human life in this world, and this includes not only the miraculous provision of sustenance and abundance, but also protection from contrary spirits that seek to frustrate their right to freedom, wealth, and health. They understand themselves to be anointed to manifest God's power in the world, to set captives free and heal the sick. In the context of Southern Africa, there is a real need for such ministries, which, in turn, makes evangelism more possible. Africans respond to miracles, which explains the rising popularity of the prophetic movements in Southern Africa. Second, Pentecostalism in Southern Africa builds upon an eschatology that places a great emphasis on heaven and hell as the destination of humanity.[26] Undergirding this eschatology is the belief that has crossed over from traditional religion that humans are essentially spiritual beings and as spirits, they live forever. So, if they live forever, it is important for people to consider where they will spend eternity after they have vacated their earthly bodies. A typical Pentecostal Christian in Southern Africa will believe that only those who receive Jesus as personal Lord and Savior and are thus born again will enter heaven and enjoy everlasting life in the presence of Jesus. All those who do not receive him will perish in eternal fire in hell, and this includes all nominal Christians in mainline denominations. Consequently, it is every Pentecostal Christian's duty to witness and evangelize. They practice the "evangelisthood" of all believers. Every believer must evangelize. Evangelism is not reserved for the evangelism team or the missions task force. And they do not only evangelize followers of traditional religion and Muslims. They also seek to proselytize members of mainline Christian denominations (e.g., Presbyterians, Anglicans, Methodists, and Catholics). As a matter of fact, mainline denominations have been their catchment area for decades, and, as one would expect, many mainline denominations have lost members to Pentecostal churches.

In addition, many believe that those who convert others to Christianity (by which they generally mean Pentecostalism) will receive a special soul winners reward. Proverbs 11:30 says, "He who wins souls is wise," suggesting that it is important to win souls even though, most probably, Solomon was not talking about evangelism.[27] Isaiah 52:7 is often used to exhort them to preach the good news to anyone who listens: "How beautiful upon the mountains are the feet of him who brings good news, who proclaims peace, who brings glad tidings of good things, who proclaims salvation, who says to Zion, 'Your God reigns!'" There are also a few other texts that shape their theology of evangelism, such as Ezekiel 3 and Ezekiel 33, both of which talk about the woes of the watchman who does not blow the trumpet to warn the city in times of danger. Pentecostal Christians understand themselves to be guards who should sound the trumpet through evangelism to save people from the devil's lure. James 5:19 is used to urge believers to value souls. It says, "Brethren, if anyone among you wanders from the truth, and someone turns him back, let him know that he who turns a sinner from the error of his way will save a soul from death and cover a multitude of sins."[28]

Another key aspect of evangelism in Southern Africa is that it is communal. In most instances, people seek to convert communities. They speak of converting communities and not just individuals. Even when they start with one person, their goal is to have families, clans, and villages of believers. In any case, when a person converts to Christianity, they are expected and encouraged to witness to their families, clans, and communities. Of course, who would want to see their family members, neighbors, and friends perish in hell? Young Christians are told to be aggressive in their evangelism so that none of their relatives and neighbors will rise on judgment day to condemn them for not sharing the good news of Christ. It is common to find families of born-again Christians who then try to evangelize their extended families, clans, and villages. At the peak of the revivals of the 1980s, there were born-again villages in Southern Malawi in which more than half of the people were Pentecostals. My own village was such—our Bible study meetings brought the whole village together.

Prayer

If there is a thing that we can say about Pentecostal Churches in Southern Africa, it is that they are praying churches. People pray like their lives depend on it—and usually, their lives actually do depend on it. Prayer retreats in the mountains are a common thing among them. Prayer is the foundational pillar that, for them, undergirds all ministry, especially evangelism. Without prayer, they believe their evangelism will be fruitless. Prayer is, for many of them, the most important evangelism tool. Many believe that evangelism is only possible if we bind the strong man, putting into practice Jesus' words in Mark 3:27, "No one can enter a strong man's house and plunder his goods unless he first binds the strong man. And then he will plunder his house." Winning souls is impossible without prayer. Planting churches is impossible without prayer. Performing miracles is impossible without prayer. All this says that anything worth doing must be borne in prayer. This they understand largely because of their spiritually sensitive worldview. They know that through prayer they touch and reorder the spirit world to their favor. They believe that prayer opens hearts to the gospel. I heard it said many times that "Prayer moves the hand that moves the world." Many believe this today. To get anything done, prayer must be front and center.

Mission

The Great Commission is understood in its most literal sense, that followers of Christ, especially Pentecostals, must go and make disciples of all nations. For this reason, mission is always connected to going, and, therefore, to migration. As General Superintendent of the Assemblies of God in Malawi, Lazarus Chakwera used to say, "The 'go' in the Great Commission means 'go.'" Many times, I heard him asking, "Which part of 'go' do you not understand? Stop analyzing it and start obeying it." As Director of Missions for the Assemblies of God in Southern Africa, he mobilized the sending of many missionary families to North Africa. This is a part of the strong missionary movement rising up in the wider landscape of Pentecostalism in Southern African that reverses the long-time trends that kept sub-Saharan Christianity as a missionary-receiving land. Today, African Pentecostals are also a missionary sending church. Their understanding of mission is generally evangelism in a foreign place, and, as such, there is a great deal of intra-national and international mission. When we factor in those Christian leaders who move from one part of a country to another part of the same country, sub-Saharan Pentecostal missionaries are many and are scattered both in their countries, in their neighboring countries, in their regions, and around the world. In the past fifty years, there have been great efforts to evangelize the few remaining unreached people groups in the region. For instance, I know of several South African missionaries working among the Yao in Malawi today, while Zimbabwean Pentecostals have been working in Angola for decades. In addition, there has also been an intentional focus on the least reached countries in the region, Mozambique and Namibia. The Living Waters Church of Malawi has focused on evangelizing Mozambique for twenty years now, in which time it has planted more than 1,000 congregations in the country. Furthermore, the Assemblies of God in Malawi has sent missionaries from the wider Southern African region to evangelize in Namibia.

This sense of mission also plays a big role in the African Diaspora. African Christians have been scattered to all parts of the earth, and they have carried with them their faith, their hunger for prayer, and their zeal for evangelism. The language of "African missionaries in the West" is often used even though, to a great extent, these African missionaries are only taking care of African Christians in the West with little intention and effort to evangelize Westerners. It is appreciated, though, that their presence in the West at a time when Western Christianity is in decline means they are witnessing just by being there. Zimbabwean churches in the U. K. are a good example. There is a strong presence of the Apostolic Faith Mission among Zimbabweans in British cities—they have around sixty congregations in the U. K. In addition, Tudor Bismarks' Jabula New Life Community Church also has a handful of congregations in Europe. Ezekiel Guti's Zimbabwe Assemblies of God (ZAOGA) congregations can be found in almost all major cities in Britain. Moreover, there are hundreds of Zimbabwean Anglicans in Birmingham, Zimbabwean Methodists in Sheffield, and Zimbabwean Presbyterians in Glasgow, to name a few.

Evangelism by the Ballot

In the 1990s, Pentecostal-charismatics started to pay attention to the societal issues that affected their members, especially politics. This started out in Zambia, where a Pentecostal preacher, Frederick Chiluba, was president from 1991 to 2002. In 1991, soon after Chiluba became president, he declared Zambia a Christian nation. Soon, evangelism by the ballot spread across Southern Africa. For instance, in the summer of 1999, a Zambian Pentecostal televangelist, Dr. Nevers Mumba, came to preach in Blantyre, Malawi. His sermon, in its entirety, exhorted Pentecostal Christians to get involved in politics because governance matters. He was on a one-man mission to encourage Pentecostal Christians to help save the continent by taking political offices, including that of the president. He accurately reflected on the social context of the Africa of the 1990s, which was, at the time, going through its second liberation, having endured decades of bad governance. He argued that Pentecostals had, for the large part, been too heavenly minded to engage in politics while many sub-Saharan nations suffered political thuggery and economic mismanagement. To prove his conviction, he formed his own political party in Zambia in 1997 that hoped to take over from a fellow Pentecostal Christian, Frederick Chiluba, in the 2001 elections.[29] For him, entire nations would perish if born-again Christians continued to avoid politics. Malawian Pentecostals listened. In the following years, many joined party politics, with a few rising to the top government positions. Pentecostal churches became a key electoral block that all presidential candidates make it a point to court, making many Pentecostal pastors a lot of money from political bribes. In 2020, one of the most popular Pentecostal preachers in Malawi, the former General Superintendent of the Malawi Assemblies of God, Dr. Lazarus Chakwera, is president.

This engagement in the public sphere, especially in the political arena, gained Pentecostalism a great deal of credibility. Success in business, career, or politics was always a testimony that was ready-made for evangelism. In Zambia, Chiluba's 1991 declaration of Zambia as a Christian nation (by which he meant a Pentecostal nation) transformed the country. That one declaration moved Pentecostalism from the margins of Zambia's religious landscape to the center of its government and political spheres.[30] Reflecting on the impact of that declaration, several Zambian leaders have said it made Pentecostalism mainstream on the country's religious landscape. According to Chammah Kaunda:

> Bishop Joseph Imakando stated in 2016 that after Chiluba's declaration, "It became fashionable to be born again. Everyone wants to be Pentecostal." Nevers Mumba added that "before [the declaration] . . . Zambia was not 89 percent Christian as it is now. The Pentecostal movement was not as rampant, and churches were not at almost every corner of this country." Another Zambian Pentecostal leader, Danny Pule (founder of Dunamis Church, former minister in Chiluba's government, and President of the Christian Democratic

Party), asserts that "Pentecostals were so few [before the declaration]. Now, the impact of the Pentecostal is so much. You know, the Baptists and others cannot ignore us. They now accept us probably as equals. Probably they want to have what we have."[31]

It seems fair to suggest that this mainstreaming of Pentecostal and Charismatic forms of Christianity leads Kaunda to begin his article with an observation that, "The rise of Pentecostalism has revolutionized the Zambian Christian landscape to the extent that there is no talk of Christianity without a conscious or unconscious reference to Pentecostalism."[32] He adds that:

> Since the mid-1990s, there has been an unprecedented expansion in Zambian Christianity, which in 2010 was the religion practiced by 86.95 percent of the population. . . . In the early 1980s, less than 5 percent of Zambia's Christian population embraced Pentecostalism. Only a decade later, this grew to about 23.6 percent. Operation World cites the number of Charismatic Christians in mainline denominations in Zambia at 25.8 percent and Evangelical/ Pentecostals at 25.7 percent. Taken together, over half of Zambia's population subscribes to a Pentecostal-Charismatic form of spirituality, and this form of spirituality represents the character of Zambian Christianity.[33]

This significant impact of Pentecostalism on Zambian Christianity is also representative of the extent to which *enthusiastic* Christianity has transformed the face of Christianity (both on the African continent but also on the global scale). With almost 700 million Christians today, Africa has the most Christians of the continents.[34] Almost one third of Christians in the world today live in Africa, and they are greatly shaped by Spirit-empowered theology in whatever tradition of Christianity they follow. It is projected that this percentage will continue to rise beyond 40 percent of world Christians by 2050, and, considering the growth rates, well over 50 percent of these African Christians will practice Pentecostal or Charismatic Christianity of one kind or another.[35] It is already quite rare to find a denomination that has not been influenced by Pentecostalism, either positively or otherwise. Those denominations that excommunicated and persecuted their charismatic members and neighbors of Pentecostals have changed many aspects of their theologies (and ecclesiology) to respond to the Pentecostals, even if that is only to prevent their members from leaving. All Pentecostal indicators of old—*glossolalia*, charismatic gifts, singing choruses and dancing, prayer vigils—have flowed over into mainline Evangelical, Reformed, and even Catholic churches all across Southern Africa.

Some Challenges to Consider

As the story of Nevers Mumba has shown, even though Pentecostalism in Southern Africa has come of age, there remain many challenges to negotiate if it is to stand on a secure footing. The greatest of these challenges, in my opinion, is the contextualization of both their theologies and their ecclesiologies. While they have theologized for themselves to a great extent, their theological thought remains tethered to European and North American Evangelical theologies. We complained about the Church of Scotland in Malawi or the Church of England in Uganda. However, today we have Hillsong-like churches in Nairobi and Bethel-like churches in Harare, and I wonder if they are theologizing and contextualizing properly even in our day and age. This Western-tethered theological thinking can be seen in their institutions of theological training. Their libraries are filled with American books. It appears they are still suspicious of theology, and where they provide their own theological education, the standards are usually below parr. They are not producing their own resources. Hardly any of them are doing church-related research. If research is to be done, it is left to Westerners to fund. Of course, they love academic titles, but they detest theological education. Consequently, and this is where the challenge lies, there remains a dichotomy today between the Pentecostal Christian in worship on Sunday at church and the same Pentecostal Christian in the marketplace on Monday. They will speak in tongues and cast out devils and, before long, receive bribes and extort the poor. It was Chiluba's Pentecostal government that was blamed for massive corruption in Zambia, the corruption that eventually "sold the country" off to China. In Kenya and Malawi, countries with 85 percent of their populations identifying as Christians, corruption is a big problem. Unfortunately for us, speaking in tongues does not translate to integrity or loving people of different tribes, or refusing to steal public funds.

This poor contextualization has also brought us the plague of prosperity-preaching and the money-grabbing prophets, high priests leading worship at the shrine of mammon in Blantyre, Harare, or Pretoria, and many other cities in Southern Africa. They outdo one another at performing dubious miracles—one of them is said to have "walked on air," another "raised a man from the dead," and yet another deposits "miracle money" into his followers' pockets or bank accounts. In the end, like the Christian capitalism that it is, these miracles sell and generate money for the prophets—they now compete in riches. The theological justification for such ministries remains shaky, and while others look for reasonable ways to respond, the prophets continue to take advantage of the poor people's hopelessness, promising them material blessings in exchange for their tithes and seed offerings. 2 Corinthians 9:7 says God loves a cheerful giver, not a dumb one. Perhaps it is high time governments responded to this extortion of the poor in the name of Christ.

Pentecostal denominations in Southern Africa are fiercely independent of one another and ferociously competitive at the same time. Needless to say, most of their leaders do not get along at all. This is characteristic of Pentecostal ecclesiology throughout the continent, as it was of the AICs. Each charismatic leader is often accountable to nobody else. The visions of many of these churches are tied exclusively to one person (and maybe his or her family) and driven by whatever brings the most money today. Those that have somewhat institutionalized have tended to do so along tribal lines. This is the Achilles' Heel of our ecclesiology. It is tribalistic, territorial, and essentially has no systemic need to diversify and engage a different "other." Our sense of independence gives us a false impression of self-sufficiency. We can speak at each other's conferences, but we cannot figure out how best to partner in the ministry in non-threatening ways. As we speak at each other's conferences, we are also exploring how to establish our own branches in our friends' territories and steal their members to help establish ours. There is still a great deal of shuffling of members (or tithers). As Bantu peoples of Southern Africa, most of us understand that *ubuntu* excels in communion. We need others if we are to be, and others need us if they are to be. Somehow, this philosophy does not find ways to influence our theologies and ecclesiologies. We would do infinitely better if we actually practiced our belief that our ministries and congregations need each other. It is especially absurd here in the diaspora that Zambians do not need to engage with Malawians just like Malawians have no need to work with Zambians or that Zimbabwean churches remain Zimbabwean churches even when they are in South Africa, Kenya, or England.

Looking Forward

Pentecostalism in Southern Africa is passing through an exciting *kairotic* moment–there are many great opportunities for growth and impact. The figures are on their side. They have the energy and human capacity to reach not just Africa but also the entire world. They also already have many Christians and potential missionaries scattered around the world. This is a great advantage. It would be helpful if their faith was translated to shalom in their societies to bear witness to the transforming power of the Spirit. The world will be looking to Africa for ecclesiastical leadership in a few generations, and I pray that when that time comes, Africa will be ready.

Notes

1 For the purposes of this essay, Southern Africa includes fourteen of the sixteen countries that form the Southern African Development Community (SADC), namely, Angola, Botswana, Comoros, Eswatini, Lesotho, Madagascar, Malawi, Mauritius, Mozambique, Namibia, Seychelles, South Africa, and Zimbabwe, the Democratic Republic of Congo, and Tanzania.

2 In various ways, African Independent Churches reflect the ministry of a voice shouting in the wilderness to prepare a way for Spirit-empowered Christianity in Africa. I suggest, therefore, that we cannot faithfully understand the post-1970 Pentecostal explosion in Africa without discussing the slow ferment of enthusiastic Christianity that had been brewing in AICs for a good one hundred years before 1970.

3 This was a main theme of Reinhardt Bonnke's evangelistic campaigns in Africa. Ron Steele's account of Bonnke's life and ministry in the 1970s and 80s was entitled *Plundering Hell to Populate Heaven*. See Ron Steele, Reinhard Bonnke: Plundering Hell and Populating Heaven (Sovereign World, 1986).

4 In the Pentecostal sermons of the 1970s and 80s, there was an emphasis on the reality of hell and the need to repent to be saved to go to heaven, all because the second coming of Christ was imminent. By the turn of the millennium, the tone had changed and started to encourage Pentecostal Christians to engage in ministries that bettered the human condition here on earth as well as preparing them for heaven. David Bosch discusses this delayed *parousia* in *Transforming Mission*. See David J. Bosch,

Transforming Mission: Paradigm Shifts in Theology of Mission (Maryknoll, NY: Orbis Books, 1991), 143.

5 I have argued elsewhere that enthusiastic forms of Christianity connect directly with the enthusiastic nature of African spirit-world-focused cultures. Thus, the more Christianity becomes African, the more it takes aspects of African culture, and therefore, the more spirit-centered it becomes. See Harvey C. Kwiyani, "Independent, Enthusiastic, and Africa: Reframing the Story of African Christianity," in Nimi Wariboko and Adeshina Afolayan, eds., *African Pentecostalism and World Christianity: Essays in Honor of J. Kwabena Asamoah-Gyadu* (Eugene, OR.: Wipf and Stock, 2020).

6 Kenneth R. Ross, J. Kwabena Asamoah-Gyadu, and Todd M. Johnson, eds., Christianity in Sub-Saharan Africa (Edinburgh: Edinburgh University Press, 2017), 3.

7 All of Africa had 9 million Christians in 1910, most of whom were in Egypt and Ethiopia, where Christianity has existed since the first Century C. E. and fourth Century C. E. respectively.

8 Ross, Asamoah-Gyadu, and Johnson, *Christianity in Sub-Saharan Africa*, 12, 14.

9 The first AICs emerged in the 1870s, in the decade before the Scramble for Africa which followed the Berlin Conference of 1884–1885.

10 This is a grounding principle discussed in Anderson's very important book, Allan H. Anderson, *Moya: The Holy Spirit in an African Context* (Pretoria: University of South Africa, 1991). Of course, this is not to claim that AICs did this without error.

11 Denis B. M'Passou, *History of African Independent Churches in Southern Africa, 1892–1992*, History of Unhistorical Churches in Southern Africa, 1892–1992 Series (Mulanje, Malawi: SPOT, 1994), 1.

12 They were, of course, preceded by John Alexander Dowie's Zion City Church that came to South Africa in 1895.

13 Allan H. Anderson, *African Reformation: African Initiated Christianity in the 20th century* (Trenton, NJ: Africa World Press, 2001), 95–97.

14 The PEW Forum on Religion and Public Life, "Spirit and Power: A 10-Country Survey on Pentecostals," PEW Research Center, October, 2006, https://www.pewforum.org/2006/10/05/spirit-and-power/, accessed August 23, 2021).

15 For instance, Pentecostalism came to Malawi through the ministry, first of Lyton Kalambule and, later, of Robert Chinguwo in the early 1930s. See

Ulf Strohbehn, *Pentecostalism in Malawi: A History of the Apostolic Faith Mission in Malawi, 1931–1994* (Zomba, Malawi: Kachere Series, 2005).

16 Todd Johnson and Gina Zurlo, *Introducing Spirit-Empowered Christianity: The Global Pentecostal and Charismatic Movement in the 21st Century* (Tulsa, OK: Oral Roberts University, 2020), 30.

17 Johnson and Zurlo, *Introducing Spirit-Empowered Christianity*, 31.

18 Johnson and Zurlo, *Introducing Spirit-Empowered Christianity*, 31.

19 Johnson and Zurlo, *Introducing Spirit-Empowered Christianity*, 32.

20 Johnson and Zurlo, *Introducing Spirit-Empowered Christianity*, 33.

21 Irving Hexham, "Isaiah Shembe: Zulu Religious Leader," *Religion* 27:4 (1997).

22 Aurélien Mokoko Gampiot, *Kimbanguism: An African Understanding of the Bible*, trans. Cécile Coquet-Mokoko (University Park, Pennsylvania: Pennsylvania State University Press, 2017).

23 Kemp Pendleton Bureau, *God's Showman: A Historical Study of John G. Lake and South African/American Pentecostalism* (Oslo: Refleks, 2004). See also, Lyton Chandomba, *The History of Apostolic Faith Mission and Other Pentecostal Missions in South Africa* (Milton Keynes: AuthorHouse, 2007).

24 In the nineteenth century, when Western missionaries came to Africa and Asia, it was hoped that they would establish self-governing, self-financing, and self-governing churches. For a detailed discussion on this, see Peter Dorn, "The Three-Self Principle as a Model for the Indigenous Church" (Masters of Divinity thesis, Concordia Seminary, 1982).

25 The impact of his work is widespread in sub-Saharan Africa. While Bonnke died in 2019, his website claims that his ministry is responsible for the salvation of 61 million Nigerians in the years between 2000 and 2017, https://reinhard.cfan.org/, accessed Sept 14, 2021.

26 An example of this urgency can be seen in Lazarus Chakwera's Eleventh Hour Institute for the preparation of evangelists and missionaries in southern Africa. That institute later became the Assemblies of God Theological Seminary and eventually transformed itself into the Malawi Assemblies of God University. For the reasoning behind the institute, see Lazarus McCarthy Chakwera, "The Development of the Eleventh Hour Institute to be Utilized as a Means of Mobilizing, Training, and Sending Missions Workers from Malawi and Nearby Countries to Unreached Peoples" (DMin diss., Trinity International University, 2000).

27 Unless otherwise noted, all scripture quotations come from the New King James Version.

28 I remember too well a sermon I heard many times in Malawi entitled "The Value of One Soul." It argued that if Jesus could die for one soul, Pentecostal Christians today should do everything humanly possible to save as many souls as they can manage.

29 Dr. Mumba's party, the National Christian Coalition (NCC), was formed in 1997. It soon changed its name to National Citizens Coalition (NCC) and again changed to the Reformed Party in 2006. He stepped down from being the senior pastor of a ministry that he had formed and had shot him to fame in Africa, Victory Bible Church, to concentrate on his dream to save Zambia by the ballot to run for president of the country in the elections that happened in 2001. In those elections, his party got a meager 2 percent of the vote. Soon after, the NCC joined the ruling party, Movement for Multiparty Democracy (MMD), and Dr. Mumba became Vice President of Zambia in 2003 during Levy Mwanawasa's tenure. He was demoted in 2004 after a small political misdemeanor. In response, he immediately declared that he would contest again in 2006 with NCC but under a new name, Reformed Party. He lost again and became Zambia's High Commissioner to Canada from 2009 until 2011. Back home in 2012, Dr. Mumba became president of the MMD, which had been in opposition after losing the 2011 presidential elections. He stood as MMD Presidential Candidate in 2015 and got 0.87 percent of the votes. He continues to lead MMD.

30 Chammah J. Kaunda, "The Making of Pentecostal Zambia: A Brief History of Pneumatic Spirituality," *Oral History Journal of South Africa* 4:1 (2016), 20.

31 Kaunda, "The Making of Pentecostal Zambia," 20.

32 Kaunda, "The Making of Pentecostal Zambia," 15–16.

33 Kaunda, "The Making of Pentecostal Zambia," 15–16.

34 Gina A. Zurlo, Todd M. Johnson, and Peter F. Crossing, "World Christianity and Mission 2021: Questions about the Future," *International Bulletin of Mission Research* 45:1 (2021), 23.

35 Johnson and Zurlo, *Introducing Spirit-Empowered Christianity*, 33.

6 Asian Pentecostal Mission and Spirituality: The Dual Quests in the Globalized World

Connie Au

Abstract

The purpose of this article is twofold. First, it aims to elaborate Pentecostal missions in urban and rural areas in Asia from the twentieth century until the present under the tide of globalization. It analyzes how Asia Pentecostals engage in urban mission in four dimensions: ethnoscape, ideoscape, technoscape, and mediascape. Regarding rural mission, it focuses on how prayer mountains in Malaysia and South Korea minister to the locals and foreigners through spiritual retreats in the natural environment. Secondly, this article illustrates Asian spirituality from ancient to contemporary times including how Asian Pentecostals deal with the world of spirits. It discusses the trend of nationalist spirituality, especially in India and China, which is politically oriented, justifying any kind of oppression imposed on the targeted religions and political opponents.

Introduction

Asia has played an essential role in the mobilization of globalization, and Asian Pentecostals ably adapt to this environment to launch missions in urban and rural settings. Furthermore, Asia is a continent enriched with multiple kinds of spirituality and religions from ancient to contemporary times. Pentecostals can also find ways to engage with Asian spirituality and survive in the oppressive nationalist spirituality fabricated by politicians. This article will first discuss the statistics of the global Christian population and the Pentecostal population in Asia. Second, it will elaborate on how Asian Pentecostals engage in missions in urban settings through the lenses proposed by the distinguished anthropologist, Arjun Appadurai: ethnoscape, ideoscape, technoscape, and mediascape.[1] Third, it will explain how Pentecostals develop rural missions through prayer mountains, with two different examples of the Malaysian tribal Pentecostals and the Yoido Full Gospel Church in South Korea. Finally, it will discuss Asian spirituality by giving an overview of this spirituality from ancient to contemporary time, how

Asian Pentecostals deal with the world of spirits, and how they approach the recent trends of nationalism in India and China.

Global Christian Population and Asian Pentecostal Population

According to a Pew Forum's survey on "The Global Religious Landscape" published in 2012, 13 percent of Christians live in the Asia-Pacific region, ranking fourth in regions that have most Christians (26 percent in Europe; 24 percent in Latin America and the Caribbean; 24 percent in sub-Sahara Africa). However, while Christians are a majority in Europe, Latin America, the Caribbean, and sub-Sahara Africa, they are minorities in the Asia Pacific region.[2] This region contains the most adherents of Hinduism (99 percent), Buddhism (99 percent), folk or traditional religions (90 percent), and other religions (89 percent). This region is also inhabited by three-quarters of the religiously unaffiliated, meaning the atheists, agnostics, and people who do not identify with any religion (76 percent). About 700 million of them live in China. Moreover, most Muslims (62 percent) live in the Asia Pacific region, compared to only 20 percent in the Middle East and North Africa and 16 percent in sub-Sahara Africa.[3]

Among the global Christian population, Johnson and Zurlo estimate that there were 644 million Spirit-empowered Christians by 2020, who constitute 26 percent of the entire Christian population in the world.[4] The Global South contributed the most to this growth, of which 19.5 percent are in Asia, 30.3 percent in Latin America, and 35.7 percent in Africa.[5] Johnson and Zurlo explain that the growth was due to the increase of independent Charismatics in the Global South in the last 120 years. They planted new churches or left the traditional denominational churches.[6]

Although Asia is not the continent with the highest growth amongst the three, Johnson and Zurlo reckon that Asia and Oceania saw the fastest growth of Spirit-empowered Christians between 1900 and 2020.[7] They estimate that there were only 4,300 Spirit-empowered Christians in Asia in 1900, which only comprised 0.4 percent of the global population of Spirit-empowered Christians. However, seventy years later, in 1970, the number had jumped to 7,564,000 (13.1 percent). By 2000, the number had increased to 87,810,000 (19.8 percent), which means 80,246,000 Asians had become Spirit-empowered Christians in just thirty years. In 2020, there were 125,395,000 (19.5 percent) Spirit-empowered Christians in Asia, meaning that 37,585,000 new converts were added in twenty years. Although the increase slowed when compared to the figure of 2000, the growth of Spirit-empowered Christians in Asia has never stopped. Johnson and Zurlo predict that the number will increase to 214,497,000 (20.8 percent) in 2050.[8]

Most Asian countries are predominantly non-Christians or atheists, except the Philippines, where Christians are the majority. Christians of whichever denomination must learn to live with the non-Christian religions,[9] especially in a country with a dominant or state religion, such as Hinduism in India or Islam in Malaysia, where public evangelism is restricted or forbidden. In atheist and communist countries like China, North Korea, and Laos, Christians have been under constant oppression together with believers of other religions for decades.

Urban Missions

Urbanization and globalization are probably each other's cause and effect—urban is the area where globalization is bred and developed; globalization accelerates the urbanization of a particular geographical area. Arjun Appadurai identifies that globalization transforms an urban area in five dimensions. First, it changes the ethnoscapes, meaning the movements of people leading to a shifting world, such as tourists, business people, legal and illegal migrants, and refugees, who are prompted by "the realities of having to move, or the fantasies of wanting to move."[10] Second, it changes the technoscapes, including the "high and low [. . .] mechanical and informational" technology.[11] Third, it changes the finanscapes, including the international flows of capital in the currency markets, stock exchanges, and commodity markets.[12] Fourth, it changes the mediascapes, meaning "the electronic capabilities to produce and disseminate information" in newspapers, magazines, movies, etc. These media spread images and narratives which are controlled and possessed by certain individuals or states to the target audiences. Finally, it changes ideoscapes, that is, "ideologies of states and counter-ideologies of movements" composed of ideas, terms, and images.[13]

Asia has been a continent materializing globalization, primarily through world trade. It offers diverse and rich natural resources, big-scale low-cost labor forces, vast lands for building factories and offices, and fewer environmental restrictions. Foreign investments from western and some affluent Asian countries have been pouring into Asia for the benefits of lower costs. Asian Pentecostals have adapted well to the urbanized and globalized environment and have seized the opportunities to launch urban missions. The following explains how Asian Pentecostals develop an urban spirituality and mission based on Appadurai's categories. Since it is not possible to acquire sources on the finances of Pentecostal churches, this work only focuses on ethnoscape, ideoscape, technoscape, and mediascape.

Ethnoscape

In modern metropolitan cities, it is no longer necessary to travel to a foreign country to launch missions to people of other cultures and ethnic groups as in the past. The pull factors of metropolitan areas draw people worldwide to look for opportunities to earn their living and to study. Asian Pentecostal churches in these urban areas tend to reach out to people of different countries, races, ethnicities, and classes. They organize multi-lingual services and employ ministers of different nationalities to serve the diversified flocks. For example, the International Christian Assembly (ICA) in Hong Kong holds multi-lingual services every Sunday, including in English, Cantonese, Mandarin, Nepali, Indonesian, Sri Lankan, and Thai. Its senior pastor is a Malaysian Chinese who is fluent in English. Its pastoral team includes ministers from Vietnam, Sri Lanka, India, South Korea, the United States, and Thailand. The Chinese ministers from Singapore, Indonesia, and Hong Kong formerly lived, worked, or studied in Australia, Canada, or the United States.[14]

International churches in Asia usually attract wealthy middle-class and professional individuals. Some of them are local, and some are expatriates sent by the headquarters of their firms in the West to work in the branches in Asia. To better serve this particular social class, the pastoral teams are formed of ministers who formerly worked in professional sectors. For example, the ministers of ICA were a lawyer, investment banker, fashion designer, architect, or professional footballer.[15] They were transplanted from their professions in the secular world into the spiritual realm. Similarly, the founder of Bethany Church in Indonesia, Niko Njotorahardjo (1949–2013), had been a businessman with a degree in architecture. He had been a consultant for educational construction and had regularly worked with the World Bank and Asian Development Bank before becoming a pastor.[16] These pastors with professional qualifications prove David Reed's observation that "Pentecostals are partners of sorts with modernity, especially in urban areas."[17]

Besides the wealthy middle class, international churches in the Asian countries that have an advanced economy also attract migrant workers from lower-income Asian and African countries who work as care-workers, domestic helpers, and small trade dealers.[18] For example, Malaysia absorbs migrant workers from Nepal, Vietnam, Africa, Indonesia, and Myanmar. They enhance the multi-lingual and multi-cultural elements of Pentecostal churches in Malaysia.[19] Hong Kong people have employed Filipina and Indonesian women to work as domestic workers since the mid-1970s. There are also workers who travel from rural to urban areas within a country. Vince Le reckons that most Vietnam Pentecostals are temporary migrant workers in the cities of Vietnam. They also work in Malaysia, South Korea, Taiwan, and the Middle East.[20] The diaspora Vietnamese and local Christian groups evangelize Vietnamese migrant workers in the host countries.[21] Among the Pentecostal congregations in Asia, there are also students from suburban areas and foreign countries. En-Chieh Chao discovers that in the Pentecostal churches in Surabaya, Indonesia, most local students came to the city from their hometowns.[22] Whether rich or poor, professional expats or manual migrant workers, suburban workers or students, migrants all look for a spiritual oasis in a foreign land to ease their loneliness and rootlessness through corporate worship and cell group meetings. Some Pentecostal megachurches offer free counseling and healing services for people of different races and religions, such as the Calvary Life Ministries of the Calvary Church, a Pentecostal megachurch in Kuala Lumpur.[23]

International Pentecostal megachurches contain the paradoxes of globalization: the local and migrants, the rich and poor, the economically and academically superior and inferior, and those whose native lands are traditionally Christian, Hindu, Buddhist, Islamic or non-religious. They also realize the harmonious utopia envisioned by globalization where people whose economic and religious backgrounds are drastically different, can worship with the same styles and songs; they are bound by the same faith in Jesus Christ, the same crisis experience of Spirit baptism, and the same practices of charisms. Such diverse individuals colorfully and vibrantly constitute urban Pentecostal churches.

Ideoscape

Asian Pentecostal leaders of megachurches share their visions and teachings on church growth and prosperity gospel through transnational networks, international conferences, church visits, and theological education. David Yonggi Cho's teaching on these two aspects have influenced many Asian and Western Pentecostal leaders since the 1970s. His "Theology of Blessings" was developed out of his impoverishment after Japanese colonialism and the Korean War in the 1950s. Cho sees the kingdom in two perspectives: "the future aspect of the kingdom" and "the present reality of the kingdom of God." He believes that the world can experience the eschatological kingdom through Christ and the Spirit, which means that the gospel is not just about hope for eternal life and salvation of the soul, but also brings about "prosperity in life and physical health and wellness that would keep the balance between spirituality and reality." He particularly sees healing as "a sign of the coming of the kingdom of God to the earth."[24]

Although the prosperity gospel has been criticized for encouraging greed and avarice, in the Asian context, it has given hope to millions of the impoverished who struggle with poverty daily and the subsequent problems such as illnesses, domestic violence, and addictions to alcohol, drugs, and gambling.[25] In 1982, Yonggi Cho spoke at a church growth seminar in Singapore which influenced Malaysia Assemblies of God leaders to launch urban ministry. Churches of more than a thousand members were established one after the other, like Glad Tidings and Grace Assembly in Klang Valley, Malaysia.[26] Eu Choong Chong reckons a significant growth of Christian population and churches can be seen in all cities in Peninsular Malaysia, especially in Klang Valley. This phenomenon is revealed by the increase of large English-speaking Pentecostal churches which have at least a thousand members.[27]

Asian Pentecostal leaders seriously consider global networking as an important tool for church growth and the spreading of Pentecostal teachings. Most megachurches in Asia have built a global network through their migrant workers and expatriates working and living in the host countries. For example, back in 1976, Yonggi Cho launched his mission in Japan and planted a branch in Osaka. In 1978, another church was founded in Tokyo, and by 1989, there were nine churches in Japan with 5,000 members, of which 90 percent were Koreans.[28] In Indonesia, Njotorahardjo had a vision for global mission in 1993, and since that time, his Bethany Church has expanded its network to 108 countries. He envisioned his churches in Indonesia and around the world to be prayer houses for its city instead of mere gatherings of believers.[29] The Bread of Life Church has founded 145 branches in Taiwan and 221 affiliated congregations in the world, of which are mainly in Asia. Services are attended by about 10,000 in the central sanctuary, while people in thirty satellite stations can join them online.[30]

Filipino Catholic Charismatic networks have also spread around the world, which can be attributed to their migrant workers. In Macau, El Shaddai plays a significant role in uniting 15,000 Filipino workers out of the total Catholic population of 30,000 among the 680,000 residents. Its branch in Macau is run by a council of four members and sixty volunteers. They organize weekly prayer meetings at Our Lady of Fatima Church with scripture reading, intercession, dancing, preaching, and sharing of their lives in this Chinese-speaking land.[31] In Japan, according to the survey conducted by the Catholic Commission of Japan for Migrants, Refugees and People in the Move in 2005, 44 percent of Catholics are Japanese, and the rest are migrants, especially from South America and the Philippines.[32] Reginald Alva observes that many people flock to charismatic prayer meetings for physical, relational, and emotional healing led by international charismatic preachers. These healing meetings are particularly helpful to the highly stressful Japanese society where suicide is common. Speakers also encourage audiences to seek repentance, forgiveness, and reconciliation, and to receive the sacrament of reconciliation, particularly for Catholics.[33] In whichever countries in the world, Catholic Charismatic's Life in the Spirit Seminar is a useful means to systematically convey Catholic teachings on Spirit baptism and charisms to both locals and migrants. Through the migrant network, the seminar efficiently expands the Catholic charismatic ideoscape around the world.

In the twentieth century, Pentecostal missionaries established theological seminaries to train local Pentecostals to be ministers. For example, the Ecclesia Theological Seminary in Hong Kong was founded by the Pentecostal Assembly of Canada's missionary, Elmor Morrison. The Asia Pacific Theological Seminary in Baguio, the Philippines, was founded by Maynard Ketcham, field secretary of the Assemblies of God (AG) for the Far East.[34] The Bethel Bible College in Punalur, India, is the oldest AG ministerial institute outside the United States.[35] The Asian Pacific Theological Association is a network of AG Bible colleges in Asia and Oceania to grant accreditation and teacher certificates and to organize regional conferences.[36] However, independent charismatic megachurches have increasingly organized their own ministerial institutes in recent years, alongside these Classical Pentecostal denominational colleges with American origins. These resourceful, independent churches train their own members to become leaders of cell groups, youth groups, and worship teams, with their own theological ethos and practices, especially regarding the exercises of spiritual gifts and evangelism. Nevertheless, independent ministerial institutes cannot completely replace the traditional Bible colleges as ministers still rely on creditable degrees from an accredited theological association or university to gain their congregants' recognition, especially in churches that target the middle class.

Mediascape

Asian Pentecostals know far too well the evangelistic power of the media and hire IT specialists to engage in media ministry. For instance, Asia for Jesus is a transnational network founded by five Taiwanese pastors (Nathaniel Chow, Ewen Chow, Jonathan Chow, Timothy Yen, and Ian Liao) and one Indonesian pastor (Philip Mantofa). This network utilizes social media, Youtube, and printed materials to reach out to the globe. Yen graduated with a degree in Entertainment Arts from California State University and is passionate about media-related ministries as he knows how media can influence the younger generation. This network produces TV programs of different themes, such as emotional wellness, prophetic ministry, worship, and the culture of God's kingdom. The affiliated worship team, Joshua Band, produces their own worship albums and translates English songs into Chinese. The network's website provides "Kingdom Culture Online School" and "Kingdom Culture Equip Course," which broadens the charismatic ideoscape by changing the traditional model of theological training in a seminary constructed with a campus, buildings, library, and community.

Media has been a crucial vehicle to spread Pentecostal teachings to the people of a particular language and age group and to virtually connect Pentecostals around the world. It enables churches to effectively reach out to young people who are major users of the latest social mediums and technology. According to the survey conducted by Pew Forum in 2012, the average age of Christians in the Asia Pacific region is twenty-eight, and they are younger than the general population (twenty-nine years old).[37] Pentecostals' openness to and investment in the latest IT media probably attribute to their appeal to the younger generation.

Technoscape

Technoscape, mediascape, and ideoscape are interrelated. Ideoscape relies on mediascape to reach out to the populace to the ends of the earth; mediascape relies on technoscape to enhance its speed, efficiency, accuracy, and visual, audio, and light effects. But more importantly, technology plays a significant and indispensable role in Pentecostal spirituality. From a small church of about one hundred members to a megachurch of several thousand, technical support staff are indispensable to ensure a smooth flow of worship. At the least, somebody has to change the slides of lyrics. The sound of the drum set, keyboard, guitar, and other musical instruments is adjusted and transmitted by the mixer, soundboard, overdrive amplifier, speakers, and microphones. These instruments are necessary for the playing of contemporary electronic music, which virtually makes every service a live concert. Professional graphic design of the slides, video, and photography projected on the large television screens through the projector enhances the visual effect on the platform and the entire worship hall. Lights of different colors create different atmospheres. Visual, audio, and light effects produced and facilitated by the hi-tech equipment and software create a mood of worship, be it zealous, be it joyous, be it meditative. All these moods are controllable and predictable.

The atmosphere created by the hi-tech equipment and technical support team prepares worshippers to receive the work of the Holy Spirit and for the exercise of spiritual gifts.[38] The human-controlled worship facilitated with expensive hi-tech equipment becomes a virtual altar for Christians to offer their sacrifice of praise to God. It is also an arena for the Spirit to satiate desire through the healing of emotional and physical pains and his direct guidance. Hi-tech worship indeed facilitates the synergy between the divine and human as well as the immediacy of the Spirit. Many churches around the world have adopted this globalized hi-tech worship style without any doubt about its homogeneity, which consequently discourages any imagination of the possibility of various distinctive Asian styles.

Rural Mission

Urban Asian Pentecostal churches embrace a diverse ethnoscape characterized by multi-cultural, multi-ethnic, and multiracial congregations constituted by a significant component of migrants. They establish an ideoscape to spread the ideas of church growth, Spirit baptism, and endowing God's blessings through global networking, denominational and independent theological institutes, and Catholic Charismatic's Life in the Spirit seminar. They keep expanding and updating their mediascape to spread their teachings and to attract the younger generation in particular. They advance their technoscape in worship, which essentially assists congregants in experiencing the presence of God. Efficiency, growth, transnationalism, and triumphalism mean that globalization values can all be found in Asian Pentecostal churches in urban settings. In other words, Asian Pentecostals can adapt to the trend of globalization and make the most of the opportunities and resources to engage in urban mission, which has delivered significant growth since the 1970s.

Urban mission does not represent the entire scenario of Asian Pentecostalism; missions launched by Pentecostals in rural areas are just as important. They fully demonstrate what Harvey Cox calls "primal spirituality"—back to the simple and basic to directly engage with the divine, without any technological, financial, and artificial media.[39] In the rural setting, the landscape overpowers the four "scapes" mentioned above; they immediately become less significant in terms of reaching out to God. Pentecostals in rural areas serve their neighbors and the urbanites through building prayer mountains—retreat facilities for people to experience God in serenity and solidarity. Prayer mountains are a significant aspect of Asian Pentecostal spirituality. The following introduces the prayer mountains provided by the tribal Pentecostals in Malaysia and the Yoido Full Gospel Church in South Korea.

Malaysia

Mount Murud in Sarawak, Borneo, is the fourth tallest peak in Malaysia, bordering Kalimantan, Indonesia.[40] A collective worship site was first developed by the indigenous Lun Bawang and Kelabit people.[41] Gradually it has become a pilgrimage site that attracts people in Malaysia and from overseas. The Lun Bawang and Kelabit people were evangelized by American and Australian missionaries in the 1930s, and Sidang Injil Borneo (SIB) was founded and has become the dominant church.[42] Due to the shared Christian faith, these indigenous people of different tribes come together to participate in prayer meetings and other religious events.

The revival that broke out in the Kelabit Highlands in 1973 remarkably transformed the lives of the community. It was started by a group of students in Bario secondary school who prayed earnestly.[43] Their spiritual fervor spread quickly to the entire Kelabit and Lun Bawang communities and even to other areas in Sarawak and Kalimantan. Many people were baptized by the Spirit, spoke in tongues, and repented of alcoholism, theft, quarrels, and other misbehaviors. They spent days praying instead of farming and going to schools, but they still gained good harvest and academic results. The Kelabits considered themselves a "chosen people" because of this revival.[44]

The Bario revival led to subsequent revivals in the 1980s. A lay leader of the Lun Bawang tribe, Agung Bangau, was well-known for his miracles, which effectively convinced the people of his teachings. He regularly went up to Mount Murud to do retreats and inspired other Christians to develop it as a prayer mountain without knowing similar initiatives in the world.[45] Many Christians were first scared of this idea, as the mountain had been known as a habitat of evil spirits. With courage, they claimed the mountain for Christian prayer, and old beliefs were eradicated.[46] The first prayer meeting was conducted on the site in July 1985.[47] Then the first church was built on the upper slopes of the mountain in 1990 and was expanded in 1992. It can accommodate 1,200 people, and other buildings for retreat were gradually constructed.[48] A biennial international revival meeting is now held and attracts hundreds of pilgrims from Malaysia and other parts of the world to participate, despite trekking through the muddy paths in the jungles with their bulky luggage for two days. They also face the possible challenge of rain and leeches.[49] Protestants from various denominations and Catholics join the SIB members to participate in services conducted in English and Bahasa Malaysia.⁵⁰ The revival meetings transform this tribal area into a multi-ethnic, multi-national, and multi-denominational carnival.

Mount Murud physically represents the shared Christian memory of the Kelabit, Lun Bawang, and other neighboring tribes, and thus strengthens their religious identity as a group of Christians who seek the Holy Spirit and lead a sanctified life. The religious ecotourism that the mountain offers connects the indigenous people with the outside world and local charismatic spirituality with global Christianity.⁵¹ As a former principal of a local primary school, Pudun Tadem, said, "We are not well-off financially, so we cannot go out to the people. But through this, people can come to us. The world comes to us."⁵²

South Korea

Praying on mountains has been practiced by adherents of Shamanism, Buddhism, Christianity, and other religions for centuries in the Korean Peninsula. During the Japanese occupation in 1910–1945, Christians escaped from oppression to the mountains. Yongdo Lee was one of the prominent figures to lead a monastic life on mountains. He prayed, fasted, and read the Bible on Kumkang Mountain.⁵³ After the liberation and the Korean War, another wave of the prayer mountain movement was started on Yongmun Mountain by Ra Woon Mong (1914–2009). He founded the Gideon Monastery and Gideon Theological Seminary, whose graduates steered the prayer mountain movement across South Korea. The number of prayer mountains increased from 207 in 1975, 239 in 1978, 462 in 1988, to 500 in 1994. Sang Yun Lee reckons that Ra's prayer mountain movement played an important role in the spread of Pentecostalism in South Korea through his messages on revivalism and the Holy Spirit movement.⁵⁴ Under the current of revivalism, a prayer mountain was founded by a Pentecostal, Jasil Choi (1915–1989), Yonggi Cho's mother-in-law and ministerial partner. She established it in Osanri village in 1973, and now it is called Osanri Choi Jasil Memorial Fasting Prayer Mountain. It contains a sanctuary that accommodates 10,000 people, twelve subsidiary chapels, as well as bedrooms, restaurants, and a cafeteria. Free shuttle buses are provided almost every hour daily to take passengers to travel between Yoido Full Gospel Church and the prayer mountain in about an hour.⁵⁵ This arrangement is ideal for urbanites who can only spare a few days to do a retreat in a natural environment. Christians from different denominations and non-Christians from neighboring countries like Japan and Taiwan, and other parts of the world go there to pray, fast, and even anticipate experiencing healing and other miracles.[56]

In most religions, mountains trigger the imagination of being the "'locations of or passages to paradise,' in essence bringing one closer to the heavens." Their heights exhort humankind living on earth to aim at higher goals in piety, virtue, and sanctity.[57] On the one hand, praying on a high mountain draws people closer to experiencing God's real presence, which is particularly emphasized in Pentecostal spirituality. On the other hand, through prayer mountains, Pentecostals in rural areas of Asia engage in a unique mission of being hospitable to the urbanites who travel to a natural environment for a retreat. They can focus on meditation, reflection on their personal lives, and intimately staying together with themselves and God. Although prayer mountains are also founded in the United States and the sub-Sahara,[58] the distinctive Asian tribal features and the ancient indigenous spiritual understanding of mountains amalgamated with Christian spirituality cannot be easily globalized.

Asian Spirituality and Asian Pentecostals

Asia is the birthplace of almost all major religions, ranging from multi-theism (Hinduism, Shinto) and pantheism to monotheism (Islam, Christianity, Judaism) and politically oriented atheism. Besides these categories, there are plenty of unclassifiable religious rituals which can be generalized as popular religion amalgamated with institutional religions, ancestral veneration, and shamanism.

From the Ancient to Contemporary Times

For instance, Chinese popular religion has selectively adopted the ethical teachings of the three major philosophical and religious streams, Confucianism, Daoism, and Buddhism, and translated them into rituals. These three streams were highly regarded by the intelligentsia, especially Confucianism, which for thousands of years was the core subject in the public examination for the literati to elevate from being a peasant to a government official. Before Christian missionaries condemned practices of popular religions as superstitious, those Confucian literati had long challenged the rituals practiced beyond the Confucian Classics, such as the *Book of Rites* and the imperial procedures to conduct sacrifices. The emperor venerated heaven and prayed for the harvest and blessings on behalf of the whole nation during festivals.

Moreover, ancient Chinese imagined the spiritual world *vis-à-vis* their earthly imperial kingdom formed by monarchy and hierarchy. Mount Mao sect, a branch of Daoism, teaches that some real historical figures and heroes were deified as "ghost gods" then promoted as heavenly gods.[59] In the hierarchical pantheon, officials of different ranks have authority over different matters, such as weather, sicknesses, and marriages of the human world. Some of them can give verdicts to spirits or human beings on whether they should be allowed to ascend to "the upper world where gods live. . . the middle world where the normal people, the religious people, or the potential god-to-be live; and the underground world or the hell."[60] This "excluded middle," in Paul G. Hiebert's term, contains "beings and forces that cannot be directly perceived but are thought to exist on this earth. These include spirits, ghosts, ancestors, demons, and earthly gods and goddesses who live in trees, rivers, hills, and villages."[61] They cohabit with humans and other natural entities "in the land of the living," to quote the Psalmist's phrase (Ps 27:13). Asians are no strangers of the excluded middle through their personal encounters with spirits, their mythology, hearsay from acquaintances, and the inhabited culture for centuries before Christ.

Some practices which bear prophetic implications like fortune-telling and *Fengshui*[62] are adopted by anyone who is concerned about their health, wealth, career, marriage, interpersonal relationships, and indoor and outdoor safety—no matter whether they are rich or poor, professional or manual workers, well-educated or illiterate, young or old, or in urban and rural environments. In recent decades, meditative exercises that emphasize the harmony between the body, mind, and spirit like Zen, Falungong, and Mindfulness, which are embedded with Buddhist or Daoist elements, have become popular in the West and have spread to non-Hindu and non-Buddhist Asian countries. Breathing and physical exercises like yoga originating from Hinduism, and *qigong* from Daoism have been practiced throughout the world. These meditative exercises are sometimes supplemented with music therapy and with tools like the Tibetan singing bowl. These meditative practices and fortune-telling methods, together with Western New Age movements and Tarot cards, are particularly welcome by the younger generations in Asia, who are skeptical about the need to participate in any institutionalized religions whatsoever.

Pentecostals and the World of Spirits

For the 2,000 years after Christ, Christianity spread eastward from Syria through the Nestorians, from Western Europe through the Catholics, and from Europe and North America through the Protestants. While some Asians were converted to this monotheistic religion, some considered Jesus as sage-like Hindu gurus or a moral figure like Confucius masters. But when the Pentecostals came, Asians were vividly introduced to the other person of the Godhead in Christianity—the Holy Spirit. They realize that despite all the spirits and ghosts in their surroundings, there is one and only one Spirit who does not harm them but delivers them from all evil bondages. Physical healing, exorcism, speaking in tongues, and baptism in the Spirit channel them through personal experiences of this *Creator Spiritus*.

For instance, the Lun Bawang people had believed in the existence of Puteri Rimba, a female spirit, on Mount Murud for generations. Some of them eye-witnessed that it was "a beautiful princess with long hair, bare feet, and black clothing who was discovered after the church was built living in a cave above the church at Mt. Murud." She also took "the form of a water buffalo" and "a beautiful woman" during church services, but exorcism did not take place immediately. After an annual Christian service in 1996 or 1997, a group of Lun Bawang women claimed to have received a message from God to cast Puteri Rimba and her daughter away from the cave where they lived. About 400 people walked from the church for about one and a half hours. Upon their arrival, they held a service and "bombed" the cave entrance with coarse salt for an hour as instructed by the two women who had received the vision from God.[63] This ritual of exorcism both symbolically and practically demonstrates that mountains are not only regarded as a sacred place but also a spiritual battleground. For generations, the Lun Bawang might not have had the courage to confront their perceived evil spirits, but their charismatic experiences empowered them to do so in a way that was consistent with their culture. Matthew Amster considers that this exorcism symbolized "their liberation from the 'time of darkness' prior to conversion." This warfare against the female spirits led by charismatic laywomen who had no priestly training in exorcism challenged the male-dominated church leadership.[64]

Pentecostals and Nationalist Spirituality

In the struggle against Western colonialism and imperialism in Asia, spirituality has been closely linked with nationalism, which unites the people of an ethnic group inside and outside a country. Peter van der Veer, a Dutch anthropologist specializing in religion and nationalism in Asia and Europe, argues that this "nationalist spirituality" implies "the essence of the people, their collective spirit, which calls our attention to the fertile connection of spirituality and nationalism."[65] It often becomes a tool to attack and oppress their political opponents. Here are two of the most obvious examples.

India

Mohandas Karamchand Gandhi adopted Hindu teachings and put them into practice through asceticism. He gradually developed a nationalist spirit to fight for independence from the British. Gandhi's Hindu national identity has never been abandoned after the independence in 1947. In 2014, the Bharatiya Janata Party, which promotes the Hindu nationalist ideology of *Hindutva* ("Hindu-ness") in a religious and cultural sense, won the election.[66] Minority religions have been under threat since this party came to power in 2014. As Peter van der Veer analogically describes, "It is the exorcism of the Muslim and Christian Other that is central to political witchcraft."[67] Among the entire Christian population, Pentecostals have been "disproportionately targeted," as observed by Chad M. Bauman, due to their active evangelism, public visibility, rapid growth, ecstatic behavior, and condemnation of Hindu gods as "idols."[68] Pentecostals are "denationalized" and "account for fully 87 percent of the targets of "everyday" anti-Christian violence."[69]

China

Ever since the Communist Party established its sovereignty in China in 1949, its form of nationalism has been imposed on all institutionalized religions, including Catholicism, Protestantism, Islam, Buddhism, and Daoism. They were forced to register with the state department and founded a patriotic association. In 2016, under the regime of Xi Jinping, new nationalist jargon and policy were adopted: the Sinicization of Religion. Xi addressed the annual religious conference of the National Working Meeting on Religions, demanding that "religions adhere to the direction of Sinicization, [. . .] interpreting rules and dogmas in a way that corresponds to the needs attached to the progress and development of contemporary China."[70] He requires that "emotional identity and the behavioral habits of each person" should be infilled with socialism. Benoît Vermander, a Jesuit scholar at Fudan University in Shanghai, succinctly summarizes the requirements of this policy:

> Religions must work towards (1) more Chinese "religious values;" (2) more Chinese religious symbols; and a (3) "more Chinese practice of the faith." A distinction is to be made: (a) Religions of foreign origin must put the stress on making behaviors, liturgy, dogmas, and cultural expression fully compatible with the political, economic, and cultural aspects of Chinese society, "forming a religion with unique Chinese characteristics, and showing a special spiritual outlook." (b) As to "local religions" (i.e., Daoism and Buddhism), "sinicizing" means to adapt to modern, socialist China and to the imperatives of the 'New Era.'[71]

Ever since the announcement of this new policy, academic institutions have conducted conferences and seminars to discuss how to integrate the party's perceived Chinese-ness into religious dogmas and liturgies. According to ChinaAid's Annual Persecution Report, the Zaozhuang Research Center on Sinicization of Christianity was founded in Shandong. China Christian Council and Three-Self Patriotic Movement in Henan established a Christianity Sinicization Research Office. Officials of Inner Mongolia issued "Implementation Plan for Promoting Adherence to the Path of Religious Sinicization in China."[72] The China Christian Council and Three-Self Patriotic Movement issued a document entitled "Principle for Promoting Chinese Christianity in China for the Next Five Years (2018–2022)," instructing that "contents of the Bible that are compatible with the core values of socialism should be deeply researched in order to write books that are popular and easy-to-understand."[73]

No matter how the scholars of religious studies interpret this new policy, for Christians at the grassroots level, in practice it means new restrictions and oppressions. Flag-raising and anthem singing are required in religious places.[74] Registered churches are pressurized to show their loyalty to the government. Portraits of Xi are hung on church walls. The Bible is to be re-translated, and verses that are perceived to challenge the regime are to be removed.⁷⁵ Books on catechism and biblical exegesis are revised. Sellers of Christian books and audio Bible players were charged with an "illegal business operation" and were imprisoned. Church wedding attendants must be over eighteen years old and register their names. Hymns are prohibited at weddings and funerals. Christian logos and crosses are removed from graveyards. Facial recognition cameras and other surveillance devices are installed in both registered and house churches. Online live streaming of preaching, worship, and theology training courses are cut off.⁷⁶ Biometric data, voice analysis, and satellite-tracking systems with the advanced 5G technology enhance the regime's capacity, efficiency, and accuracy to inspect the local people and foreigners.⁷⁷

Based on the collected data and stories, ChinaAid concluded that persecutions against Christians "intensified" in 2020, including against the elderly, adults, and children; urban and rural churches; Three-self and house churches; local pastors and missionaries.⁷⁸ It is assumed that ecstatic behavior, healing, speaking in tongues, and so on, which have been labeled as superstitious for years, are now even more sensitive.⁷⁹ Vermander foresees that the goal of the Sinicization of religions is to develop "national sacredness" and a civil religion, "making the country the object of the citizens' adoration, teaches them that service done to the State is service done to its tutelary god." Han Chinese and minorities will be united with "love and fear" for the party.⁸⁰ With this new policy, the Chinese Communist Party has created a nationalist spirituality that is party-centered and masqueraded with the term "Sinicization," which may give outsiders the first impression of tracing the roots of traditional Chinese culture and religions, i.e., indigenization, instead of what it actually is: a new all-encompassing scheme of oppression assisted by advanced technology.

Conclusion

From the early twentieth century to the present, Pentecostals have never stopped being passionate for the kingdom of God, and this passion has spread to Asia through Western missionaries and church periodicals. Although the way Asian Pentecostals interpret the kingdom of God and Pentecostal theology may have varied, they share the faith of experiencing the power of the Holy Spirit here and now, be it affectionate feeling (e.g., supreme joy, ecstasy, the release of grief); be it miraculous manifestations (e.g., healing, exorcism, words of wisdom and knowledge); be it psychological empowerment to face everyday challenges.

Asian Pentecostals engage in urban mission within the ethnoscape, ideoscape, mediascape, and technoscape shaped by globalization for the sake of expanding God's kingdom on earth. They reach out to the urbanists of different educational, economic, social, religious, and professional backgrounds and generations. They establish prayer mountains with their unique local culture in the natural environment for people from different corners to connect and re-connect with God and their inner selves. They have learned to practice their Pentecostal faith in the continent full of a variety of spirituality and spirits and the latest invention of nationalist spirituality, targeting political opponents. Asia is full of the paradoxes of modernity and pre-modernity, secularity and religiosity, and rural and urban dynamics. Its political climate is ever-changing since most of the Asian countries are non-democratic but ruled by dictators or military leaders. Asians keep learning to live with these paradoxes and adapt to the governments' policies, whether moderate and restrictive, depending on the authorities' own interests. Asian Pentecostals do the same.

Notes

1 Arjun Appadurai, "Disjuncture and Difference in the Global Cultural Economy," *Theory, Culture and Society* 7:2–3 (June 1990), 297–299.
2 Pew Research Center, "The Global Religious Landscape," December 18, 2012, https://www.pewforum.org/2012/12/18/global-religious-landscape-exec/, accessed April 22, 2021.
3 Pew Research Center, "The Global Religious."
4 Johnson and Zurlo use this term to refer to the "broadest interpretation of the Pentecostal and Charismatic Movement worldwide." Todd Johnson and Gina Zurlo, *Introducing Spirit-Empowered Christianity: The Global Pentecostal and Charismatic Movement in the 21st Century* (Tulsa, OK: ORU Press, 2020, limited pre-publication edition), 6.
5 Johnson and Zurlo, *Introducing Spirit-Empowered Christianity*, 38–39.
6 Johnson and Zurlo, *Introducing Spirit-Empowered Christianity*, 93.

7   Johnson and Zurlo, *Introducing Spirit-Empowered Christianity*, 35.

8   Johnson and Zurlo, *Introducing Spirit-Empowered Christianity*, 39.

9   Peter C. Phan, *Asian Christianities: History, Theology, Practice* (Mary Knoll, NY: Orbis, 2018), 246.

10 Appadurai, "Disjuncture and Difference," 297.

11 Appadurai, "Disjuncture and Difference," 297–298.

12 Appadurai, "Disjuncture and Difference," 298.

13 Appadurai, "Disjuncture and Difference," 299.

14 International Christian Assembly, "Pastoral Team," https://icahk.org/pastoral-team, accessed April 9, 2021.

15 International Christian Assembly, "Pastoral Team."

16 David Reed, "From Bethel Temple, Seattle, to Bethel Church of Indonesia: Missionary Legacy of an Independent Church," in Michael Wilkinson, ed., *Global Pentecostal Movements: Migration, Mission and Public Religion* (Leiden: Brill, 2012), 107.

17 Reed, "From Bethel Temple," 103.

18 For migrant workers in Asian Pentecostal and charismatic churches, please see my article: "Globalization and Asian Pentecostalism in the Twenty-First Century," *Pneuma: Journal of the Society for Pentecostal Studies* 42:3–4 (2020), 1–21.

19 Denise A. Austin and Lim Yeu Chuen, "Critical Reflections on the Growth of Pentecostalism in Malaysia," in Denise A. Austin, Jacqueline Grey and Paul W. Lewis, eds., *Asia Pacific Pentecostalism* (Leiden: Brill, 2019), 209.

20 Vince Le, "The Pentecostal Movement in Vietnam," in Amos Yong and Vinson Synan, eds., *Global Renewal Christianity: Asia and Oceania Spirit-Empowered Movements—Past, Present, and Future* (Lake Mary, FL: Charisma House, 2016), 184.

21 Le, "The Pentecostal Movement in Vietnam," 193.

22 En-Chieh Chao, "Counting Souls: Numbers and Mega-Worship in the Global Christian Network of Indonesia," in Terence Chong, ed., *Pentecostal Megachurches in Southeast Asia: Negotiating Class, Consumption and the Nation* (Singapore: ISEAS-Yusof Ishak Institute, 2018), 57.

23 Jeaney Yip, "Reaching the City of Kuala Lumpur and Beyond: Being a Pentecostal Megachurch in Malaysia," in Terence Chong, ed., *Pentecostal Megachurches in Southeast Asia: Negotiating Class, Consumption, and the Nation* (Singapore: ISEAS-Yusof Ishak Institute, 2018), 85.

24 Sang Yun Lee, "The Kingdom of God in Korean Pentecostal Perspective," in Amos Yong and Vinson Synan, eds., *Global Renewal Christianity: Asia and Oceania Spirit-Empowered Movements—Past, Present, and Future* (Lake Mary, FL: Charisma House, 2016), 151.

25 Wonsuk Ma, "David Yonggi Cho's Theology of Blessing: Basis, Legitimacy, and Limitations," *Evangelical Review of Theology* 35:2 (2011), 146.

26 Timothy T. N. Lim, "Pentecostalism in Singapore and Malaysia: Past, Present, and Future," in Amos Yong and Vinson Synan, eds., *Global Renewal Christianity: Asia and Oceania Spirit-Empowered Movements—Past, Present, and Future* (Lake Mary, FL: Charisma House, 2016), 216.

27 Chong Eu Choong, "Pentecostalism in Klang Valley, Malaysia," in Terence Chong, ed., *Pentecostal Megachurches in Southeast Asia: Negotiating Class, Consumption, and the Nation* (Singapore: Yusof Ishak Institute, 2018), 100, 103.

28 David Hymes, "Toward a History and Theology of Japanese Pentecostalism," in Amos Yong and Vinson Synan, eds., *Global Renewal Christianity: Asia and Oceania Spirit-Empowered Movements—Past, Present, and Future* (Lake Mary, FL: Charisma House, 2016), 167.

29 Reed, "From Bethel Temple," 107.

30 Iap Sian-Chin and Maurie Sween, "Pentecostal and Charismatic Christianity in Protestant Taiwan," in *Global Renewal Christianity: Asia and Oceania Spirit-Empowered Movements*, 135.

31 *La Croix International*, "Charismatic Prayer Group Unites Filipino Migrants in Macau," March 16, 2021, https://international.la-croix.com/news/religion/charismatic-prayer-group-unites-filipino-migrants-in-macau/13974, accessed April 10, 2021.

32 Reginald Alva, "Catholic Charismatic Renewal Movement and Healing in Japan's Religious Culture," *Claritas: Journal of Dialogue and Culture* 5:1 (March 2016), 43.

33 Alva, "Catholic Charismatic Renewal," 44.

34 Asia Pacific Theological Seminary, "About the Seminary: History," https://apts.edu/seminary-profile/history/, accessed April 12, 2021.

35 Johnson and Zurlo, *Introducing Spirit-Empowered Christianity*, 57.

36 Asia Pacific Theological Association, "About APTA," http://apta-schools.org/about/, accessed April 12, 2021.

37 Pew Research Center, "The Global Religious Landscape," December 18, 2012, https://www.pewforum.org/2012/12/18/global-religious-landscape-christians/, accessed April 22, 2021.

38 Connie Au, "'Pentecostal Spirituality: Beliefs, Ethos, Practice," in Frank Senn, ed., *Protestant Spiritual Traditions*, vol. 2 (Eugene: Wipf and Stock, 2020), 170–171.

39 Harvey Cox, *Fire from Heaven: The Rise of Pentecostal Spirituality and The Reshaping of Religion in the Twenty-First Century* (New York: Addison-Wesley Publishing Company, 1995). See his chapter, "Shamans and Entrepreneurs: Primal Spirituality on the Asian Rim," 213–242.

40 Carolyn Hong, "Seeking God in Peak Pilgrimage," The Straits Times, January 26, 2015, https://www.straitstimes.com/asia/se-asia/seeking-god-in-peak-pilgrimage, accessed April 20, 2021.

41 Matthew H. Amster, "New Sacred Lands: The Making of a Christian Prayer Mountain in Highland Borneo," in Ronald A. Lukens-Bull, ed., *Sacred Places and Modern Landscapes: Sacred Geography and Social-Religious Transformations in South and Southeast Asia* (Tempe, AZ: Arizona State University Program for Southeast Asia Studies, 2003), 131–134.

42 Amster, "New Sacred Lands," 134–135.

43 Amster, "New Sacred Lands," 137–138.

44 Amster, "New Sacred Lands," 138–139.

45 Amster, "New Sacred Lands," 141.

46 Amster, "New Sacred Lands," 150.

47 Hong, "Seeking God."

48 Amster, "New Sacred Lands," 143.

49 Hong, "Seeking God."

50 Amster, "New Sacred Lands," 143–144.

51 Amster, "New Sacred Lands," 133, 152.

52 Hong, "Seeking God."

53 Julie Ma, "Prayer Mountain Movement, Korea," in Michael Wilkinson, Connie Au, Jörg Haustein, Todd Johnson, eds., *Brill's Encyclopedia of Global Pentecostalism Online* (Leiden: Brill, 2021), https://referenceworks.brillonline.com/entries/brill-s-encyclopedia-of-global-pentecostalism/prayer-mountain-movement-korea-COM_044993?s.num=0&s.f.s2_parent=s.f.book.brill-s-encyclopedia-of-global-pentecostalism&s.q=Prayer+Mountain+Movement%2C+Korea, accessed April 22, 2021.

54 Sang Yun Lee, "Ra, Woon Mong," in *Brill's Encyclopedia of Global Pentecostalism Online*, https://referenceworks.brillonline.com/entries/brill-s-encyclopedia-of-global-pentecostalism/ra-woon-mong-

COM_039349?s.num=0&s.rows=20&s.mode=DEFAULT&s.f.s2_parent=brill-s-encyclopedia-of-global-pentecostalism&s.start=0&s.q=%28ra+woon+mong%29, accessed April 22, 2021.

55 Sang Yun Lee, "Choi, Jasil," in *Brill's Encyclopedia of Global Pentecostalism Online,* https://referenceworks.brillonline.com/entries/brill-s-encyclopedia-of-global-pentecostalism/choi-Jasil-COM_039338?s.num=0&s.f.s2_parent=s.f.book.brill-s-encyclopedia-of-global-pentecostalism&s.q=Choi%2C+Jasil; "Osanri Choi Ja-sil Memorial Fasting Prayer Mountain," DCEM, http://www.davidcho.com/NewEng/PrayerMountain.asp, accessed April 21, 2021.

56 Julie Ma, "Influence of Pentecostal Spirituality to Asian Christianity," *Asian Journal of Pentecostal Studies* 23:2 (August 2020), 112.

57 Amster, "New Sacred Lands," 133.

58 See Orji Boniface Ifeanyi and Odeh Lemuel Ekedegwa, "Moutain Worship and Quest for Miracles: A Study of Some Selected Miracle Mountain Prayer Ministries in Igboland," in Soede Nathanael Yaovi, Patrick U. Nwosu, Akiti G. Alamu, et al., eds., *Ori-Oke Spirituality and Social Change in Africa: Contemporary Perspectives* (Bamenda: Langaa Research and Publishing Common Initiative Group, 2018), 393–404.

59 Samuel Hoi-Kee Ooi, "A Study of Strategic Level Spiritual Warfare from a Chinese Perspective," *Asian Journal of Pentecostal Studies* 9:1 (2006), 151.

60 Ooi, "A Study," 151.

61 Paul G. Hiebert, "The Flaw of the Excluded Middle," in Robert L. Gallagher and Paul Hertig, eds., Landmark Essays in Mission and World Christianity (Maryknoll, NY: Orbis Books, 2009), 183.

62 Feng shui is the romanization of two Chinese characters, 風 (wind) and 水(water). It is a Chinese geomancy for auspicious purposes by seeking the harmony between the universe, heaven, earth, and humanity in architectural sites, such as tombs, temples, residential apartments, offices, etc., and interior design.

63 Amster, "New Sacred Lands," 148.

64 Amster, "New Sacred Lands," 149.

65 Peter van der Veer, *The Modern Spirit of Asia: The Spiritual and the Secular in China and India* (Princeton: Princeton University Press, 2014), 41.

66 Chad M. Bauman, "Pentecostals and Interreligious Conflict in India: Proselytization, Marginalization and Anti-Christian Violence," *PentecoStudies* 16:1 (2017), 13.

67 Van der Veer, *The Modern Spirit of Asia*, 137.

68 Bauman, "Pentecostals and Interreligious Conflict," 18–19, 21.

69 Bauman, "Pentecostals and Interreligious Conflict," 10.

70 Benoît Vermander, "Sinicizing Religions, Sinicizing Religious Studies," *Religions* 10:137 (2019), 3.

71 Vermander, "Sinicizing Religions," 3–4.

72 ChinaAid Association, "ChinaAid's Annual Persecution Report 2020 (January – December 2020)," https://drive.google.com/file/d/1FcV6rElfBYtM7cFpKspV2b0kE8pTgJ31/view, 43, accessed May 7, 2021. A long list of seminars held across the country is published in the report on pages 3–4.

73 Vermander, "Sinicizing Religions," 5.

74 Vermander, "Sinicizing Religions," 4.

75 Thomas Harvey, "The Sinicization of Religion in China: Will Enforcing Conformity Work?" *Lausanne Global Analysis* 8:5 (September 2019), 5.

76 ChinaAid Association, "Annual Persecution Report," 44–45.

77 Harvey, "The Sinicization of Religion," 6.

78 ChinaAid Association, "Annual Persecution Report 2020," 41.

79 David C. Schak, "Protestantism in China: A Dilemma for the Party-State," *Journal of Current Chinese Affairs* 40:2 (2011), 78.

80 Vermander, "Sinicizing Religions," 18.

7 Resurrecting Europe's Christian Heritage: Opportunity for the Spirit-Empowered

Arto Hämäläinen

Abstract

Europe: Once a Christian stronghold, it is today characterized by decreasing numbers of Christians in its traditional churches. However, Pentecostal-charismatic Christians are growing in number. Does this signify a new future for Christianity in Europe? Can Europe once again become a power for change in the world where the gravity of Christianity is now in the Global South? The trends in Europe move in opposing directions: Secularism versus a new interest in religion, freedom of religion versus militant atheism, a call for unity versus increasing national interests, liberal anti-biblical values versus conservative biblical family and marriage models, the need for more laborers to come to Europe versus a phobia of refugees and immigrants coming into Europe. At the same time, many new Europeans portray a vibrant aspect of Christianity through their living faith while some others represent the unreached people groups. How can the Spirit-empowered churches in Europe respond effectively to these challenges? Are they able to work together? Are they prepared to meet emerging persecution or discrimination? How can they overcome cultural challenges? In order to evaluate the vision of mission leaders for spreading the gospel to the unreached people in the world, two surveys were taken of these European Pentecostal mission leaders by the writer. The results were attained by using both quantitative and qualitative points of view. This study will reflect on whether the future impact of European Pentecostals in world missions will echo the ministry of Carey, Taylor, or early Pentecostal missionaries sent from this continent in the last century.

Has Europe ever been Christian?

Europe has been labeled as a Christian continent. How true is that? The answer depends on the criteria. If the starting point is formal church membership, then according to a 2010 survey, only five of the fifty-seven European countries did not have a Christian majority. In thirty-four countries, Christians represented 70 percent or more of the population. In that sense, Europe was still very Christian. However, at the same time, the percentage of Christians was decreasing by 0.3 percent per year.[1] The problem with this view is that many who belong to the church are not really committed, and their membership is only a formality, with no personal conviction or commitment to faith.

The PEW Research Center published a survey in 2018 in order to determine what percentage of the population in Europe could be considered "highly religious." What was meant by that term? There were four criteria: Attending religious services at least monthly, praying daily, believing God in absolute certainty, and stating that religion is very important to them. The survey showed that the people in Central and Eastern Europe are generally more religious than Western Europeans. Only about one in ten in France, Germany, United Kingdom, and several other Western European countries were considered "highly religious." The Czech Republic, Estonia, and Denmark were noticeably less religious than most Central and Eastern European countries.[2]

Another way to analyze the situation is to use the definition of Evangelical as a starting point. Who is an Evangelical? The Encyclopedia of Evangelicalism defines it in the following way: "Evangelicals are Christians who (1) believe in the centrality of conversion or a 'born again' experience in receiving salvation; (2) believe in the authority of the Bible as God's revelation to humanity; and (3) have a strong commitment to evangelism or sharing the Christian message."[3]

Comparing the percentage of Evangelicals in the different continents, Europe is the weakest:[4]

North America	26.8 percent
Pacific	17.8 percent
Africa	17.2 percent
Latin America	16.7 percent
Caribbean	14.3 percent
Asia	3.5 percent
Europe	2.5 percent

Together with Asia, Europe places at the bottom of these statistics. Africa, the Caribbean, Latin America, and the Pacific are much more

Christian, not to even mention North America. The question then is whether Europe has ever really been Christian in the Evangelical sense. The method in which it was Christianized did not always correlate with early church missions. Nominal membership replaced genuine commitment. The Constantine era brought freedom to practice Christian faith, but at the same time, brought laziness toward sacrificial missions and the temptation to combine political power with the favored religion. The result was not necessarily "highly religious" people, but just "officially" Christians and, in more recent times, secular and liberalized Christians. For a long time, the United Kingdom was a stronghold of Evangelicalism in Europe, but now, in many ways, it is following the decreasing trend of Christian emphasis such as is found on the continent. In 1970, it ranked second in the world, with 23.3 percent of its population being identified as Evangelicals. However, in 2010 it disappeared from the top ten list.[5]

The entire picture of Europe is not that dark, however. Several countries have experienced revival movements. The word "revival" has been used in different ways. Timothy K. Beougher defines it as ". . . a special movement of the Spirit of God in which he renews the hearts of believers."[6] This means that the starting point is the awakening of Christians to pray and seek God. All revival movements initially have been prayer movements. God's fire begins from the inside, spreading outward. It is centrifugal, like all the missions of God in New Testament times.

David W. Smith has reflected on the different understandings of spiritual renewals. He points out that at the beginning of modern missions, "in those parts of the world where Christ had never been named, the category of 'revival' gave way to a new emphasis on 'mission.'"[7] Revival and missions became closely connected. At the same time, revival was emphasized as a means of making nominal Western Christians into real believers.[8]

Europe as a continent has never experienced a 'great awakening' type of revival.[9] However, Jan Hus in the Czech Republic, Tyndale in England, Waldenses in Italy, France, and other countries, Huguenots in France and elsewhere, Anabaptists, Hutterites, Baptists, Pietists, Mennonites, Moravians, Quakers, Methodists, the Salvation Army, Plymouth Brethren, the Keswick movement, the Welsh revival, and finally, the Pentecostal movements and charismatic renewal have caused spiritual movements that have swept over countries and even larger areas of the continent of

Europe, changing the lives of a huge number of people. Their influence has also touched other continents through the missionary vision, which has often been born as a natural consequence of increased Bible-based spirituality. Sometimes these movements have led to the birth of new denominations, but there are several examples of evangelistic movements inside the traditional churches. The Nordic countries of Finland, Norway, and Sweden have often benefitted in this way during the last centuries. For example, the Läsare movement in Sweden, Hauge's influence in Norway, and the revival movement of the Lutheran priest Laestadius especially touched the northern parts of Finland, Norway, and Sweden 200 years ago. The last movement was the cause of a major social change for many people in the North who were bound by alcoholism which was the source of much misery.

Although many revivals have touched several countries in Europe, there has never been a Europe-wide revival on this continent. Is the time now ripe for revival? The coronavirus pandemic has been a source of facing existential questions. It has also awakened many Christians to pray. Will this lead to a new spiritual breakthrough in Europe and on other continents?

In the mid-1990s, American theologian Harvey Cox, wrote that "We are definitely in a period of renewed religious vitality, another 'great awakening' if you will."[10] Both of the large Pentecostal umbrella organizations, the World Assemblies of God Fellowship (WAGF) and the Pentecostal World Fellowship (PWF), have named the 2020s as a Decade of Revival. How can this be realized in Europe? What are the obstacles that must be overcome?

Challenges in the European Context

Stuart McAlister, a Scottish Evangelical leader with great experience in evangelizing Europeans, finds that modernity's secularizing project has motivated autonomous and good human beings to use reason and science in building a better world. Darwin, Freud, Marx, and the prophets of the market have been building a worldview that is quite gospel resistant. Dualistic thinking dominates Europeans. Everything is divided into sacred and secular issues, and the former is a private matter which should not be brought into public forums.[11]

McAlister states, "The reduction of faith to personal piety and privatistic belief is a tragedy of major proposition." He points to the fact that young people have grown up with a sense of interdependence.[12] The churches need to find a balance between the pressure to keep spiritual life inside the walls of the church or home while also answering the desire to do things together and publicly. Interdependence also leads to consideration of the best style of leadership. Strict top-down leadership may not allow enough space for the wide sharing of ideas, visions, strategies, and implementation.

In 1943, Henri Godin and Yvan Daniel published a book in France entitled *La France Pays de Mission* (France, a country of mission). They were concerned about the condition of Christianity there. The dominating factors in France were neopaganism, atheism, secularism, unbelief, and superstition.[13] The French revolution paved the way for religious freedom. At the same time, it promoted secularism by separating religion from public life. France has gone through different phases in implementing these principles, from very strict division in the beginning to state-supported activities later. Religious freedom has created space for free churches with the result that between 1970–2009, Evangelical churches have established 1,100 new churches. That means a new church has been established every eleven days.[14]

David E. Bjork reflects on the future of Christianity in Europe. He talks about the "exculturation" of it by referring to French sociologist Danièle Hervieu-Lèger. According to Hervieu-Lèger, Christianity has lost its influence in French society through the process of secularization.[15] The situation in other Western European countries is similar to that of France. Secularization does not mean that people are no longer interested in spirituality. They may still randomly pray and may practice some Christian ceremonies for burials and weddings. However, for example, religious practices diminished by 50 percent in Belgium by the end of the 1990s.[16]

Bjork divides European Christianity into three categories: the believers, the pilgrims, and the converts. Believers in this classification are those who are "passively carried to the Christian faith," which means they were baptized as infants. Pilgrims are those "caught up in a movement of personal growth and development." A convert "experiences a complete reorientation of his or her life."[17] The first two categories are usually connected to traditional churches. The convert in a free church context is a person meeting Christ as Savior for the first time. For persons in traditional churches, he/she can be a member of the church but lacks a personal relationship to Jesus as Savior. Because traditional churches believe every person who is baptized as an infant is a Christian, evangelizing such people is understood as proselytism by many in those churches. Evangelicals, including Pentecostals, have quite often been criticized and have faced opposition based on that understanding.

However, today proselytism is defined as unethical ways to convert a person to a new religion or denomination. The need for a personal relationship with Jesus, having a living faith, is understood, and emphasized more and more in traditional churches. Renewal movements are appreciated. At the same time, many in the traditional churches keep thinking that all those baptized by them "belong" to them. Some may admit that all people need a personal relationship with Jesus, and anyone who can contribute to that happening is valued. The strongest interpretation seems to be the doctrine of canonical territories of Orthodox Christianity. This means that other Christian proclaimers are not welcome in their area.

Although we need to be respectful to all others no matter their religion, it is not acceptable to prevent the preaching of the gospel freely and publicly in the EU, where we have religious freedom. However, unethical ways to persuade people are not in accord with the nature of the gospel and the Bible. From the Pentecostal point of view, every person has a right to hear the gospel and make his/her decision about following Christ. This is likened to a human rights issue according to John 3:16. No one is excluded from the right of access to the kingdom of God if he/she believes in Jesus. That is why the Empowered21 movement has as its goal: "That every person on Earth would have an authentic encounter with Jesus Christ through the power and presence of the Holy Spirit . . . by Pentecost 2033."[18]

Many Europeans put their trust in science. They do not need God because they think that science has all the answers. A naturalistic explanation based on the Newtonistic experimental results has dominated thinking until post-modernistic philosophy challenged that. Actually, Einstein was shaking the old paradigms. Many modern Europeans are not taking note of the very character of science, the fact that science is continually correcting itself. Many things in the Bible which earlier were considered unscientific have now proved to be true, according to recent research.[19] Apologetics of this nature is needed in Europe to help release people from the bondage of wrong dependence on science which prohibits their finding of biblical truth.

Today, the European worldview is strongly postmodern. The old Enlightenment project with knowledge based on reason and empirical evidence has been challenged. Postmodernism rejects modernity's assumption of its own superiority. This leads to emphasizing tolerance and cognitive and moral relativism.[20] Without absolute truth, there is no real gospel. 'No other name than Jesus by which to be saved' does not fit the postmodern paradigm. It has no metanarrative like the Bible with God in action from Genesis to Revelation. The postmodern person has no faith in a grand metanarrative.[21] How then can he/she be reached? Lesslie Newbigin aptly summarizes: "I believe that the whole of experience in the natural world, in the world of public affairs, of politics, economics, and culture, and the world of inward spiritual experience is to be seen as one whole in the light of this disclosure of the character and will of its Creator."[22] Europeans need God back in their lives.

Jacques Delors, as president of the EU Commission in 1990, gathered leaders together to reflect on what is the heart and soul of Europe.[23] The same question is valid today. The EU is still on its way to finding the answer. Delors was serious in seeking the spiritual dimension for the European soul. He states, "If in the ten years ahead of us we do not succeed in giving Europe its soul, a spiritual dimension, true significance, then we will have been wasting our time. That is the lesson of my experience. Europe cannot live by legal argument and economic know-how alone."[24]

The EU has a spiritual heritage. The French promoter of European cooperation, Robert Schuman, saw in his original dream of Europe a "community of peoples deeply rooted in basic Christian values."[25] Schuman was actually the architect of the EU together with German Konrad Adenauer. Both were devoted Christians. They attended prayer gatherings in Caux, Switzerland, where a Lutheran evangelist, Frank Buchman, was a key figure.[26] Those meetings melted the ice in the relationship between Germany and France after WWII. Because of the future development of a more secular emphasis in the EU, this spiritual beginning of the EU is now a little-known fact. How can that heritage be brought to light again? Where are the voices being raised for it?

New Europeans

People have been on the move, especially from the South to the North and North-West. This has changed the demographics of Europe in the last half-century. In 2002, Philip Jenkins observed that the British had drawn labor from Jamaica and Pakistan and the French from Algeria and West Africa. His prognosis was that half of the population in London would be non-white by the end of the twenty-first century, and that the white population will be in the minority in Great Britain as a whole.[27] Jenkins wrote his view long before the great migration of people in the mid-2010s when refugees and immigrants were flooding into Europe from Syria, Iraq, Afghanistan, Eritrea, and several West African countries. Germany had 1.0–1.5 million, United Kingdom 800,000–1.2 million, Italy 500,000–700,000, and France 300,000–400,000 unauthorized migrants in 2017.[28] This challenged the governments but also the churches.

Many churches understood the presence of these new people on the continent as part of God's plan. They were to serve them and show God's love by word and deed. As a result, thousands of Muslims have received Jesus Christ as their Savior, been baptized, and are now active members in the churches. Some of the arriving people were already believers. Many Asians, Africans, and Latinos have come to Europe, not on the crest of the big migration around 2015, but earlier or later; not as refugees but seeking a better future for themselves and their families. The lack of workers in many EU countries has encouraged this. People from Africa and Latin America particularly were already believers before leaving their home countries, and in some cases, also those from Asia. Many of them are motivated to be a presence as a missionary or evangelist in the European context. The latter type of new Europeans creates a challenge to the existing churches. Can the believers really integrate into the existing churches? Is there enough intercultural understanding? On the other hand, have the new arrivals enough flexibility and readiness to adapt to a new culture? Do the existing churches have a proper structure to involve the new workers from other countries? Is proper training and mentoring available?[29]

The new Europeans are also facing the challenge of the new generations. The first generation of immigrants keep close contact with their home country. For instance, often, the link to the African church is closer than to the existing national church in Europe. Cultural otherness creates a desire to keep their own culture and traditions. However, the next generation, which is being educated in a new cultural context, are no longer very connected to the continents from which the immigrant generations came.

Caleb Opoku Nyanni has researched the second-generation Pentecostals in the United Kingdom. These people originated from the Church of Pentecost in Ghana. He found that not only was the style of worship a challenge to the second generation, but also the understanding of the doctrine of the Holy Spirit had a different emphasis to them. The first generation, with the strong spirit-dominated world view of the Ghanaian culture, stressed the power of the Holy Spirit against the evil spirits. The second generation in the European context no longer had felt that challenge was so central. For them, the Holy Spirit, besides being the power for missionary purpose, was especially a friend.[30]

The new Europeans can contribute much to Europe. Their spirituality is often much stronger in keeping the supernatural nature of God's work which is realized in healings and other miracles.[31] It is no wonder that some of the largest Pentecostal-charismatic churches in Europe are led by African pastors. The blessing could be even greater if the intercultural approach was stronger. In too many cases, the new Europeans concentrate only on reaching people of their own culture. There is an option for an Antiochian breakthrough. Just as some Jews there crossed the divide between Jews and Gentiles in the early days of the church, some foreign-background churches in Europe can adopt a different approach to reach Europeans, their new neighbors.

The flow of people into Europe from Asia, Africa, and Latin America has either fertilized, challenged, or worried Europeans, depending on their viewpoint. Some immigrants are motivated by the spiritual challenge of the continent. They have been sent as missionaries or were motivated toward ministry once in their new country. Their ultimate success is very much a matter of cultural integration.

Response of the Pentecostal Leaders Concerning the Spiritual Change in Europe

I took a survey of classical Pentecostal leaders concerning their understanding of the present spiritual situation and their vision for the future of Europe. This took place in March-April 2020, and included eleven countries: Belgium, Finland, Germany, Greece, Italy, Lithuania, Netherlands, Poland, Spain, Sweden, and Switzerland. All respondents were leaders of the main or major Pentecostal denominations.[32] The questions were sent to all Pentecostal European Fellowship (PEF) member church leaders in Western Europe (covering Northern, Western, Central, and Southern Europe according to the PEF categories). The responses represent all mentioned sub-areas.

In the first question, the leaders were asked to identify the most urgent spiritual needs in their country. At the top were spiritual awakening, including planting new churches, stronger collaboration between the churches, and tools in dealing with the increasing ideology of secularism, atheistic humanism, and unbiblical ethical values. All issues that require renewed structures, strategies, and updated adequate training programs.

The second question was intended to find out whether the Pentecostal churches would be able to give a relevant answer to the challenges in Europe and, if not, what should be changed. It is evident that there is a need for closer collaboration on both the national and international levels. Usually, there are several Pentecostal denominations in a country. They, however, do not necessarily collaborate, even though they all may be members of the PEF. Churches of different ethnic backgrounds often seem to be living life on their own, many still being connected to their former home countries and church movements.

The gifts of the Spirit, the treasure of the Pentecostal tradition, seem to be underused. Closely related to this is the importance of prayer and fasting and of understanding the importance of spiritual warfare. The balance between Spirit leadership and structural forms of the work also seems to require attention in pastoral education. A sound theological foundation together with sensitive openness to the spontaneous work of the Holy Spirit is a combination with sustainable results in the lives of the people.

Globally in 2020, classical Pentecostals numbered 118, 865,000.[33] In 2010, there were 5.9 million in Europe, with a growth rate of 2 percent.[34] Can they become an agent of change in Europe? The secret of Pentecostal growth, as Mark Hutchinson observes in France, is due to evangelism efforts by ordinary Pentecostal believers. About 60 percent of the growth among French Pentecostals since WWII has been of this type.[35] The

Spirit-Empowered Christians numbered 644 million globally in 2020,[36] with 21 million in Europe.[37]

The generational gaps in European Pentecostalism need more attention. The younger generation is not very interested in denominations. Believers, young and old, need to realize that achieving concrete results in evangelizing and missions requires some kind of structure. Having just fellowship together is easier than establishing a new church together.

The third question of the survey dealt with mutual contribution for spiritual change in other European countries. All respondents were very committed to that. Their contributions include enhancing mutual prayer support for getting and sending new missionaries, building strategic partnerships in evangelism and world missions, and in leadership training, strategic planning, church planting, revitalizing the churches and serving the communities in a holistic way. The Pentecostal leaders want to see the Pentecostal identity to be strengthened in all these actions.

The willingness to contribute efforts in reaching all people in Europe with the gospel seems to be great. However, do serious obstacles exist on the way to revival? Can missions and evangelism take place in the atmosphere of religious freedom? That was the focus of the fourth question. Pentecostal leaders see some clouds in the sky, although Article Ten in the EU Charter of Fundamental Rights states: "Everyone has the right to freedom of thought, conscience, and religion. This right includes freedom to change religion or belief and freedom, either alone or in community with others and in public or in private, to manifest religion or belief, in worship, teaching, practice, and observance."[38]

Christian schools, in some instances, face challenges from the governments, causing questions as to whether religious freedom is truly practiced. Some tensions can also be noticed in the media. Sometimes outdoor evangelism is complicated because of restricting regulations. Freedom of speech is challenged if you cannot use the Bible as the basis for ethical guidelines. The entry of missionaries coming from other continents to Europe is also sometimes a challenge. In Belgium, for instance, there have been several cases where work permits and visas have been difficult to receive, although they are invited and recommended by their European partner churches. Additionally, a new threat is growing inside the churches themselves. The coronavirus pandemic has isolated people, and the risk is the increase of inward-looking "only-Jerusalem" churches (Acts 1:8). Another coronavirus consequence is economic damages. Are churches able to follow the Macedonian example? "In the midst of a very severe trial, their overflowing joy and their extreme poverty welled up in rich generosity" (2 Cor. 8:2). My own country of Finland was left in poverty during and after WWII. However, a strong mission vision started to grow, leading the first Pentecostal pioneers to Ethiopia, Eritrea, Thailand, and Uruguay, and among the first ones to many other countries.

The Role of Charismatic Movements and Independent Churches in Europe

The number of Christians is decreasing in Europe. According to Operation World statistics, in 2010, the rate of decrease was −0.3 percent.[39] Still, about 71 percent of Europeans were identified as Christians in 2010.[40] The Evangelical and independent Christian churches grew 1 percent in 2010, and Pentecostal churches grew 2 percent. The same growth rate (2 percent) also took place in the charismatic churches.

The charismatic movement is not very well coordinated in Europe. There is no umbrella organization in Europe like the Pentecostal-Charismatic Churches of North America (PCCNA). The lack of an organized entity of Charismatics in Europe has challenged the forming of the Empowered21 movement in Europe. It has not been easy to connect the independent congregations or subgroups in the historical churches for any coordinated efforts. The Spirit-empowered wing of European Christianity, however, seems to be quite strong. The latest statistics show 21 million people belong to this group.[41]

The only organization trying to somehow build bridges between Pentecostals and other Spirit-empowered movements has been the European Pentecostal Charismatic Research Association (EPCRA). It had its last conference at the Missionsakademie at the University of Hamburg in 2018. The conference proceedings were published in 2020 with Regnum Books, Oxford, with the title, *Conviction in an Optional Society*. The chairman of EPCRA, Jean-Daniel Plüss from Switzerland, strives to eliminate the divide between academia and spirituality.[42] The EPCRA chairman has regular contacts with the Charismatic Community Chemin Neuf. It began in the early 1970s when a number of Catholic priests were baptized in the Spirit and began to meet regularly in an apartment in Chemin Neuf Street in Lyon, France. The community grew quickly. The Chemin Neuf Community is ecumenical, comprised of about 70 percent Catholic and 30 percent from other Christian churches and communities. There are a number of other charismatic groups in Europe that do similar work.[43] The crucial questions are how can the Pentecostal-Charismatic collaboration be developed, and what kind of influence can it achieve in Europe? Because of some historical tensions and negative experiences, Pentecostal churches in certain countries are mistrustful of traditional churches. To overcome these obstacles, there needs to be open and sincere mutual dialogue.

A large potential for future development is slumbering in the immigrant churches. Joseph Ola, in his article about African Christianity in Europe, pointed out Kwiayani's observation in 2017. It states that the 14 percent minority made prominently of migrants forms 60 percent of church attendance in a global city like London.[44] The challenge is how that potential can reach people outside their own ethnic sphere. Can the spiritual power existing in African and other migrant churches decisively touch Europe? The Pentecostal Redeemed Christian Church of God (RCCG) has 800 churches in the UK and gathers 50,000 people for its festival. This kind of development is not only taking place in the UK. Stian Sørlie Eriksen reports that there are 1,000 immigrant churches in Germany and 300 in Norway.[45]

European Pentecostals as Changemakers in World Missions

The number of Pentecostal-charismatic Christians in Europe has grown in the past fifty years. In 1970, they numbered 5 million. Fifty years later (2020), they numbered 21 million.[46] Can these Christians continue as changemakers in Europe and influence the positive development of world missions globally?

I took a survey among the mission organizations or mission departments of the national Pentecostal churches in Europe. The responders are all members of the Pentecostal European Mission (PEM), which is the coordinating body for the mission activities of the Pentecostal European Fellowship (PEF). Of the twenty-eight full member organizations in PEM, twenty-one of them responded to this inquiry which was made in the spring of 2021. Thus, more than two thirds of the members responded, giving the possibility to make referential and trustworthy observations. The aim of the survey was to discern whether PEM organizations have a vision and motivation for spiritual change in Europe and the world. The missionary personnel of PEM organizations can be numbered between 1,500–2,000. The total number of PEM member missionaries who responded to the survey was 1,454. However, based on previous information in oral and written reports, the above-mentioned estimate of missionary manpower can be made.

The survey unveiled a clear desire of the PEM member organizations to reach the untouched areas and people groups. They are interested in focusing on people living in or coming from the Middle East, Central Asia, North Africa. As one example, Romania's APME (mission organization) alone wants to see at least 200 long-term missionaries working among unreached people groups, especially in the Muslim context, by 2030.

A very clear focus is the least reached in Europe. This continent has sixteen countries with less than 1 percent of the population in each country being Evangelical Christians. These countries are Albania, Andorra, Austria, Bosnia-Herzegovina, Croatia, Cyprus, Czech Republic, Greece, Lichtenstein, Luxemburg, Northern Macedonia, Montenegro, Poland, San Marino, Serbia, and Slovenia.[47]

The increased blend of ethnic backgrounds is opening new possibilities to the churches. Many of the 7,000 unreached people groups are represented in Europe. In 2010, the Pentecostal European Mission (PEM) identified a goal for its members to reach 200 unreached people groups (UPG) in Europe and globally by 2020. The result was even better. At least 280 of the UPGs were included in the programs of the PEM members. The Gypsies, often referred to as Roma, are found all across Europe and make up the largest ethnic minority on the continent. There are 11 million Gypsies living in Europe. Centuries of discrimination, including systematic extermination by some twentieth-century fascist regimes, have helped keep them marginalized second-class citizens. The good news is that it is now estimated that half a million to one million are followers of Jesus. Large Roma revivals have taken place in France, Spain, and in some areas in Eastern Europe. In Finland, 10 percent of the Roma people are believers.[48] Turkey, Japan, and Thailand are countries in which the number of Evangelical Christians is very low. The total population in 2021 of these countries is over 260 million. Fortunately, these three countries are included as a priority for mission efforts by several PEM organizations.

The future goals presented in the survey indicate that classical Pentecostals have a serious desire to see the Great Commission more effectively fulfilled. They want to see unreached to be reached, and Christianity to be moved from Southern and Central Africa to North Africa, Middle East, and Central Asia, and touch all of Asia's Hindu, Buddhist, and Islamic regions. They pray that the wind of the Holy Spirit would also penetrate to the last Communist fortresses along its way.

Conclusion

Can the 2020s become a decade of revival in Europe? The biblical pattern for change has never been based on numbers and physical power as the prophet Zechariah clearly states: "Not by might nor by power, but by my Spirit . . ." (Zech 4:6). Jesus knew that it was possible to change the world with twelve people if they were filled with the power of the Holy Spirit. If that was true with such a few people, it should not be too difficult a task for 6 million classical Pentecostals and for 21 million Spirit-empowered Christians in Europe.

There are several barriers in Europe that need to be overcome by the power and wisdom of the Spirit. The worldview of Europeans is a mix of modern and postmodern thought. A portion of the population is still reason-oriented and has problems in understanding spiritual truths which do not exist in the world of empirical science. That attitude has led many to become atheists or agnostics. Some of them need well-grounded Christian apologetics. Others need to be confronted by the power of the Spirit of God to understand the supernatural possibility of the triune God to forgive sins and perform signs and wonders such as healings. This is also medicine for the wounds of secularized and liberalized Europeans whose God is money and welfare and who believe that tolerance is the answer to all ethical questions without any reference to biblical moral values. To be able to answer the needs of people, Pentecostal and charismatic churches must allow the Holy Spirit to rekindle the fire, the gift of the Holy Spirit. This is the treasure they have received by the grace of God: the work of the Holy Spirit in its full empowerment. The Pentecostal distinctive leads the churches to become witnesses of the risen Lord Jesus.

European churches need more cultural sensitivity in meeting people from other continents. This includes meaningfully addressing those adherents of religions like Islam, Buddhism, and Hinduism. The expertise of missionaries with experience in meeting those religions and worldviews is needed now. The unreached people groups are now coming to the doors of European homes. The stream of immigration is not only bringing unreached people but also many Christians are coming, among whom are the Pentecostal-charismatics. Many of them still stay closely connected to their home countries and denominations. The challenge is for successful integration into the Christian family of Europe. Can the immigrant churches reach not only their own people but also other Europeans? Can they become multicultural in their approach? And are the existing Pentecostal churches ready for this collaboration? The new European Pentecostals have spiritual riches that are urgently needed in Europe. The social challenges will surely increase in the post-coronavirus age. Will the Pentecostal-Charismatic churches show the love of Jesus Christ in a holistic way in the everyday life of people in Europe?

Can European Pentecostals have an impact on the world? In the past, missionaries sent from the European Pentecostal churches and mission organizations have caused a change that has influenced millions of people. The desire of the Pentecostal mission directors in Europe reflects the same attitude as their forerunners. They believe in reaching unreached people in the whole world and finishing the task given to them by Jesus. The Pentecostal-charismatic response to the needs of Europe and the world is not necessarily complicated. The Pentecostal leader of Sweden summarized it in a very simple way. It is a "spiritual revival with a refreshed love for Jesus."[49] It is not a question of technique. It is all about relationship.

Notes

1 Jason Mandryk, *Operation World* (Colorado Springs: Biblica Publishing, 2010), 73–75.

2 "How Do European Countries Differ in Religious Commitment?" Pew Research Center, December 5, 2018, https://www.pewresearch.org/fact-tank/2018/12/05/how-do-european-countries-differ-in-religious-commitment/, accessed April 27, 2020.

3 Randall Balmer, *Encyclopedia of Evangelicalism* (Westminster: John Knox Press, 2002), 196–197.

4 Mandryk, *Operation World*, 28, 43, 45, 47, 57, 73, 83.

5 Gina A. Zurlo, "Demographics of Global Evangelicalism," in Brian C. Stiller, Todd M. Johnson, Karen Stiller, Mark Hutchinson, eds., *Evangelicals Around the World – A Global Handbook for the 21st Century* (Nashville: Thomas Nelson, 2015), 43.

6 Timothy K. Beougher, "Revival," in A. Scott Moreau, ed., Evangelical *Dictionary of World Missions* (Grand Rapids: Baker Books, 2000), 830–833.

7 David W. Smith, *Against the Stream – Christianity in the Age of Globalization* (Leicester: InterVarsity, 2003), 54.

8 Smith, *Against the Stream*, 54.

9 The first Great Awakening took place in the United States in the 1730s and 1740s and the second from the 1790s onward. John Wolffe, "Who Are Evangelicals? A History," in Brian C. Stiller, Todd M. Johnson, Karen Stiller, Mark Hutchinson, eds., *Evangelicals Around the World: A Global Handbook for the 21st Century* (Nashville: Thomas Nelson, 2015), 26–27.

10 Harvey Cox, *Fire from Heaven: The Rise of Pentecostal Spirituality and Reshaping of Religion in the Twenty-First Century* (Boston: Addison-Wesley, 1995), xvi.

11 Stuart McAlister, "Younger Generations and the Gospel in Western Culture," in William D. Taylor, ed., *Global Missiology for the 21st Century* (Grand Rapids: Baker Academic, 2000), 368.

12 McAlister, "Younger Generations," 369.

13 Risto Jukko, "Vallankumouksesta Välinpitämättömyyteen," *Lähetysteologinen Aikakauskirja* 11 (2009), 68.

14 Jukko, "Vallankumouksesta Välinpitämättömyyteen," 73.

15 David E. Bjork, "The Future of Christianity in Western Europe," *Missiology* 34:3 (2006), 309–310.

16 Bjork, "The Future of Christianity," 311–312.

17 Bjork, "The Future of Christianity," 316–318.

18 Empowered21 Brochure (Tulsa, OK: Empowered21 Headquarters), 5.

19 The Finnish archeologist Eero Junkkaala mentions in his book *Faktaa vai Fiktiota* (Helsinki: Uusi Tie, 2006), 72–73 how the dynasty of David had been questioned long time. The argument was that it lacks any evidence outside the Bible. However, the archeological findings in Dan in 1993 challenged fundamentally that view. Text in one stone confirmed the existence of the king David and his rule.

20 Paul G. Hiebert, *Transforming Worldviews: An Anthropological Understanding of How People Change* (Grand Rapids: Baker Academic, 2008), 214.

21 Hiebert, *Transforming Worldviews*, 215.

22 Lesslie Newbigin, *Foolishness to the Greeks: The Gospel and Western Culture* (Grand Rapids: Eerdmans, 1986), 89.

23 Edy Korthals Altes, *Heart and Soul for Europe: An Essay on Spiritual Renewal* (Assen: Van Gorcum, 1999), 4.

24 Altes, *Heart and Soul for Europe*, 172.

25 Jeff Fountain, "A Christian Europe(an): The Forgotten Vision of Robert Schuman," *Encounters Mission Journal* 36 (March 2011), https://encountersmissionjournal.files.wordpress.com/2011/08/fountain_2011-03_schumann_and_europe.pdf, accessed April 27, 2020.

26 Jeff Fountain, *Juuret Syvällä* (Tampere: Päivä Osakeyhtiö, 2016), 63, 69.

27 Philip Jenkins, *The Next Christendom* (Oxford: University Press, 2002), 96–97.

28 Jon Henley, "Up to 4.8m Unauthorized Immigrants in Europe in 2017 – Study," *The Guardian*, November 13, 2019, https://www.theguardian.com/world/2019/nov/13/4m-unauthorised-immigrants-in-europe-in-2017-study, accessed August 2, 2021.

29 Arto Hämäläinen, "The Significance of the Refugees and Asylum Seekers to the European Pentecostal Church," *Journal of the European Pentecostal Theological Association* 39:2 (November 2019), 122–123.

30 Caleb Opoku Nyanni, "Second-Generation African Pentecostals in the United Kingdom," *JEPTA* 20:1 (April 2020), 40.

31 Hämäläinen, "The Significance of the Refugees and Asylum Seekers," 120–121.

32 The respondents were Mika Yrjölä/Finland, Daniel Costanza/Belgium, Johannes Justus/Germany, Ilias Chatzieletheriou/Greece, Carmine Napolitano/Italy, Rimantas Kupstys/Lithuania, Machiel Jonker/Netherlands, Marek Kaminski/Poland, Juan Carlos Escobar/Spain, Daniel Alm/Sweden, and Marco Hofmann/Switzerland.

33 Todd M. Johnson and Gina A. Zurlo, *Introducing Spirit-Empowered Christianity – The Global Pentecostal and Charismatic Movement in the 21st Century* (Tulsa, OK: ORU Press, 2020, pre-publication edition), 46.

34 Mandryk, *Operation World*, 75.

35 Mark Hutchinson, "Evangelicals in Western Europe," in *Evangelicals Around the World*, 391.

36 Johnson and Zurlo, *Introducing Spirit-Empowered Christianity*, 46.

37 Johnson and Zurlo, *Introducing Spirit-Empowered Christianity*, 47.

38 Martina Prpic, "Religion and Human Rights," European Parlimentary Research Service, December 2018, https://www.europarl.europa.eu/at-your-service/files/be-heard/religious-and-non-confessional-dialogue/events/en-20181204-eprs-briefing-religion-and-human-rights.pdf, accessed April 27, 2020.

39 Mandryk, *Operation World*, 75.

40 Mandryk, *Operation World*, 75.

41 Johnson and Zurlo, *Introducing Spirit-Empowered Christianity*, 30.

42 Correspondence between Jean-Daniel Plüss and the author of this article in April 2020.

43 Correspondence between Jean-Daniel Plüss and the author of this article in April 2020.

44 Joseph Ola, "'Strangers' Meat is the Greatest Treat': African Christianity in Europe," 2019, https://www.academia.edu/41993424/_STRANGERS_MEAT_IS_THE_GREATEST_TREAT_AFRICAN_CHRISTIANITY_IN_EUROPE?email_work_card=title, accessed April 27, 2020.

45 Stian Sørle Erikson, "Immigrant-Majority Church Relations in the West: Separate Worlds or Bridges Over Troubled Waters?" *Lausanne Global Analysis* 8:4 (July 2019), https://www.lausanne.org/content/lga/2019-07/immigrant-majority-church-relations west?utm_source=Lausanne+Movement+List&utm_campaign=d696be5e4d-RSS_Best_of&utm_medium=email&utm_term=0_602c1cb67d-d696be5e4d-91726457, accessed April 27, 2020.

46 Johnson and Zurlo, *Introducing Spirit-Empowered Christianity*, 47.

47 Mandryk, *Operation World*, 73.

48 Deborah Meroff, *Europe: Restoring Hope* (Linz: OM Books, 2011), 30.

49 Daniel Alm, the Chairman of the Swedish Pentecostal Church, in his reply to the survey concerning PEF leaders.

8 Focusing on the People of the Margins in Latin America: A New Approach to Social Concern

Miguel Alvarez

Abstract:

Pentecostalism has been studied from different angles and in different contexts. This time we will look at it from the context of Honduras, particularly at the way Pentecostals approach ministry among people in the margins. The discussion takes into consideration the example of the incarnated Christ who served in a context of poverty. Such a combination of arguments will help us to deal with some issues of poverty against the background of the scripture, as this deals with the current situation of some Latin American communities.[1] In the end, we will engage the redemptive action of Christ in favor of the poor and marginalized (Luke 4:18). This idea sets some foundations for understanding the theology of mission as practiced by the Pentecostal community. This chapter also refers to the general context of Pentecostal mission and seeks to add more resources to the study of the mission of God.[2]

Introduction

Pentecostalism has about a century of history in the continent of Latin America. In general, the first Pentecostals of Latin America trace their origin to two streams that are largely accepted by most Pentecostal historians. The first was brought by Pentecostal missionaries from North America. These came with a strong Evangelical background. The second stream of Pentecostalism was initiated among local free Evangelical congregations. One example is the 1909 Pentecostal movement that began in Chile when Methodist believers received the baptism of the Holy Spirit.[3] Another movement took place later in Brazil in 1914, when a group of Evangelical believers had their own Pentecostal experience.[4] These free Pentecostal movements took place after the teachings and practices of holiness by some Methodist congregations that settled in Latin America before the Pentecostal awakening took place in the region. In each case, all of these Pentecostal movements were established and grew strong among the poor people of Catholic societies and cultures.

Pentecostalism appeared as a providential act of the grace of God in favor of the poor and marginalized people of Latin America. This is so because Pentecostalism became a movement of the poor. In the Pentecostal congregations the poor found hope and support, which led them to overcome not only their spiritual struggles but also their social and economic limitations. In its approach to the poor and marginalized, the Pentecostal message found fertile ground in the region. At some point, Pentecostals were able to capitalize on what was earlier initiated by the Evangelical movements in the area.[5] According to Calixto Salvatierra Moreno:

> The twentieth century witnessed the rise and development of Pentecostalism. This movement generated the formation of new expressions of religion across the Americas, which had a sociological, anthropological, and spiritual influence on contemporary societies. Pentecostalism innovated and created various ways to express the religious beliefs that significantly affected the culture and spiritual ethos of humanity in Latin America.[6]

The Pentecostal lifestyle brought explosive numerical growth in most depressed and marginalized areas of large cities. Pentecostalism made the message of the gospel relevant to the poor, the sick, the depressed, and the weak. The message was simple, yet powerful enough to convince people about the relevance of the gospel. The activity of the supernatural was observed in most congregations. Pentecostalism became instrumental in finding a solution to civil war, natural disasters, disease, and the need for spiritual deliverance. Henceforth, Pentecostals in Latin America speak of grace as the intervention of God on behalf of the poor. In the power of the Holy Spirit, the persecuted may obtain deliverance from their enemies and find a solution to any source of affliction or adversity.[7] For Pentecostals, living in the Spirit denotes spiritual enablement, daily guidance, forgiveness, and protection in the midst of trouble. Pentecostals also emphasize the importance of simplicity. For them, living in a community and sharing their lives with other people is the testimony of the grace of God actively operating in the congregation.

This kind of Christianity shook the pre-existing religious establishment in the area. Churches and Christian leaders had never seen this church model before. Naturally, the first reaction was to oppose it. The Pentecostal worship style made them nervous. The impartation of spiritual gifts among the congregants was completely different from the church order that they had experienced before. Eventually, Pentecostal worship and ministration permeated most Evangelical, Protestant, and Catholic churches. Thus, this influence could also be interpreted as an act of the grace of God to revitalize the church in Latin America. Through the imprints of Pentecostalism, churches have become more dynamic in evangelism, social action, and the development of the laity in ministry.

New Dynamics of Mission

Es que lo llevamos en la sangre (it is that which we carry in our blood); this seems to be a negative attitude used by many Latin Americans to justify misfortunes and tragedies that happen to them. Thus, understanding the people of this region requires knowledge of this cultural epithet and other traditions that have long stood with the culture. Transforming the negative into a positive mentality requires an injection of hope.[8] Through the transformational message of the gospel, God's people are now bringing such hope.

In the particular context of Central America, the area suffers different degrees of chronic features of underdevelopment that manifest through endemic political corruption and unbearable administrative bureaucracies.[9] Admittedly, there are different terms that can be used to classify the Latin American countries according to their national wealth. Whether it is Honduras at the bottom of such lists, or Chile at the top, they all are part of a continent that struggles to reach higher levels of progress, despite the entire region being rich in natural resources. Moreover, Christianity has been present in the region for more than five centuries. What makes this background so difficult? In this section, we will look at the history of the region through the lenses of anthropological, sociological, cultural, and spiritual factors.

In Honduras, for example, recent years have witnessed severe conditions of political corruption coupled with natural disasters that have forced people to create their own survival devices. For example, the youth turned to gangs at the arrival of the twenty-first century.[10] Months later, the drug-lords bought the gangs. The gang-drug[11] combination made Honduras one of the most violent countries in the world.[12] Current reports show that the drug industry has now permeated elite government and military officials. Consequently, this evil has reached some of the most significant leaders and influential people of the country.[13]

Mission in the Margins

History shows that conditions in Honduras have alarmingly increased the number of people living in poverty. Corrupt political leaders have perpetuated and nurtured this social problem.[14] The Honduran economy shows severe imbalances in the distribution of wealth. The rich are becoming richer, and the poor are getting poorer. In the legal system, officials continue to struggle in the application and realization of justice. As a result, the number of poor and marginalized continue to increase. The failure of the judicial system creates unbearable conditions for the promotion of humanity.[15] The first decade of the twenty-first century saw Honduras emerge as one of the poorest and most violent countries in the world.

In search of better conditions of life, a significant number of young people migrated to the United States. Recent migration data reports that most rural communities of Honduras were left with grandparents taking care of grandchildren. As natural consequences of migration, marriages are destroyed, families split, and children grow up without parents. The new generation is growing without parental figures at an unnerving rate and moving forward into an uncertain future.

As a result of severe measures taken by new immigration laws in the United States, thousands of undocumented immigrants have been deported to their homelands.[16] Upon returning to their country, migrants are faced with a new decision. They either return to the United States, or they join a gang. Gangs are already associated with the drug-trafficking industry in the country. Tragically, the government agencies that assist the deportees have nothing to offer to them in the re-entry process.[17] The government does not have the political strength, financial capability, or honorable stance to overcome this need. Under the present conditions, Honduras seems to be very vulnerable and with little hope for the future. Foreign assistance and financial aid are needed. However, people will have to be re-educated through a new system of values that will save the country from self-destruction. Therefore, it is under these circumstances that Pentecostals are expected to play a major role in the solution to the problems of society.

Pentecostals on the Scene

Pentecostalism in Honduras has grown significantly in recent years. This growth can be observed mainly through high numbers in church attendance which is currently seen in a significant number of recently established congregations. In addition, these new churches and ministries have impacted local communities in a number of fields that benefit humanity. Why is this happening? There may be many reasons that explain it, but I focus this discussion on the Pentecostal service to the community.[18] Much has been said about the response of Pentecostalism towards disaster, poverty, and social unrest in the country. Historically, Hondurans have responded positively to the Pentecostal message of hope in times of crisis.[19] However, such a message has had a positive impact due to the significant service provided by Pentecostals in the communities. Pentecostal believers are committed to a devoted life that serves the community in obedience to the Great Commission (Matt 28:19).

Pentecostals have learned to depend on prayer and fasting for most of their actions.[20] They believe these disciplines are necessary in order to sharpen their focus on ministry. In the local congregations they are taught that holiness is the standard of life for God's people. They also realize how important it is to experience sanctification and the baptism of the Holy Spirit. Such experience enables Pentecostals to serve effectively and prepares them well to serve people in their communities.

Pentecostals believe that if every believer uses his or her priestly call from God, then each one is capable of serving people effectively. This notion leads them into a prayerful life as the main source of spiritual enrichment. This discipline is highly esteemed and remains active at all levels of Christian service.[21] Pastors and local church leaders emphasize the importance of prayer and fasting. The purpose is to strengthen believers in their personal spirituality and to enable them to serve people effectively.

Community and Discipleship

As we have seen, Pentecostals teach that personal conversion to Christ, sanctification, and the baptism of the Holy Spirit enable believers to be effective in ministry. They are capable of and empowered to reach out to the needy, the poor, and the marginalized.[22] Once people respond to the preaching of the gospel, those who accept Christ are consolidated into the congregation through a program that leads new believers into solid discipleship. These actions create a culture of evangelism and discipleship, which is intentionally planned and executed through community service. Most believers are part of a small group where they experience most of their Christian life. As a result, local communities are transformed. Local leaders grow in faith and become capable of influencing local authorities for the good of people. Thus, civil authorities are now paying attention to the voices of Pentecostal congregations.[23] Pentecostals are now taking part in the decisions and plans of local authorities.

Facing Destructive Forces of Evil

It is clear that this kind of spiritual influence causes positive effects in society. For instance, Honduras is facing one of the most dramatic situations in its social and spiritual realms. There are two extremes that can be clearly identified: on one side, there is the transforming power of the gospel, and on the other, there is the destructive source of evil that remains strong in the country.[24] The church seems to be growing strong, and it continues to transform people's lives and communities. However, it seems that evil also continues to manifest its destructive power over those who remain apart from the gospel.

There is a spiritual conflict battling for the control of the country. Evil increases through violence, death, destruction, and immorality in economic, social, and political structures. However, the church intensifies prayer and Christian action for the sake of those who are the direct victims of such evil schemes.[25] Because of this spiritual conflict, Honduras is now going through a historical, spiritual battle.[26] Pentecostals understand this well, so they are intentionally increasing and intensifying their prayer. They have no doubt that the Holy Spirit is at work in the transformation of the country.

Identifying Evil Agents in Political Structures

Political authorities that democratically enter into power are capable of manipulating the country's constitutional order once they are in position.

They do this so that they can remain in control of the government without term limits. The situation becomes worse with the support of the international community.[27] The international community practices double standards toward governments and countries depending on the interests of those who control politics. Thus, corruption is found at all levels and seems to have permeated most political structures.

This phenomenon is clearly observed in several Latin American governments. Such political structures and personalities deform the culture of economics, social relationships, and people's moral behavior. This reality has given birth to new forms of evil such as drug trafficking, gangs, and diverse forms of violence. Civility has been severely affected by the negative power of corruption at all levels. Honduras is undergoing one of its darkest times in history under the attack of these evils. As previously mentioned, the country has been recently labeled as one of the most violent ones in the world. Similar situations are also taking place in other Central American nations and Mexico, which are also known as drug-dealing states.

The Spiritual Response of the Church

Pentecostals have understood the serious responsibility that they have assumed under the circumstances of this time. For them, there is no turning back in their commitment to the truth of the gospel.[28] In the midst of corruption, poverty, and violence, they are aware of their role in the redemption of their nation – the opportunity is now. Daniel Chiquete argues that Pentecostals who are aware of this situation are now mobilized to evangelize the poor, the weak, and the marginalized.[29] They focus their efforts to spread hope for new life conditions. This hope becomes the main source of strength to counterattack the destructive forces of evil. They realize victory is possible if they observe and practice their faith. They can do this by showing solidarity with those who are hurting.

Pentecostals are also practicing an intelligent reading and interpretation of the scriptures. Such reading strengthens their commitment to the Great Commission, even when this means sacrifice or suffering. Their personal relationship with the Holy Spirit keeps them focused on their mission. The Holy Spirit makes them strong in the battle against evil. In the church, the altar is still occupied by the poor, the weak, the sick, and the marginalized. That is one reason why Pentecostal congregations continue to witness effectively and win people for Christ.

The Challenge of Social Evils

Pentecostals have been criticized for claiming large numbers of adherents, yet the country remains one of the most violent and corrupt in the region. Such criticism does not seem to be accurate. It does not report what actually happens with the two extremes that struggle for control. Pentecostals are using every way possible to counterattack the forces of evil.[30] As stated earlier, prayer has intensified, and social work has increased dramatically and intentionally in most communities.[31] Assistance to the poor and marginalized has also been intensified. Believers are making every effort p to advance the transformational power of the gospel in politics and socio-economic terrains.

Poverty, marginalization, and insecurity about the future lead people to a search for ultimate answers. Pentecostals come from the most marginalized segments of society. The movement was born in the midst of the poor masses. It represents the voice that articulates the revelation and hope the Holy Spirit has given to those who had no other voice. In some circles, Pentecostalism has been referred to as a revolution of the poor.[32] For them, there cannot be a dichotomizing between theory and praxis in a world of poverty and insecurity. Here, theory arises from praxis to further praxis that eventually leads to change and to the building of a different society. It is the community of faith that determines the destiny and ultimate answers that edify believers. The community sends a prophetic message to the world to find answers in the incarnated Jesus.[33]

Pentecostals have made a significant impact in the process of evangelization of Latin America. Pentecostals understand evangelization as the action of proclaiming the gospel of Jesus Christ as the fulfillment of the Great Commission. Such proclamation reaches out to every man and woman who is in need of spiritual salvation. Once the message is accepted, it adds transformation to the individual and his or her world.[34] For Pentecostals, the first responsibility of a believer is to look for the salvation of others, especially those who are close, such as relatives and friends. This thrust generates new conversions that continue to grow in numbers.

Once a community is impacted by the gospel, in most cases, transformation starts at home and at the *barrio*. Believers no longer participate in worldly activities and other scenarios of evil. These events are multiplied from one community to another. Congregations continue to grow, and spiritual revival is seen mostly through a devoted prayer life. A subsequent outpouring of the Holy Spirit then takes place with the manifestation of spiritual gifts in the life and ministry of those who believe.

Such growth also brings about social transformation. New converts leave behind old paradigms of life and look for new options and possibilities.[35] This Pentecostal growth has reached higher levels of influence. Entire communities have changed by the influence of Pentecostal life and spirituality.[36] The results are visible and can be seen in the family, schools, and social relationships. Once the inner circle of relationships is won for Christ, the next step is to reach out to other families and communities, so the cycle continues to multiply.[37]

Grace, Peace, and Justice

Although there are still challenging levels of injustice, Christians in Latin America are making every effort to influence transformation in their communities. They know that this can be possible through the implementation of the principles of the gospel. In recent years, violence has claimed thousands of lives. Many young people have died or have been mistreated at the hands of gangs and drug trafficking.[38] Insecurity causes people to migrate to safer places. Weak economies cause the search for better options at other sites of the world. Political instability forces people to flee for safety. Administrative corruption has driven people against political authority. All these social evils hurt society and raise a legitimate demand for social justice and peace that can only happen when civil authority is held accountable under civil law.

As Christianity grows in Latin America, a new generation of leaders has begun to lead the church. They are aware of the challenges ahead of them. Therefore, in order to respond to the social needs of the countries, they are preparing solid discipleship programs with the principles of the gospel that are preparing the church for the future. They also know that transformation happens over the course of time. They will have to invest strategically in younger generations.[39] True peace and justice will occur under the lordship of Christ in the new societies.

Concluding Remarks

This chapter has looked into the manifestation of God's redemptive grace among the Pentecostal communities in Latin America through the lens of Honduras. This region of the world has experienced the incarnated Christ through the service of his disciples in the context of poverty. Christian leaders of this region seem to understand that there is more work to be done by the church in order to reach true transformation in society. They realize that the initiative of grace comes from God himself. He loves the Latin American people and wants all of them to experience redemption through Christ. Many people have responded to God's offer, yet the work of redemption and transformation remains unfinished.

Fortunately, the implementation of the grace of God among the Latin American people continues to expand. God's gift of grace faces opposition from the forces of evil in positions of authority and in control of the economy. Nevertheless, God's people continue to take a stand against this evil in the power of the Holy Spirit, which makes that grace relevant to the communities. At this point, I think that the key to succeeding in this endeavor is to endure hardship, be patient, and trust God and his grace on behalf of the people he so loves in Latin America.

Notes

1 Ample information on this subject was documented on the occasion of the VIII Encounter of the Study Commission of the History of the Church in Latin America in Lima, Peru. Presided by Enrique Dussel, several scholars provided a broad approach to mission among the poor in the region. See Enrique D. Dussel, "Resistencia y Esperanza: Historia del Pueblo Cristiano en América Latina y el Caribe," in Pablo Richard, ed., *Materiales para Una Historia de la Teología en América Latina* (San José, Costa Rica: Dei-Cehila, 1981), 641–650.

2 The most recent scholar who began to organize the history of mission in the context of Honduras was Medardo Mejía, *Historia de Honduras*

(Tegucigalpa, Honduras: Editorial Universitaria, 1983). His work sets the anthropological, cultural, and religious basis to understand the history of Honduras since the days of the Colonia Española. This Roman Catholic scholar argues that Christianity could be examined from a non-religious point of view.

3   See, "The Beginnings of Pentecostalism in Chile," in Stanley M. Burgess and Eduard M. van der Maas, eds., *The New International Dictionary of Pentecostal and Charismatic Movements* (Grand Rapids: Zondervan, 2010), 102–103.

4   Laura Premack, "The Holy Rollers are Invading Our Territory: Southern Baptist Missionaries and the Early Years of Pentecostalism in Brazil, 1910–1935" (Master of Arts Thesis, University of North Carolina, 2007).

5   Miguel Álvarez, "Latin American Mission, Then and Now," in Miguel Álvarez, ed., *The Reshaping of Mission in Latin America* (Oxford: Regnum Books, 2015), 1–5.

6   Calixto Salvatierra Moreno, "Catholic and Pentecostal Convergence on Practical Theology and Mission," in *The Reshaping of Mission in Latin America*, 65.

7   A good book on this topic is Amos Yong, *In the Days of Caesar: Pentecostalism and Political Theology* (Grand Rapids: Eerdmans, 2010), 238–251. Yong offers a thorough discussion on the role of Pentecostal empowerment in the incarnational and redemptive mission of God over civilian freedom.

8   Emilio Núñez and William Taylor, *Crisis and Hope in Latin America: An Evangelical Perspective* (Pasadena, CA: William Carey Library, 2012), 102–103. The authors discussed the theme of racial inheritance and its influence over mentality and traditional thinking among Latin Americans.

9   Sebastian Edwards, *Crisis and Reform in Latin America: From Despair to Hope* (Oxford: Oxford University Press, 1995), 29. The author discusses how external economic pressures and domestic policies have affected the political behavior of Latin Americans in recent years.

10 Jon Wolseth, *Jesus and the Gang: Youth Violence and Christianity in Urban Honduras* (Phoenix: University of Arizona Press, 2011), 68–71. Wolseth takes individual case studies in Honduras to discover the motivation behind gang members in the inner city.

11 Margot Webb, *Drugs and Gangs* (New York: Rosen Publishing, 1998), 39–49. The author discusses the relationship between drugs and gangs. It also explains how this relationship has generated a powerful illegal industry worldwide.

12 Rita James Simon, *A Comparative Perspective on Major Social Problems* (Oxford: Lexington Books, 2001), 36. She found updated information with reference to violence in Central America. Unfortunately, at that time, Honduras was one of the deadliest countries in the world.

13 Thomas P. Anderson, *Politics in Central America: Guatemala, El Salvador, Honduras and Nicaragua* (Westport, CT: Greenwood Publishing, 2003), 13–15.

14 On the matter of political corruption in Honduras, see the article of Michael Radu, "The Other Side of Democratic Transition," *Democracy at Large* 2:3 (2006), 28–30.

15 For extensive information on work among the poor and marginalized in Honduras, see Vilma Elisa Fuentes, "Reconstruction: An Opportunity for Political Change," in Marisa O. Ensor, ed., *The Legacy of Hurricane Mitch: Lessons from Post-Disaster Reconstruction in Honduras* (Phoenix: University of Arizona Press, 2009), 100–128.

16 Vladimir López Recinos, "Desarrollo Migración y Seguridad: El caso de la Migración Hondureña Hacia los Estados Unidos," *Migración y Desarrollo* 11:21 (2013), 65–105.

17 Daniel Álvarez, "No More Violence: Renewal Theology Reflections on Violence in the Context of Honduras and its Immigrants to the United States," in Sammy Alfaro and Néstor Medina, eds., *Pentecostals and Charismatics in Latin America and Latino Communities* (New York: Palgrave Macmillan, 2015), 81–95.

18 See, for instance, Daniel Chiquete, *Haciendo Camino al Andar: Siete Ensayos de Teología Pentecostal* (San José, Costa Rica: DEI 2007), 32. The author offers fresh ideas of the approach of Pentecostals in service to the community. See also Harvey Cox, *Fire from Heaven: The Rise of Pentecostal Spirituality and the Reshaping of Religion in the 21st Century* (Burlington: De Capo Press, 1995), 82.

19 Andrés Tapia, "Growing Pains: Evangel Latinos Wrestle with the Role of Women, Generation Gaps, and Cultural Divides," *Christianity Today* 40:2 (February 1995), 38–41.

20 See, Miguel Álvarez, "The South and the Latin American Paradigm of the Pentecostal Movement," *Asian Journal of Pentecostal Studies* 5:1 (2002), 135–153.

21 Dario López, *Pentecostalimo y Transformación Social* (Buenos Aires: Ediciones Kairos/FTL, 2000), 29. López is one of the first scholars to address the issue of transformation from the margins of society.

22 For a discussion of the personal transformation of Pentecostal lives in Latin America see, Miguel Álvarez, *Hermenéutica: La Palabra, El Espíritu y la Comunidad de Fe* (Cleveland, TN: CPT Press, 2021), 56.

23 Wilma Wells-Davies, "La Naturaleza de la Conversión Pentecostal en la Argentina: Implicaciones Missionológicas," in Daniel Chiquete and Luis Orellana, eds., *Voces del Pentecostalismo Latinoamericano* (Concepción, Chile: Red Latinoamericana de Estudios Pentecostales, 2009), 157–178.

24 Wolfgang Bühne, *Explosión Carismática* (Terrassa, Spain: Editorial CLIE, 1994), 141. The author does a critical analysis of the doctrines and practices of the so-called "three waves" of the Holy Spirit. He studied the most current trends of Charismatic and neo-Pentecostal leaders and churches.

25 About the fervent prayers of Pentecostals in favor of peace and against the forces of evil in Honduras, see Joseph F. Manning, *Cristianismo Milenario* (Ciudad de México: Editorial Pax, 2001), 94.

26 María Ramírez Nieves, *Ángeles en Guerra Espiritual* (Bloomington, IN: Palibrio, 2012), 56. The author presents evidence of spiritual warfare, such as demonic deliverance, healings, and miracles that take place in the context of Pentecostal congregations of Honduras.

27 By "international community," Hondurans understand the associations or groups of nations that gather together for common purposes. The United Nations represents the largest body of nations worldwide. In Latin America, there is the American Organization of States. Cf. the behavior of the international community as observed by Gary Goertz and Paul F. Diehl, "International Norms and Power Politics," in Frank W. Wayman, and Paul F. Diehl, eds., *Reconstructing Politics* (Detroit: University of Michigan Press, 2001), 101–122.

28 Edward Cleary, "Latin American Pentecostalism," in Murray W. Dempster, Byron D. Klaus and Douglas Petersen, eds., *The Globalization of Pentecostalism: A Religion Made to Travel* (Eugene, OR: Wipf & Stock), 127–145.

29 Chiquete, *Haciendo Camino al Andar*, 124.

30 See, for instance, Juan Driver, *La Fe en la Periferia de la Historia* (Ciudad Guatemala: Semilla, 1997), 76–81.

31 Bernardo Campos, "In the Power of the Spirit: Pentecostalism, Theology, and Social Ethics," in Dennis A. Smith and Benjamin F. Gutiérrez, eds., *In the Power of the Spirit: The Pentecostal Challenge to Historic Churches in Latin America* (Ciudad Guatemala: CELEP, 1996), 41–50. Campos' main interest is to examine the role of Pentecostalism in the context of

marginalization, which is the typical social and economic condition of Pentecostals in Latin America.

32 See, for instance, R. Andrew Chestnut, *Born Again in Brazil: The Pentecostal Boom and the Pathogens of Poverty* (New Brunswick: Rutgers University Press, 1997), 5–9.

33 Driver, *La Fe en la Periferia*, 78.

34 On the matter of Pentecostalism and evangelism in Latin America see, Yara Monteiro, "Congregación Cristiana en Brasil, de la Fundación Centenario: La Trayectoria de una Iglesia Brasileña," in Daniel Chiquete and Luis Orellana, eds., *Voces del Pentecostalismo Latinoamericano* (Concepción, Chile: RELEP, 2011), 90.

35 Evidence of this kind of transformation could be found in the work of López, *Pentecostalismo y Transformación Social*, 78–83. See also, Luis Orellana, "El Futuro del Pentecostalismo en América Latina," in Daniel Chiquete and Luis Orellana, eds., *Voces del Pentecostalismo Latinoamericano* (Concepción, Chile: RELEP, 2011), 141–156.

36 See Lillian Kwon, "Pentecostal Impact Growing in Latin America," The Christian Post, November 9, 2006, https://www.christianpost.com/news/pentecostal-impact-growing-in-latin-america.html, accessed May 2, 2022.

37 López, *Pentecostalismo y Transformación Social*, 82.

38 Carlos F. Cardoza-Orlandi and Justo L. Gonzalez, *To All Nations from All Nations: A History of the Christian Missionary Movement* (Nashville, TN: Abingdon Press, 2013), 389.

39 Enrique Pinedo, "Mission and the Children of Latin America: A Historical Perspective from the Latin American Congress of Evangelization – CLADE," in *The Reshaping of Mission in Latin America*, 103–116.

9 The Unfinished Task in North America and its Impact on Spirit-Empowered Christianity

Daniel D. Isgrigg

Abstract

This study explores the state of evangelism in North America, particularly the Spirit-empowered Church in America. Charted through the history of evangelism movements, most of which originated in North America, this essay will look at those movements, their impact on the church, and some theological reasons why North America has not been more effective in its own evangelistic efforts.

Introduction

Before taking my present job in academia, I spent twenty years in ministry in a local Spirit-empowered church, seven years as a lead pastor of a church of eighty people. These pastoral years were good, but hard. As much as I loved the people, as a small church, we struggled to grow in a town that boasted over 1,000 churches and many mega-churches. The challenges of the average pastor are immense, but what made my experience particularly frustrating was that in seven years as the pastor, we averaged less than one salvation per year. Of course, the Great Commission was a priority and said we believed the baptism in the Spirit was for effective witness. We were very active in outreach ministry, conducting over a dozen outreaches per year. But these efforts yielded very few salvations. I found that many of my neighbor churches were reaching people at an astounding pace. In the end, I had to come to grips with the fact that some churches are better at reaching people than others.

The reality that some Christian traditions are better at evangelism than others is also playing out on the global stage. Spirit-empowered Christianity is demonstrating that it has a distinctive advantage in church growth. According to Todd Johnson and Gina Zurlo, Spirit-empowered Christianity (SEC) now numbers 644 million people worldwide, a growth of nearly ten-fold in the past half-century.[1] For many Pentecostal denominations, the growth is particularly significant in the Global South.

For example, in Latin America, Pentecostal and Charismatics have grown from 4 percent of the Christian population to 29.4 percent.[2] There are similar trends in other regions of the world. In 2020, Spirit-empowered Christianity represented 35.7 percent of Christians in Africa, 30.3 percent of Christians in Latin America, and 19.5 percent of Christians in Asia.[3] These global trends have contributed to SEC becoming the fastest-growing religious movement worldwide.

North America, however, is a different story for evangelism. Headlines declaring the decline in the church have been a regular occurrence in religious media. Since 1999, church membership in American has declined from 70 percent in 1999 to 47 percent in 2020.[4] This fact is particularly difficult to understand for those who study the unprecedented growth worldwide of the Pentecostal and Charismatic.[5] This study will explore the state of evangelism in North America, particularly the Spirit-empowered Church in America. Charted through the history of evangelism movements, most of which originated in North America, this essay will look at those movements, their impact on the church, and some theological reasons why North America has not been more effective in its own evangelistic efforts.

To the Ends of the Earth

Evangelism has always been a major tenet of the Christian faith. The idea that the whole world could be evangelized stretches back to the gospels themselves with Jesus' famous prediction, "This gospel of the kingdom shall be preached in all the world as a witness to all nations, and then the end will come" (Matt 24:14, ESV). The thrust of evangelistic efforts to reach the world in obedience to Jesus' Great Commission continued into every period of Christian history. In fact, David Barrett has documented 788 different formal plans to reach the world for Christ by Christian communities in the past two millennia.[6] Yet, Barrett laments, all of these plans failed to finish the task in their generation.

The twentieth century opened with a significant re-emphasis on evangelism, which became the catalyst for a number of modern attempts to finish the task. In 1855, A. T. Pierson wrote an article in the *Missionary Review* with a "Plan to evangelize the world."[7] Pierson's Northfield Conferences combined eschatological zeal with the missional impulse to preach the Evangelical gospel to the ends of the earth before the coming of the Lord. This was followed by John R. Mott, the Methodist layman who published his classic work *The Evangelization of the World in this Generation* in 1900. Many missiologists were animated by his charge to mobilize the global Christian world to unite to reach the lost. The enthusiasm came to a head in 1910 at the Edinburgh World Missionary Conference, where Protestant missionaries organized and committed to completing the task of evangelism within a decade. While great energy was generated, it ultimately fell short of its goal, as others had done before. But Edinburgh did inspire the founding of other ecumenical movements such as the World Council of Churches and the International Missionary Council.[8]

The missionary impulses of Pierson and Mott naturally influenced the founding of the Pentecostal movement in the early 1900s. Animated by an eschatologically motivated impulse, Pentecostals sought to reach as many people as possible before Jesus returned. Azusa Street Mission attendees were filled with the Spirit and spoke in unknown languages, with the expectation that they were empowered to take the gospel to the world. Though Spirit-baptism was an inner work of the Spirit, it was primarily concerned with the outward witness to the whole world. Taking the gospel to "every creature" was a top priority and the reason for the Spirit's empowerment.[9] Allan H. Anderson comments, "[Pentecostalism] is above all else a missionary movement—this premise enables us to understand the primary motivation for its global expansion through the twentieth century."[10] But the missional impulse often placed more emphasis on missionaries evangelizing the world rather than reaching their own continent of North America.

The evangelization impulse is seen clearly in the formation of the Assemblies of God in 1914, where one of its goals was mutual cooperation in the effort of preaching the "whole gospel for the whole world." At the second General Council held in November 1914 at the Stone Church in Chicago, the AG committed themselves to prioritizing evangelism. They passed a resolution that said, "We commend ourselves and the movement to him for the greatest evangelism that the world has ever seen."[11] Yet, over the next few generations, Pentecostalism remained relatively on the margins of the North American landscape. Between WWI and WWII, the AG stabilized but grew only marginally. It wasn't until the post-WWII era that significant growth took place as Pentecostals began to experience upward mobility in the post-war boom. It is in this era that departments of missions and evangelism were established, shifting the evangelistic enterprise to missionaries rather than serving as the overall mission of the fellowship.

In the post-World War II era, the American church saw a resurgence in attendance from 30–50 percent of the population.[12] Much of the mid-century growth was due to new forms of mass evangelism. Evangelicals like Billy Graham and Pentecostal healing evangelists like Oral Roberts pioneered the method of mass evangelism. Roberts, who became famous for mainstreaming healing on television, never saw healing as his primary mission. His ministry of deliverance was in the mode of the traditional evangelist. To emphasize this, in 1953, Roberts launched the "Million Souls Crusade" with the goal of winning a million souls to Christ per year. This wasn't secondary to healing for Roberts; rather, it was his "first, second, third and last goal. Besides that, I have no other."[13]

A significant moment came in 1966 when Billy Graham and *Christianity Today* hosted the Berlin Congress on Evangelism which brought together an international delegation of Evangelical missionaries and evangelists to re-ignite the church toward the unfinished task. The motto was "one race, one gospel, one task," a theme that emphasized overcoming sectarian and racial walls that prevented the church from uniting in mission. Carl F. H. Henry commented:

> If Christians around the world heed the plea of the congress to unite in a bold and winsome presentation of the Good News, the twentieth century world will be spectacular, confronted with a prospect of peace and hope and joy that men and women of all races and lands may share.[14]

Following this congress was Lausanne Congress on Evangelism in 1974 that began the Lausanne Movement focused on uniting Evangelicals toward the common goal of "total evangelism of the world."[15] It turns out that Lausanne was just the beginning of efforts to increase evangelism as the twentieth century was coming to a close.

Toward A. D. 2000

In the 1970s–1980s, leaders from several prominent Christian evangelism and mission movements converged to discuss an effort to coordinate world evangelization efforts leading up to A. D. 2000.[16] The gathering included Keith Parks, David Barrett, Luis Bush, Thomas Wang, and Jay Gary, who met together to brainstorm on what it would take to "finish the task" prior to the turn of the millennium. The result is the following commitment:

> In light of the unfinished task, but with a quiet confidence in the possibilities for the completion of world evangelization if Christians cooperate with one another; and in light of the fact that many Christian denominations and organizations are already using A.D. 2000 as a milestone; it is hereby resolved that in the near future a small world-level consultation of Christian leaders be convened to focus on A. D. 2000.[17]

David Barrett, the noted missiologist and statistician, did extensive research to document that there were some 250 initiatives between Pentecost A. D. 33 and 1900. In each case, efforts to evangelize the world were launched and fizzled within a generation.[18]

However, the momentum toward A. D. 2000 was gaining momentum as several significant efforts at world evangelism were already underway. One effort was led by religious broadcasters who aimed to preach the gospel by radio to every nation by 2000. The Southern Baptist Convention launched its "Bold Mission Thrust" in 1976 with a target of world evangelization by 2000. In 1976, Ralph Winter started the U. S. Center for World Mission focused on unreached people groups. Roman Catholics also caught the evangelism vision in 1978 when Pope John Paul launched a major evangelism effort called "Evangelism 2000" led by Spirit-filled Catholic Tom Forrest. Also, in the late 1970s, Bill Bright launched the Jesus Film as an evangelism effort called "New Life 2000" to introduce every nation to Jesus in their native tongue.[19] In 1980, the World Consultation on Frontier Mission was held in Edinburgh with the goal of "A Church for Every People by the Year 2000." All total, some thirty different organizations and denominations had set their sights on evangelizing the world by A. D. 2000.

The Decade of Harvest

In the Spirit-empowered movement, several major evangelism initiatives were also taking place in the various Pentecostal denominations. Each one recognized the importance of the upcoming millennial moment and placed an emphasis on the last decade as a special era of evangelism. Most notably was the Assemblies of God's "Decade of Harvest," which focused on American evangelism based on foreign mission principles. Others included The Church of God (Cleveland, TN) initiative called "Decade of Destiny," the "Mission 2000" effort in the Pentecostal Assemblies of Canada, and the "Church Target 2000" initiative in the International Pentecostal Holiness Church.[20]

Beyond these classical Pentecostal movements, the charismatic renewal community was mobilized by Vinson Synan, the Pentecostal historian who became the leader of the Spirit-filled ecumenical evangelism movement called the North American Renewal Service Committee (NARSC). Synan joined with various charismatic renewal communities to host a Global Congress on the Holy Spirit and World Evangelism Conference to take seriously the mandate of world evangelization.[21] The NARSC leaders set a goal of reaching half of the global population with the gospel by A. D. 2000. For Spirit-empowered believers, the missional emphasis of the Spirit made the turn of the century a perfect target for finishing the task. Synan noted in 1988, "If Christians, who are filled with the Holy Spirit and who are given evangelistic gifts are not able to win the world Christ, who else will be able to rise to the challenge? If not us, who?"[22] Conferences continued through the 1990s until the final one was held in 2000, after which NARSC was dissolved and the various ecumenical charismatic leaders went their separate ways.

As ecumenical convergence movements dissolved and cooperation for world evangelism once again waned, a new convergence movement was about to be birthed out of the centennial celebration of the Azusa Street Revival in 2006. Organized by Church of God of Prophecy pastor and evangelist Dr. Billy Wilson, the Azusa Centennial brought together 50,000 people from 115 nations to celebrate the outpouring of the Holy Spirit at Azusa and to pray for a fresh outpouring on a new generation for a new millennium. The Centennial was more than just another Holy Spirit conference. It was a convergence moment in which Spirit-filled leaders saw the value of cooperation towards reaching a new generation.

Out of the Azusa Centennial was birthed a vision for a new convergence of Spirit-empowered movements called Empowered21. Wilson assembled a Global Council of Spirit-empowered leaders who prayed and dreamed together about a goal for E21: "That every person on earth would have an authentic encounter with Jesus Christ through the power and presence of the Holy Spirit by Pentecost 2033."[23] In the tradition of previous movements, E21 emphasized the purpose of the Spirit-empowered life was to evangelize the world with the gospel in obedience to the great commission. Today, it is mobilizing global constituents toward this goal through regional councils meeting on a regular basis to cooperate and consult together on how to "finish the task" in this generation. Can this be accomplished in the next decade? That remains to be seen, but like previous movements, E21 is calling the church back to the mandate to evangelize the world for Jesus Christ in this generation.

Despite the cyclical resurgence of these missional initiatives, Global Christianity has remained fairly static in the last fifty years. While Christians have increased from 1.2 billion in 1970 to 2.5 billion in 2020, that growth has failed to keep up with global population growth, with the percentage of global Christians remaining stagnant from 32.4 percent in 1970 to 32.3 percent in 2020.[24] The demographics of the global Spirit-empowered movement today are no doubt impressive. But we must be realistic in our account of what is taking place. The reality is that despite the past century of convergence movements seeking to cooperate toward the goal of evangelization, the unfinished task remains largely unfinished, especially in North America.

The Unfinished Task in North America

Though the global Spirit-empowered movement has seen tremendous growth in the past half-century, North American Spirit-empowered Christianity has not kept pace with the world. Of the 644 million global Spirit-empowered believers, only 67 million are located in North America, placing North America fourth among the six continents.[25] While the total number increased from 2000–2020 by 14 million, the total percentage of believers declined from 12.1 percent to 10.5 percent. Overall, Pentecostals and Charismatics in the United States have increased from 13.8 million in 1970 to 65 million in 2020 but have failed to keep up with population growth.[26]

While much of the leadership for the global evangelistic efforts have been from North America, North American Christianity has not particularly benefitted from these evangelism initiatives. Many church statisticians have sounded the alarm that the church in America is in decline.[27] The Pentecostal efforts at evangelism had mixed results leading up to A. D. 2000. For example, Edith Blumhofer and Paul Tinlin noted that the AG's Decade of Harvest fell well short of its goals of 5 million new converts and 5,000 new churches.[28] All total, AG adherents only grew by less than 400,000 during that decade and have climbed steadily to a modest, yet less than expected, growth of 1.1 million since 1990.[29] At the same time, the goal of 500 churches was equally disappointing as the number of churches declined from 8,988 in 1990 to 8,801 in 2000; a net loss of 187 churches. The AG was not the only major Pentecostal denomination to struggle. The International Pentecostal Holiness Church saw moderate growth from 1,475 churches in 1989 to 1,868 churches in 2000, including an increase of over 60,000 members.[30] While these gains were certainly welcome, they fell below their stated goals and expectations set by the millennial benchmark.

What these numbers tell us is that North America, while slowly growing, lags largely behind the global landscape of growth. For example, from 2009–2019, Assemblies of God (U. S.) adherents climbed from 2.9 million to 3.2 million, an increase of 13.1 percent.[31] Conversions over this same period climbed from 440,803 to 487,322, a growth of 10 percent.[32] The church is growing, but growth among ethnic minorities, rather than evangelization, is the leading cause. The total population of White adherents remained relatively flat—from 1,853,632 to 1,849,688 yet declined in total percentage from 70 percent to 56 percent. Over the same period, Hispanic adherents went from 428,747 (16 percent) to 739,001 (23.2 percent).[33] Yet, this isn't to say that growth is directly tied to evangelism among ethnic populations. Ethnic language districts in 2018–2019 saw a decline of 5.1 percent in conversions.[34] This means that while the AG is experiencing more diversity, which is positive, growth has stagnated among most of its congregations overall.

In Canada, Pentecostals and Charismatic are not fairing any better. The total number of Spirit-empowered believers more than tripled from 709,000 in 1970 to 2,300,000 in 2000.[35] Yet that growth has stagnated since, marking 2,500,000 in 2015. For example, the Pentecostal Assemblies of Canada, perhaps the largest Pentecostal body, has seen only modest growth in the last twenty years, from 220,000 in 2000 to 240,000 today.[36] Michael Wilkinson notes that Pentecostalism reached its peak in 1991 with over 435,000 Pentecostal believers, but has since declined as many Pentecostals joined independent neo-Pentecostal or charismatic groups like the Vineyard.[37] It is notable that Spirit-empowered believers have outnumbered Evangelicals for the past two decades as a percentage of the total population, but that percentage is comparatively small at 6 percent.

If there is growth in the Spirit-Empowered Movement, it is taking place in the independent networks of charismatic churches around North America.[38] These networks, sometimes called New Apostolic Reformation (NAR), operate by a different set of values than traditional Pentecostal communities. Brad Christerson and Richard Flory studied these networks and noted that they have a different missional focus than the traditional mission of evangelism. Primarily, they "Seek to transform society as a whole rather than saving individual souls and building congregations."[39] Contrasted with early Pentecostals, who saw themselves as an end-time missional movement, charismatic churches are often focused internally on advancing the prosperity of believers and the church network itself to grow personally, organizationally, and societally. While these factors have drawn members from Pentecostal circles into their ranks, it has also appealed to America's ethos of neo-liberal self-actualization. These churches offer innovative religious experiences that can be customized in ways that benefit the religious consumer. In this way, the goals of building the kingdom are commoditized by offering personal enrichment and success rather than motivating individuals toward accomplishing evangelization for the gospel's sake.[40]

Factors Shaping North American Evangelism

Why has Christianity in North America been in decline while Spirit-empowered Christianity is expanding globally? I want to suggest three factors that have challenged evangelism efforts among Spirit-empowered communities. These factors seem to have impacted every generation's effectiveness in fulfilling the Great Commission. But, particularly for this new generation, these factors are increasingly central to any effort to re-invigorate evangelization in North America.

Premillennial Eschatology

Pentecostalism was birthed out of the phenomenon of baptism in the Holy Spirit. But this experience was set in a larger eschatological and restorationist metanarrative known as the Latter Rain. Pentecostals believed the emergence of the last days phenomenon of Spirit-baptism and speaking in tongues was a sign that earth was in its final days before Christ's coming. This dispensational metanarrative was semi-cessationist in that they understood that what was lost during the decline of the church was being fully restored in anticipation of the coming millennial reign of Christ.[41]

The Latter Rain eschatological paradigm presented Pentecostals with two competing tensions. On the one hand, Pentecostals imagined an increase in glory from the outpouring of the Spirit that would make evangelism possible before the coming of Christ. They believed the restoration of the baptism in the Holy Spirit was the beginning of a worldwide global outpouring to bring in the end-time harvest. Pentecostalism was not a movement that evangelized; it was thought to be God's primary vehicle of global evangelization.

At the same time, the eschatological narrative had an equally pessimistic orientation. Rooted in premillennialism, Pentecostals rejected the postmillennial idea of progress that expected the Spirit to renew the world through the church. Instead, the dispensational aspects of premillennial convinced them that the conditions on the earth were to get worse, not better. Peter Prosser comments:

> Dispensationalists became a self-fulfilling prophecy. With the present dispensation winding down, Pentecostals recognized that sin was increasing and wickedness. In not looking for change, except for the worse, everything around them and among them would naturally tend to get worse.[42]

You can see how these ideas would stifle evangelistic efforts as a lost cause. This cognitive dissonance between evangelistic success and fatalistic failure has little been recognized in Pentecostal circles. But it is a key tension that has motivated, or demotivated, evangelist efforts.

One turn in this orientation was to shift a view of the eschatological mandate: "This gospel shall be preached in every nation as a witness, then the end shall come" (Matt 24:14, paraphrased). On the positive side, this verse could imply that the gospel will be successful at some point when every nation is reached in fulfillment of the promise that "The earth will be filled with the knowledge of the Lord as the waters cover the sea" (Hab 2:14). This verse would imply that the gospel could reach the whole world. However, the eschatological mandate could also be interpreted by those who have a fatalistic view by implying that a witness of the gospel must reach one portion of every nation of the world rather than success in evangelizing the whole world. This was the strategy in the A. D. 2000 approach to make sure that every nation had some gospel witness in some form in order to fulfill the mandate. This was the approach taken by media companies such as radio broadcasters and television networks like Trinity Broadcast Network.

But perhaps a third approach is warranted that would avoid the tensions inherent in both approaches to the eschatological mandate. What if the goal of reaching the whole world is not a prediction but rather a challenge to every generation to take responsibility for reaching the world they have inherited? In this way, the eschatological mandate is not a goal of evangelization, per se. It is the motivation for evangelization for each successive generation. The failure of previous generations to win the world for Jesus should not deter this generation from believing that such a goal is possible. Nor should that failure be used as an excuse to limit evangelization efforts to filling a quota of the evangelized among every people group. Jesus is still coming, and North America is still worth reaching. Every year, North America grows and changes. Just as the global population rapidly expands through globalization, population growth, and migration, the nature of the church's understanding of "every nation" continues to shift. Therefore, generational contextualization is extremely important, as each generation takes up the mandate and reaches their generation in the ways that reach their generation. It is this idea that leads us to the next hindrance and possibility in evangelization.

Baptism in the Holy Spirit and Mission

One of the hallmarks of Spirit-empowered Christianity is its belief in Spirit-baptism as an empowering encounter with the Holy Spirit to be witnesses (Acts 1:8). Early Pentecostals understood this experience in a missional way, so much so that the languages they spoke by the Spirit were thought to be explicitly for their missionary endeavors. However, this emphasis shifted in the Charismatic Renewal and Independent charismatic movements toward the personal benefits of Spirit-baptism above its missional benefits. As a result, self-improvement has become the goal rather than the salvation of the lost. I dare say this inward focus has lessened the Spirit-empowered believer's missional impulse to reach the lost. This has no doubt had consequences on personal evangelism and the overall growth of the past few decades.

Pentecostals have tended to focus highly on missionary endeavors for the expansion of Christianity globally. As Allen H. Anderson notes, "Just as Spirit Baptism is Pentecostalism's central, most distinctive doctrine, so mission is Pentecostalism's central, most important activity."[43] But, the baptism in the Holy Spirit was never supposed to be empowerment just for missionaries; it was the power of evangelization for everyday believers living missionally in their own contexts. Pentecostals were called to be missional, not just missionaries.

The good news is a significant shift has taken place in recent generations as younger people are more drawn to missional Christianity rather than simply gospel proclamation. While this trend excites fear by some that mission will replace evangelism, the truth is that global growth is taking place primarily because the global Spirit-empowered Christianity worldwide is far more engaged with social issues than in Western contexts.[44] Because global missions work has successfully integrated the gospel and social engagement, this has filtered down to North American Pentecostals denominations adding compassion ministry to their statements on evangelization.[45] Missionaries have long invested in missional partnerships as the means of contextualizing the gospel. Says Robert Priest, "A high proportion of mission today involves the synergy of global partnerships across such marked socio-economic divided, partnerships mobilized on behalf of human need and of Christian witness."[46] If missions work is successfully rooted in compassion ministry, why would evangelism on the local level be any different?

The shift from "missions" to "mission" is an important one for the growth of evangelism in North America. Christians need to see evangelism not as a calling or office in the church but as the daily mission of the believer. Robert Priest comments:

> In contemporary understandings, the task of living missionally is thought to belong to all believers, not merely religious professionals. Furthermore, there is a pervasive recognition that missional presence is best accomplished through the full body of Christ and that lay Christians living out their various vocational commitments in ways that establish a visible Christian presence is a critical component of authentic witness.[47]

Missional living is a Spirit-empowered concept. The idea that the Spirit makes us witnesses does not have to fit the old paradigm of evangelistic crusades and or preaching on the street corner. The Holy Spirit empowers believers in every generation to live everyday lives in which the kingdom of God is present in power, in mission, in speech, in friendship, and in vocation.

What is taking place is a shift in what is understood as evangelism, especially among Millennials and Gen Z. It is easy to see that this generation is struggling with conventional models of evangelism. A Barna Report found that 47 percent of Millennials believed it was "wrong to share their faith." That is a sobering statistic. However, it doesn't tell the whole story. The study also notes that 96 percent of Millennials report that sharing their faith is important, and 94 percent say that people coming to Jesus is the "best thing that could happen" to a person they love.[48] As one millennial reflected on evangelism:

> It is certainly a tragedy that communication of this beautiful message of Jesus' love and grace has become associated with colonialism, cheap manipulation, and obscurant dogmatism . . . evangelism, sharing of the good news of Jesus, honestly stands in need of holistic overhaul both of method and of content.[49]

Rather than seeing evangelism as an event done by ministers, Millennials and Gen Z see their lives as missional and want their lives to be engaged in things that matter. In this way, Craig Spring notes they are uniquely equipped to evangelize. "Millennial Christians have more non-Christian friends than any other prior generation. They're more plugged into the reality of the world."[50] So evangelism is of high priority, but younger Pentecostals are looking for new models of evangelism that differ from outdated evangelization paradigms.

By way of contrast, personal evangelism among Boomer Generations has also continued to fall steadily. One Barna study notes that less than 50 percent of the Boomer generation engages in personal evangelism, compared to 65 percent of Millennials in 2013. Says Barna, "While the evangelistic practices of all other generations have either declined or remained static in the past few years, Millennials are the only generation among whom evangelism is significantly on the rise."[51] That statistic has grown even higher more recently as 80 percent of Gen Z has shared Christ with someone in the past year.[52] While on the surface, it appears evangelism is in decline, there is reason to hope for the future of evangelism in this new generation, even if it looks different from generations past.

Politicizing the Gospel

One thing that is clear in North America is that the church has become less evangelistic as it has become more political. This is a huge problem facing Evangelicalism, including Spirit-empowered communities. While politics is always extremely divisive, the exponential growth of Pentecostalism has benefited from North America's stable political situation. As William Kay notes, Church growth is often the result of stable political environments when the church can evangelize unhindered by governmental control.[53] The presence of political peace following WWII led to significant growth in Pentecostalism and led to the emergence of Charismatic Renewal movements.

But political stability is far from what we are experiencing today. While North America is largely free from military conflict on its shores, internal political polarization is causing great rifts in Spirit-empowered communities today. This political climate has bled into the church, a phenomenon not experienced by early Pentecostals, who were fairly neutral on societal politics for the first few decades.[54] The movement towards conservative political alignment among Spirit-empowered churches mirrors trends in Evangelicalism. This became apparent in the U. S. during the election and administration of President Donald Trump. While Evangelical ministers have served as presidential advisors in the past (both Republican and Democrat), the Trump Administration was the first to marshal support from Spirit-filled ministers such as Paula White, Stephen Strang, Jentzen Franklin, and Lance Wallnau. Leah Payne and Erica Ramirez note that "Pentecostal-charismatic faith-based media moguls have enjoyed unprecedented access to the White House during Trump's tenure. In return, they have showered the president with praise and loyalty."[55] The benefits of mainstreaming Spirit-empowered leaders were enormous. For the first time, Pentecostals and Charismatics, who in previous generations had been marginalized, were suddenly welcomed into the White House. The presence of Spirit-empowered leaders in Presidential functions also meant that elements of Pentecostal spirituality were in full display in prayer meetings and rallies.

While Pentecostal denominations were not particularly vocal in support of the president, support from Charismatic ministers was no surprise to Arlene Sanchez-Walsh, who recognizes that prosperity-leaning charismatic figures "appreciate showmanship, wealth, and spectacle."[56] President Trump's controversial style mirrored the leadership aesthetics of independent Charismatic ministers who celebrate their ability to "Break away from constraints imposed by traditionally organized" groups, like Pentecostal denominations.[57] Many Evangelicals and Spirit-empowered believers admired him for just such a leadership style.

Whatever benefits were gained in the psyche of Spirit-empowered believers by this legitimization, the detrimental effects upon the witness of the church cannot be ignored, particularly with younger Christians. As the controversial candidate and president was lauded by many, others within the movement were disenchanted by a candidate whose past was littered with obvious contradictory values to Pentecostal morality and ethics. This cognitive dissonance, particularly in the minority Pentecostal communities, was indeed disenchanting.[58] For many younger Pentecostals who were already struggling with a distaste for culture wars, the Trump presidency became enigmatic of the fatigue many have felt over the idea that Christianity should be aligned with political parties.

In abandoning the politicization of Christianity, younger Evangelicals have questioned Evangelical Christianity in North America as it exists today. Some studies show that Millennials and Gen Z are rapidly moving toward the "nones" category. It is true that a 2017 Pew Research poll found that "Millennials are more likely than older adults to take liberal positions on social and political issues."[59] This is largely because younger generations are more ethnically diverse and tend to have a less conservative outlook on political and social policy.[60] But it is more than that. Like early Pentecostals, they are rejecting the postmillennial impulse to Christianize America through politics. They have a passion for seeing God's kingdom as a priority over any political or social kingdom.

Political conservatives often attribute the liberalization of the younger generation to the erosion of biblical worldview among America's youth. But this is not a fair characterization, especially among Spirit-empowered communities. This generation appears to be outpacing older generations in their commitment to the core of Pentecostal sensibilities. The Barna Group reports that 38 percent of younger generations rank speaking in tongues as part of regular worship services as a high priority, an amount over twice as much as the reported 14 percent of Boomers.[61] This phenomenon is exemplified by the prayer and worship movement led by Spirit-filled ministries at Bethel and the International House of Prayer. These two movements, and others like them, have ignited the spiritual passion of this generation, whose churches are arguably exhibiting more Pentecostal aesthetics than their Boomer parents.[62]

Conclusion

As the religious landscape of North America continues to change, the church faces a crisis of decline that only vigorous evangelistic efforts can reverse. The Spirit-Empowered Movement is leading the way globally as it effectively draws people into the kingdom of God. If the North American church wants to see similar results, it must draw on the things that have distinguished Pentecostal and charismatic growth worldwide. Now more than ever, baptism in the Holy Spirit is needed to empower the church to accomplish the evangelization of the world. We must realize that the next-door neighbor is equally important as the 10–40 window. Second, as the Spirit re-ignites believer's passion for evangelization, we understand we live in light of Jesus' coming and his great commission. God's kingdom is coming to earth. Our responsibility is to take the gospel to every nation before that kingdom comes. It is that urgency that keeps the church on task to fulfill the great commission. But it is also that eschatological orientation that buffets the church from trading the Spirit's passion for the kingdom for a false political kingdom on this earth. North American Christians need to evaluate how passion for political kingdom building has hindered its witness. We need to embrace a vision of evangelism fueled by a passion for the kingdom of God above all other kingdoms that would distract us from fulfilling our mission. If each generation can take seriously its responsibility to take the gospel to every person's world, including our own continent, then we will answer the call to the global eschatological mission.

Notes

1 Todd M. Johnson and Gina A. Zurlo, *Introducing Spirit-empowered Christianity* (Tulsa, OK: ORU Press, 2020) ebook, ch. 2.

2 Todd M. Johnson, and Gina A. Zurlo, eds., "Latin America," *World Christian Encyclopedia Online*, http://dx.doi.org/10.1163/2666-6855_WCEO_COM_0102, accessed June 27, 2021.

3 Johnson and Zurlo, *Introducing Spirit-empowered Christianity*, ch. 2.

4 Jeffrey M. Jones, "U. S. Church Membership Falls Below Majority for First Time," Gallup, March 29, 2021, https://news.gallup.com/poll/341963/church-membership-falls-below-majority-first-time.aspx, accessed July 31, 2021.

5 "U. S. Membership Report 2000–2010," Association of Religion Data Archives, https://www.thearda.com/rcms2010/r/u/rcms2010_99_us_name_2000_ON.asp, accessed July 19, 2021.

6 David Barrett and James W. Reapsome, *Seven Hundred Plans to Evangelize the World* (Birmingham, AL: New Hope, 1988). This work was part of the Southern Baptist Convention A.D. 2000 missions thrust.

7 David B. Barrett, *Evangelize! A Historical Survey of the Concept* (Birmingham, AL: New Hope, 1988), 27.

8 Tormod Engelsviken, "Role of the Lausanne Movement in Modern Christian Mission," in Lars Dahle, Margunn Serigstad Dahle, and Knud Jorgensen eds., *The Lausanne Movement: A Range of Perspectives* (Oxford, UK: Regnum Books, 2014), 24–44.

9 Allan H. Anderson, *Spreading Fires: The Missionary Nature of Early Pentecostalism* (Maryknoll, NY: Orbis, 2007).

10 Allan H. Anderson, *To the Ends of the Earth: Pentecostalism and the Transformation of World Christianity* (New York: Oxford University Press, 2013), 2.

11 "General Council Great Success," *Christian Evangel*, December 5, 1914, 3.

12 George Hawley, *Demography, Culture, and the Decline of America's Christian Denominations* (Lanham, MD: Lexington Books, 2017), 3.

13 David E. Harrell, Jr., *Oral Roberts: An American Life* (Bloomington: Indiana University Press, 1985), 120–121.

14 Carl F. H. Henry, "The Good, Glad News," *Christianity Today* 9:2 (October 28, 1966), 2.

15 Engelsviken, "Evangelical Perspectives," 3–4.

16 Jay Gary and Olgy Gary, *The Countdown Has Begun: The Story of the Global Consultation on A. D. 2000* (Rockville, VA: A. D. 2000 Global Service Office, 1989).

17 Gary, *The Countdown Has Begun*, 26.

18 David B. Barrett, *Evangelize! A Historical Survey of the Concept* (Birmingham, AL: New Hope: 1987), 9.

19 Jay Gary, *The Star of 2000* (Colorado Springs: Bimillennial Press, 1944), 44. Thomas Wang, "By the Year 2000: Is God Trying to Tell us Something," in Luis Bush, Jay Gary, and Mike Roberts, eds., Toward A.D. 2000 (Rockville, VA: Global Consultation on World Evangelism, 1989), 1–3.

20 Vinson Synan, "A. D. 2000 Together: A Pentecostal/Charismatic Explosion," in Jay Gary and Olgy Gary, eds., *The Countdown Has Begun: The Story of the Global Consultation on A.D. 2000* (Rockville, VA: A. D. 2000 Global Service Office, 1989), 122–134.

21 Vinson Synan, *Where He Leads Me: The Vinson Synan Story* (Franklin Springs, GA: LifeSprings Resources, 2019), 160–173.

22 Vinson Synan, "If Not Us, Who? If Not Now, When?," *A.D. 2000 Together* 2:5 (Fall 1988), 2.

23 Vinson Synan and Billy Wilson, *As the Waters Cover the Sea: The Story of Empowered21 and the Moment it Serves* (Tulsa, OK: Empowered Books, 2021), 81–85.

24 Todd M. Johnson and Gina A. Zurlo, eds., "World Christianity, 1900–2050," *World Christian Encyclopedia Online*, http://dx.doi.org/10.1163/2666-6855_WCEO_COM_0102, accessed June 27, 2021.

25 Johnson and Zurlo, eds., "Pentecostals/Charismatics, 1900–2050" *World Christian Encyclopedia Online*, http://dx.doi.org/10.1163/2666-6855_WCEO_COM_0102, accessed June 27, 2021.

26 Johnson and Zurlo, eds., *Introducing Spirit-empowered Christianity*, chapter 4.

27 George Hawley, *Demography, Culture, and the Decline of America's Christian Denominations* (Lanham, MD: Lexington Books, 2017), 10, points out that between 1972 and 2014, the percentage of fully committed believers to the church (attending more than once a week) in North America remained essentially the same.

28 Paul B. Tinlin and Edith L. Blumhofer, "Decade of Harvest or Decline: Dilemmas of the Assemblies of God," *Christian Century* 108:27 (1991), 684–687.

29 "AG U. S. Adherents 1975–2019," General Council of the Assemblies of God, https://ag.org/About/Statistics, accessed June 27, 2021.

30 "International Pentecostal Holiness Church Membership Data," Association of Religion Data Archives, https://www.thearda.com/Denoms/D_997.asp, accessed July 19, 2021.

31 "AG U. S. Adherents," General Council of the Assemblies of God, https://ag.org/About/Statistics, accessed June 27, 2021.

32 "AG ACMR and Related U.S. Statistics, 2009–2019," General Council of the Assemblies of God, https://ag.org/About/Statistics, accessed June 27, 2021.

33 "AG USA Adherents by Race, 2001–2019," General Council of the Assemblies of God, https://ag.org/About/Statistics, accessed June 27, 2021.

34 "AG U. S. Conversions 2018–2019," General Council of the Assemblies of God, https://ag.org/About/Statistics, accessed June 27, 2021.

35 Johnson and Zurlo, eds., "Canada," in *World Christian Encyclopedia Online*, http://dx.doi.org.oralroberts.idm.oclc.org/10.1163/2666-6855_WCEO_COM_02CAN, accessed July 30, 2021.

36 Johnson and Zurlo, eds., "Canada," in *World Christian Encyclopedia Online*, http://dx.doi.org.oralroberts.idm.oclc.org/10.1163/2666-6855_WCEO_COM_02CAN, accessed July 30, 2021.

37 Michael Wilkinson, "Pentecostalism in Canada: An Introduction," in Michael Wilkinson, ed., *Canadian Pentecostalism: Transition and Transformation* (Montreal, Canada: McGill-Queen's University Press, 2009), 5–6

38 Brad Christerson and Richard Flory, *The Rise of Network Christianity: How Independent Leaders are Changing the Religious Landscape* (Oxford: Oxford University Press, 2017).

39 Christerson and Flory, *The Rise of Network Christianity*, 147.

40 Christerson and Flory, *The Rise of Network Christianity*, 160, note that the organizational structure of the Independent Network Churches allows them to change quickly, innovate, and gain the "market share" of believers in North America and globally.

41 Daniel D. Isgrigg, "The Latter Rain Revisited: Exploring the Central Metaphor in Pentecostalism," *Pneuma* 41:3–4 (2019): 439–457.

42 Peter Prosser, *Dispensationalist Eschatology and Its Influence on American and British Religious Movements* (Lewiston: Edwin Mellen Press, 1999), 152.

43 Anderson, *Spreading Fires*, 65.

44 Donald E. Miller and Tetsunao Yamamori, *Global Pentecostalism: The New Face of Christian Social Engagement* (Berkeley: University of California Press, 2007).

45 An example is the Assemblies of God revision in 1999 of Pentecostal Mission and Social Concern. See Vinay Samuel and Chris Sugden, eds., *Mission as Transformation: A Theology of the Whole Gospel* (Eugene: Wipf and Stock, 1999), 112–118.

46 Robert J. Priest, "A New Era of Mission is Upon Us," in A. Scott Moreau and Beth Snodderly eds., *Evangelical and Frontier Mission: Perspectives on the Global Progress of the Gospel* (Oxford: Regnum, 2011), 297.

47 Priest, "A New Era of Mission," 301.

48 "Almost Half of Practicing Christian Millennials Say Evangelism is Wrong," Barna: Faith and Christianity, February 5, 2019, https://www.barna.com/research/millennials-oppose-evangelism/, accessed June 27, 2021.

49 Andrew F. Bush and Carolyn C. Wason, *Millennials and the Mission of God: A Prophetic Dialogue* (Eugene OR: Wipf & Stock, 2017), ebook, Chapter 7.

50 "ChurchPulse Weekly Conversations: Craig Springer on the State of Evangelism," Barna: States of the Church, June 10, 2021, https://www.barna.com/research/cpw-springer/, accessed July 19, 2021.

51 "Is Evangelism Going out of Style?" Barna: Faith and Christianity, December 17, 2013, https://www.barna.com/research/is-evangelism-going-out-of-style/, accessed August 22, 2021.

52 Daniel Silliman, "Gen Z Wants to Talk About Faith," *Christianity Today*, August 13, 2021, https://www.christianitytoday.com/news/2021/august/gen-z-evangelism-faith-conversations-jesus-barna.html, accessed August 22, 2021.

53 William K. Kay, "The Future of Global Pentecostalism: Demographic Trends, Geopolitical Realities, Ideologies, and Eschatological Models," *Journal of the European Pentecostal Theological Association* 40:3 (2020), 87–103.

54 Daniel D. Isgrigg, "Interpreting the Signs of the Times: How Eschatology Shaped Assemblies of God Social Ethics" (Annual Meeting, Society for Pentecostal Studies, St. Louis, Missouri, March 2018).

55 Leah Payne and Erica Brand Ramirez, "President Trump's Hidden Religious Base: Pentecostal-charismatic Celebrities," Religion News Now, August 27,

2020, https://religionnews.com/2020/08/27/president-trumps-rnc-religious-base-pentecostal-charismatic-kari-jobe-paula-white/, accessed July 8, 2021.

56 Arlene Sanchez-Walsh, "Don't Forget Trump's Pentecostal Fans," University of Chicago Religion and Culture Forum, February 18, 2018, https://voices.uchicago.edu/religionculture/2018/02/18/dont-forget-trumps-pentecostal-fans/, accessed July 19, 2021.

57 Christerson and Flory, *The Rise of Network Christianity*, 125–126.

58 Aaron Earls, "The Vast Majority of Pentecostals Feel this Way About President Trump," CharismaNews, October 11, 2018, https://www.charismanews.com/us/73567-the-vast-majority-of-pentecostal-pastors-feel-this-way-about-president-trump, accessed August 22, 2021.

59 Jeff Diamant, "Though Still Conservative, Young Evangelicals are More Liberal than their Elders on Some Issues," Pew Research Center, May 4, 2017, https://www.pewresearch.org/fact-tank/2017/05/04/though-still-conservative-young-evangelicals-are-more-liberal-than-their-elders-on-some-issues/, accessed July 19, 2021.

60 Patrick Fisher, "The Generational Gap in Presidential Approval for Donald Trump," *Journal of Political Science* 48 (2019), 47–69. points out that the Boomer generation is 79 percent white, whereas the Millennial generation is 59 percent and Gen Z 52 percent.

61 "Christian Millennials are Most Likely Generation to Lean Toward Charismatic Worship," Barna: State of the Church, July 23, 2020, https://www.barna.com/research/worship-preferences/, accessed July 19, 2021. See also, "How Different Generations View and Engage with Charismatic and Pentecostal Christianity," Barna: Faith and Christianity, March 29, 2010, https://www.barna.com/research/how-different-generations-view-and-engage-with-charismatic-and-pentecostal-christianity/, accessed July 23, 2020.

62 See John Weaver, *New Apostolic Reformation: History of a Modern Charismatic Movement* (Jefferson, NC: McFarland and Co., 2016).

III
Strategic

10 Home and World Evangelism: Nigerian Church with Islam and Internationalization

Samson A. Fatokun

Abstract

The task of evangelism and discipleship, which is called the Great Commission, plays a significant role in the advancement of Christianity as a global missionary religion. This study particularly examines the roles hitherto played by the Nigerian church with its Spirit-empowered Christianity in reaching out to the Islam-dominated northern part of Nigeria as well as in cross-boundary evangelism across the globe. This is done with a view to assessing the extent to which the special mandate of evangelism given by Christ to all, irrespective of tribes, nations, language, and culture, has been fulfilled by Spirit-empowered Christianity in the Nigerian church in the face of fierce opposition by Islam in Northern Nigeria and the growing secularization across the world. Historical and descriptive methods are employed in data analysis and discussion. The chapter brings to the limelight the extent of the successes, the challenges, as well as the way forward in three areas: carrying the gospel of salvation to strongholds of Islam in Northern Nigeria, the internationalization of missions by the Nigerian church, and enriching Spirit-empowered evangelism in the twenty-first century Christianity in Nigeria.

Introduction

The Great Commission, which is the final mandate given by the Lord Jesus to his disciples, forms the most significant discipleship mandate ever given by any religious leader in world history. That Jesus backed up this mandate with the bestowal of the Holy Spirit upon the disciples to confer an enabling grace to effectively carry out the commission is a perfect example of the Master-Servant Effective Commission Model. Thus, its historical emergence situated within the context of the coming down of the Holy Spirit on the day of Pentecost makes Christianity far more than being a nominal religion. It is a Spirit-empowered religion with equally a Spirit-empowered commission. Within this context, this chapter explores how Spirit-empowered mission has been able to launch an aggressive spiritual invasion on Northern Nigeria—the reputed home of Islam– through strategic evangelism, and how the Nigerian church has

180 The Remaining Task of the Great Commission

been able to carry the gospel of Christ across Nigerian borders to other countries of the world. In this regard, the missionary activities of different foreign missions and home-based missions from Southern Nigeria in evangelizing and Christianizing Northern Nigeria are examined alongside the successes and challenges so far encountered in preaching Christ to the Muslims and indigenous religious adherents in the North. Similarly, this chapter takes a critical look at the roles played by the Nigerian church in cross-national/cross-boundary missions with the view to assessing the impacts so far made by the church in the internationalization of mission. The chapter closes with a conclusion and recommendations on the way forward in Nigerian home and global missions within the context of Spirit-empowered Christianity.

Spirit-Empowered Christianity and Evangelism in Nigeria with the Islam-Dominated Northern Region

Nigeria's first contact with Spirit-empowered Christianity dates back to the sixteenth-century Portuguese missionary enterprise. Portuguese missionaries visited the Benin Kingdom in 1514[1] and the Warri Kingdom in 1555.[2] However, owing to the miscarriages of that enterprise, Christianity in the Benin kingdom continued to fade away until, finally, the Benin church disappeared, leaving only shrines called "altars of God," which were absorbed into the traditional religion.[3] On the other hand, Christianity thrived in Warri in the 1570s on political grounds and remained there for more than two hundred years until it equally faded away.[4] Thus, the first Christianity planted in pre-colonial Nigeria vanished without any continuity with modern times.[5]

A lasting planting of Spirit-empowered Christianity in Nigeria began in the nineteenth century through real missionary movements/societies formed in Europe and North America as products of the spiritual revivals in those two continents.[6] Unlike the earlier Roman Catholic enterprise, which was after what it could gain from the people, these new movements were truly evangelistic in their outreaches and were more preoccupied with what to give to have souls saved for Christ than targeting material things to gain from them. Thus, these missionary societies recorded more lasting success in their evangelistic outreaches as they employed appropriate socio-economic evangelism strategies as means of communicating the gospel message of salvation to their target audience. These include the provision of social amenities, Western education, primary health care services, the introduction of legitimate trade outlets, and the improvement of the agricultural system. They were meeting the immediate social and economic needs of the opened doors of the hearts of the people rather than faulty strategies employed by the earlier enterprise.

The first Protestant missionary to arrive on the shore of Nigeria on a purely evangelistic mission was the Reverend T. B. Freeman of the Wesleyan Mission. He arrived on September 24, 1842. He was followed by the Church Missionary Society on December 17, 1842[7] the Scottish Missionary Society of the Church of Scotland in 1844, the American Baptist Missionary Society in 1850,[8] and the Roman Catholic Mission in 1860. These were followed by a host of other missionary societies, especially from Europe and North America. Towards the end of the nineteenth century and the beginning of the twentieth century, Nigeria witnessed the emergence of the Nigerian brand of African Independent/Indigenous churches, followed by the rise of Pentecostal churches.[9] These also have contributed a great deal to fulfilling the mandate of the Great Commission in Nigeria.

In the Christianization of the Islam-dominated northern part of Nigeria, Spirit-empowered Christianity has, for close to two centuries now, made several attempts through both foreign and home-based missionary societies/movements. Different church denominations in Nigeria, including mainline, Nigerian independent church denominations, Pentecostal-charismatic churches, and non-denominational mission organizations,[10] have over the years, in their missionary expansion drive, taken up the task of reaching out to the Muslims in the Islam dominated the northern part of Nigeria with the gospel of Christ. Different evangelism outreach methods employed included the use of broad-daylight street to street evangelism with the jingling of handbells, early morning cries, marketplace evangelism, bus evangelism, prison, and hospital evangelism, open-air crusades, and organized villages/towns/cities mission outreaches, and other relevant methods. Some of these employed the use of social packages, such as free medical tests and care, entrepreneurship training, food and clothing distributions, and other strategies of attracting the gospel recipients. In fact, some of the churches and para-church ministries in the Southwest, Southeast, and South-South geo-political zones have organized evangelism outfits devoted to missions in the North. These strategies have been yielding very productive in converting the Muslim North to Christ.

Today, there are well-established church denominations of all types in Northern Nigeria. The Muslim North equally today has a good competing number of indigenous Northern Christians who are ministers of the gospel, disseminating the gospel of Christ with rigor among their own people, using every available means. Different missions have indeed contributed to this. The Church Missionary Society, a missionary arm of the Church of England, was the first to open up the northern part of Nigeria for evangelism through 1841, 1854, and 1857 British Explorations of the Niger in which Samuel Ajayi Crowther (an ex-slave who later emerged as the first African Anglican Bishop) played an active role in its success.[11] Through his instrumentality, the Niger Mission was established in 1857 with the sole aim of witnessing Christ to the indigenous Northern Muslims, with foundation mission stations at Lokoja, Bida, and Zaria.[12] As part of his evangelism strategies, Ajayi Crowther studied some of the languages of the indigenous Northern tribes and committed them to writing, and equally did translations of some Christian materials for effective mission among the Northern Muslims. This pioneering work of the Church Missionary Society laid the foundation for evangelism in Northern Nigeria, upon which other church denominations in Nigeria were built.

Many other Christian missions embarked on Spirit-empowered evangelism in the Muslim-dominated cities, towns, and villages of Northern Nigeria, using the provision of social welfare facilities as evangelism strategies, particularly the provision of Western education and improved health care services such as the building of dispensaries, hospitals, and leprosarium. Notable among missions that followed up the opening up of the Niger for evangelism are United Missionary Society, with stations in Ilorin, Kontagora and Zuru, Sudan United Mission in Plateau and Bornu, Roman Catholic Mission at Benue and Plateau, Dutch Reformed Church Mission, particularly in Jukunland and Wukari, the Lutheran Mission (Adamawa and Muri), and other small missions.[13] The Church of the Brethren, which in Hausa is called *Ekklesiyar Yan'uwa a Nigeria* (EYN), literally translated as "Church of the Children of the Same Mother in Nigeria," is one of the largest evangelistic mission churches in the North with over 160,000 members, 450 ministers, and 403 congregations (local assemblies).[14] Similarly, the Church of Christ in Nations (formerly, Church of Christ in Nigeria), which in Hausa is *Ekklesiyar Kristi A Nigeria*, is another largest evangelistic mission church in northern Nigeria with eleven provinces, ninety-eight regional church councils, and foreign missions in nine countries, from its headquarters in Jos, Northern Nigeria.

Very significant among the earliest Christian missions, which played a foundation-laying role in opening up the Islamic North of Nigeria for a Spirit-empowered Christianity, is Sudan Interior Mission, which is known today with the same acronym as 'Society for International Mission,' owing to its internationalization of mission from Nigeria.[15] This mission devoted its outreaches basically to the evangelization of Northern Nigeria, which to the foreign missionaries who pioneered the association was regarded as Sudan, hence, the name 'Sudan Interior Mission.' In later years, it became one of the largest in Northern Nigeria, covering a wider geographical territory more than any other single mission in the Islamic Northern Nigeria, with vibrant mission stations in Nupeland, Gbagyiland, Southern Zaria, Jos-Plateau, Bauchi, Tangale-waja, Hausaland, Bornu, Kabba, and Ilorin.[16] In Jos alone, where the national headquarters of the church arm of the mission, named Evangelical Church Winning All, is situated, there are over 130 local assemblies.[17]

Other mainline denominational churches in Nigeria like the Methodist, Presbyterian, Baptist, Seventh Day Adventist, and a host of Nigerian independent churches also took the evangelistic mission works to the North with the primary aim of converting Muslims to the light of the gospel of Christ, using the different social strategies previously mentioned and other related social and economic incentives to attract Muslims to the blessings of salvation through Christ. Today, in many choice places in Northern Nigeria, there are a good number of diocesan, district/area, provincial, and state/regional headquarters of mainline as well as Nigerian indigenous, Pentecostal, and charismatic church denominations. These are present across all the states of Northern Nigeria, believed to be core Islam territories. That is to say, the gospel of salvation has been successfully preached, and strong churches have been established amidst hostilities in Northern Nigeria.

The Apostolic Church Nigeria (TACN), which is the pioneer classical Pentecostal denomination in Nigeria, was the first to preach a Pentecostal brand of Christian evangelistic gospel in Northern Nigeria. TACN's efforts at evangelizing the Islam-dominated North date to the 1920s when the indigenous group that adopted this British-based Pentecostal denominational name (TAC) was still under its earlier adopted label 'Faith Tabernacle Congregation.'[18] Between 1925 and 1930, branches of Faith Tabernacle churches were established in the North, with principal centers at Kaduna, Zaria, Jos, Kano, Markurdi, Kafanchan, and Minna. Attempts to reach the Muslim North with a Spirit-empowered message of the cross were made possible through the missionary activities of some members of the church from the South who went to the North for business activities and job transfer. Some of those who were on transfer to the North as civil servants particularly seized the opportunity afforded them by their secular profession turned lay evangelists among the Muslims in the midst of whom they dwelt and interacted daily. In other words, TACN's earlier attempt at evangelizing the Muslim North was not a product of a direct missionary activity pioneered by ordained ministers. Rather, it was the laypeople with burning zeal for evangelism who took seriously the task of reaching out to the yet unreached Muslims in the North, following the scriptural clarion call on those who have been saved from arising for the salvation of the North.[19] Methods of evangelism employed included one-on-one witnessing, group and individual street-to-street evangelism, holding of crusades under trees, open fields, and marketplaces. These people, from a pure Evangelical and Pentecostal background, preached the gospel with burning passion and succeeded in pioneering a Pentecostal brand of Spirit-empowered Christianity. This was done amidst hostility from the fanatic Muslims, who constantly launched direct attacks on their immediate family members and burnt down their places of worship. This was aside from language challenges which they had to contend with by learning the indigenous languages of the different Northern tribes.

Apart from towns and cities evangelism in the North, in the year 2006, as a way of reaching out to the yet unreached indigenous people in the remote places of the Muslim-dominated lands of Northern Nigeria, the authorities of The Apostolic Church Nigeria developed a new evangelism model of reaching out directly unto the indigenous Northern Muslims and traditional worshippers in rural areas (places tucked away from the main roads) through the setting up of a 'Home Mission Department.'[20] This team, under the leadership of Pastor J. B. Coker and Elder Banji Mayowa, has successfully established indigenous mission stations among the Tiv and Igala tribes of Benue and Kogi States, the Hausas of Kano, the Gbaji/Gbari tribe of Kaduna, Niger, and Abuja, among others. The team, which took up from Lagos in the South, embarked on learning the indigenous languages of the different tribes in the North among whom they are evangelizing and equally began training some of the indigenous converts as missionary agents among their own people. Between 2006 and 2017, this Home Mission, in its evangelistic outreaches to the interior North, has succeeded in establishing additional 113 local assemblies in the remote places in the core North and has equally established more Apostolic Church primary schools as part of its evangelism outreach scheme in several villages that previously had no schools.[21] Today, TACN, as the first classical Pentecostal denomination in the country, has been able to firmly establish a strong presence of the church in Northern Nigeria with a total of twenty-one administrative area headquarters (the equivalent of dioceses), with an average of over 500 local assemblies.

A host of Nigerian charismatic churches, in their evangelism zeal, equally took the gospel of Christ to Northern Nigeria with a view to reaching out to the indigenous Northern Muslims. Some of these churches used strategic evangelism planning method in their mission outreaches to the Northern Muslims, launching out with a well-planned and well-equipped evangelistic team from respective denominations from the South. Some of these charismatic/neo-Pentecostal Nigerian churches registered their evangelistic presence in the North and got branches of their church denominations planted through the evangelistic activities of their members from the South who went for their one-year compulsory National Youths Service Corps in Northern states. For instance, the Deeper Life Bible Church got established in Northern Nigeria in 1985 through the evangelistic zeal of its National Youth Service Corps members who were serving in the North that year.[22]

While today, evangelism in the Muslim North is still surrounded by intense persecution, especially in the core North, where Islam is very strong, Christians have developed coping mechanisms instead of retreating from preaching the gospel of Christ. Missionaries in the North take preaching Christ as similar to signing a self-death warrant amidst the Boko-Haram insurgence, Fulani Banditry, and general hostility from the indigenous Northern Muslims. The media is full of records of untold hardships confronting Christian evangelism in the North. There are daily records of killings, targeted basically at Christian communities, all as a reprisal for bringing the gospel of Christ to the Islam North.

The Nigerian Church and International Missions

The Nigerian church has been at the forefront of international missions in Africa for decades. A number of Nigerian Pentecostal churches have succeeded in opening viable branches of their church denominations and mission outreach stations in neighboring West African countries, other parts of Africa, Europe, North America, South America, Australia, Asia, and even in the Caribbean Islands. As a result of aggressive transnational evangelism, today, several Nigerian pioneered Pentecostal church denominations are found in virtually every city in Europe, North America, Australia, and the Caribbean.

Israel Olofinjana observed that the 1960s witnessed the formation of African Pentecostal churches in England.[23] This was a direct result of the independence of African nations in the 1960s from their European colonial masters. The independence gave opportunities to Africans, among whom Nigerians ranked highest, to visit European countries for studies and work, and many of these, especially from Nigeria, became involved in evangelism and church planting, duplicating the home-based church type in Europe. The first of the churches planted by Nigerians in Britain as African Instituted Churches (AIC) was the Church of the Lord (Aladura) from Nigeria, planted in 1964 by Apostle Adejobi in South London. This was followed by churches including Cherubim and Seraphim Church in 1965, the Celestial Church of Christ in 1967, Aladura International Church (founded by Rev. Father Olu Abiola in 1970, with branches opened in France, Italy, and Germany), and Christ Apostolic Church of Great Britain established in 1976.[24]

The 1980s and 1990s witnessed a new form of Spirit-empowered evangelism in Europe and North America with the emergence of neo-Pentecostal churches in Nigeria, whose members carried a new evangelical zeal to European nations in their quest for fulfilling the mandate of the Great Commission in Matthew 28:19. Consequently, several Nigerian classical Pentecostal, neo-Pentecostal, and charismatic churches opened mission stations across Europe and North America. Notable among these were branches of Gospel Faith Mission International, which opened in London in 1983, and subsequently in Belgium, while the Deeper Life Bible Church of W. F. Kumuyi opened in the United Kingdom in 1985, and subsequently in Belgium, the Netherlands, and Luxemburg. Additionally, New Covenant Church of Reverend Paul Jinadu opened in the United Kingdom in 1985–1986, and by 2010, it had risen to forty-one branches across the United Kingdom.[25] The Redeemed Christian Church of God, which began evangelical activities in the United Kingdom in 1988–1989, is today the fastest-growing brand of Nigerian trans-national mission church in the United Kingdom with well over 400 parishes in the United Kingdom and other branches spread across the world, including Germany, Norway, Spain, Austria, Sweden, Holland, Italy, France, Portugal, and Denmark.[26]

Besides the above, the 1980s and 1990s saw an influx of Nigerian print and electronic media evangelists and teachers in different continents (most especially Europe and North America), operating as freelance ministers in what is called "reverse mission," by ministering on invitation in different church programs like crusades and conferences, through which they contributed in a great deal to fulfilling the mandate of the Great Commission. Notable among these Nigerians were the Late Arch-Bishop Benson Idahosa (Idahosa World Outreach), Bishop David Oyedepo (Living Faith Outreach), Bishop Francis Wale Oke (Sword of the Spirit Ministries), Dr. Uma Ukpai (Uma Ukpai Evangelistic Association), Abubakar Bako, a former Muslim (Logos Rhema Foundation), Apostle Samson Ayorinde (World Evangelism Bible Church), and Bishop Mike Okonkwo (The Redeemed Evangelical Mission).[27] A host of these have, through their cross-boundary evangelism, successfully planted and consolidated their Nigerian brand of Spirit-empowered Christianity in different nations of the world.

The missionary activities of Sudan Interior Mission which originally started activities in Nigeria and formed the Evangelical Church of West Africa (ECWA) among the Muslim-dominated northern areas of Nigeria, later engaged in further internationalization of its mission by extending her mission outreaches to other places in Africa and beyond. These include such places as Ethiopia, Sudan, Niger, Cote d'Ivoire, Republic of Benin, and Ghana, where national churches were established. This internationalization of mission led to the change of the full meaning of the acronym ECWA – from "Evangelical Church of West Africa" to "Evangelical Church Winning All," with the view to accommodating other branches opened outside Nigeria and West Africa.

The Apostolic Church Nigeria (TACN), as the pioneering classical Pentecostal denomination in the history of Nigerian Christianity with its origin dating to the 1918 indigenous revivalist movement (Precious Stone Society), equally played a leading role in trans-national evangelism. Between 1936 and 2017, TACN was involved in foreign missions to African countries, North America, Asia, and Europe, which subsequently led to the opening of mission fields in those places, some of which today are now autonomous. The places TACN has successfully carried out trans-border evangelism, with subsequent church planting, include Gold Coast, Ghana in 1936, and Benin Republic in 1944,[28] which as of 2016 had a total of 842 assemblies divided into forty administrative areas.[29] TACN equally extended her trans-national evangelism mission to Cameroon in 1949,[30] which as of 2015 had some 780 assemblies cared for by about 400 indigenous pastors and 700 elders,[31] as well as to the Republic of Togo in 1953,[32] and Sierra-Leone in 1957.[33] Other cross-national evangelical outreaches of TACN within Africa include Cote d'Ivoire in 1987, Tanzania in 1992, Kenya in 2000, South Africa in 2000, Uganda in 2002, and Lesotho in 2002. In the 1980s, TACN extended her evangelistic mission to North America, which resulted in the opening of assemblies of the church in places like Houston, Texas, and New Jersey, respectively, before the close of that decade.[34] Today, through continuous evangelical works, The Apostolic Church North America Mission Field is made up of five districts and twenty-six assemblies, all still under Nigerian control of the foreign mission. In a similar tone, the church opened a mission station in Canada in the 2010s, while her evangelistic activities to Israel dated back to the 1990s, which resulted in planting a branch of the church in Tel Aviv.[35] The first indigenous church of The Apostolic Church Nigeria in the United Kingdom was established in Liverpool in 2014, followed by Manchester in 2015 and London in 2016.[36] Carrying out evangelistic activities in the United Kingdom by Nigerians is a good demonstration of a 'kinsman-redeemer evangelism model' now that branches of TAC established by the European founding fathers of the church are closing down due to present spiritual decline across the once-Christian Europe. As S. G. Adegboyega has noted,[37] not less than forty European missionaries worked in different parts of Nigeria between 1931 and 1981 for the consolidation of the apostolic church work consequent upon affiliation of the indigenous Nigerian group with the European Pentecostal denomination in 1931.

This evangelistic invasion has its consequences on global religious and political scenes. As noted by Babatunde Adedibu,[38] the twentieth century has witnessed the redrawing of the political map of Christianity as global South Christianity is now globalized. The prevalence of diversities of expressions of the Christian traditions in the West, particularly from Africa, is one of several from the global South.

Summary and Conclusion

The Nigerian church, in her home and international evangelistic mission, has been able to successfully entrench a Spirit-empowered Christianity in the Muslim-dominated Northern Nigeria, the stronghold of Islam, in spite of continuous hostility, marginalization of indigenous Christian converts, and incessant persecutions with loss of lives and properties which history cannot accurately account for. In fact, a good number of Christian converts in the North have suffered greatly from Boko Haram insurgence and Fulani kidnapping and banditry. Several church buildings have been set ablaze by the Muslim opposition to entrenching a Spirit-empowered Christianity in their Islamic domain. In spite of these oppositions, there are currently well-established denominational churches and trans-denominational mission agencies with strong footings in the Islamic North. Equally, the Nigerian church has thrived in cross-border evangelism with the planting of branches of Nigerian churches, particularly in Europe and North America; continents known in history as pioneers of Christian missions in Nigeria. This "payback in the evangelistic mission" by Nigeria in trans-national mission has put the Nigerian church right in the position of an "evangelistic kinsman-redeemer," especially to the once-Christian Europe, which is currently facing the growing challenge of spiritual decay due to secularism.

On the other hand, a critical assessment of Nigeria's international missions to the Western world reflects more chaplaincy services to the African minority communities. Nationals have not been adequately witnessed to. There is, therefore, the need for Nigeria's cross-national evangelism to give due consideration to assimilating the socio-cultural dispositions of the nationals in its packing and dissemination of the gospel message without losing its fundamental truths. This will go a long way in making the white majority more receptive to the gospel and its power.

Furthermore, for a more productive Spirit-empowered evangelism and entrenching a long-lasting Spirit-empowered Christianity in home and international missions, the Nigerian church needs to improve on its social welfare evangelistic mission packages. Effective communication of a spiritual gospel of liberation to the socio-economically deprived, spiritually and socially oppressed, and emotionally depressed, especially in the Muslim North of Nigeria and elsewhere across the globe, equally requires adequately meeting the immediate social, economic, and emotional needs of the people.

Notes

1 Toyin Falola and Biodun Adeniran, *Islam and Christianity in West Africa* (Ile –Ife: University of Ife Press, 1983), 83. See also A. F. C. Ryder, "Portuguese Missions in West Africa," TARIKH 3:1 (1969).

2 See E. O. Babalola, *Christianity in West Africa* (Ibadan: BRPC, 1988), 5–6. See also E. A. Ayandele, "Traditional Rulers and Missionaries in Pre-Colonial West Africa," TARIKH 3:1 (1969), 23.

3 For details see J. F. Ade Ajayi, *Christian Missions in Nigeria: 1841–1891 The Making of a New Elite* (London: Longmans, Green & Co. 1965).

4 Deji Ayegboyin and S. A. Fatokun, *The Church in West Africa* (Ibadan: Baptist Press, 2018), 23.

5 S. A. Fatokun. "Christian Missions in Nigeria before the Wake of Pentecostalism: A Historical Evaluation," in S. A. Fatokun, ed., *Christianity and African Society* (Ibadan: Book Wright Publishers, 2013), 45.

6 Stephen Neil, *The History of Christian Missions* (London: Penguin Books, 1986), 214.

7 Modupe Oduyoye, *The Planting of Christianity in Yorubaland* (Ibadan: Daystar Press, 1969), 257.

8 For details see Travis Collins, *The Baptist Mission of Nigeria 1850–1993: A History of the Southern Baptist Convention Missionary Work in Nigeria*

(Ibadan: Associated Book Makers Nigeria, 1993), 6–11; S. A. Ajayi and J. T. Okedara, *Thomas Jefferson Bowen: Baptist Missionary to Nigeria, 1850–1856* (Ibadan: John Archers Publishers, 2004).

9   Fatokun, "Christian Missions in Nigeria," 43–52.

10 For example, the Great Commission Movement of Nigeria – a mission organization which began in Nigeria in 1969 at the University of Lagos by Rev. Yemi Ladipo, with national headquarters in the North – Jos, Plateau State.

11 S. A. Fatokun, "Missionary Activities of Samuel Ajayi Crowther in Yorubaland and Lokoja Area (Niger Mission)," *TRANSFORMATION: Crowther Journal of Theology and Missions* 2 (July 2018), 28.

12 Fatokun, "Missionary Activities," 28.

13 Yusufu Turaki, *Ethno-Religious Crises and Conflicts in Northern Nigeria* (Jos: Yusuf Turaki Foundation, 2017), 93.

14 Church of the Brethren, "Global Mission and Service: Nigeria," http://www.brethren.org/, accessed July 9, 2021.

15 S. A. Fatokun, "Sudan Interior Mission and the Emergence of the Evangelical Church Winning All in Nigeria," *Nigerian Journal of Church History and Missiological Studies* 1:1 (2019), 30.

16 Turaki, *Ethno-Religious Crises and Conflicts*, 93.

17 Fatokun, "Sudan Interior Mission," 39.

18 For full details on the origin of the Pentecostal denomination that today became known as The Apostolic Church Nigeria, see S. A. Fatokun, ed., *A Pentecost from Africa to Europe, From Europe to Africa: History and Distinctiveness of The Apostolic Church Nigeria, 1918–2017* (Ibadan: Global Estida Publications, 2017).

19 S. A. Fatokun, "Origin of the Apostolic Church in the Old Northern Region of Nigeria: African Indigenous Missionary Efforts and European Participations," in Fatokun, *A Pentecost from Africa to Europe*, 154; See also J. O. Akinsanya, "A Brief History of The Apostolic Church in Zaria Area," in S. A. Fatokun, ed., *TACN Nigeria Golden Jubilee 1931–1981* (Ibadan: Global Estida Publishers, 2017), 8.

20 E. O. Olowoyeye, "Rural Mission of The Apostolic Church in Northern Nigeria," *Nigerian Journal of Church History and Missiological Studies* 1 (2019), 30.

21 D. A. Oyeleke, "The Apostolic Church Nigeria and Home Missions," in *A Pentecost from African to Europe*, 342.

22 I. S. Ukoha, "Northern Nigeria Deeper Life Bible Church Experiment with Church Indigenisation, 1994-2019: A Historical Perspective," *Nigerian Journal of Church History and Missiological Studies* 1:1 (2019), 113.

23 Israel Olofinjana, *Reverse in Ministry and Missions: Africans in the Dark Continent of Europe* (Milton Keynes: AuthorHouse, 2010), 36–37.

24 Olofinjana, *Reverse in Ministry and Missions*, 37.

25 Olofinjana, *Reverse in Ministry and Missions*, 38.

26 Olofinjana, *Reverse in Ministry and Missions*, 38.

27 S. A. Fatokun, "African Independent Churches in the Diaspora and the Challenges of Migration to Christian Mission, in S. A. Fatokun, ed., *Christianity and African Society* (Ibadan: BookWright Publishers, 2013), 108–109.

28 Interview with Pastor Djotto Mamase, National Secretary, The Apostolic Church Republic of Benin, August 1, 2018, Lagos, Nigeria.

29 Fatokun, "The Apostolic Church Nigeria and Foreign Missions," 316.

30 S. A. Fatokun, "Pentecostalism in Cameroun and Nigeria's Cross-Border Influence," in Vinson Synan, Amos Yong, and J. Kwabena Asamoah-Gyadu, eds., *Global Renewal Christianity* vol. 3 (Lake Mary, Florida: Charisma House, 2015), 72.

31 Fatokun, "Pentecostalism in Cameroon," 73.

32 Fatokun, "The Apostolic Church Nigeria and Foreign Missions," 317.

33 Fatokun, "The Apostolic Church Nigeria and Foreign Missions," 318.

34 Fatokun, "The Apostolic Church Nigeria and Foreign Missions," 322.

35 Fatokun, "The Apostolic Church Nigeria and Foreign Missions," 323.

36 Pastor Dotun Davies, "TAC LAWNA UK Mission Field Report," n.p.

37 S. G. Adegboyega, *A Short History of The Apostolic Church in Nigeria* (Ibadan: Rosprint Press, 1979), 77.

38 Babatunde Adedibu, "Prospects and Challenges: Migration, Identity in Christ, and Integration of Britain's Black Majority Churches," *Spectrum: Journal of Contemporary Christianity and Society* 2:1 (April 2017), 94.

11 Low-Income People Discipling the Poor: Low-Fee Christian Schools Fulfilling the Great Commission

Makonen Getu

Abstract

This study seeks to shed light on the less or non-recognized role of low-income Christian proprietors of low-fee independent Christian schools in the realization of the Great Commission supported by Edify in eleven countries in Africa, Asia, and Latin America. In their partnership with Edify, these Spirit-empowered proprietors' endeavor to promote Christ-centered education in and through their respective schools to disciple students who, in turn, will disciple the nations as they serve in leadership and other capacities in their adulthood. The presentation is based on material collected through interviews with school proprietors and the author's personal experience in the facilitation of Edify's programs.[1]

Introduction

"Go therefore and make disciples of all the nations, baptizing them in the name of the Father and of the Son and of the Holy Spirit, teaching them to observe all the things that I have commanded you" (Matt 28:18–19).[2]

This was the Great Commission Jesus gave his disciples before ascending to heaven, instructing his followers to continue doing what they saw him doing in his ministry throughout the ages until his second coming. The goal was to make disciples of all the nations who would observe the things that Jesus commanded and pave the way for establishing God's kingdom on earth as it is in heaven: a new creation under the rulership of Jesus in which sin is no more, and death has no power. This is at the heart of Jesus' ministry and is the method that was meant to be applied related to baptism in the name of the triune God and the teaching of the gospel. Baptism in the triune God implies repenting of sins and choosing to give one's life to God unto discipleship by responding to the call (Matt 3:2). It means salvation and reconciliation with God through repentance and acceptance of Jesus Christ as personal Savior and Lord. The acceptance of Jesus as Lord and Savior means putting off old thoughts and practices and putting on new ones. It means undergoing a Jesus revolution, which in turn means a revolution in the minds and hearts of men.

What does mind revolution mean? It means at least two things: being transformed by the renewing of the mind (Rom 12:2) and taking captive every thought to obey Christ (2 Cor 10:5) Why the mind? Because as the Bible says, "as a man thinks so is he" (Prov 23:7). Human beings think as they are taught and act as they think. Every battle between good (God) and evil (the devil) is won or lost in the mind.[3]

What does heart revolution mean? It also means at least two things: creating a clean heart and renewing a right spirit within us (Psalm 51:10) and removing the heart of stone and receiving a heart of flesh (Ezek 36:26). Why the heart? Because as the Bible says, "the heart is fully set to do evil" (Eccles 8:11). Before mind and heart revolution comes, salvation comes, and before salvation comes, repentance comes, and before repentance comes, God's word comes. Salvation is preceded by faith, and faith comes by hearing the word.

Jesus brought about mind and heart revolutions by preaching and teaching the gospel, recruiting and training/discipling his followers, and performing miracles in the midst of difficult circumstances. When he ascended to heaven, he commissioned his disciples to continue doing the same things with emphasis on making disciples of all nations with the help of the Holy Spirit. In response to this mandate of the Great Commission by Jesus, his followers continuously attempt to both individually and collectively disciple the nations. While some have been recognized, others have not. The role of low-fee independent Christian proprietors in discipling the nations, however, is unknown or little known.

The purpose of this study is to examine the work of discipling the nations carried out by low-fee independent Christian schools in marginalized communities in Africa, Latin America, and Asia with reference to those supported by Edify, a Christ-centered NGO founded in 2009 in San Diego, in the United States. In other words, the study seeks to examine how low-income people disciple people living in poverty in line with the Great Commission and how their effort has been strengthened by their partnership with Edify.

Who are the Discipling Agents and the Discipled?

The discipling agents referred to in this study consist of low-fee independent school proprietors who operate schools to create access to education for children living in poverty. Some are micro, small, and medium-scale social entrepreneurs, and others are pastors of low-income churches. They are male and female of varying ages and educational backgrounds. Some are retired teachers with experience in education. However, the majority lack experience in the field of education. Nonetheless, they share a common interest in providing access to quality education to children in poverty. Unlike public schools, Christian school proprietors offer Christ-centered education because they believe that education in the absence of God is not complete as it focuses only on shaping the mind and not the heart (character). By teaching the values and principles of Jesus as part of the curricula, they use education as a tool for evangelism and Christ-centered character development—discipling.

The discipled social groups include school proprietors, school leaders, teachers, students, and community members. The school proprietors and leaders are discipled in order to understand God's purpose for their schools and make sure that they create a conducive biblical framework for the effective promotion of Christ-centered education. This includes having a proper curriculum for and practical support given to the teaching of biblical values and principles in their respective schools. The teachers are discipled in order to understand God's purpose behind their role in educating students in the knowledge of Christ and pointing them to salvation, deepening their faith and growing into Christ-likeness. The students, in turn, are discipled in order to strengthen their biblical knowledge, evangelize among their peers inside and outside schools, and undertake outreach activities within their respective families and communities both in word and deed.

Edify contributes towards the work of discipling the agents of discipleship in low-fee independent Christian schools by offering and facilitating Christ-centered training activities in partnership with both national and international training organizations. Some of the main training topics include biblical worldview, biblical integration, servant leadership, early childhood development, business management and accounting, leadership for learning, student-centered pedagogy, discipleship formation and administration skills, youth leadership skills, and education technology. The training events are planned and organized by Edify field staff in consultation with school owners and leaders.

Throughout its eleven years of service, Edify has supported 7,033 low-fee independent Christian schools, trained 40,480 school leaders and teachers, and impacted 1.9 million students in seven countries in Africa (Burkina Faso, Ethiopia, Ghana, Liberia, Rwanda, Sierra Leone, and Uganda), three countries in Latin America (the Dominican Republic, Guatemala, and Peru) and one country in Asia, specifically Northeast India.[4]

Discipling Activities in Low-fee Independent Christian Schools

In his book *Teaching Redemptively,* Donavan Graham stresses the need for Christian schools to create a framework in which education is given in a holistic and not a divided manner. This means both the secular and sacred aspects of life are taught, and citizens are prepared for both earthly (temporal) and heavenly (eternal) kingdoms.[5] This is what the Christian schools supported by Edify seek to do. Among other things, they create strategic and coherent daily and weekly devotional and worship systems and practices for all stakeholders to participate in schools. The stakeholders involved here include school proprietors, leaders, support staff, teachers, and students.

School Proprietors and Leaders

The biblical knowledge and skills acquired by school proprietors and leaders through the various trainings equip them to create favorable conditions for Christ-centered education in their respective schools. The school proprietors employ Christian teachers committed to teaching Christ-centered values. They run School Transformation Committees responsible for ensuring Christ-centered education is promoted in such a way that all the stakeholders are involved, and the relevant training skills are acquired for in-school (onsite) training.

They also lead in a Christ-like manner and thereby disciple the people they lead by example. This means the leaders manifest love, humility, integrity, accountability, honesty, justice, and servant leadership in their service—they lead in and through love as Christ did. The leaders, in Christ-like service, evangelize and disciple more through their actions than through just their words. They use words appropriately in line with St. Francis of Assisi's famous quote to "Preach the gospel at all times and use words when necessary."

Teachers

Of all the things that are essential to high-performing schools, nothing is more important than the teacher, including what the teacher knows, believes, and can do. A teacher's skill makes a difference in student performance, not only in achievement scores but also in students' sense of fulfillment in school and their feelings of well-being.[6] Being at the front-line, the teacher is the interface and the key link, the deliverer of all goods and services offered by the school to the children. Through her/him all knowledge is diffused, minds and hearts are molded, academic achievements are made, and student well-being is maintained. One could simply say that the teacher is the school, and the school is the teacher. She/he is the role model for students.

Christian teachers play a vital role in the work of discipling children in poverty who are attending low-fee independent Christian schools. They treat teaching as mission, teaching as unto the Lord (Col 3:23). They recognize that "the fear of the Lord is the beginning of wisdom, and knowledge of the Holy One is understanding" (Prov 9:10), and feed students not only with the academic knowledge, but also with the knowledge of God. In other words, they engage in evangelism and discipling. They do this by teaching the word of God and by being role models for their students.

Discipling through Teaching the Word of God

As part of their effort to discipling students, Christian teachers engage in various Christ-centered activities. What follows are some examples of such activities.

Christian teachers lead and participate in school devotionals, prayers, and worship. In most schools, devotionals, whether they are done on a daily or weekly basis, are often planned, facilitated, and led by committed Christian teachers. In such events, they share the word of God, organize students to sing and worship, share testimonies, and compete in verse memorization. They lead devotions in their respective classrooms. They also integrate biblical perspectives in their lesson plans.

In secular schools, education is offered in a divided way. The secular is separated from the sacred. In fact, there is both official and private opposition to the teaching of Christ in schools. The humanist movement led by such prominent figures as Richard Dawkins, the author of the *God Delusion*, for example, not only opposes the provision of Christ-centered education but also works to bring up children who reject the existence of God. Despite the permission to have classes on religious studies, teaching Christ is forbidden in public schools. In some countries, this applies even in private schools. In counteracting the secular move, teachers in Spirit-empowered low-fee independent Christian schools are actively engaging in evangelism and discipling the poor by bringing God into the classroom and teaching the values and principles of Jesus in both Muslim and Christian countries in line with the Great Commission.

In Christian schools, it is commonly held that the "goal of education is to train children to know Jesus Christ as Lord, to know his word as truth, and to be equipped that they may serve his purposes and fulfill the destiny for which he created them."[7] This, however, does not mean that Christian teachers stop teaching academic subjects and give Evangelical sermons in the classroom. On the contrary, Christian teachers are trained to do both and do them with excellence. They are encouraged to teach mathematics, physics, chemistry, biology, history, English, arts, business, and other topics with academic vigor, discipline, and standards so as to enhance the students' understanding and knowledge of the topics studied as per the relevant curriculum and deliver them skillfully and professionally as unto the Lord.

At the same time, teachers go beyond the secular way of delivering their teaching and deliberately plan to provide biblical perspectives in all the subjects they teach. Seeing academic subjects from a biblical worldview and demonstrating to the students how these reveal the character and nature of God, creation, humankind, moral order, and purpose is tantamount to biblical integration. This is bound to broaden the content and basis of learning. Taught with biblical perspective, mathematics and science become more integrated, more interesting, and more exciting. Biblical integration enables the students to think biblically and critically and serves as a powerful way of knowing that God is the truth and the source of all knowledge. The students' perspective and understanding widen their knowledge and wisdom, enabling them to excel in their academic performance and character development. In order to achieve this, the personal commitment of the teacher to "Jesus Christ is the basis for teaching our students to walk in God's ways and delight in his faithfulness."[8]

Participating in School Transformation Committees

School Transformation Committees are composed of school proprietors and representatives of school leaders, teachers, support staff and students, and some cases even parents. The main task of STCs is to facilitate the participation of all stakeholders in transformation as a whole-school business under the leadership of the school proprietor. The specific tasks include developing a training plan, recruiting suitable trainees for external training for implementing in-school (onsite) training by trained staff, mobilizing the necessary support for training and Discipleship Clubs, and monitoring and evaluating discipling activities. Comprising the largest number of trained personnel by Edify, teachers undertake most of the onsite training activities.

Facilitating Formation and Administration of Discipleship Clubs

Teachers also participate in helping students with the formation and administration of Discipleship Clubs (DCs) in schools. Although the clubs are for, of, and by the students and are organizationally student-led, Christian teachers initially help them with the establishment and running of the clubs. They also take an active role in guiding and teaching the Bible. Outside the classroom, the DCs constitute an important platform for teachers to disciple students. The DCs also serves as a leadership training ground for the students as they take roles in planning, organizing, and leading small groups.

Youth Leadership Training Camps

Christian teachers play an active role in helping with the planning, preparation, and execution of youth leadership training camps. In these camps, student leaders are gathered to do biblical studies, pray, and worship over a period of five to seven days. These are opportunities for the youth to grow deeper in their faith and relationships with God and one another. They represent another platform for teachers for discipling students.

Participating in Salvation

"No one can come to me unless the father who sent me draws them" (John 6:44). All salvation is done by grace through the Holy Spirit. No one can make the salvation of others happen. The teachers, however, play an important role in the salvation process by exposing students to the word of God and the teaching of Jesus before, and by supporting and praying for them during and after salvation.

Discipling by Example: Living the Faith

Biblical integration in the classroom and participating in school-based faith activities are necessary components of Christ-centered education but not sufficient. Students do not learn only from the theoretical and experiential knowledge that teachers deliver through lectures, supervision, and assessments. They also learn from the teachers' overall character and attitudes: their being present and their practical engagement in school-based faith activities. Students learn from how the teachers present themselves and how they are both as teachers and as human beings. That is, their works are other important sources of Christ-centered education. In this regard, being is teaching. "Imitate me as I imitate Jesus," said Paul (1 Cor 11:1). The students hear what their teachers are saying, and they see what they are doing. The former is abstract, and the latter is visual. Learning by imitation, that is, internalizing what students see and observe, tends to be more powerful than learning by hearing. To achieve this and enhance Christ-centered education effectively, teachers display qualities that inspire, encourage, equip and empower children so as to make them feel that they are respected, valued, and contributing members of the school system. Some of the qualities that teachers apply in discipling students by example are as follows.

Teachers give attention. students need to feel that their teachers pay attention to what they think, say, do, and feel. They need to be noticed. They need to feel loved and cared for. When they are sad, they need to be counseled. When they are sick they need to be visited, and when they succeed they need to be celebrated. When they need help with their work they need to be assisted. When they experience the act of attention by their teachers individually and/or communally, they find joy in learning and perform better and will pay attention to others too.

Every child is special. Students have different talents, gifts, challenges, and temperaments. While caring for and paying attention to the general student body as a whole is key to student-centered learning, Christian teachers recognize that every child is special, has unique needs and needs special attention. Teachers learn that distinguishing the different conditions and levels of learning among students, adapting teaching approaches, and working with students accordingly will bring the best out of students.

Teachers see and treat all equally. Students are different in many areas such as in looks, stature, knowledge, gender, performance, and communication. Christian teachers see all through the eyes of Jesus. All are one in Christ. All are accepted, treated, and served fairly and equally, without favoritism and nepotism.

Teachers share appreciation. Students thrive when anything they do or say, small as well as big things, are appreciated by their teachers. Telling a child 'Yes, you can' speaks volumes in how that child sees himself/herself. They feel uplifted. When they grow in the culture of being valued and appreciated, they will recognize and appreciate and thereby uplift others.

Teachers forgive. Like anyone else, students make mistakes and do wrong things that might cause disappointment and anger among teachers. In such instances, teachers should express bold love by firmly and constructively confronting the problems and by forgiving students for any wrongdoing. The students feel loved when they are forgiven. By exercising forgiveness, teachers create a culture of bold love accompanied by logic in the minds of students, which students then apply in the next generation as a form of conflict resolution.

Teachers show integrity. Teachers are expected to "walk the talk," that is, keep promises. Students feel loved when teachers are honest with them and keep their promises. This includes keeping time in class for giving feedback. This makes students feel respected and loved.

Teachers give their best. This is about the efforts, including lesson planning and preparation, teachers make to deliver quality education. When students see that their teachers are seeking to give the best, they feel worthy and loved. They then do what they have experienced themselves, giving their best to others.

Teachers practice conflict resolution. They do this by taking the time to address any relationship and behavioral issues among students in the classroom through constructive discussion and mutual understanding and not through unexplained physical or other forms of punishment.

Teachers provide a non-threatening environment. This is about releasing and freeing students by creating a non-threatening learning environment. Students thrive, learn, and perform better when they feel confident about thinking freely, taking initiative, expressing curiosity, daring to make mistakes without being threatened, and where they know their teachers are approachable and friendly. Teaching in a non-threatening environment is a powerful means of enhancing critical thinking.

All in all, by translating their faith, that is, imitating Jesus, in practical terms, Christian teachers disciple students to be caring, appreciative, forgiving, loving, honest, integrated, accountable, diligent, just, humble, non-threatening, and walking humbly with God. They become role models, thereby discipling students by example.

Students

Jesus made the disciples who followed him fishers of men by teaching them the essentials of the gospel. As his followers, Christian teachers teach students to do the same. How do Christian students undertake their role of discipling the nations?

In-schools

"All Scripture is God-breathed and is useful for teaching, rebuking, correcting and training in righteousness" (2 Tim 3:16). During their school life, students do two things. First, they take part in school-based Christian activities, including devotional events, Discipleship Clubs, and youth leadership training camps to study the Bible, pray, and worship as a community. In other words, they equip themselves with biblical knowledge and discipling skills and deepen their faith as they are trained in righteousness.

Second, they undertake evangelism activities among their peers within their respective schools. They reach out to students of different religious orientations by giving testimonies in both word and deed. In the former case, they share the gospel, distributing Christian literature, encouraging others to join Discipleship Clubs, and attend youth leadership training camps. In the latter case, they mobilize material and moral support to students in need as an expression of love and care.

Outside of Schools

In addition to what they do in discipling their fellow students within schools, Christian students undertake outreach activities in their respective communities. They share the gospel with people on the streets and marketplaces. They also provide community services such as cleaning streets, clinics, and hospitals as well as visiting the sick and vulnerable. In other cases, they mobilize funds and other material resources, donating to orphanages and other charity organizations. They practice the culture of giving and serving to others and thereby pursue their act of evangelizing and discipling the nations.

Why Disciple People in Poverty?

Planting churches, preaching the gospel, teaching the values and principles of Jesus, and leading people to salvation are important components of the Great Commission. However, the heart of the Great Commission is discipling the nations. In the words of Darrow Miller, this means "'laying' kingdom principles and a biblical worldview as the founding order or ethos of a people."[9] Christian schools are in the business of discipling people in poverty, and Edify is boosting their efforts to do so through the provision of loan capital, education technology, and training, with the ultimate goal of building flourishing godly nations. School leaders and teachers are discipled to disciple students who, in turn, disciple their communities and nations in both their youth and adulthood. As a result, schools have been improved and expanded to give sustainable Christ-centered education, more access and quality education have been offered, and employable and God-fearing citizens have been generated.

Low-fee independent Christian schools run by low-income Christian men and women supported by Edify produce God-fearing citizens. These are new creation people (1 Peter 2:10). As Paul writes, they have "put on the new man which was created according to God, in righteousness and true holiness" (Eph 3:24). In their adulthood, the discipled youth become useful in society through the professions they have acquired, such as agriculturists, economists, political scientists, doctors, and anthropologists.

As they discharge their responsibilities by applying the Christ-centered values they gained during the discipling process, they go through their education (lower and higher alike), they disciple the nations, they multiply themselves (Gen 1:28; 2:15), as they serve in the framework of the Great Commission. They become salt and light to those who do not believe by doing things and loving others with honesty, humility, and integrity as Jesus did. Herein lies the long-term contribution and impact of discipling people in poverty by low-income and low-independent Christian school owners, permeating the social, economic, political, and spiritual aspects of all society and creation with biblical values and building flourishing godly nations in the fulfillment of the Great Commission.

It is worthwhile to distinguish between the two phases of the new creation. The first refers to the phase of followers of Christ, that is, people living in submission to his ordinances in the sinful world. They are in this world but not of it, and by doing that, they create communities of people who live in obedience to God side-by-side with the people who deny him and live under human-made values and principles.

As they serve "in holy conduct and godliness" in a sinful world, they contribute to "hastening the coming of the day of God" (2 Pet 3:11–12). This is the second and final phase of the new creation, whereby the first earth and heaven are dissolved, and a new heaven and earth is formed. This phase represents the establishment of God's kingdom under the full control and rule of Jesus Christ, where sin is no more, and people are fully reconciled with God and one another (Rev 21:3–4).

In the short term, the promotion of Christ-centered education through low-fee independent schools with the enabling support offered by Edify might be seen as a program of mere evangelistic activities focused on teaching the gospel and saving lives from the bondage of sin. These are all the means and must-do things but do not constitute the end. In the long-term, however, the promotion of Christ-centered education is done with the purpose of fulfilling the Great Commission goal of discipling the nations and establishing God's kingdom.

Conclusions

Several conclusions could be drawn from the collective and individual stories presented in this study. Education is a great tool for evangelism and discipling children into God-fearing citizens who, in turn, disciple the nations in Christ-like ways as they serve with love, justice, accountability, honesty, humility, transparency, and good stewardship in their adulthood. Education becomes more profoundly impactful when it is offered in an integrated manner. Education is complete when it is given in such a way that the secular and sacred are not divided, both academic and character excellence is pursued, and Christ-centered education is promoted.

Teaching is a mission, as is learning, and teachers are missionaries in their own right. When teachers teach as unto the Lord and students learn as unto the Lord, effective discipling happens in and through schools. The teachers use the classrooms as a church as they teach about Christ in an integrated manner, and the students use the school grounds as a mission field as they evangelize their fellow students. Together, they go out into the communities and share the gospel in accordance with the Great Commission.

Evangelism and discipling the nations are not only the prerogative of established churches and mission groups. It can also be undertaken through schools. Evangelism and discipling the nations are not only done by the theologically trained and professional messengers. It can also be done by teachers and students who have not gone through biblical or theological colleges and have no missional training. All that is required is vision, passion, obedience, and commitment to participate in the mission of Jesus in earnest and truth. Evangelism and discipling the nations is not only done by the wealthy, strong, and long-experienced establishments. It can also be done by low-income, weak, and inexperienced establishments. Low-income, vulnerable, and inexperienced as they are, the low-fee independent Christian schools owners operating in communities in poverty, as presented in this study, constitute good evidence.

Togetherness, i.e., interdependence, is key to the success of low-income, vulnerable, and inexperienced change-makers in accomplishing their mission. In solving the problem of the widow with a jar of oil, Elijah told the widow to go out and borrow empty jars from her neighbors and pour the oil into the empty vessels. She did as Elijah told her and sold the oil, paid her debt, and she and her sons lived on the rest. The widow was able to solve her immediate problem and ensure her long-term sustenance with the little she had and the help she received from her neighbors (1

Kings 18:8–15). In a similar vein, the low-income and low-fee independent Christian school proprietors have been able to undertake their discipling program through the promotion of Christ-centered education more effectively with the support they received from Edify.

Any partnership involves mutuality. Edify is not only a giver but also a receiver as much as the low-fee independent Christian school proprietors are also receivers and givers. Through the low-fee independent schools, Edify has access to fulfilling its own calling of participating in the realization of the Great Commission and building God's kingdom. Edify has also gained knowledge and experience from serving together with the low-fee independent school proprietors; Mutual learning and growing together through serving one goal and one God together. Both Edify and the low-fee independent Christian schools are givers and receivers.

Notes

1 My appreciation goes to the Edify Christian Transformation and Training Officers for their assistance in undertaking the field interviews.
2 All biblical references are from The New King James Version (Nashville: Thomas Nelson Publishers), 1983.
3 T. Marshall, *Free Indeed Fullness: Fullness for the Wholeman, Spirit, Soul, and Body* (Aukland: Orama Christian Fellowship Trust, 1975), 3.
4 "Edify: Impact," https://www.edify.org/impact, accessed June 8, 2021.
5 Donovan Graham, *Teaching Redemptively: Bringing Grace and Truth into Your Classroom* (Colorado Springs: ACSI Purposeful Design Publications, 2009), 58.
6 Jon Saphier et al., *The Skillful Teacher* (Acton, MA:Research for Better Teaching, Inc., 2008), 45.
7 David Freeman, *Diamonds Lost in the Sand: Gems of Wisdom for Educating Our Children* (Bulverde, TX: True North, 2015), 40.
8 Harro Van Brummelen, *Walking with God in the Classroom: Christian Approaches to Teaching and Learning* (Colorado Springs: ACSI Purposeful Design Publications, 2009), 49.
9 Darrow Miller, *Discipling Nations: The Power of Truth to Transform Cultures* (Seattle: YWAM Publishing, undated), 69.

12 The Spirit-Empowered Mission of Chinese House Churches

Evan J. Liu

Abstract

Research to understand the Spirit-filled mission of the underground Christian churches in China has been widely explored in the global Christian world. Many believe that the first-century church revival and mission model with the outpouring of the Holy Spirit has been inherited well by Chinese Christians. This article aims to clarify what features of the Spirit-empowered mission are manifest by Chinese underground churches, how those features operate in the house church mission movement to the world, and what observations I have obtained from my personal involvement in establishing the ministries in China. This study will discuss that the Spirit-filled revival mission derives from the witnesses of Chinese churches persevering through the special time period. This study also posits the essential condition for incubating the spiritual transformation among the house churches is to build a wholehearted God-seeking community with sound biblical teaching and spiritual exercise. When a temple community (*ecclesia*) can embrace the gospel of Jesus with love, sacrifice, prayer, perseverance, and mission, the spiritual empowerment will outpour, and the spiritual revival will happen.

Acts 1:8 "But you will receive power when the Holy Spirit comes on you, and you will be my witnesses in Jerusalem, and in all Judea and Samaria, and to the ends of the earth." (NIV)

Rapid Christian Growth in Modern China

Christianity entered China around AD 635, and it was not widely accepted by the Chinese until China underwent twenty years of political movements, including the Great Cultural Revolution (1956–1976). When China reopened its doors to the world in 1980, the Chinese Christian population did not die off but instead increased from 700,000 before 1949 to 3,000,000. Later, this number rocketed from 3,000,000 to 70,000,000 until 2004.[1] According to the China Religious Year Book, the number of Chinese Protestants in 2018 was estimated to be 38 million, but this count does not include many underground Protestant believers.[2] Some organizations boldly estimate about 100 million Christians total in China.[3] If we assume that 100 million is the number of Christians in China, then 22 percent are the Chinese Three-Self Patriotic (TSP) and underground Catholic members (totaling around 22 million), 38 percent are the TSP protestant believers (around 38 million people), 0.01 percent are the Chinese Orthodox adherents (around 10,000 people), and an estimated 40 percent are then underground Protestant Christians. Namely, around 40 percent of Christians attend unregistered Protestant churches that are called family churches.[4] At the same time, of course, there is an unknown number of Protestant Christians who may go to both the TSP churches and the underground churches or some family churches that are under the umbrella of local TSP churches.

Modern political persecution has caused the Chinese to see humanity's sinful nature more clearly and put their hope in Christ's salvation. Throughout Christianity's history, church revival was always generated from persecutions and trials, just as Jesus' resurrection burst forth from his passion through crucifixion and death. The unchangeable pattern of suffering and revival in Christian belief continues to prove true, especially in China. The severe persecution accelerates a more wholehearted Chinese acceptance of the Christian redemptive doctrine that Jesus suffered on the cross to save the Chinese and forgive all their sins and debts. Someday, they will enter a real, beautiful land without pain and persecution — the kingdom of God.

Many house churches do not agree with the government's attempt to control Christianity using political power and insist on the separation of religion from politics. The guarantee of religious freedom in the general sense is written in the constitution, but it has never been specified in any laws regarding how this freedom can be implemented in the Christian church's activities. Registration of religious groups has turned out to be a tricky policy, so that only a tiny portion of the house churches are registered under the recognition of the Three-Self state churches. There have been no house churches that have registered as legal and independent churches ever since China allowed religious activities to be restored in 1980.[5]

At present, most family churches are non-denominational though they may bear some marks from the influence of the foreign missionaries and evangelists. They have no problem ordaining their own women to be pastors and accept female pastoral ministry. Some family churches may claim them to follow certain foreign traditions, such as the Western Reformers or Baptists, but this is not very common. In some of the family churches that follow certain foreign traditions, women are forbidden from teaching adults or doing pastoral ministry. However, overall, the indigenous family churches prefer to be a witness of their Chinese Christian faith through their own style of worship and ministry. They wish their religious practices to be recognized and protected by the government someday, and they do not fear suffering for the sake of their faith as they pray for the government to regard them as good citizens with understanding rather than misunderstanding.

Persecution, Revival, and Mission

Chinese underground churches had been accustomed to all kinds of prosecutions under strict governmental supervision. Arrest, property forfeiture, and harassment cannot intimate them to stop, and they easily perceive all these miserable experiences as receiving good credit for bearing the cross with Jesus Christ. With the belief that someday they will be rewarded by God in heaven for denying the world and persevering in trials, a good number of newly founded underground seminaries continue to increase every year, even though they could face the possibility of being shut down and getting their staff arrested. The conviction that underground Christian education is approved by God and not by man has greatly encouraged many Christian churches and organizations to take risks in China.

The rise of Chinese Christianity was, to a large extent, due to the rapid growth of Christians in villages from 1985 to 2005. The religious passion of Christian farmers enlarged their ministry perspective and left them in contemplation of what they were missing in their previous Christian beliefs and ministry. The pilgrimage path in front of those farmers was narrower than that of Christians in cities, but the former demonstrated an even greater power of hope than the latter. That is why Christianity has really found its deep root since the 1980s in China because the power of faith approached the lowest societal level and expanded like a wildfire that could not be controlled by the government.

Before 2000, underground churches focused their mission primarily on domestic China, and after 2000, the mission focus began to shift from China to other countries. Two international mission movements originated from Chinese house churches and are well known around the world as Back to Jerusalem (BTJ) and Mission China 2030 (MC2030). Back to Jerusalem is a mission movement initiated by Pastor ShaoTang Yang and GuQuan Zhang in the 1940s, which bears the gospel witness and walks on the Silk Road from the west of China toward other countries until Jerusalem. When they founded Northwest Spiritual Fellowship (NSF) in 1946, Pastor Zhang's family was sent to Xinjiang province, the western corner of China. When the communist party took power in 1949, the missionary work in Xinjiang was quickly shut down by the government. The members of NSF in Xinjiang faced arrest and imprisonment in 1951, and pastor Zhang was martyred right before he was released out of prison in 1956. Simon Zhao, a member of NSF, was detained in the prison of Kashgar for 20 years (1951–1971). After some years of living in Xinjiang after he was released from prison, Simon Zhao moved to the middle part of China and began to proclaim BTJ's vision in many places in China. The vision ignited many house church leaders, and they also advocated it by promoting churches to reach out to the lost souls in China as far as possible.[6]

From the 1990s, BTJ's vision has greatly expanded by the house churches in the middle part of China. It emphasizes that Chinese Christians should receive the evangelistic token from Western missionaries and send out 100,000 missionaries to the Islamic countries and Israel. The advocates of BTJ are deeply convinced that Jesus' *parousia* will surely happen right after the Chinese churches can convert the Muslims and Jews. This movement has widely been propagated by many Chinese rural underground church leaders from the 1980s to now.[7]

Three Chinese leaders, Peter Xu, Brother Yun, and Enoch Wang, inherited Simon Zhao's vision of BTJ and promoted BTJ among their churches for a pan-China mission. After Brother Yun escaped from China to Germany in 2001, he boldly proclaimed BTJ's vision in Europe and predicted that one million missionaries would be sent out to the world by Chinese house churches sooner or later.[8]

Instead of the Back to Jerusalem movement, which was promoted by the village house churches, Mission China 2030 was applauded by the intellectual house churches in megacities. The focus of the MC 2030 movement is that the Chinese churches should pay off the gospel debt owed to the Western Protestant missionaries who came to China in 1807 and were expelled from the country in 1952. There were approximately 20,000 Protestant missionaries who came to China during 1807–¬1952 and taught Chinese people to know Jesus Christ, so the aim of Chinese family churches is to equally send out 20,000 native missionaries to other countries by the year 2030. The movement founders were primarily from the underground churches of megacities of China, and they were all highly educated, representing the elite Christian classes in the urban house churches.[9]

Back to Jerusalem and Rural Revival During the 1980s to 2000

Peter Xu was the founder of All Range house church in the middle of China, whose members were estimated to be tens of thousands in the 1990s. Later, Peter Xu also became the major leader of the Back to Jerusalem gospel mission movement. He was arrested many times by the government, and after his last imprisonment of several years, beginning in 1997, he escaped from China to the United States in 2002 under the escort of the United States government.

I had an interview with Peter Xu in August of 2017 at his house in Colorado, and he shared his understanding of how the village house churches underwent such a huge revival from 1980 to 2002. He emphasized that the secret of revival allied with suffering, witness, and gospel commission without fear. He had done many supernatural services since the 1970s and witnessed many healing miracles upon the sick. Peter Xu was a charismatic leader who practiced healing and deliverance with strong confidence. Peter tells his story that when he was a little child, he received a vision from heaven at the side of a small river. In the vision, he saw the heaven open with three old men with white robes standing on high. Then each of them brought out a book and held the book to pray. Later, the three old men disappeared, and Peter began to meditate on the vision in his heart from that time on. Due to his spiritual openness, Peter believed in spiritual images, dreams, prophecies, and other phenomena. When he founded All Range church in the 1980s, the church also received spiritual transformation with weeping and mourning for many days. Later, this spiritual weeping even became a sign for the church to discern whether a believer had experienced a born-again process. Therefore, the church was also called 'Born-Again' by others.

In 2002, when I went to the province in the mid of China where Simon Zhao, Peter Xu, and Brother Yun previously served, I also experienced the strong Spirit-filled atmosphere within different village churches. There were so many revival meetings every month, and hundreds of village Christians gathered for worship, prayer, and study in just one meeting. They usually lived together in a huge house for two weeks, and all the gatherings were held in the basement so that no sound could be heard by neighbors for security reasons. Every day they got up at 5:00 am for prayer and worship until 7:00 am. The preaching session proceeded from 8:30 am to 12:00 pm. After a lunch break, another preaching session would continue from 1:30 pm to 5:30 pm. They sang hymns in the evening and went to bed around 9:00 pm. When I preached among them, I sensed the strong spiritual presence, and even my preaching had to change according to the impromptu spiritual work. As I observed, such Pentecostal fire was ignited by each day's sincere worship and prayer, and many of the believers fasted through the whole process of training. Due to their wholehearted seeking of the Lord, the atmosphere was totally changed and filled by the easy-touching presence of God.

The catalyst of village churches' revival was the Holy Spirit. When the spirit-filled revival and mission swept the rural areas after the 1980s, numerous Chinese grassroots people began to embrace Christianity widely. Poverty and sickness become the threshing point for Chinese farmers to experience the spiritual miracles and open their hearts to follow Jesus. Many village church leaders told me almost similar stories about how the revival began to sweep their areas. It always started with miraculous healing and deliverance. There were many sick families with demonic possession in their areas because of severe idolatry and hygienic situations. When people got a sickness or psychological disorder, they did not have enough money to receive medical treatment. Thus, they had to seek spiritual mediators or monks for protection and restoration. However, their situation then became even worse. Finally, when they heard that Christian pastors could do healing and deliverance, they invited pastors to help them as the last attempt. To their surprise, all the bad situations changed radically to goodness, the sick were restored, and the mental illness was cured with the demons cast out from the oppressed by the evangelists. This brought repentance among the whole village with the giving up of idolatry and other sins. A revival began to sweep the whole area with the people's eagerness to listen to the evangelists. The Chinese village revival sounds very similar to the narrative version that happened in the Samaritan village according to Acts 8:5–17. The evangelists usually encouraged those new Chinese believers to pray earnestly for God's forgiveness and outpouring of his Spirit. When the Holy Spirit filled the believers, they were usually full of joy and manifested some spiritual gifts such as speaking tongues, prophecy, and interpretation of tongues.

The Chinese village revival fire was also accompanied by persecution. The believers used many ways to secure their meetings, but they were still sometimes discovered by the local government. Their property would be forfeited once they were accused of attending illegal religious meetings, and they could be put into prison for several months or several years, depending on what leading role they played in organizing and operating the meetings.

I investigated some typical rural churches during 2002–2004 and found that although the revival fire did not quench at that time, many young adults had left their churches for megacities to improve their physical lives, hoping for financial prosperity. Those who were left in the churches were the elderly, teenagers, and mothers of young children. However, God can make all things work together. Quick after the rural revival, the spiritual fire also went into cities along with such massive urbanization. Many young adult Christians from rural areas later formed the urban laborer' churches when they finally settled down in cities.

Mission China 2030 and Urban Revival from 2000 to 2018

Mission China 2030 movement debuted in September of 2015 in Hong Kong for the first international convention. The movement was initiated by the Chinese urban house church leaders primarily from Beijing and Shanghai, such as Ezra Jin from Beijing Zion Church, Daniel Li from Beijing Great Commission Church, and Quan Cui from Shanghai All Nations Church.[10]

MC2030 had very good momentum at the beginning and mobilized many mainland Chinese family churches to participate. However, the movement radically declined after the government shut off Beijing Zion Church, which had the leading role in it. Since the movement has not been widely supported by overseas Chinese churches, its continuing outcome and influence could hardly be recognized today.

I have met the three major leaders of Mission China 2030 from 2012 to 2019. Ezra Jin and Daniel Li studied at Fuller Theological Seminary in Pasadena, California, and they both embraced the Evangelical study of the Bible and the charismatic practice of the ministry. When SARS hit the east coast of China in 2003, the attendants of Chinese churches increased rapidly in cities.

Quan Cui was a charismatic leader, and he was called by God to Shanghai in 1999 to plant churches. He founded All Nations Church in Shanghai, which experienced a great revival in 2008 through weekly prayer meetings when the people worshiped the Lord freely with speaking tongues and other spiritual gifts for several hours without stopping. When the Holy Spirit touched the congregation, repentance and manifestation occurred. Then the whole church was overwhelmed by the great transformation and increased from 200 to 2000 people in the next two years. From 2011 to 2012, the church faced much persecution due to its large congregational size. When the government came to tear down the church, the revival fire also decreased, and many members lost. When I met Quan Cui in 2013, he was still very excited about building numerous cell churches in Shanghai for a great network, but when I met him again in 2019, he seemed exhausted by some developing issues, which meant that the church could not go back to the previous quick growth anymore. He noted that he now only focuses on developing good quality small churches without being bothered by their numbers, calling these seedbed churches.

Ezra Jin was invited to minister to a small church composed of Chinese Koreans in Beijing in 2007. This church later grew very quickly and became the largest house church with hundreds of members named Zion Church. This church's quick growth was owed to the strong spiritual work, which had impacted the intellectuals in Beijing in many ways. Zion church tried to balance the operation between Evangelical theology and charismatic practice, so the church was very positive towards speaking in tongues, prophecy, and other spiritual practices. When I taught among them in 2017, there were some members who were also using healing and deliverance as an efficient way to pray for other people. From the pulpit side, Zion church was very Evangelical about interpreting God's words, and from the mission side, it was open to charismatic operations. Once again, the church's revival incurred persecution. Zion church was forced to quit its leased gathering space under tremendous pressure from the government at the end of 2018. Later, the church became small groups and encouraged the members to do walking worship.

Due to the difficulty of developing a church in public space, many house churches must rethink their strategies and are willing to explore new ways of pursuing the supernatural. This also becomes a point to which small Evangelical churches strive. Many house churches were conformable to doing healing and deliverance, and they trusted the charismatic prayer power. In recent years, many Evangelical churches, including some Catholic churches, have been passionate about studying supernatural healing from some international ministry schools, and these schools usually teach the ways of healing popular in the Western charismatic circle.

Furthermore, many house churches also embrace the five-fold ministry concept derived from Ephesians 4:11 and believe apostolic and prophetic ministry is still functional in today's mission. They refuse cessationism and insist the five-fold ministry church be healthy and functional like the first-century New Testament churches. They also discard supersessionism and believe that many Jewish people will believe Jesus after the saved Gentiles reach the certain number destined by God (Rom 11:25–26).

Prominent Spirit-Empowered Ecclesiastic Signs

I have participated in establishing house churches in China since 2001, and from my observation, a spiritual revival sign usually comes from passionate preaching, evangelism, healing, deliverance, and speaking in tongues. When a house church has been established for one to two years, there will often be a turning point for the church to grow with spiritual empowerment if the church receives the outpouring of spiritual baptism. After planting churches in several cities of China, I observed a similar pattern that, when people earnestly prayed for each other for healing and deliverance, the miracles would happen. When people made confession and repentance, they would feel the bondage fall and experience a heartfelt sense of joy.

When a believer's spiritual eyes are opened to see visions, and they begin to speak in tongues, his or her heart will undertake a great shift to break through a mental block. On many occasions, when I see people speak in tongues and receive healing from the Holy Spirit, they are full of joy and thanks. Then their lives manifest a great change with a strong desire to seek the Lord and grow in the Spirit. This charismatic breakthrough creates good soil in people's hearts so that the words of God can quickly multiply after being sown into it.

Another charismatic sign is the revival of the connection with the Jewish root. In recent years, traveling to Jerusalem for conferences and tourism has become popular among Chinese churches. Many Christians go to Jerusalem and claim to receive special visions or hear God's voice in the holy land. Also, many Chinese churches are beginning to keep the Old Testament festivals and weekly Sabbaths, believing that connecting with the Jewish root in this way is to please God and walk on his reviving path.

Chinese churches also attend different charismatic conferences held in Hong Kong, Taiwan, or some cities of China. They use social chatting tools to forward lots of prophetic messages translated from foreign prophetic centers to their friends. Social media has become a powerful tool for Chinese believers to seek charismatic trends and follow prophetic tones.

From 2018 to 2019, I began to direct the planting of prayer houses in several cities of China, and finally, there were three prayer houses established in three different cities of China. When I planted the Chinese house of prayer (CHOP), I aimed to equip intercessors, revive a passion for God, and take spiritual warfare for city transformation by making CHOP the mission temple of God. In CHOP, Chinese intercessors met together and prayed from morning to evening every day, intertwined with worship, speaking tongues, vision-sharing, prophecy, fighting a spiritual battle, and teaching. Many of them claimed to receive fresh anointing and vision from God, and they were full of hope to break through their spiritual bondages and win spiritual battles in their lives. However, when so many good signs occurred among CHOP, the spiritual interruption also came with the appearance of the local authorities checking what was going on in the apartment leased by CHOP.

Finally, a CHOP on the east coast of China was closed at the end of 2019 due to severe persecution, but it had left a good legacy to the local churches, and many believers' lives were opened to see the real presence of God and dedicate their lives to follow him. Later, the fire from this closed CHOP was transferred from the east coast to the northern part of China, which became a mini-Pentecostal mission movement. This CHOP's attempt is a mini-Pentecostal outpouring that testifies that revival and persecution usually come together from the spiritual realm when people's lives are changed by the Spirit-empowered community.

Eschatology, Temple Community, and Conclusion

Many house churches earnestly seek spiritual gifts for doing church ministries, and they believe China to be the primary nation used by God to reach out to the global Muslims and Jews so that the Great Commission can reach its finish line and Christ's millennium kingdom will finally come after the seven years of terrible catastrophe (Dan 9:27). They primarily firmly hold the pre-historical millennium view and believe there will be a third temple to be established in Jerusalem in the future. They also foresee artificial intelligence technology will be used by the anti-Christ power to control the world according to the last book of the Bible (Rev 13:18), and then the seven years' calamity will sweep the whole world with the rapture of God's chosen.

House churches proudly proclaim them to be the true temple of God because they worship him with a true heart. They believe that the temple community is the authentic dwelling place for the Holy Spirit, and that Chinese churches shall carry the gospel of Jesus to all nations someday to finish the last race of the great commission before the *parousia*. They emphasize that the temple community should be filled with spiritual power and love. Moreover, in my view of how a revival can keep moving, one essential character is the sustenance and development of the Spirit-filled community, which could be a five-fold ministry church, twenty-four-hour prayer house, or intercessional fellowship for spiritual warfare. This Spirit-filled community needs to embody several features. First, it embraces lots of worship and prayer every day for a good number of hours to bring forth a strong spiritual anointing and atmosphere. Second, the community members are used to participating in healing, deliverance, and spiritual warfare. Third, lukewarm Christians should repent and receive revival (the second blessing, according to some Pentecostal scholars) with their spiritual eyes open. Fourth, when the anointing of the spiritual presence, angelic cooperation, truthful teaching, and holy relationship accumulates, life transformation will take place, and many people's faith will increase rapidly. Fifth, prophetic vision, evangelism, and the spiritual battle will also be released into the community so that the unity and love of the community will be tested. Once the community can survive the spiritual trials with strong love and unity, they can be delegated by the Holy Spirit for mission and evangelism toward other areas (Acts 13:1–3).

In conclusion, the Spirit-filled mission in China has manifested in diverse ways, and the supernatural spiritual communities generate widely in China now. Many Chinese Christians will be reborn through these spiritual temple communities with a new wineskin and new knowledge of God. Predictably, a large spiritual empowering mission movement from China will be birthed from the supernatural incubational communities and sweep other nations with signs and wonders in the coming decade.

Notes

1 John S. Peale, *The Love of God in China: Can One Be Both Chinese and Christian?* (New York: iUniverse Inc., 2005), 84–88.
2 Lauren B. Homer, "Registration of Chinese Protestant House Churches Under China's 2005 Regulation on Religious Affairs: Resolving the Implementation Impasse," *Journal of Church and State* 52:1 (2010), 61.
3 Philip Jenkins, *The Next Christendom: The Coming of Global Christianity* (Oxford: Oxford University Press, 2007), 88.
4 Lauren B. Homer, "Registration," 62. The Pew Research Center's 2011 report on global Christianity estimated that there were 58 million Protestants in China, see "Global Christianity – A Report on the Size and Distribution of the World's Christian Population," December 19, 2011, https://www.pewforum.org/2011/12/19/global-christianity-exec/, accessed February 17, 2022.
5 Liao Yiwu, *God Is Red: The Secret Story of How Christianity Survived and Flourished in Communist China* (New York: HarperCollins, 2011), 157–180.
6 Huang Jianbo, 自东而西—西北灵工团史述及思考: https://www.holymountaincn.org/article/jiaohuilishi/20081120/283.html, accessed March 21, 2020.
7 Paul Hattaway, "A Captivating Vision: Why Chinese House Churches May Just End Up Fulfilling the Great Commission," *Christianity Today* 48:4 (2004), 84; cf. Ezra Jin, *Back to Jerusalem with All Nations: A Biblical Foundation* (Eugene: Wipf & Stock, 2016).

8 Paul Hattaway, *Back to Jerusalem: Three Chinese House Church Leaders Share Their Vision to Complete the Great Commission* (Downers Grove: Intervarsity Press, 2003); Brother Yun and Paul Hattaway, The Heavenly Man: *The Remarkable True Story of Chinese Christian Brother Yun* (Grand Rapids: Monarch Books, 2002).

9 Andrew T. Kaiser, *The Rushing on of the Purposes of God: Christian Missions in Shanxi Since 1876* (Eugene: Wipf & Stock, 2016), 255–256.

10 Composed by GCCI (Great Commission Center International), *Great Commission Journal* 119 (Dec 2015), 20–22, http://www.globalmissiology.org/gcci/Chinese/b5_publications/GCB/2015/Dec/p20.pdf, accessed March 12, 2022.

13 God's Mighty Work in the Graveyard of Missions: Transformation Breaking Forth Among the Bhojpuri People of North India

Victor John, with Dave Coles

Abstract

This chapter describes the background and development of the church planting movement among the Bhojpuri people of North India. It covers the socio-religious setting of the Bhojpuri region, a brief history of the movement, and challenges experienced in evangelism and church planting. It also gives an overview of work and development in evangelism, discipleship, leadership development, church planting, and multiplication strategies, along with examples of power encounters in missions, the Holy Spirit's works through healings, deliverance, and signs and wonders. The chapter concludes with an overview of some lessons learned for others to consider.

Introduction

In the past twenty-five years, God has done great work in bringing many people out of darkness into light, into saving a relationship with their Creator through the Lord Jesus Christ. The details of his work in the Bhojpuri Church Planting Movement and related movements can be found in the book, *Bhojpuri Breakthrough: A Movement that Keeps Multiplying.*[1] In this chapter, we will highlight just a few aspects of this great work of God.

The Socio-Religious Setting of the Bhojpuri Region

God's glory in this movement shines even brighter against the backdrop of this area's history. The Bhojpuri area of India is fertile in many ways, not just in its soil. A great many religious leaders and gurus were born here. Gautama Buddha received his enlightenment and gave his first sermon in this area. Yoga and Jainism originated here as well. In the past, this region was very hostile to the gospel, which was viewed as foreign. It was known as "the graveyard of missions." When the foreignness was removed, people started accepting the good news. Yet even with all the Lord has done in recent decades, we still need to bind the strong man through prayer (Matthew 12:29). The Bhojpuri area has been described as a place of darkness, not just by Christians but by non-Christians as well. Nobel laureate V. S. Naipaul, after traveling mostly in Eastern Uttar Pradesh, wrote a book entitled *An Area of Darkness*,[2] describing well the region's pathos and depravity.

Ironically, the whole Gangetic Plain is very fertile. A person can just throw seeds on the ground, and they will grow. Every year, the rain washes away the dead soil, and the flood brings fresh minerals from the Himalayas. Thus, the land is very fertile, and water is abundant. Yet, poverty and the caste system have kept people under bondage. Many people look at the fertile soil and wonder why there is so much inequality and wickedness. Why do so many people die of hunger while millions of tons of grain rot or get eaten by rodents? A dark power has worked to keep people poor and divided and to keep Christianity from flourishing here.

For over 150 years, from the time of William Carey (in India 1793–1834), the British suppressed Christian outreach in the region so they could maintain a better face for themselves and continue to profit through business. Seeing white missionaries sitting with Indians humiliated the elite British rulers. They did not want missionaries to associate with common people as this caused embarrassment to the British Raj. After those years of opposition, in forty years of work among the Bhojpuri, only eighty–ninety people had been baptized. Many of the missionaries during that period were territorial and controlling. They thought they had to keep the work in their own hands for it to flourish. They did not believe in passing on training to local leaders. Also, many of the missionaries only reached people with little influence in their communities – not decision-makers. These people became nice Christians, but they didn't have leadership qualities; nothing in their life or their caste background had given them the confidence to exercise leadership.

On the positive side, missionaries brought the good news and brought hope for the lowest people in society, and they tried to sow the good news in abundance. They established a Christian identity, but one marred by foreign dependence and lack of indigenous leadership. Indians who became Christians remained very dependent on foreign personnel and resources. Their mindset prevented them from functioning without outside assistance. Foreigners commonly pastored the churches. Indian Christians thought only Western missionaries could evangelize or lead a church.

In Northern India, the few Christians were especially weak and dependent: a tiny minority in a vast sea of Hindus and Muslims. The mindset was "us versus them." "Us" meant a small minority lacking resources and adequate leadership. Hence, they focused entirely on surviving as Christians rather than going out to share with others. Suspicion reigned toward non-Christians who came to the churches. If a non-Christian walked into a church, the church members would think, "Who is he? Is he a spy? Why is he here?" rather than "Is he a seeker? Might he be open to hearing about the Lord?" Their deep suspicion overrode any motivation for outreach.

The church in India was also very westernized in language, culture, and style of worship. They did not connect with the vast majority of the people around them. Instead of using the local Hindi word for God, they used the English word for God. This kind of Christianity, the only Christian message available until the early 1990s, offered no real hope for reaching the Bhojpuri or other groups in Northern India.

A Brief History of the Bhojpuri Movement

In 1994, only a handful of Christian organizations were working in the Bhojpuri region. Those that existed were quite territorial and focused on literature-based evangelism, which was very popular at that time, despite the fact that much of the literature was in Hindi, and the majority of the population were non-literate Bhojpuri speakers. We chose to focus instead on obedience-based discipleship. This new approach to evangelism brought negative reactions from established organizations. But the Lord brought along a group of men who had gotten excited about using a Bhojpuri-language approach.

We invited all nearby pastors and church leaders, including Roman Catholics, to the first Bhojpuri Consultation, held in Varanasi in 1994. In this consultation, we shared our vision for the Bhojpuri church: culturally appropriate churches which have a local flavor and are Bible-based. The idea behind the Bhojpuri vision was to eliminate the territorialism of the old-fashioned approach to evangelism and church planting. The new concept would facilitate an umbrella for better communication of vision, methods, and implementation among those committed to or open to the vision. A holy fire was kindled among the eighty leaders who participated.

We began a systematic survey of all the Bhojpuri districts to learn who was doing what and to assess the task before us. The survey showed that out of nearly 100 million Bhojpuri people, only about 10,000 (0.0001 percent) called themselves Christians, and most of these were not very serious about their faith. By this time, what had previously been my personal vision quickly became a shared vision among many individuals and groups. We launched prayer mobilization and prayer walks, and one group brought in a full-time prayer team. We did not start with a blueprint for how the ministry would unfold; everything has been evolving through the years.

We began a one-month training on discipleship and leadership in three different cities. The idea was to form a group of leaders who would be ready for the harvest when it happened, equipped with a shared DNA for church multiplication. Within two years, a good pattern had been established to carry forward the vision by anyone and everyone who was interested. Working in the Bhojpuri language drew upon not only language but also culture, history, and everything these people represented through songs, music, and drama. This approach had been missed in the past. We recognized the Bhojpuri language as an integral part of the core of the Bhojpuri people.

As the number of fellowships multiplied, we launched the first Bhojpuri song book in 1998. It contained songs of worship and instructions on baptism, child dedication, marriage, and funerals, including appropriate Bible verses for use with each occasion. This was received with much enthusiasm and greatly strengthened the local worshiping communities. It facilitated the use of a wider variety of worship songs since people no longer had to depend entirely on the memory of songs in Hindi translated from other languages. It also built a broader sense of unity, as all Bhojpuri fellowships could sing similar songs in their worship times.

The real breakthrough with significant numbers occurred in 1998, when we released the first edition of the Bhojpuri New Testament. After this, the movement began to grow exponentially. In the beginning, the work was very small, but now it has become very large. The Bhojpuri movement started with hard work, commitment, and a great vision. Now millions and millions of Bhojpuri people are following Jesus.

Challenges in Evangelism and Church Planting

At the same time I began working among the Bhojpuri in 1992, Hindu fundamentalists began a new push to spread radical Hinduism.

Spiritual Challenges

The extremists destroyed a sixteenth-century mosque in Uttar Pradesh, one of the two major provinces where the Bhojpuri people live. Destruction of the mosque, which had been built on the site of the mythological birthplace of the Hindu god Rama, signaled that the Hindus meant to challenge all attempts for control by Christians or Muslims. They also launched a campaign against Christians and Muslims. The Hindu fundamentalists' design was to prevent any evangelists from entering villages. Some Christian groups at that time were pumping in money and holding meetings that brought in famous foreign evangelists. They planned and announced how many Hindus and Muslims would be won to the Lord. They held citywide meetings and posted billboards about healing campaigns. I kept telling Christian leaders, "This is all coming to an end. You need to change your strategy." As I had anticipated, that ministry approach ended with a wave of persecution.

More religious TV programs began being broadcast in the early 1990s. It seemed that any channel you turned to had a Hindu holy man lecturing. Yoga also became very popular in the early 1990s. Restrictions began to be imposed on building church buildings. Thus, several things happened at the same time I was struggling to begin the visible work among the Bhojpuri.

Satan wants to destroy the work of God, and one of his favorite methods is to discourage God's people so that they lose heart and give up. Persecution is often part of Satan's strategy to bring discouragement, and it comes in many different ways. Though none of our people have been killed, some of them have been beaten up and put in jail. Others have had their property damaged.

Urban Challenges

As God blessed the movement among the Bhojpuri and we shared with others about that work, some people gave us this challenge, "All your ideas work in the village, but they won't work in the city." When I led seminars in Western countries, I could see people thinking, "It won't work here." Urban work differs from rural work in many ways. Rural work is community-based, with more socially homogeneous groups, so in one way, it is much easier. Urban work tends to be fragmented and disconnected. Most people are not local; they have arrived from villages or other states, so the community has many layers to consider.

One of the first challenges we had in urban work was that many organizations and people came to training thinking we would give them financial assistance. We said, "No, we're trying to help you serve effectively." Some could not understand and started complaining, "These guys don't help financially; they only give training!" We explained: "We're not a funding agency. We can't give you money."

The second challenge is that urban people often have a lot of transitions and frequently relocate. Maybe to pursue higher studies, to take a better job somewhere else, or to get married. They are always on the move. In rural areas, you often meet the same people in the same places, and change occurs slowly. Even when people move away, their families remain. When we start a church in a rural village, people do not generally move away without some special reason. The village is their home. But in an urban area, people often move around. When someone moves, they disappear; the whole family relocates. We had to overcome this major challenge. In an urban setting, we might only have two or three years to impact a person before they move away. That could be seen as a setback: we prepare people, then after a while, they move away. At the same time, this mobility can become an advantage. Wherever these people go, they can start something new. They spread the good news and the church planting movement concept wherever they move to next.

The third kind of challenge has come from traditional churches. For example, we trained a girl from a traditional church who started six groups within a few months. Then, in about half a year, those six groups became eight groups. At that point, she came to the attention of her pastor, who completely absorbed her ministry. Her church considered it a big deal to have eight groups get launched. However, out of eight groups, they could only maintain two churches. Now that girl no longer does disciple-making at all. She completely lost her passion for this when the church people gave her honor and status. We consider that a setback, not because she does not work with us, but because she no longer does the great work she could have done to make disciples and launch groups of new believers.

A fourth challenge is that sometimes when pastors became "successful," they felt satisfied and lost interest in seeing the good news spread. Some of the pastors we taught about the church planting movement felt very happy when their churches got to 200 or 300 members. When they reached 300, they thought, "That's enough; no more is needed. I've got enough to survive," so they did not continue with serious outreach. Once their church filled up, they stopped focusing on church planting.

Work and Development in Evangelism

God has called us to pioneer planting fellowships among whole communities. Community Learning Centers (CLCs) have opened countless doors for accomplishing this goal. A CLC enables leaders to focus on lost people and effectively connect with them. Through the CLC, we reach out and "incarnate" Christ's love to people who would otherwise never hear the good news or see it lived out in their context.

Our first Community Learning Centers opened in 2008, and these have changed the playing field for leadership development. We train local leaders first to act as change agents, second, to use the CLC programs to do good to all people (Gala 6:10), and third, to locate the "person of peace" (Luke 10:5; Matt 10:11) within their local communities. By meeting needs in the community and solving local problems, CLC leaders build strong relationships in the community, always with the objective of advancing God's kingdom. CLCs embody a holistic approach to serving. Each CLC aims to provide access to the community, discover the person of peace, provide resources, implement locally relevant holistic service, and meet the needs of the people where they live. When needs are being met, the good news of the kingdom finds fertile soil, and CLC leaders can begin the process of disciple-making and multiplication. Using the CLC approach, the good news has been planted in places that were previously barren ground.

Over the years, many people have observed that when an evangelist goes to a place just for evangelism, no one wants to help him when problems arise, or someone objects to what he is doing. However, the Community Learning Center approach establishes a positive connection with people in the community. Then, if somebody raises a problem with the work, those who have been helped defend the CLC leader.

The Community Learning Center leader does not begin by doing spiritual ministry. They focus first on meeting the community's felt needs. During the months while starting the CLC, they note who seems spiritually open, but they do not share the good news at that time. The CLC leader only stays in a location for six months to one year and then moves to another location. During the leader's time on site, some local people often ask him to come to their home, saying, "I would like to know why you are here. I sense you are genuine, and you have something more to tell me." On other occasions, a prayer for healing or deliverance triggers an opportunity for discipling an individual or a whole family. When a person shows interest, the CLC leader begins sharing the good news. As the Lord works in the person's heart through the scripture, they become believers. With the new believers and those who are open to the Lord, the leader starts a house fellowship and raises up local leaders to shepherd the group.

Community Learning Centers serve as a flexible tool the Lord has given us to meet the needs of the lost, open doors for the gospel, and lay the foundations for effective leadership. We give God all the glory for his work through CLCs to touch people's lives, facilitate and accelerate church planting movements, and bring transformation to this part of the world.

Work and Development in Discipleship

We train people from the very start in obedience as a lifestyle; obedience to God's word, not to a specific human leader's interpretation of the word. Obedience is vital because too many Christians have gotten educated way beyond our level of obedience. Therefore, before we start imparting a lot of knowledge, we start helping disciples to obey. Instead of telling a new person do's and don'ts, we help them discover who Jesus is and how to follow him. By learning and growing together in groups, believers have natural accountability to one another to apply the word in daily life.

We first give new disciples basic training on how to reach out and how to give their testimony. We teach leaders (those who have started one or two worshiping communities) the next goal: how to start multiplying leaders. As the fellowships grow, we provide advanced leadership training twice a month for three months for leaders who lead multiple houses of worship communities. This advanced leadership training teaches how to start raising "discipler-makers." Not just making disciples or just making disciplers, but making disciple-makers. This is a key focus of our overall leadership development. We use Discovery Bible Studies as an approach to inductive Bible study for training believers and training leaders. Our basic pattern uses four simple questions to help people develop a routine of hearing and obeying God:

1) What does this passage say? (How do I put it in my own words?)
2) What is the main principle in this passage?
3) What should I do to obey this passage? (How do I apply it in my life?)
4) Who can I teach what I have just learned?

When people make a commitment to Christ, they learn to pray and experience God's power in their life. In that discipling process, they also share with their family and friends, so that while they are making commitments, they are also preparing others to do the same. Then, they start coming to fellowship and become part of the church. Sometimes they also get inspired to start a new fellowship. We involve people in prayer and Bible study and in fellowshipping with believers continuously as part of the discipling process. We also share with them our testimonies of how to grow, how to pray, and how their faith can be sustained. Then we share how to handle tough situations when they come. Our "Curriculum for New Disciples" gives new believers a basic knowledge of the Bible (concerning God, humanity, sin, salvation, and the word of God) and how to apply these truths for spiritual growth and obedience to the word of God. It also equips them to reach out to the lost and start the process of discipleship with others. This course aims to preserve the purity of the good news while applying it in varied cultural settings. We designed it for teaching in an interactive way where the participants/disciples discover these truths from the Scripture, preferably in groups, to ensure accountability. We focus not so much on acquiring knowledge as on encouraging each disciple to obey the word of God in practical everyday life. The natural outcome is a church-planting movement when disciples make disciples of others, and this process continues consistently.

Leadership Development

We look for two essential qualities in a leader: a heart for God and a heart for lost people. These reflect Jesus' Great Commandment to love God with all your heart and love your neighbor as yourself (Matt 22:37–39). A leader is a disciple, and a disciple has a lifetime of learning until death. We do not present catchy things such as "ten steps to becoming a leader." We encourage obeying the word of God, which involves application in one's character and life. A leader needs a close relationship with God that nurtures the vision and the shepherd's heart and helps him or her become compassionate and caring. It does not require a three-month course in pastoral care. We do teach that later, but we have a simpler version for all the local leaders. A leader does not become qualified because they have a Ph.D. or DMin or something like that. In our organization, leadership is functional rather than positional. A leader is a person who leads someone to succeed in whatever ways possible, so they, in turn, can lead others. We avoid the mindset of positional leadership. Our staff members do not use titles like "Reverend" or "Pastor." We just say, "You are a leader." Our avoidance of titles intimidates some people, but it works. It is both radical and biblical. Jesus said, "Whoever wants to be great must be a servant of all." If you will not go down, there is no way up. The prime example is Christ himself, who is in very nature God, humbled himself (Phil 2:3–11). This changes the whole focus of leadership.

Right from the beginning, we eliminate the idea that you get a position, and then you get money and all kinds of benefits. We focus on bi-vocational leadership, and we encourage people to have some trade in accordance with their skills. If they already have a trade, we encourage them to continue in that and then lead people. A movement cannot depend on salaries and money. A movement has to depend on God and bi-vocational leaders. If we started paying leaders, it would kill the movement (and we do not have the money anyway).

We do not train leaders by using a textbook; we use examples from everyday life to equip leaders for living Jesus' way in everyday situations. We start with life teaching such as, "What does the word of God say about the issues you are facing right now?" We focus on reproductive leadership through mentoring relationships. After each training, we provide ongoing mentoring for leaders, and we help them multiply. Leadership has two parts.

First is ongoing field training. Every month we give three to five days of reproducible training, passed on all the way to the grassroots. Leaders find creative ways to pass on the training to those they lead during a few days each month. The second part is apprenticeship. We never work alone, we always have another believer with us so that when a leader does ministry, someone else watches and learns. We always encourage leaders to take along some of those they are mentoring. Empowerment is a key element of our leadership training. We aim to empower leaders from day one.

Evaluation is another aspect. As leaders, we continue to evaluate and build relationships with those we lead. In Luke 10, we read about the disciples returning to Jesus and excitedly sharing their ministry testimony, "Even the demons are subject to us in your name!" Jesus evaluated and said, "Don't rejoice because demons are subject to you; rejoice that your names are written in heaven" (10:17–20). When leaders share their testimonies, I always evaluate, considering: "Are they on the right track, or are they too caught up in their success?" Our leadership always has that element of helpful evaluation. Like Jesus, we want to lift people's focus to a higher level as part of their leadership development. One important factor, which we have not left in our leadership training, is the God-reliance. We help leaders rely on God and always focus on him. We tell them, "Whatever success you get, stay focused on God. He is the hero of every story, not you."

Work and Development in Church Planting and Multiplication Strategies

We pioneer churches in unreached areas and continually focus on how to bring the good news to additional unreached peoples and areas. This fuels the continual growth and expansion of the movement. We enter pioneer areas with the goal of sustainable ministry. This includes sensitivity to the Lord's leading in finding any local partners the Lord might already have in that area. We do not hope or claim to be God's final answer for spreading the good news. We want others to own the ministry. Accordingly, we invest in local people, stakeholders who will take ownership, who have passion for reaching their own people, and are not just looking for personal gain. This approach has enabled the movement to survive and thrive. If we owned it, we would not have been able to carry it. We do not manage it; that would be impossible. In all our programs and all our work, we strengthen local leaders. That frees us to move into new pioneer areas.

Multiplication happens from day one. It is not a matter of a church getting too big, so they have to split. Everyone in the church is motivated; everyone is intentional. Multiplication does not depend on the main pastor. While a leader cares for the twenty to fifty people in one church, someone in the church starts another church connected to that church. Anyone in the church can plant a new church: a member or one of the leaders. In fact, we do not call people elders or pastors because of the baggage that comes with those titles. Other than leading in the weekly worship service, everyone views the pastors very much as equals in the congregation. Everyone produces disciples: the pastors, elders, and members all produce disciples.

When we share the good news with people, we tell them from the beginning, "Whatever blessing we receive, we have to share with others." In the same way, we tell leaders, "Whatever we learn, we have to share with others." Consequently, when people take the initiative and start a new church, they pass on the same blessings they have received. We have found that simple biblical patterns multiply much more effectively than brilliant human ideas. Multiplication happens naturally, when everyone takes ownership, everyone feels empowered, and everyone obeys God's commands.

Power Encounter in Missions: the Holy Spirit's Work through Healings, Deliverance, Signs, and Wonders

People in India are spiritual. The majority in India talk about demons and spiritual powers much more than Christians do. Those beings play important roles in key elements of life and culture: times of birth, marriage, death, and worship. Normal family life includes significant involvement in demonic activity, with amulets and rituals designed to maintain spiritual equilibrium. Christ redeems every aspect of life, but many traditional Christians overlook the everyday implications of those aspects. However, we focus on transforming people through the truth of the gospel. When Jesus sent out his disciples, "he gave them power and authority to drive out all demons and to cure diseases, and he sent them out to proclaim the kingdom of God and to heal the sick" (Luke 9:1–2).

We equip and encourage disciples to apply the Holy Spirit's power for living out discipleship in everyday life, including key times such as birth, marriage, death, and worship. Christ comes into those situations as the Savior who delivers us from demonic powers. He is all-powerful over all demonic forces. We see the power of his kingdom transforming culture through the life and witness of his people.

Healings

In one area, a pregnant woman had a lot of complications, and her doctor said, "It's possible she won't survive." Two of our leaders went and prayed for her as the Lord led them day after day. On the second day, while they were on their way to the hospital to pray, they fell off their scooter and had scrapes and bruises all over. They said to each other, "This is bad, but let's go and pray first, then come back and get some first aid." When they finished praying and left, they found they had no more bruises; they were completely healed! For four days, they regularly went to pray for the woman and then said, "Tomorrow morning, everything will be okay." That is exactly what happened. The woman was healed and had a normal delivery, which opened a door for the good news. The patient next to this woman in the hospital, seeing and hearing all that happened, put her faith in the Lord.

Deliverance

Deliverance from demons also plays a role in opening doors for the good news to advance. For example, at the Bhojpuri conference in 2014, a woman began to manifest demonization. She wanted to believe in Jesus but was struggling. In her home village, people feared her because she used to run around with a knife, threatening people. When she began to manifest at the conference, some people tried to lead her out to the prayer tent so she would not disrupt the meeting. However, she was so strong she threw ten men off. I was on the platform speaking at the time, and she challenged me to fight her. The leaders began to pray over her and then managed to take her to the prayer tent and pray for deliverance. When she went home, her whole village changed as they saw the transformation in her life. One year later, she brought to the Bhojpuri conference 250 people she had won to the Lord through her testimony and discipled.

In our context, signs and wonders always follow wherever the gospel is preached. We have seen divine intervention in difficult situations, and healings and power encounters have been experienced wherever churches have sprung up. Miracles happen quite commonly in the movement, but we do not focus on those. We focus on obeying God and doing what he commands to show his glory on earth. We do pray and fast, asking God to do mighty works and show himself as the Living God. But we do not have a formula as if X amount of prayer and fasting brings Y, the resultant increase in the likelihood of a miracle. We do not do special things to twist God's arm so he will act. We draw near to him because he is our loving Father, and he does great things because he is a mighty Savior.

Lessons Learned for Others to Consider

We aim for transformation according to biblical commands and the values of God's kingdom. We do not want to extract people from their families or change their lifestyles to match the patterns of a foreign culture. We do not try to change people's culture because that does not help proclamation of the good news; it hinders it. Biblical transformation advances the spread of the good news, whereas importing foreign patterns hinders it.

God's Work through Local People

Sustainable church planting includes connecting with the culture well enough that the good news does not look or feel like a foreign religion. The sustainable church-planting initiative helped many workers and organizations begin ministering in ways that better fit the local context. Over the past five years, 80 percent of those who have come to faith have come through the testimony of local believers they knew. Only 20 percent have come to faith because of a leader's initiative. If a pastor or leader goes somewhere and shares his testimony, people may think, "He came here to share this to try to convert us." Nevertheless, any local believers can share their testimony as part of everyday conversation. People feel more inclined to listen to those testimonies. Everyday witness plays a very important role in the spread of the good news.

God uses holistic service to transform whole communities. When God's love becomes visible in everyday life, the power of the good news becomes tangible. When God's children live in ways that bless the community around them, that lifestyle opens doors for the good news, proclaims the good news, and manifests the good news.

Diminishing Persecution

Many times, Christians are persecuted because they attack other people's religious practices and beliefs. Some people spend more time criticizing the culture than they do preaching the good news. We teach believers to respect the culture, not destroy the culture. We encourage people to celebrate events and holidays with their neighbors and share their concerns. If their neighbors are vegetarians, we encourage believers to respect that.

Some Christian groups have big buildings and big facilities. This creates jealousy and makes them an easier target for persecution. This happens especially when they do not have much relationship with the local people or if their connections mainly focus on business matters. We prefer to use existing (normal) buildings in the community and utilize any of our facilities as community resources.

Some groups of Christians wear special religious uniforms. If any problem arises, others can easily identify and attack them. The groups involved in the Bhojpuri movement and related movements tend to live pretty much like everyone else, wearing everyday clothes just as they did before and eating the same food. Someone looking from the outside cannot easily see the difference. The difference is in heart, attitudes, and godliness, not external markers. This helps believers avoid unnecessary persecution. Enough persecution comes because of obedience to the good news; we do not want to do things that make it easier.

An Easily Reproducible Process

Leaders need to make sure the entire church planting process is the following:

- Simple. It should not be something complicated that only a few people can do. Jesus taught things that anybody can understand and follow. One of the best compliments we have ever received on our church planting method teaching is: "It's so simple!"
- Doable. It doesn't help to portray the process as something spectacular, saying things like, "For 500 days I prayed. I fasted for weeks." Instead, in social interventions, we encourage leaders to initially do something that will bring fruit in just a couple of days. That increases their faith so they can later do something with the whole community that will bear longer-

term fruit. All kinds of people can plant churches. If the process is simple, educated people can do it as well as illiterate people. But if it's complicated, only a few experts can do it.
- Visible. "You watch while I do it, then you do it, and I will watch."
- Reproducible. Work must be done in such a way that it reproduces itself. Otherwise, everything will die with the first generation. We aim to make it so people say, "I can do this too," not so they say, "I could never do what you're doing."
- Sustainable. We always aim to take ourselves out of the picture. We serve in such a way that the work will not collapse when we are not around. We tell leaders: "If others aren't doing what you're doing, it will collapse without you." We need to equip others to do what we do. Jesus did not create dependency; he gave his disciples authority. We do not want to do anything that creates a dependency on us. Jesus is the bridegroom; we are just his friends. The best man helps until the wedding, but he doesn't go on the honeymoon! People need to depend on Jesus from day one.

Conclusion

The Lord has done marvelous work in bringing millions to himself through the Bhojpuri church planting movement and related movements. He deserves all praise for inspiring the ministry approaches used and infusing them with the power of his Spirit. Disciples have multiplied disciples, and churches have reproduced generations of new churches. The Lord has transformed individual lives, families, and villages through the power of the gospel breaking forth in a former graveyard of missions. We give him glory for his wonderful works in our day.

Notes

1 This chapter includes excerpts from Victor John with Dave Coles, *Bhojpuri Breakthrough: A Movement that Keeps Multiplying* (Monument, CO: WigTake Resources, 2019). Excerpts from pages 3–6, 8–9, 11–12, 17, 33–35, 40–41, 49, 51, 57–58, 63, 67, 70, 84, 103,105, 114–115, 118–119, 158–165, 180–181, 188–189, 195, 198–199, used by permission.

2 V. S. Naipaul, *An Area of Darkness: A Discovery of India* (New York: Vintage Books, 1964).

14 Extroversion of Worship: Spirit, Worship, and Witnessing

Thang San Mung

Abstract

Within the rise of Pentecostal-Charismatic revival, the contemporary worship practice was born. It even became a primary contributor to the phenomenal growth of the movement and its popularity in recent decades. However, it also has its downside. A crucial aspect of biblical worship may sometimes be missing. It is in the aspect of witnessing that some fail. In their honest attempt to entertain themselves in such an exuberant worship environment, their practice turns to introversion that shies away from witnessing. This chapter will present two separate Myanmar stories to address these issues. This study is more than a report of the issue. It is also a biblical homily, reasoning that witnessing is an integral component of Spirit-empowered worship. Therefore, significant biblical, liturgical passages such as Isaiah 60:1–3, the Lord's Prayer from Matthew 6, and 1 Corinthians 14:23–25 are set used to address the issue.

Introduction

Since its early conception in the late nineteenth century, the Pentecostal revival was marked by the festive worship phenomena that were so strange to the pre-existing religious cultures.[1] Moreover, in the 1960s, the Jesus People movement joined the revival. Since then, the Jesus People's pop music style has helped the Pentecostals to significantly modify their worship practices in many ways. This matrix of revival and pop music has become an undeniable factor for Pentecostal popularity by meeting the pop-cultural appetite of the time.[2] In such a way, the Pentecostal revival has brought this worship dimension with its lively style to public attention. It has even become a major academic discipline in many prestigious seminaries across the globe. In addition, contemporary worship culture has more to do with contemporary churches worldwide. For example, Natural Church Development has recently done a statistical report on global church growth. The report covered wide-ranging research of over more than 45,000 churches of different sizes and denominations in seventy countries of for twenty-plus years.[3] According to the report, "inspiring worship" has played a significant role both in the quantitative and qualitative growth of healthy churches.[4] This lively worship practice, also called empowered worship, has now become a sweeping movement that penetrates denominational boundaries and cultural barriers.

However, it has its own spots for criticism.[5] This study would like to discuss the issue that some practices seem to be missing in the entertainment-like performances on the stage. Therefore, this study will examine two contrasting case stories from Burma/Myanmar, reflecting the role of worship practice in each case. Then, an exposition of selected Bible passages, also known as liturgical "worship" passages, including Isaiah 60:1–3, Matthew 6:9–13, and 1 Corinthians 14:23–25, will follow. The rationale is to discover the role of empowered worship in mission formation and evangelism and to respond to contemporary practices concurrently.

Introversion or Extroversion: Two Burma/Myanmar Cases

Is worship introversion or extroversion? The answer is that both can happen. However, Spirit-directed worship should be extroverted. To address this issue, two Burmese/Myanmar stories are presented here.

Story One: Full Gospel Assembly and its Gospel Impact

Full Gospel Assembly (FGA), the fastest-growing church in Myanmar, was established by a former Assemblies of God pastor, Rev. Dam Suan Mung, in Yangon, in 1987. After thirty years of persistence under a countrywide political dictatorship, the church became one of the largest churches in Yangon, with more than 6,000 members. At present, there are several satellite campuses in more than sixty locations. More than 400 ministers are currently working under Pastor Mung's leadership, as the Full Gospel Bible Training Center also produces new preachers annually. According to Thang D. Lian, whose Ph.D. dissertation dealt with Pastor Mung's ministry, more than 2,250 preachers have already been trained at this school.[6]

Lian claims that Pastor Mung's spiritual influence and the impact that FGA has on Myanmar Christianity are many. He summarized all collected data into five categories, and of these, contemporary worship is the most remarkable.[7] Furthermore, Lian commented that under Pastor Mung's leadership, FGA had produced worship songs in Burmese, meaning in own melodies.[8] Thangtawng, a worship pastor, once said that in the early days, they had to copy the melodies from others like Integrity music and Hillsong and translate the lyrics into Burmese, but no more now.[9] Additionally, worship practice is not just about internal church affairs and personal piety. It is a form of extroversion in reaching out to the neighboring community and making a gospel impact on broader society.

In 2019, the Full Gospel Assembly worship team became the first to present their gospel music as an open-air program in downtown Yangon. While this is normal for others, it marked the first time for Myanmar to enjoy such freedom since the military dictatorship took power in 1962. Indeed, the praise and worship moment at FGA is more than entertaining the congregations. It is missional in practice.

Story Two: Van Kunga and a Dancing Religion

The Full Gospel Assembly story is not the first time Myanmar experienced Pentecostal revival. Myanmar/Burma's first contact with Pentecostal revival has an early date. However, the political turmoil and internal ethnic conflicts have damaged its chances for the past forty-plus years. Despite this conflict, a revival story of the early day is still circulating among the locals in the Northwestern region of Myanmar.[10] The revival was a spark of what the neighboring Mizo, a later federated state in Northeast India, had experienced. It was said to be connected through missionaries to the Walsh and the Scottish revival of the late nineteenth century.

The revival, known as *Hlimsang* in local designation, was strong among the Mizos, and it soon penetrated Chin Hills, the inhabited area of Zomi.[11] The Assemblies of God missionaries Glen Stafford and Walter Erola were still in the land at the time. When the missionaries received the news in 1963, they sailed upstream to Kalay and visited the area. They established five local assemblies and assigned a local pastor, Van Kunga. However, due to a government order, Stafford and Erola could not stay long as they had soon to leave the country.

The local assembly assigned to Van Kunga still survives as a small community. According to a later historical narrator, however, this community could not make much gospel impact on society. They remain just a "dancing religion," as called by the locals.[12] The designation of "dancing religion" might refer to their celebrative worship on the surface, while reflecting the only impression that they could give the wider community about their faith. Their worship likely has no greater effect than entertaining themselves. In other words, it is indeed introversion, shying away from the wider world and therefore absenting themselves from providing a gospel impact to the neighbors.

John Piper once asserted worship as the ultimate goal of mission.[13] He continued, saying that worship should, however, still be mission-oriented. In this way, mission and worship go hand-in-hand. Christian mission ends in worship, and worship inspires mission in return. Therefore, this study states that worship is extroversion in practice. It aims to actively engage in the broader community by the power and gifts of the Spirit and become a light to the nations.

A Light to the Nations: Isaiah and Old Testament Vision

Public interest in Isaiah as a part of Christian worship is not new. Patriarchal writings like *1 Clement* (96 CE), the *Epistle of Barnabas* (70–135 CE), and *2 Clement* (c. mid-second century CE) indicate their influence on early Christian liturgical practices.[14] Especially for the prophet Isaiah, the personal worship encounter of "the majestic presence of God" in chapter 6 is a turning point in his life.[15] This story was an important liturgical theme and a model for early Christians, as it remains for Christians today.[16] In addition, Witvliet claims that Isaiah is a "workhorse of Christian liturgy, ranking with Psalms [as] the most frequently cited."[17] For instance, apart from the throne-room encounter of chapter 6, the canticles of chapter 12, and the Servant Song of chapter 53, passages such as 43:1–7, 44:6–8, and 61:1–3 are always part of traditional Christian daily and Sunday liturgies.[18] Next to the Psalms, Isaiah is indeed the book of worship in the Old Testament.[19] Accordingly, the prophet's worship theme is evident in the whole book with the concept escalating to a climax at the end (chapters 56–66).[20] Regarding this consummating part, Goldingay asserted the crucial role of the two internal sections, 59:21–60:22 and 61:1–62:12, by calling the "two great central sections," in which 60:1–3 is an essential pericope.[21] Structurally, the passage is thus a good choice for our current "worship" discussion.

In a general reference to chapter 60, Shalom Paul once elaborated on the future glory of Jerusalem related to worship as follows:

> Chapter 60 is composed of one uninterrupted eschatological prophecy delineating a plan for the rehabilitation, reconstruction, and all-pervasive glory of future Jerusalem. In this prophecy of salvation, Deutero-Isaiah

describes the radiant light that will cover Jerusalem, a beacon all nations shall follow. On their journey, the nations shall bring with them all types of trees for the reconstruction and adornment of the temple, shall rebuild the walls, serve in the sanctuary, and praise the God of Israel.[22]

In another book, *Isaiah for Everyone,* Goldingay also posited a similar view. He believed that the fulfillment of those prophecies would occur in conjuncture with rebuilding both the wall, a sign of messianic redemption, and the temple, which was a sign of worship.[23] Both in view of literary structure and conceptual framework, it is fair to say that chapter 60 is like a culmination of all those "worship" prophecies of preceding chapters. Thus, two keywords from the passage are noted here. They are "the glory" of YHWH who would dwell in the temple (v. 1) and "your light" to which nations would come (v. 3).

R. Jamieson et al. defined the "glory" as more than the so-called shekinah glory but "the glory of the Lord in person."[24] It is his personal presence, as Shalom Paul also asserted.[25] The prophecy here is that God's glorious personal presence would rest with his people during the eschatological temple worship in Jerusalem. Concerning the fulfillment, Goldingay observed a crucial connection with the present ministry of the Spirit, namely the indwelling of the believers.[26] This reading of present connection aligns with what Jesus Christ said about true worship in John 4:23–24 (especially 14–16). In reference to this impending ministry of the Spirit, Jesus stated that true worship is more than space or time. It is something that should be done "in the Spirit and truth." In this sense, the prophecy of God's glorious personal presence should be taken as already fulfilled in the Spirit-empowered worship of the present church that awaits its final completion in the eschatological temple worship.

However, this prophetic message cannot be completed unless the fulfillment of the following crucial words, "your light," to which nations would gather, is taken seriously. Goldingay explained that this prophecy refers to "the nations' acknowledgment of Yahweh" and is another central theme of this section that somehow culminates the previous prophecies like Isaiah 40–55.[27] In the interest of this study, it is the most evangelistic missional statement in the book of Isaiah. In simple words, God's glorious presence would rest in Jerusalem among his people with the rebuilding of the wall and the temple. This prophetic fulfillment will not only be for the Israelites alone but also for all the nations to enjoy God's presence.[28]

It is all about the Spirit-empowered worship in the messianic age that Isaiah, as an Old Testament prophet, has envisioned. Therefore, it is not an overstatement to say that Isaiah's vision of Spirit-empowered worship has an evangelistic missional outlook. It is extroversion in practice indeed.

Evangelistic Significance of the Lord's Prayer: Jesus' Teaching

The central role of the Lord's Prayer in the life and worship of the early church is no question.[29] Apart from Jewish sources, it is the pattern they received from Jesus to formalize their liturgical rites. By referring to some archeological findings, Kistermaker dated the widespread use of the Lord's Prayer even before 79 CE.[30] He assumed that "it soon became part of the liturgy in the entire church," as the *Didache* has the Lord's Prayer in Matthean form.[31] Undoubtedly, the Lord's Prayer has received the central attention of liturgical practices of the church for two thousand years.

In light of some Christian practices, Roy Hammerling further contended for early Christian belief in the "power of the Lord's Prayer." He said that they believed the prayer "could produce what it asked for, namely, daily bread, the forgiveness of sins, and deliverance from temptation and evil." He then related the belief to later generations, saying that they also eventually thought of the prayer as "endowed with divine mystery and power."[32] However, a closer look into the Lord's Prayer would give another impression. Kerry Irish once criticized the way many used the Lord's Prayer as a "magic incantation" but described praying it as an "exercise in understanding Christian theology."[33] Likewise, the use of the Lord's Prayer is still more than a theological treaty. As Amanda du Plessis asserted, it is also another tool for pastoral care.[34] Indeed, the prayer's aim and purpose are beyond all the words in the sentences. This study thus aims to read what missional engagement the prayer has reflected and how.

The Lord's Prayer was never given for use only as a sacred rite but for a greater purpose. For instance, it has a global perspective in view, action steps in the project, and inclusive tones in practice. With this in view, three crucial expressions of the prayer that concern the disciples' evangelistic missional engagement are in focus here. The first is "your kingdom come." Referring to this specific prayer, Jack Hayford once connoted that "all prayer should somehow invite his will to work earthward."[35] It suggests that God's will is to promote the redemption that Christ accomplished through the church on earth.[36]

According to Craig Keener, Jesus' prayer here implies two aspects—present and eschatological future. Keener clarified that this prayer is not only a "prayer of submission to God's will in this age" but also a reminder of God's perfect restoration of his rule in the future.[37] However, this future perspective does not lack the present aspect. D. A. Carson explained that God's kingdom is already "breaking in under Christ's ministry, but it is not yet consummated till the end of the age." Therefore, Carson continued, "To pray 'your kingdom come' is simultaneously to ask that God's saving, royal rule be extended now as people bow in submission."[38] In other words, this prayer has a broader community in perspective. It is to this broader community that the disciples should bring "God's saving, royal rule" to welcome its final completion.

The second prayer line is "your will be done on earth." It is the other part of the previous "kingdom" prayer. "In the consummated kingdom," Carson commented, "it will not be necessary" to speak about God's righteous will. "For then God's will . . . will be done," as it is now in heaven.[39] Further, in referring to God's perfect will in the creation, Keener also noted a similar final restoration concept. He said that "Jesus' kingdom prayer even more explicitly reminds us that God in the kingdom will restore the perfect purpose for which he formed the world in the beginning."[40] However, the intriguing lesson in the prayer is the active role that the disciples should always take. It reminds them to seek God's kingdom and helps it come into their community.

This active engagement is most evident in the third "forgiveness" prayer that says, "forgive us, as we forgive." The prayer of forgiveness here is a paradox. As Warren Wiersbe warned, a simple reading of it might appear that God's forgiveness is earned by forgiving others. However, Wiersbe clarified, "if we have truly experienced God's forgiveness, then we will have a readiness to forgive others."[41] Only after knowing that God always forgives is someone bold enough to ask God's forgiveness and strong enough to forgive others.[42] By forgiving others, anyone can assure oneself of really knowing God's forgiveness. Put another way, God's forgiveness inspires a forgiving relationship between each other, and forgiving each other affirms God's forgiveness is on display.

Therefore, as John Lange commented, the Lord's Prayer basically concerns "the existing relation between man and God," upon which all the prayer lines rest as the outworking of that vertical relationship.[43] It is really what many might call the gospel lifestyle that is actively engaged in the broader community as an outworking of what one received from God. That engagement is none other than displaying the forgiving love of God and his "saving rule" to others. Therefore, it is not an exaggeration to say that Christ had a vision of missional engagement in view when he taught this prayer to the disciples.

Furthermore, the Gospel narrator himself has this vision throughout the composition. All the later stories unfold this, as evidenced in passages like 8:10–13, 24:14, and 28:16–20. Indeed, the Lord's Prayer, in its true sense, is more than a liturgical practice. It embodies more than all the words could contain in the recitation. It enlightens one's theological understanding on the one hand, as it envisions a missional engagement of Christ's disciples in witnessing their faith on the other hand.

Finally, it is appropriate to say that praying the Lord's Prayer is more than a "magic incantation." It portrays a life submitted to God's sovereign rule. That is what a worshipful life truly means. The Lord's Prayer will continually be a valued liturgical practice of the church. At the same time, it will also remain an inspiration to instill a spirit of missional engagement in the hearts of those who genuinely pray for it. Beyond these, it is also a biblical "worship" pattern that Jesus Christ has constituted from which contemporary worship cannot excuse itself.

Revival, Gifts, and Conversion: Corinthian Paradigm

To pick up a prototype church from the New Testament for contemporary Christianity, the church in Corinth might be a common choice. William Cook once claimed that:

> The book of 1 Corinthians, written in the middle of the first century, is amazingly relevant. From the standpoint of pastoral ministry, it may be the most contemporary of Paul's letters. Many pastors only think they have a difficult church until they read 1 Corinthians.[44]

Revival fantasy, power abuse, misuse of spiritual gifts, and heated division are among many Corinthian problems that contemporary churches are also confronting. Amidst this backdrop, liturgical issues are among the hottest in 1 Corinthians as talks on the topic occupied about one-third of the space in the epistle. Thus, 1 Corinthians 14:23–25, a passage on worship, gifts, and witness, is a good selection. Structurally, B. C. Johanson posited 1 Corinthians 14:23–25 as "Paul's swift rebuttal" to the Corinthian question posed in v. 22a, to which Mark Taylor commented that Paul's answer would be, "No!"[45]

The possible situation for the rebuttal in the Corinthian church is, as Lowery commented, "they apparently poured forth their gift of tongues in unrestrained fashion," which newcomers found ridiculous.[46] Paul's primary interest is more than the gifts. For instance, Gordon Fee would say that Paul's concern is the "edification of the church" that rule the "zeal" of the members.[47] For Ben Witherington, propriety and solemnity are the priority. For these, he stated "intelligibility" and "order" are necessary.[48]

Above all, Taylor's evangelistic concern is worth noting. Paying attention to the immediate literary context, Taylor noted that Paul's final concern here is "the conversion of the unbeliever."[49] Wiersbe also has similar reading that looks beyond the internal concern of mutual edification as mostly commented. He argues:

> Paul's final application was to the unsaved person who happened to come into the assembly during a time of worship (1 Cor 14:21–25). Paul made here another point for the superiority of prophecy over tongues: a message in tongues (unless interpreted) could never bring conviction to the heart of a lost sinner. In fact, the unsaved person might leave the service before the interpretation was given, thinking that the whole assembly was crazy.[50]

Further, Wiersbe defines Paul's concern of edification itself as an encouragement "to major on sharing the word of God so that the church will be strengthened and grow."[51] Therefore, what this study wants to infer is that Paul's vision of Spirit-filled worship with the demonstration of gifts is extroversion in practice. For instance, verse 23 opens the sentence with "to assemble" in a direct reference to worship gathering. Then, in the closing statement of verse 25, the expectation is that empowered worship would bring even the "unbelievers" to repentance. It is Paul's ministry paradigm for the use of gifts in worship.

Therefore, concluding notes regarding Corinthian abuse of spiritual gifts in worship can be drawn as follows. Their use of spiritual gifts in the past was only meant inwardly, as for themselves. It was just for self-gratification, self-commendation, and self-sustenance. However, the pastoral directive of Paul is an outward focus. Its implication is extroversion, reflecting an evangelistic missionary outlook. That is, to bring others to repentance during the worship gathering. It is evangelistic engagement indeed.

Conclusion: Not to Shy Away from But to Engage With

Inspiring worship could truly create a time of personal piety and spiritual nourishment for genuine spiritual seekers. Moments of Spirit-filled worship can truly bring a time of refreshment and mutual edification within the body. It is a time of revival and renewal. However, this revival moment can also lose its meaning if not well directed. It can become an end in and of itself. Further, all that it could bring can become no more than self-entertainment, as seen in the case labeled "dancing religion." This is no fault of the revival. It is the responsibility of the worshippers to work out their spiritual experience in the community.

Worship, if truly Spirit-filled, is extroversion in practice, as the prophet Isaiah once proclaimed. It concerns shedding its light on the nations so that its light should not end within itself. Furthermore, it is also what Jesus Christ had already envisioned when he taught his disciples how and what to pray in the Lord's Prayer. This prayer never misses how to bless others and make the gospel impact on the broader community, while never losing sight of meeting one's daily needs. Indeed, Jesus never taught his disciples to shy away from the world. Rather, he taught them to engage with the world and even bring it to repentance.

The liturgical paradigm that Paul set forth for the Corinthian church for the proper use of spiritual gifts during worship is that of engagement with others who are not yet believers. Therefore, worship should not only be for one's personal piety and own entertainment; that is an end in itself. Worship gatherings should still invite and accommodate non-Christians. It should not be less than bringing someone to repentance as the gospel demanded. In other words, worship should always be at least an open occasion for someone who would like to come to the Lord. In that sense, what is happening with Full Gospel Assembly, as previously noted, is worthy of our consideration.

Finally, "Is worship introversion or extroversion?" Introversion in terms of shying away from the world is not what Spirit-filled worship truly means. Rather, it is engagement in practice. It has a witnessing aspect in its application. Therefore, worship, where spiritual gifts are manifested, should be the best occasion when many could find salvation. Any public gathering for worship should always be a place where many are well-equipped to engage in the world and make the gospel impact on the broader community. In that sense, worship is extroversion indeed.

Notes

1 See Ligon Duncan, "Traditional Evangelical," in J. Matthew Pinson, ed., *Perspectives on Christian Worship: 5 Views* (Nashville: Broadman & Holman, 2009), 12; S. D. Harrison and Jessica O'Bryan, eds., *Teaching Singing in the 21st Century* (New York: Springer, 2014), 323; and G. Raymond Carlson, "The Priority of Pentecostal Worship," *Enrichment* (Winter 1996), 14–15.

2 Similar observations are made in Donald E. Miller, *Spirit and Power* (Oxford: Oxford University Press, 2013), 7; and Wolfgang Vondey, *Pentecostalism* (London: Bloomsbury, 2013), 129.

3 Christian A. Schwarz, *Natural Church Development: A Guide to Eight Essential Qualities of Healthy Churches* (St. Charles, IL: ChurchSmart, 2012), 3–5.

4 Schwarz, *Natural Church Development*, 32–33.

5 See Thang San Mung, "Worship as Lifestyle: An Exegetical Study of Ephesians 5:15–20" (a paper presented for Biblical Interest Group at the 45th Annual Meeting of the Society for Pentecostal Studies, San Dimas, CA, 2016).

6 All the statistical reports are taken from Thang D. Lian, *When God Calls a Man: The Making of a Spiritual Leader* (Yangon, Myanmar: Thang Deih Lian, 2020), 1-2.

7 Lian, *When God Calls*, 63-64.

8 Lian, *When God Calls*, 65.

9 See, https://www.facebook.com/thangtawngWorship, accessed March 21, 2021.

10 See Thang San Mung, "Intensity and Extensity of Revival: A Critical Review of Christianity and Pentecostal Movement in Myanmar" (a paper

presented at the Historical Interest Group at the 48th annual meeting of the SPS, Hyattsville, MD, 2019).

11 For more on Hlimsang revival, see "Influence of Khasi Revival," in Wikipedia contributors; "History of Christianity in Mizoram," in Wikipedia, https://en.wikipedia.org/w/index.php?title=History_of_Christianity_in_Mizoram&oldid=826283463, accessed June 20, 2018.

12 Thuam K. Thang, *History of Pentecostal Movement* (Tedim: Bethel Bible College, 1993), 20.

13 John Piper, *Let the Nations Be Glad! The Supremacy of God in Missions* (Grand Rapids: Baker, 2003), 17–43.

14 Clement quoted in Claire L. Partlow, "What Isaiah Means for Christian Worship: Reading Scripture after Roberts Wilken's *The Church's Bible Series*," *Journal of Scriptural Reasoning* 16:1 (June 2017), 1–19.

15 Abstracted section, "Prophets," from Ph.D. seminar notes by Dr. Wonsuk Ma, Seminar in OT Theology, Oral Roberts University, Tulsa, OK, Fall 2020.

16 Partlow, "What Isaiah Means," 3–12. Partlow noted Isaiah's influences in both the form and the content of Christian worship. Also see Chris Atkins, *The Isaiah Encounter: Living an Everyday Life of Worship* (New York: MJ Publishing, 2016), 3–25; John D. Witvliet, "Isaiah in Christian Liturgy: Recovering Textual Contrasts and Correcting Theological Astigmatism," *Calvin Theological Journal* 39 (2004), 135–156.

17 Witvliet, "Isaiah," 136.

18 Witvliet, "Isaiah," 136–137.

19 Jacqueline Grey, "The Book of Isaiah and Pentecostal Worship," in Lee R. Martin, ed., *Toward a Pentecostal Theology of Worship* (Cleveland, TN: CPT Press, 2016), 27–46.

20 Treating chapters 56–66 as the final part of the book is not the interest of this study; overlaying what is mostly known is the only intention. For more on the structure, please, see David L. Petersen, *The Prophetic Literature, An Introduction* (Louisville: Westminster John Knox, 2002); Marvin A. Sweeney, "The Latter Prophets," in Steven McKenzie and Matt P. Graham, eds., *The Hebrew Bible Today: An Introduction to Critical Issues* (Louisville: Westminster John Knox, 1998).

21 John Goldingay, *Isaiah* (Grand Rapids: Baker Books, 2012), 337.

22 Shalom M. Paul, *Isaiah 40–66: Translation and Commentary* (Grand Rapids: Eerdmans, 2012), 514.

23 John Goldingay, *Isaiah for Everyone* (Louisville: Westminster John Knox, 2015), 232.

24 R. Jamieson, A. R. Fausset, and D. Brown, *Commentary Critical and Explanatory on the Whole Bible*, vol. 1 (Oak Harbor, WA: Logos, 1997), 498.

25 See notes in Paul, *Isaiah*, 518.

26 For more, see in Goldingay, *Isaiah for Everyone*, 231.

27 Goldingay, *Isaiah*, 338.

28 Goldingay, *Isaiah for Everyone*, 231–232.

29 In this study, the Matthean variant is focused. For more, please, see Craig S. Keener, *The Gospel of Matthew* (Grand Rapids: Eerdmans, 2009), 214–215.

30 Simon J. Kistemaker, "The Lord's Prayer in the First Century," *Journal of Evangelical Theological Society* 21:4 (December 1978), 323–328. Also see Roy Hammerling, "The Lord's Prayer in Early Christian Polemics to the Eighth Century," in Roy Hammerling, ed., *A History of Prayer* (Leiden, Netherlands: Brill, 2008), 223–241; Willy Rordorf, "The Lord's Prayer in the Light of its Liturgical Use in the Early Church," *Studia Liturgica* 14:1 (March 1980), 1–19.

31 Kistemaker, "Lord's Prayer," 327.

32 Hammerling, "Lord's Prayer," 223.

33 Kerry Irish, "The Lord's Prayer: A Study in Christian Theology," *Faculty Publications – Department of History, Politics, and International Studies* 91 (June 2019), 91.

34 Amanda du Plessis, "The Lord's Prayer as a Paradigm for Restorative Justice in Brokenness," *In die Skriflig/In Luce Verbi* 50:4 (August 2016), 1–6.

35 Jack W. Hayford, *Prayer is Invading the Impossible* (Orlando: Bridge-Logos, 1977), 124.

36 Hayford, *Prayer*, 125.

37 Keener, *Matthew*, 220.

38 D. A. Carson, *Matthew* (Grand Rapids: Zondervan, 1984), 170.

39 Carson, *Matthew*, 170.

40 Keener, *Matthew*, 220.

41 Warren W. Wiersbe, *The Bible Exposition Commentary*, vol. 1 (Wheaton: Victor Books, 1996), 26.

42 See notes in John P. Lange and Philip Schaff, *A Commentary on the Holy Scripture: Matthew* (Bellingham, WA: Logos, 2008), 126.

43 Lange and Schaff, *Matthew*, 123–126.

44 William F. Cook, III, "Twenty-First Century Problems in a First Century Church: 1 Corinthians 5–7," *Southern Baptist Journal of Theology* 6:3 (Fall 2002), 44–57.

45 B. C. Johanson, as quoted in Mark Taylor, *1 Corinthians* (Nashville: B&H, 2014), 342.

46 David K. Lowery, "1 Corinthians," in J. F. Walvoord and R. B. Zuck, eds., *The Bible Knowledge Commentary: An Exposition of the Scriptures* (Wheaton: Victor Books, 1985), 539. See also the comments of Gordon Fee, *The First Epistle to the Corinthians*, rev. ed. (Grand Rapids: Eerdmans, 2014), 750–761.

47 Fee, *First Corinthians*, 732; Walvoord and Zuck, eds., The Bible Knowledge Commentary, 540.

48 Ben Witherington III, *Conflict, and Community in Corinth: A Socio-Rhetorical Commentary on 1 and 2 Corinthians* (Grand Rapids: Eerdmans, 1995), 285.

49 Taylor, *1 Corinthians*, 343.

50 Wiersbe, *Bible Exposition* 1, 614.

51 Wiersbe, *Bible Exposition* 1, 614.

15 The Role of the Holy Spirit in the Great Commission through the Lens of Migration in the Middle East

Stavros Ignatiou

Abstract

Migration has been seen by many as a great opportunity and challenge to the existing Christian family and established religions in the area. It created an evangelistic edge which in turn resulted in the spiritual and numerical growth of the established local church. Migration also proved to be a challenge to the strong existing religious environment and, at the same time, became a major contributing factor to both contextual and theological challenges. Due to migration, the Great Commission became central to the local body of believers. The challenges of the newcomers were great, but the challenges of the resulting rapid social changes were even greater. In all of these, the Holy Spirit's presence became mandatory as never before. As migration continues and rapid social changes along with it, the demand for immediate intervention of the Holy Spirit through the Spirit's gifting becomes even greater. Seeking the Holy Spirit's guidance is more evident amongst local believers than ever before. This study will examine the role of the Holy Spirit employed by the local body of Christ and the extent of Spirit-empowerment that makes the Great Commission successful. It will also examine to what extent the local body of believers acts missionally in the shadow of migration.

Introduction

Many understand Acts 1:8 as part of the Great Commission: "But you will receive power when the Holy Spirit comes on you, and you will be my witnesses in Jerusalem, and in all Judea and Samaria, and to the ends of the earth."[1] The Great Commission is enabled by the power of the Holy Spirit. We are to be Christ's witnesses, fulfilling the Great Commission in our cities (Jerusalem), in our countries (Judea and Samaria), and anywhere else God sends us (the ends of the earth). Throughout the book of Acts, we see how the apostles began to fulfill the Great Commission, as outlined in Acts 1:8. First, Jerusalem is evangelized (Acts 1–7), then the Spirit expands the church through Judea and Samaria (Acts 8–12), and finally, the gospel reaches "the ends of the earth" (Acts 13–28). Today things have shifted. We have shifted from going to coming. The "Unevangelized" are coming to us by the thousands. We are living in a world on the move. People move because of war, poverty, physical dangers, fear, or even for the experience of adventure. The people of God became migrants for different reasons. Nevertheless, God was working with them while they were on the move (Exodus). In this chapter, we will examine how the power of the Holy Spirit is still engaged in this global migrant movement, particularly in the Middle East.

The Holy Spirit and the Great Commission

On the day of Pentecost, a promise was fulfilled. Lesslie Newbigin, a missionary, pastor, apologist, theologian, and ecumenical statesman, referring to the day of Pentecost, says, "The disciples are now given the same anointing that Jesus received at his baptism."[2] He continues, "It is thus an act of the sovereign Spirit of God that the church is launched on its mission."[3] Here, Newbigin is comparing what happened on the day of Pentecost with the same anointing that Jesus received at his baptism. The Bible states, "For he whom God has sent speaks the words of God, for God does not give the Spirit by measure" (John 3:34).

It is known how Jesus performed his ministry while on this planet; by that anointing, miracles and signs and wonders were performed. This same Jesus, when talking to his disciples, said, "Most assuredly, I say to you, he who believes in me, the works that I do he will also do; and greater works than these he will do, because I go to my Father" (John 14:12). The above statements not only make it evident that the Great Commission, which was started by Jesus himself, was carried out in the power of the Holy Spirit's anointing, but that it will continue to be carried out in the same power via his disciples and their disciples until the end comes.

The Pentecost event was certainly the inauguration of the New Testament church. Arthur F. Glaser, Dean Emeritus of the School of World Missions at Fuller Theological Seminary, states, "on that day, the New Testament expression of the people of God, the church, was formed and empowered for its worldwide mission."[4] Alan Hirsh, the founding director of Forge Mission Training Network, says:

> Most people, when asked about how they think the early Christian movement grew so remarkably, answer that it was largely because they

were true believers–that there was a real and abiding authenticity to their faith and that they, therefore, accessed the power of the Holy Spirit that was available to them.[5]

According to Alan Hirsh, "true believers" somehow know how to access the power of the Holy Spirit. That, of course, is a result of an "abiding authenticity to their faith." They believed in what Jesus promised them, and that led them into a relationship with the person of the Holy Spirit. If we refer to the first disciples of Jesus and later apostles as true authentic believers, then today's disciples are expected to be characterized as a people of miracles to an even greater degree. Let us not forget the words of Jesus concerning "greater things than these . . ." (John 14:12).

Pentecost was not just an experience; Pentecost was, as Newbigin puts it, "the same anointing that Jesus received,"[6] which was obviously as necessary then as it is today. The biblical account reveals to us in story after story how the Holy Spirit enabled the New Testament believers to do church mission work. The Acts of the Apostles contains a list of such examples. The Holy Spirit and his power in Philip's incident with the Ethiopian eunuch (Acts 8:26-40), the Holy Spirit in the Ananias incident with Paul (Acts 9:10–19), the story of Peter and Cornelius (Acts 10:1–20), and, of course, the power of the Holy Spirit in all missional endeavors with the Jews and to the Gentiles.

Samuel Escobar, a leading Latin American theologian, reflecting on the initiative of the Holy Spirit in relation to missions, states, "The Biblical pattern stresses the presence and power of the Holy Spirit in the life of the church as the source of missionary dynamism."[7] Escobar lists five very important points for missions:

First, "the word of promise becomes a reality by the work of the Holy Spirit."[8] Escobar is here referring to the fulfillment of prophecy in the person of Jesus. This man, Jesus, is real, and his appearance is due to the power of the Holy Spirit. Johannes Nissen, a professor of New Testament exegesis at the University of Aarhus, referring to the role of the Holy Spirit in mission, says, "The Holy Spirit makes Christ more present, more comprehensible, more transforming. In its Spirit-prompted mission to the world, the church discovers the meaning of the Word made flesh."[9] 'Christ more present,' 'Christ more comprehensible,' 'Christ more transforming,' 'Christ more fulfilling:' all of what we still need in today's world. Christ —the one who, according to Apostle Paul, every true believer is supposed to imitate (1 Cor 11:1) — was all of the above by the power of the Holy Spirit.

Second, "The ministry of Jesus is possible by the Power of the Holy Spirit."[10] Here, Escobar is referring to the manifestations of the Spirit "centered in or around Jesus as though in preparation for a mighty dispersion."[11] In this sense, Escobar is talking about Jesus' birth, his baptism, the way he was led by the Spirit in the desert to be tempted, and so forth. In all of these manifestations, one thing becomes crystal clear, and that is the dependency of Jesus on the Holy Spirit to accomplish his mission. Escobar goes on to say, "It is arrogant for missionaries to plan strategies based entirely on human logic and calculation if the Savior and Lord accomplished his mission only through the power of the Holy Spirit."[12]

Third, "God uses people with the power of the Holy Spirit."[13] Escobar says that "if the Spirit of God is in action, it is not only in spectacular ways, according to methods prescribed in manuals but also in the daily actions of faithful service . . ."[14]

Fourth, "Jesus teaches about the work of the Holy Spirit in mission."[15] From the very beginning of his teaching, Jesus aimed to prepare his disciples for the coming of the Holy Spirit. He would go, but his father would send another comforter who would help the disciples to continue what Jesus had started. The Holy Spirit would remind the disciples of what Jesus had taught them (John 14:25–26). The Holy Spirit would lead them into all truth, and furthermore, would tell them things that Jesus did not (John 16:12–13).

The Holy Spirit's role becomes even more essential in our day and age. Evelyn A. Reisacher, associate professor of Islamic Studies and Intercultural Relations at Fuller seminary, in discussing encounters between Christians and Muslims, states in her book, *Joyful Witness in the Muslim World*, that the "Bible does not provide details on how to interact with the Muslims simply because Islam did not exist in biblical times. Muhammad was born over 500 years after the death and the resurrection of Christ."[16] That is one more reason to rely on the Holy Spirit, who knows all things and can lead us into all truth for any given situation, at any time, and at any age.

Finally, "The growth of the church in numbers and depth is the work of the Holy Spirit."[17] In this last point, Escobar relates the growth of the newborn church from the day of Pentecost. He argues that the "dynamism" of the Spirit actually "pushes" the church forward. Apart from the Philip incident as described at the beginning of this section and the opening of Peter's eyes to a different aspect of mission, Escobar ascribes the sending of missionaries to Antioch to the Holy Spirit.

Becoming Missional

As shown above, the Holy Spirit enables and empowers the church to be missional. To explain what a missional church is, we need to see the church from the inside out. What is the church? Edmund P. Clowney, an adjunct professor of practical theology, president of a seminary, and prolific writer, claims that "according to the Bible, the church is the people of God, the assembly of the body of Christ, and the fellowship of the Holy Spirit."[18] Will Mancini, in analyzing the mission of the church, speaks about its missional mandate: "From the biblical perspective, the church's mandate is anchored in the sent-ness of Jesus Christ, reflected in the Great Commission as the church's sent-ness to the world."[19] Alan Hirsch speaks of a church as a living organism. He believes that the growth of the church is metabolic; it "feels like a movement, has a structure as a network, and spreads like a virus."[20] In summary, a missional church is the "people of God," "the assembly of the body of Christ," and the fellowship the people of God have with the Holy Spirit. Furthermore, a missional church is a church with a missional mandate, a church that is sent into the world. The missional church is indeed a "movement," and it "spreads like a virus."

One can say that all of the above terms are absolutely biblical but cannot be carried out without the help of the Holy Spirit. The church cannot be missional in the absence of the Holy Spirit. The following stories will enable us to see "reality" and will hopefully enable us to see exactly what is happening on the ground in missions. Moreover, it will help us to understand if missionaries, the contemporary disciples of Jesus, think missionally.

Real Stories –Testimonies

These testimonies were taken from refugees I have personally had contact with. They have all consented to give their testimonies on one condition, and that is their anonymity.[21] All of them have turned from Islam to Christianity. These testimonies, in my opinion, give an insight into how the Holy Spirit was introduced to the newcomers and how the newcomers perceive it. Moreover, these testimonies will help us to evaluate, recommend, and even develop new approaches when it comes to evangelization and missions. We will also recognize the work of the Holy Spirit in each and every testimony. The following testimony is from a refugee I will call "Q":

> Someone stuck a little booklet in my food package. It was a New Testament in the Arabic language. I got curious, so I took it out and started to read. It was the first time that the New Testament had come into my hands, so I started reading it. Little by little, I became more interested in reading the book. Ten days later, someone invited us to a place where we could hear more about the New Testament. It was a Christian NGO where we had the opportunity to participate in New Testament classes. There I understood more about Jesus Christ. In a short period of time, I invited Christ to become the Lord of my life.

> I was the first one from our family that became a Christian. My wife was not persuaded. She was very resentful and even hostile to the idea of me becoming a Christian. During that time, our fifth and youngest son became very sick. My wife challenged me. 'Where is your Christian God now?' she asked me. In her desperation, she said, 'If your God heals my boy, I will believe.' That same night our seven-year-old boy was miraculously healed. After that, all the members of my family invited Christ to become the Lord of their lives.

"M" is a Kurdish man in his late forties who came to know Christ as his Lord and Savior after having a vision. According to his description, he saw a star falling into the sea as he was waiting on the shore to get in a boat and flee Turkey with his eleven family members. That star, after falling into the sea, emerged as a cross. That vision was accompanied along by a voice saying, "Don't get into the boat." That caused "M" to stop his family from getting into the boat. After that incident, he took them all back to Istanbul.

When he arrived back in Istanbul, he came to a Christian church building, and on the front wall of that church, he recognized the same cross of his recent vision. Based on that vision, he started searching for Christians. In the meantime, he shared his dream with others. "M" today is leading a group of 110 Kurdish people who came to know Jesus as a result of his testimony.

"M" explained to me that the voice he heard and the vision he had were all acts of the Holy Spirit. "M" came to this conclusion by reading his new Arabic Bible. By that time, he knew that the Holy Spirit moves on people, gives them visions, and speaks to them. "M" claims that he is leading his group by the power of the Holy Spirit. He himself, after that initial experience, has seen miracles in his personal life and in the lives of those he leads. Evidence of that is the rapid numerical growth of his group. "People are getting saved very easily," he explains. "It is not my testimony alone," he continues, "it is definitely the power of the Holy Spirit that brings people to Jesus."

"R" is from Aleppo, Syria, and is married with three kids and one on the way:

> I used to live in the Muslim community where we always heard the Imam speaking more about hell and fear instead of mercy or salvation. He was talking more of a problem than a solution. That did not feel right to me. I was thinking, what kind of God is this? Why does this God want so much to punish us? Why did he create us in the first place? I knew that there was somehow a mistake in all of this.
>
> One day I went to work in the fields with some Christians who told me that they were walking a different path, a path of love. I observed them, and I found out that they were different. Somebody gave me the New Testament, and I started reading it. In there, I saw a big difference between the Koran, Islam, and what I used to believe. I saw the possibility of finally finding happiness and peace elsewhere. I was convinced.
>
> When my family and I made it to Athens, I called a Christian friend in Istanbul and told him that I needed to know more about Jesus the Messiah. He directed me to contact some Christians, and, in the meantime, I continued reading the Bible. The turning point for me was my fellowship with believers in Athens who were genuinely eager to help me in whatever I needed to survive. Their love in practice really touched my heart. Eventually, my whole family chose to walk in the path of the Messiah.

There are more testimonies to be shared, but space would not allow me. However, there are some common trends, which the table below throws light on.

Findings – Common Threads

The following chart will give an overview of the interview findings. It is a summary of common causes or reasons which led Muslims to their new faith. This chart is not exhaustive, it is nevertheless important for the reader to get a general idea.

Reasons Muslims have been led to Christ

SOMETHING IS WRONG WITH ISLAM
- It was impossible to accept Islam as the word of God
- Religion of fear and humiliation
- There is no love in Islam.
- Islam was a lie.

CHRISTIAN PROXIMITY, HELP, AND/OR BEHAVIOR
- I called a Christian- These people helped us.
- I went to my neighbor who was a Christian.
- Received food and blankets and a home.
- Went to a Christian NGO.

DREAMS AND VISIONS
- I saw a man full of light.
- I saw a cross.
- I saw a face within the sun.
- I heard a voice.

NEW TESTAMENT
- I read the NT.
- I read the NT.
- I read the NT in ten days.
- Started reading the NT.

MIRACLES
- My son was miraculously healed.
- I asked the Lord not to hear the Imam.
- Supernatural Healing

The Baptism of the Holy Spirit in Mission

Some of the reasons which played a decisive role in leading Muslims to Christ described above can be easily recognized and ascribed to the Holy Spirit's work. Healing, salvation, dreams, and visions are all the work of the Holy Spirit according to biblical teaching and theology. However, according to my observation, in all follow-up cases, there was not any intentional teaching, prompting, or encouraging towards new believers regarding the person of the Holy Spirit, the baptism of the Holy Spirit as referred to in Acts 2, and the gifts or charismata as mentioned in 1 Corinthians 12:8–10. According to the biblical account, the person of the

Holy Spirit, the baptism in the Holy Spirit, and the charisms or gifts of the Holy Spirit are three major and central factors of the NT missions. People who led the follow-up of the new believers were fearful about teaching on the Holy Spirit and his gifts, his manifestations, and especially on the baptism of the Holy Spirit as a separate experience in the new believers' journey.

As stated, the reason for the lack of such teachings is fear. This was observed among many leaders, even those who can be classified as Pentecostals. But what are the real reasons for avoiding teaching new believers about the person, the gifts, and the manifestation of the Holy Spirit?

First is the confusion on the teaching of *glossolalia* – the speaking in other tongues. Second, many erroneous approaches to the Holy Spirit baptism have led people to intentionally leave it out of the follow-up teaching with the excuse that the new believers will eventually find out for themselves what is good and what is not good for them. In referring to the baptism of the Holy Spirit and miracles, Nissen notes that "the activity of the Holy Spirit is considered to be an extraordinary and obviously supernatural phenomenon." He goes on to say that "this fact provokes a number of difficult questions." What Nissen says is perfectly understandable. It is obvious that any supernatural activity will cause questions in the human mind. That is actually the reason why Peter took his time while he had his pre-Cornelius vision. Nissen continues: "the story of Peter's encounter with Cornelius is especially significant in the light which it throws on the sovereign work of the Spirit in Mission." He goes on to say that "Peter realizes that a power greater than his own has broken down the fence which protected devout Jews from the uncleanness of the heathen world."[22]

Is Pentecostalism a Problem?

What is Pentecostalism? According to BBC research done in 2006, "Pentecostalism is a form of Christianity that emphasizes the work of the Holy Spirit and the direct experience of the presence of God by the believer."[23] Stan Guthrie, a former editor of *World Pulse* and managing editor of *Evangelical Missions Quarterly*, states, "The numbers of Pentecostal Christians in the world would suggest that Pentecostalism has been around for centuries. The truth is that modern Pentecostalism is only about a century old."²⁴ However, as he continues to say, "the first Pentecostals, looking back to the day of Pentecost when the Holy Spirit was given to the church (Acts 2), believed that the gifts of the Spirit remain operative for the church today."²⁵ H. D. Hunter, as quoted by Guthrie in reference to Pentecostalism, reports, "The movement that ensued was ridiculed by many outsiders as the religion of the economically deprived, and socially disinherited, the psychologically abnormal and the theologically aberrant."²⁶

In any case, this "new movement," as described by many, started with Jesus. In the Gospel of John, Jesus announces his impending departure to his disciples; something that the disciples, I would imagine, did not like. Nevertheless, Jesus presents his imminent departure as an advantage to his disciples. These are his very words: "Nevertheless I tell you the truth. It is to your advantage that I go away; for if I do not go away, the Comforter will not come unto you; but if I depart, I will send him to you" (John 16:7)."

Conclusion and Recommendations

Howard A. Snyder with Daniel V. Runyon, in writing about renewal movements, state: "The history of renewal teaches us about the renewing work of the Holy Spirit and renewal movements show that deep renewal often begins at the periphery, or the margins, of the church."²⁷ As Snyder talks about a movement, my mind goes to the movement of the Holy Spirit. In essence, Christianity was always meant to be a movement despite the intentional or unintentional efforts to turn it into an institution. However, movements can also fade away unless something keeps them moving.

What would be something that can keep a movement moving? My answer is the Holy Spirit. The movement began with Jesus, its founder, but it will end with the Holy Spirit. The Holy Spirit came after Jesus had gone to continue what Jesus started. As Jesus made disciples, so the Holy Spirit will make disciples. But what is discipleship? Ivan Illich, an Austrian philosopher and theologian, as quoted by Alan Hirsch, said, "We can only live change: we cannot think our way to humanity. Every one of us, every group, must become the model of which we desire to create."²⁸ I think this is the heart of discipleship. Having in mind what Ivan Illich said, I believe that the church, in general, has drifted away from the essence of discipleship. Discipleship has been reduced to an intellectual transmission of knowledge which is only one side of the coin. The other side, which is "doing" or "modeling," is greatly missing. I really believe that new converts must be discipled by teaching and doing, which by the way, was the "Jesus way" with respect to the Holy Spirit and the "things of the Holy Spirit." Moreover, discipleship cannot be complete unless it "is communicated through life itself."[29] The above-described discipleship process has missed the element of modeling. Not to mention that discipleship, in this case, has to do more with conversion than life in the Spirit. I suspect that people cannot do what they cannot see.

Intentional teaching on the Holy Spirit is unquestionable. This can be done by taking into consideration certain contextual elements depending on who will be the target group. Furthermore, the modeling aspect of the discipleship on the Holy Spirit becomes crucial. As Alan Hirsch puts it, "It should be obvious by now that the quality of the church leadership is directly proportional to the quality of discipleship."[30] Moreover, we have to constantly remind ourselves of the Great Commission commandment. Discipleship is not just for the few but is intended for everyone.

As previously mentioned, we cannot avoid Jesus' way of developing disciples into missional leaders. As Hirsch believes:

> The founding of the whole Christian movement, the most significant religious movement in history one that has extended itself through the ages, and into the twenty-first century, was initiated through the simple acts of Jesus investing his life and embedding his teaching in his followers and developing them into authentic disciples.[31]

Discipleship was "the very task into which Jesus focused his efforts and invested all of his time and his energy, namely in the development of that motley band of followers on whose trembling shoulders he lays the entire redemptive movement that would emerge from his death and resurrection."[32]

It can be easily seen that consistency was one of the key elements in Jesus' discipleship method. "The dilemma we face today in regard to this issue is that while we have the historical language of discipleship, our actual practice of discipleship is far from consistent, and as a result, this mismatch tends to obscure the centrality of the problem."[33] Bearing this in mind, I believe mentorship to be the modern word for discipleship. Mentorship in light of discipleship becomes vitally important in developing missional leaders.

Notes

1 Unless otherwise noted, all scripture references are from the New King James Version (Nashville: Thomas Nelson, 1982).
2 Lesslie Newbigin, *The Pen Secret: An Introduction to the Theology of Mission* (Grand Rapids: Eerdmans, 1995), 58.
3 Newbigin, *The Pen Secret*, 58.
4 Arthur F. Glasser, *Announcing the Kingdom: The Story of God's Mission in the Bible* (Grand Rapids: Baker Academic, 2003), 259.
5 Alan Hirsh, *The Forgotten Ways: Reactivating the Missional Church* (Grand Rapids: Brazos Press, 2006), 85.
6 Newbigin, *The Pen Secret*, 58
7 Samuel Escobar, *The New Global Mission: The Gospel from Everywhere to Everyone* (Downers Grove, IL: InterVarsity Press, 2003), 118.
8 Escobar, *The New Global Mission*, 120.
9 Johannes Nissen, *New Testament, and Mission Historical and Hermeneutical Perspectives* (Frankfurt: Peter Lang, 2006), 93.
10 Escobar, *The New Global Mission*, 121.
11 Escobar, *The New Global Mission*, 121.
12 Escobar, *The New Global Mission*, 122.
13 Escobar, *The New Global Mission*, 122.
14 Escobar, *The New Global Mission*, 122.
15 Escobar, *The New Global Mission*, 123.
16 Evelyn A. Reisacher, *Joyful Witness in the Muslim World: Sharing the Gospel in Everyday Encounters* (Grand Rapids: Baker Academic, 2016), 23.
17 Escobar, *The New Global Mission*, 124.
18 Edmund P. Clowney, *The Church: Contours of Christian Theology* (Leicester, UK: InterVarsity Press, 1995), 28.

19 Will Mancini, *Church Unique: How Missional Leaders Cast Vision, Capture Culture, and Create a Movement*, (San Francisco: Jossey-Bass, 2008), 120.

20 Hirsh, *The Forgotten Ways*, 25.

21 All interviews were held in Athens Greece in May 2020.

22 Nissen, *New Testament and Mission*, 59.

23 BBC, "Religions: Pentecostalism," https://www.bbc.co.uk/religion/religions/christianity/subdivisions/pentecostal_1.shtml, updated July 2, 2009, accessed October 6, 2020.

24 Stan Guthrie, *Missions in the Third Millennium: 21 Key Trends for the 21st Century* (Milton Keynes: Paternoster Press, 2000), 140.

25 Guthrie, *Missions in the Third Millennium*, 140.

26 Guthrie, *Missions in the Third Millennium*, 142.

27 Howard A. Snyder and Daniel V. Runyon, *Decoding the Church: Mapping the DNA of Christ's Body* (Eugene, OR: Wipf & Stock, 2011), 80.

28 Hirsh, *The Forgotten Ways*, 101.

29 Hirsh, *The Forgotten Ways*, 115.

30 Hirsh, *The Forgotten Ways*, 119.

31 Hirsh, *The Forgotten Ways*, 102.

32 Hirsh, *The Forgotten Ways*, 102.

33 Hirsh, *The Forgotten Ways*, 103.

16 Saturation Church Planting: Towards a New DAWN?

Raphaël Anzenberger

Abstract

Whole-Nation Saturation Church Planting strategy (SCP) was the "Cadillac" of missions strategy in the late 1990s. Heralded by C. Peter Wagner as "The best and most effective delivery system for getting church growth principles to the grassroots on an international scale" and by Ralph Winter as "The most basic strategy of all strategies," SCP was in full motion within the WEA, Lausanne and AD2000 movements. Dawn Ministries, founded by Jim Montgomery, carried the task to promote SCP across continents. Although the movement collapsed in the 2000s, the global church is once again experimenting with SCP strategies through initiatives like Global SCP, Christ Together, and National Church Planting Process. This study will explore the genesis of SCP, review the current SCP praxis and offer four trends in SCP which might very well become new markers for missions practice in the future years.

"Go therefore and make disciples of all nations, baptizing them in the name of the Father and of the Son and of the Holy Spirit." Matt 28:19

Many will remember Ralph Winter's famous ten-minute presentation at the 1974 Lausanne Congress that gave shape to a renewed reading of Jesus' commands in Matt 28:19:

> Winter clarified for us that the scriptural references to nations actually refers to the *panta ta ethne* or people groups. He and others began to speak of the idea of missiological 'closure' among these people groups. This simply refers to the idea of finishing. Their idea was that the irreducible, essential mission task of making disciples in every people group was a completable task. In fact, it was one of the only tasks given to God's people that had a completable dimension to it.[1]

During the same era, another missiologist gave a more practical reading of Jesus' command. His name was Jim Montgomery, founder of the DAWN (Disciple a Whole Nation) movement. For Montgomery, discipling a nation in a geopolitical sense was also a way to reach all peoples within predetermined geographical, ethnic, and cultural spaces. He wrote:

> Are these competing ideas for world evangelization? DAWN has placed particular emphasis on the idea of mobilizing the whole Body of Christ for making disciples of all the people groups within the borders of a whole country. Its concern is that there might be a witnessing congregation in every village and city neighborhood for every ethnic, linguistic, and social group, for every class and kind and condition of man in the country. By definition, then, DAWN is designed to reach all the unreached peoples of a nation.... In this respect, DAWN is right in the flow of the unreached people's movement.[2]

In other words, if Winter understood Jesus' command as a bottom-up disciple-making movement (from *ethne* to nation), Montgomery saw it as a top-down church planting saturation movement (from nation to *ethne*). The two missiologists were friends and shared office space at the Center for World Missions, along with Peter Wagner, who labeled DAWN as "the best and most effective delivery system for getting church growth principles to the grassroots on an international scale."[3]

This study will explore the historical and missiological impact of the Whole-Nation Saturation Church Planting strategy (SCP) as it relates to the current conversation regarding mission strategies. Although DAWN disappeared from the missions grid in the late year 2000, there is a resurgence of SCP strategies in different parts of the world. What does the Spirit say to the church? How can we reconcile the top-down SCP approach with bottom-up Disciple Making Movement (DMM) practices? Are the two profoundly antagonistic, or is there apostolic genius in keeping the two in healthy tension? What if Winter and Montgomery were arguing for convergence of apostolic and institutional energies, which would reflect the dynamic of early church movements where these two lines of ministries were operating in full convergence?[4]

Historical Development of Saturation Church Planting

Montgomery started his missionary life studying the explosive growth of the Four-Square Movement in the Philippines. The goal was to map out the denominational strategy that could, in turn, inform other denominations on church growth principles. Through a series of careful interviews with local, regional, and national leaders of the movement, Montgomery found that the Four Square growth resulted from sensitivity to the authority and strategy of the Holy Spirit, no missionary control, no dependence on paid workers, training and use of the laymen, acceptance of small results before a larger response is expected, desire to take full advantage of the response of receptive peoples, and emphasis on multiplying churches rather than institutionalism.[5]

This study settled the foundation for future DAWN thinking. First, the idea was formed that careful study of church growth principles in one area, whether geographical or denominational, could provide valuable insights to the church at large to further expand its reach. Second, Montgomery emphasized the need for ongoing systems to further church planting, even if they were not perceived at first as a "predetermined strategy."[6]

The Birth of DAWN

The Discipling of a Nation (1980) was Montgomery's first attempt to put his vision in writing, with the added voice of Donald McGavran. It was here that the concept of DAWN emerged:

> Early in 1966, while traveling in the midday heat by Banca (outrigger canoe) for three hours between two islands of the Philippine archipelago, I was suddenly overwhelmed by the conviction that the peoples of this nation could be discipled. This had been my hypothesis since studying at the Institute of Church Growth (then in Eugene, Oregon) the year before.[7]

Montgomery unpacked his thesis using the Philippines as a case study and advocating for other nations to join the movement: "We trust that in all those regions and nations where discipling the whole is clearly possible, our proposal becomes a rallying point. We pray that the vision will spur all missionary-minded Christians on to bold, courageous action."[8] Montgomery identified the need to make a theological case for DAWN, but it was McGavran who finally penned the rationale:

> The question of whether the discipling of a whole nation is God's will must be answered. For Christians, it is supremely important. Unless discipling a whole nation is God's will, Christians will not begin it. If it is, they will spend life and treasure to complete it. Is discipling a whole nation God's will? That is the key consideration.[9]

Surveying both Old and New Testament passages, McGavran concluded that "The discipling of all the peoples that comprise each whole nation was clearly God's will according to the scriptures."[10] As a result, Montgomery challenged the global church to embrace Saturation Church Planting as the means to "work systematically toward the completion of the command 'to make disciples of all nations.'"[11]

To the often-heard argument: "Hasn't Saturation Church Planting always been the approach since the time of Carey?"[12] Montgomery pointed to McGavran's research that showed how far too often breakthroughs in SCP resulted in the church giving too much attention to issues arising within its own structure, hence derailing the original objective of SCP. Montgomery assumed that adopting SCP on a national scale required dramatic changes in the way Evangelical groups operated, including in-house policies regarding finance, evangelistic methods, training of ministers, and releasing of laypeople. Montgomery advocated for greater alignment of political structures within organizations as well as operational strategies that served the sole purpose of SCP within a nation. In short:

> Research on a larger basis must be continuously carried out by denominations and service agencies on regional and country-wide bases to discover larger groupings of unreached peoples and communities. Denominations must set challenging church planting goals, not only in terms of their size but also in terms of the task that remains in saturating their area or country with churches. Then they must devise plans and allocate resources insufficient strength to reach their goals.[13]

In 1989, Montgomery released *DAWN 2000: 7 Million Churches to Go*, a definitive treatment on the DAWN movement. In the foreword, Peter Wagner predicted that the book "will certainly take place as one of the premier missiological works of the closing years of the twentieth century."[14] Here, the roots of DAWN were more clearly expressed:

> DAWN has picked up where Gerber left off. Using more advanced church growth technology, more extensive research, a broader base of coordination, a longer-term and more demanding process, and an extensive accountability system, Jim Montgomery represents a second generation that has added many improvements to Vergil Gerber's basics. Goal setting, for example, remains a key internal dynamic of DAWN.[15]

According to *DAWN 2000*, another source of inspiration for the framework was the Only Way Movement in the Philippines, which was an Evangelism in Depth (EID) strategy that Montgomery helped launch in 1970. Yet, he claimed that his model went beyond previous strategies since:

> DAWN (1) is built on thorough contextual and institutional research, (2) is a long-range strategy of up to twenty-five years or more rather than a one- or two-year program, (3) emphasizes completing the task of the Great Commission in a country rather than just proclamation or growth, (4) includes the more recent understanding of people groups and the discipling of the still unreached groups in a given country, (5) mobilizes the whole body of Christ around a nationwide goal rather than a number of set activities, (6) focuses on saturation church planting rather than saturation evangelism, (7) puts denominations and local churches to work in their own backyards rather than pulling resources out of the Church into unified projects and (8) encourages parachurch organizations to work truly alongside churches in developing their evangelism and church planting ministries. [16]

Montgomery argued that DAWN "worked" because:

> It divides the world into manageable segments, does the necessary research, mobilizes the whole body of Christ around an appropriate goal for its segment, and distributes the work to effective structures already in existence. We feel DAWN puts together in a synergistic relationship twelve powerful ingredients that combine to make it a mighty force for the planting of 7 million more churches and ultimately for the completion of the Great Commission.[17]

By "manageable segments," Montgomery referred to the "harvest force" on the one hand (the whole body of Christ) and the "harvest field" (all the nations of the world that need to be disciples)[18] on the other hand. The concept of "harvest field" and "harvest force" were driving factors in future DAWN research.[19]

Then the End Will Come (1996) was the last book written by Montgomery on the DAWN strategy.[20] Twenty-two years had passed since the first DAWN project in the Philippines. The vision was now shared across one hundred nations, covering 85 percent of the world's population. The *DAWN 2000* book had been translated into ten languages. The momentum was strong. Montgomery, more than ever, believed that:

> . . . DAWN strategy comes from the heart of God, that it is based on solid biblical and missiological principles, that the churches and nations of the world are ripe for such an approach, and even that this is a primary strategy for the completion of the Great Commission and the end of the age.[21]

With the AD2000 National Initiative Movement, the Joshua Project, and the Beyond Movement fully embracing a DAWN-type strategy at the end of 1995, and with DAWN receiving the endorsement of the three major international Evangelical bodies concerned for world evangelization, the Lausanne Committee for World Evangelization, the World Evangelical Fellowship and the Global Consultation on World Evangelization,[22] it seemed that nothing could stop the movement: "With the worldwide Body of Christ united on an Saturation Church Planting strategy like this, we could have this whole task wrapped up well before AD 2010."[23]

Saturation Church Planting Thinking after DAWN

Montgomery passed away in 2006 and Dawn Ministries, which supported the DAWN vision across the world, closed its door two years later.[24] But SCP thinking continued to be developed across the world, especially through Saturation Church Planting Global, Christ Together, and National Church Planting Processes.

Saturation Church Planting Global and the Concept of Antioch Church

Saturation Church Planting Global (SCPG) was pioneered in 1996 by Dwight Smith, a protégé of Jim Montgomery. SCPG was an attempt to improve missiological gaps within the DAWN model:

> SCPG was asked by national church leadership in the UK and Spain to follow up on DAWN efforts. As we carried out those efforts, I noticed several things about the DAWN strategy that initial euphoria can ignore. A few important criteria affect whether the discipleship of a whole nation is realistically achievable in the short run, and these principles became embedded in my philosophy of saturation church planting.[25]

SCPG is currently involved in fifty-five countries around the world, with the aim to see by 2060 a developed network of "Antioch churches"[26] in ten regions around the world, primarily focusing on pivot nations, that is, countries that have geographic influence in the midst of a significant number of contiguous nations. In order to accomplish this vision, SCPG sought to repurpose or plant gospel-centered churches, exhibiting seven characteristics of "Antioch churches" and having the ability to carry the vision of Saturation Church Planting across a state or region of that nation with the aim of telescoping into neighboring countries. Each pivot nation would define how many "Antioch churches" were needed across districts/cities/regions. For instance, India has twenty-nine states, and SCP aimed at twenty-nine "Antioch churches," one per state. In the United States, it was to be implemented along city lines as opposed to state borders, in partnership with Christ Together.

Christ Together and the Concept of Gospel Saturation

Christ Together was championed in 2011 by Jerry Gillis, a protégé of Dwight Smith. Christ Together represents a third-generation development of SCP strategy since DAWN. Rather than working at a macro-country level, Christ Together aims to unify the church in a given city (*meso*-level) to consistently demonstrate and communicate the gospel of Jesus Christ to every man, woman, and child. It uses the strategy of gospel saturation, which encourages local churches to own the lostness of an identified people in a defined place, ensuring that every man, woman, and child within that group has repeated opportunities to see, hear, and respond to the good news of Jesus Christ.[27]

In order to fulfill this vision, Christ Together pursues four priorities: mobilization: God's people taking responsibility for the lostness of a defined people in a defined place; transformation: God's people transformed into the image of Christ, resulting in gospel-renewal of lives, communities, and cultures; multiplication: God's people continually reproducing disciples, leaders, and churches for the Gospel Saturation of a place; and collaboration: God's people partnering with all the expressions of his church for the gospel saturation of a place.

In his conversation with this author,[28] Gillis gave more insights into his model. Gospel saturation is preferred to church planting saturation because church planting can often miss the missional impulse of evangelizing all peoples within a definite area. In other words, evangelism is at the forefront as opposed to church planting. Christ Together also uses the Saturation Church Planting Global "circle of accountability" language to educate local churches on the importance of "owning the lostness of the people within their reach." Christ Together moves into a city whenever they identify an apostolic leader whose heart aches for the spiritual lostness of his or her city. This leader is keen to use his or her church as a resource for other churches to seek gospel saturation of their first circle of accountability. This church qualifies as a Saturation Church Planting Global "Antioch church."[29]

National Church Planting Processes and Continental Process

At the same time that Christ Together developed SCP strategies in North America, a group of church planting leaders from seven European nations has met regularly to share best practices on national church planting processes in Europe. Out of these gatherings, a framework[30] was established to help develop National Church Planting Processes (NC2P) across Europe. The goal of NC2P in a given nation is to work towards a reality in which the majority of the body of Christ cooperates with one another for the purpose of seeing churches multiplied in all of the nation's geographic, ethnic, and cultural spaces.

NC2P is usually propelled by vision casting, then it moves towards consensus building and momentum in new strategic activity until it reaches a tipping point. This results in measurable progress in church planting through evangelism, winning people for Christ. The tipping point takes place when a process is underway involving collaboration and momentum, church planting is helping cause net growth in new Evangelical churches and total Evangelical attendance nationally and in each of its geographic, ethnic, and cultural spaces, and there is a cooperation of the majority of Evangelical denominations and agencies.[31] NC2P involves mutual learning, shared training materials, and common information through research.

Empirical research and focus group conversations carried out from 2011 to 2017 have revealed four mission-critical components, vital to the implementation of a national church planting initiative in Europe: a national leader for whom the initiative is a top priority, motivating information and communication about the national process, a gathering place to foster and implement the vision at the macro and *meso-*level, and ongoing church planting systems for recruiting, assessing, training and coaching church planters. Nineteen European countries have joined the movement, and five are in conversation to enter the process.

The Missiological Implications of Saturation Church Planting Strategy

In a sense, Saturation Church Planting strategies have matured. Saturation Church Planting Global saw the need to develop a *meso*-level to achieve micro saturation, Christ Together preferred using gospel saturation rather than Saturation Church Planting terminology to ensure missional engagement of local churches towards saturation, and NC2P sought to better integrate church planting systems in its model. Overall, four trends in Saturation Church Planting can be extrapolated from the emergence of these new SCP strategies.

To Whom: From Reaching the Unreached People Groups to Reaching the Cities

Whereas Lausanne I raised awareness about unreached people groups, Lausanne III identified the next "missions challenge" as reaching the cities of the world:

> Cities are crucially important for the human future and for world mission. Half the world now lives in cities. Cities are where four major kinds of people are most to be found: (i) the next generation of young people; (ii) *the most unreached peoples* who have migrated; (iii) the culture shapers; (iv) the poorest of the poor.
>
> We discern the sovereign hand of God in the massive rise of urbanization in our time, and we urge church and mission leaders worldwide to respond to this fact by giving *urgent strategic attention to urban missions*. We must love our cities as God does, with holy discernment and Christlike compassion, and obey his command to 'seek the welfare of the city,' wherever that may be. We will seek to learn *appropriate and flexible methods of mission that respond to urban realities*. (Cape Town Commitment II.D.4, italics added).

Here, the link between unreached people groups and citywide urban strategy is clearly stated: by reaching out to cities, the church will reach to some of the most unreached peoples of this world. It is of no surprise, therefore, that numerous movements have begun establishing strategies and "methods of mission that respond to urban realities" like City to City, Movement Day movement, and City Gospel Movement, to name some of the most global. In fact, Gillis from Christ Together notes that some movements place unity at the center of their strategy, while others focus on social causes, prayer, or church planting. He argues that the most effective way to reach out to the city is through gospel saturation, namely through the local church taking responsibility for the lost people living in its circle of accountability. Church planting might be the means to reach out to them, but it is not the only necessary means. For Gillis, movements that only put church planting at the center of their agenda miss the mark of reaching out to all people.

With Whom: From Information to Collaboration

For DAWN, a congress was where shared research and goal setting was brought to the forefront. Today, the trend is towards greater collaboration among Saturation Church Planting players. Cross-institutional partnership for the sake of missions became the driving force behind CT and NC2P, where "learning together" is a core aspect of the task of missions.

In a sense, the question in the 1990s was what is to be done to finish the task (information-based)? The question today becomes how could we, the church, finish the task? The reason for this shift may reside in the fact that missions, particularly in the West, raise more challenges than opportunities. The difference between church planting and SCP is saturation. In other words, it is one thing for each denomination to plant a church in each city of a nation, but it is another to plant churches to achieve saturation of that same city. SCP requires a higher degree of research, methodology, shared training, and praxis. Learning Communities in NC2P, for example, help church denominations to come together and to look for solutions together, acknowledging the reality that no one has yet found the way to saturate all spaces.

This trend towards collaboration is to be celebrated for it fosters greater unity in the Evangelical body and beyond. Yet if DAWN's "research" acted as a prophetic message and "goal-setting" as faith, where does one find the same impetus today? There is a growing skepticism towards goal setting as if the obligation of the church should not be framed around goals but rather around the means to achieve those goals. In other words, the question becomes what the church need to do in order to create the conditions necessary to achieve those goals. As Smith would often ask in his SCP consulting, what does God want? What would it look like if God did what he wanted to do?

In a certain sense, one could argue that alignment with *Missio Dei* has replaced goal-setting. The emphasis nowadays is more on "how do we join God in his mission" (God-focused) rather than "how do we accelerate missions?" (church-focused). This shift also reflects a shift from church growth theory (1960–1990) to missional theology (2000–present). However, keeping the two in tension might be a new way forward. Missional theology should not be afraid to ask research questions and for goals to be set in order to continually keep the vision of finishing the task at the forefront of world missions.[32]

How: From Top-Down Systemic to Bottom-Up Organic

If DAWN was the product of sound "engineering thinking," the trend today is towards greater flexibility and agility of systems and processes. This shift influenced DAWN itself. The rise of Church Planting Movements (CPM), and later DMM, shifted the emphasis from systemic SCP (thirteen steps towards a DAWN movement) to organic SCP thinking (four necessary components towards an NC2P2 movement). The goal has always been to provide the impetus for movement, but the path has changed.

This shift in strategy and thinking can be explained in terms of generational differences. Indeed, church growth proponents were fluent in systemic thinking. It also fitted their generational bent. With the philosophical crisis of Cartesian epistemology and the gradual collapse of Western missions, the need to look and learn beyond the West has brought fresh impetus to modern missions. The solution was sought from where the growth is happening, which is the majority world. CPM strategies have emerged from Africa and Asia and have been applied with a variety of successes in the West.

In a sense, the move from top-down systemic rationale to bottom-up organic thinking in missions is clearly a move from rationalism to pragmatism. Yet, both thought processes reach the same limitations: if all rationalized processes cannot be applied everywhere, then not all local successes can be implemented globally. What missions needs are more reflective practitioners who can assess experiences with sound missional thinking, always keeping in mind that scriptures should remain the main foundation. Furthermore, the gap between top-down and bottom-up thinking must be compensated for by developing the *meso*-level, as is the case in Saturation Church Planting Global and Christ Together. The *meso*-level will act as the logical place where reflective practitioners can act with one foot in praxis and the other in theory. The *meso*-level also allows for the development of experimental models that can be tested before being used at the macro level.

Who: from Institutional to Apostolic

The fourth and last trend in Saturation Church Planting is the move from institutional to apostolic leadership. This author recalls a conversation with Chad Smith, son of Dwight Smith, who piloted an SCP process in Ukraine. After many attempts, Chad Smith came to the conclusion that institutional leaders were not the key to unlocking SCP in a given country. The key rather was finding and empowering apostolic leaders, who were often found operating on the margins of the institution. Mobilizing these leaders, along with the resources of their "Antioch church," would provide greater impetus towards SCP than simply relying on national leaders, who were often either corrupt or too far removed from the reality of their base to provide the necessary leadership. This "wake-up call" constitutes the general backbone strategy for Saturation Church Planting Global today.

It is of no surprise that apostolic leaders tend to emerge at the *meso*-level, having gained enough traction at the *micro*-local level to raise awareness of their "success" at the regional level while staying away from the *macro*-national and institutional levels (which are often perceived "corrupt" or "irrelevant" to the task of missions). Yet, apostolic movements need the institution if they are to last. Moreover, institutions need apostolic movements to revive their thinking and praxis. This author believes that it is the task of SCP to create a space where these two types of leadership can meet for mutual edification. *Macro*-institutional leaders often overestimate their capacity to lead SCP at the *micro*-local level, while *meso*-apostolic leaders often overinflate their actual capacity to lead SCP at the *macro*-national level.

Conclusion

These four trends (reaching the cities through bottom-up collaboration under apostolic impulse) in SCP are the markers of missions today. It might explain why the World Evangelical Alliance (WEA), under the leadership of Bishop Efraim Tendero, who led DAWN 2000 in the Philippines,[33] sought to initiate and strengthen SCP projects in each nation globally. It might also explain why the Lausanne Movement Church Planting Issue Group[34] recently adopted SCP as a way forward in promoting global missions strategy. Surely, a movement that is now taking place in eighty countries around the world cannot be taken for granted. What is the Spirit saying to the church? Is this the dawn of a new DAWN? Did the grain have to fall in the ground and die before giving birth to a new impetus for Saturation Church Planting strategy? Will it grow thirty, sixty, one-hundred-fold in the years to come? May the Spirit continue to lead us in his ways.

Notes

1. Paul Eshleman, "World Evangelization in the 21st Century," https://lausanne.org/content/world-evangelization-in-the-21st-century," accessed June 16, 2021.
2. James Montgomery, "How DAWN tackles the Great Commission," *DAWN Report* 6 (March 1988), 9.
3. James H. Montgomery, *DAWN 2000: 7 Million Churches to Go* (Pasadena, CA: William Carey Library, 1989), 11.
4. David Bosch offers the following insight: "At an early stage, there were indications of two separate types of ministries developing: the settled ministry of bishops (or elders) and deacons, and the mobile ministry of the apostles, prophets, and evangelists. The first tended to push early Christianity toward becoming an institution; the second retained the dynamic of a movement. In the early years in Antioch, there was still a creative tension between these two types of ministries. Paul and Barnabas were at the same time leaders in the local church and itinerant missionaries, and apparently, they resumed their congregational duties as a matter of course whenever they returned to Antioch." *Transforming Mission* (Maryknoll, NY: Orbis Books, 2008), 51.
5. James H. Montgomery, *Fire in the Philippines* (Carol Stream, IL: Creation House, 1975), 130–4.
6. Montgomery, *Fire in the Philippines*, 42.
7. James H. Montgomery and Donald A. McGavran, *The Discipling of a Nation* (Milpitas, CA: Global Church Growth, 1980), 13.
8. Montgomery, *The Discipling of a Nation*, 170.

9 Montgomery, *The Discipling of a Nation*, 17.

10 Montgomery, *The Discipling of a Nation*, 21.

11 James H. Montgomery, "Can We Disciple Whole Countries," *Evangelical Missions Quarterly* (January 1984), 3, https://emqonline.com/node/1280, accessed October 2, 2017.

12 Montgomery, "Can We Disciple Whole Countries," 3.

13 Montgomery, "Can We Disciple Whole Countries," 4.

14 James H. Montgomery, *DAWN 2000: 7 Million Churches to Go* (Pasadena, CA: William Carey Library, 1989), vii.

15 Montgomery, *DAWN 2000*, viii.

16 Montgomery, *DAWN 2000*, 92.

17 Montgomery, *DAWN 2000*, 99.

18 Montgomery, *DAWN 2000*, 107.

19 "In order to be good stewards of God's grace, we must have the facts – see the true picture. Yesterday's truths are often today's fiction. Accurate, up-to-date information about ourselves (the Harvest Force) and our context (the Harvest Field) is needed," Bob Waymire, Foreword in Roy A Wingerd Jr. *The DAWN Research Handbook* (Colorado: Dawn Ministries, 2001), vii.

20 Montgomery would later publish *I'm Gonna Let it Shine: 10 Million Lighthouses To Go* (Pasadena: William Carey Library, 2001), a Mission America Lighthouse movement project to encourage each home to become a missional community. Montgomery believed that this micro-strategy for evangelism, centered around house units, could be the way to implement DAWN in North America.

21 James H. Montgomery, *Then the End Will Come* (Pasadena, CA: William Carey Library, 1996), xi.

22 Montgomery, *Then the End Will Come*, 188.

23 Montgomery, *Then the End Will Come*, 195.

24 For a complete reading of the reasons behind the close of the Dawn Ministries, see Raphael Anzenberger, "Whole-nation SCP: Towards a new Dawn?" (Ph.D. diss., Columbia International University, 2020), ProQuest Dissertations & Theses Global.

25 Dwight Smith, "SCP Story," https://www.scpglobal.org/story, accessed October 25, 2019.

26 By "Antioch Church," SCPG means seven characteristics: (1) target driven, (2) measurable incarnate values, (3) people empowerment intensive, (4)

laterally postured, (5) interdependent leadership, (6) Antioch related to other churches, and (7) telescoping, a posture of missions directed at facilitating indigenous leadership in distant locations.

27 For further information, see the Christ Together website, https://christtogether.org/.

28 Interview with Gillis, Feb 1, 2019, Nice, France.

29 SCPG will refer leaders to Christ Together in the United States to carry out an SCPG strategy.

30 More on the NC2P framework at nc2p.org, accessed May 20, 2021.

31 At least 70 percent of the Evangelical body of Christ.

32 To what degree does the fact that the Lausanne Movement, which has included the former AD2000 objectives – the Gospel for every person, a Church for every people – into its new missions objectives, confirm the need to balance mission with missions for the sake of God's purposes?

33 Efraim M. Tendero, "The Philippines Model," AD2000, http://www.ad2000.org/gcowe95/tend.html, accessed August 23, 2017.

34 Lausanne Movement, "Church Planting: The Most Effective Evangelistic Methodology Under Heaven https://lausanne.org/networks/issues/church-planting, accessed May 20, 2021.

17 Spirit-Empowered Youth Evangelism with Christians Together: Lessons from *An Tobar Nua*, Ireland

Tomasz Białokurec

Abstract

Current shifts in the spiritual and cultural landscape of Ireland call for new approaches to Christian mission. The advancing secularized culture has challenged Christians in Ireland to revamp their strategies for cultural engagement in order to adapt the gospel proclamation to the ongoing transformation of the Irish milieu. The contribution of ecumenical, outreach-oriented communities to the project of a new evangelization of Ireland will be evaluated through the case study of the cross-denominational ministry of *An Tobar Nua*. The remaining task of the Great Commission will be analyzed from the perspective of Spirit-empowered youth evangelism carried out by this ministry with the aim of helping young people in their search for the ultimate meaning of life. In the course of the study, we will attempt to define the Spirit's role in empowering ministry leaders as well as in building a Christian community characterized by unity in diversity. The relevance of servanthood and credible witness for missionary enterprise will be examined. Finally, we will present a preliminary analysis of the significance of relationality for the ministry of reconciliation conceptualized within a trinitarian framework.

"The Light will shine in the not so distant future and many have I chosen as bearers of the Light. Do not be afraid, do not fear the mission, but seek it with all your heart. My Spirit will be poured out to bring life to this land. My blood has been shed, and it will purify and wash anew. My servants, I will send, and my words will be given to them. I will open the doors."[1]

Introduction

The Bible pictures God thirsty for a relationship with every single person created in his image. Jesus reveals his Father's desire to be known by all. The Spirit of love makes this life-transforming relationship possible. This study aims to present a relational model of Spirit-empowered youth evangelism carried out by Christians from diverse faith backgrounds. We will begin our inquiry by drawing the cultural context of contemporary Ireland, focusing on the rise of secularism and its impact on Irish culture. The clash between declining Christendom and all-pervading secularism will be interpreted from the perspective of their opposing claims to the entirety of human life. The quest to restore the eroded meaning of existence will bring us to the relational nucleus of evangelism. We will investigate the need for a new evangelization of this traditionally Catholic country that has been relocated on the map of global Christianity. Some testimonies will be featured to illustrate the dynamics of the Spirit's empowerment and guidance in the missionary endeavor.[2] *An Tobar Nua*, a ministry headquartered in Galway City, will be showcased as an example of the new paradigm of mission where Christians from different denominations join their efforts to re-evangelize Ireland. We will provide a biblical framework for our analysis of the remaining task of the Great Commission, particularly in relation to youth.

A Battle for the Meaning of Life: Evangelizing a Secular Culture

Since the Western world entered a secular age, the relevance of religious faith in our lives has been questioned: "The Western secular society that has converted to modern secularism through the Enlightenment constitutes a new unbelieving missionary field for Christians. . . . The European Christian root was being eroded by rising secularism and humanism."[3] Along with the Christian root of our culture, the very meaning of existence became eroded. Western secular societies have been exposed to:

> The specter of meaninglessness; that as a result of the denial of transcendence, of heroism, of deep feeling, we are left with a view of human life which is empty, cannot inspire commitment, offers nothing really worthwhile, cannot answer the craving for goals we can dedicate ourselves to.[4]

The very possibility of reaching beyond our earthly concerns has been challenged, giving rise to "a widespread sense of loss here, if not always of God, then at least of some transcendent meaning that would elevate our existence beyond the limited horizon of the material world."[5]

Human existence robbed of its transcendent orientation inevitably becomes deprived of meaning. Young people are most affected by the phenomenon of rapid secularization since, in this crucial season of life, one is searching for the answers to fundamental questions and tends to get interested—or disinterested—in the matters of faith. Youth are exposed to a secular worldview of nonfaith or, quite often, some form of indifferent belief disengaged from real life. "We live in the times of indifferent faith. ... Nonfaith is a worldview and attitude that does quite well without any religious faith and, at the same time, affirms this finite world."[6]

Ireland is an important landmark in the bleak landscape of the post-Christendom West. We face the rapid disappearance of religion from the public sphere. Old demarcation lines separating different forms of Christianity lost much of their relevance on the new map of a secular Ireland. The secularized culture is becoming more and more hostile to the Christian faith: it would not be an exaggeration to call it anti-Christian. Worse still, it claims the right to shape all the spheres of human life, including family and education. Indeed, we are caught in the clash between two competing forms of belief:

> A most important case of an encounter of faith with faith in the Western world is the encounter of Christianity with forms of secular belief. For secularism is never without an ultimate concern therefore, the encounter with it is the encounter of faith with faith.[7]

The encounter of these two types of belief generates an urgent need for re-evangelization of this once missional country. The cradle of the world missionary movement has turned into a missionary field.[8] And yet, the rich legacy of Christianity is still alive on the Emerald Isle. The embers of faith wait to be rekindled to spread new spiritual fires across the country.

Closing the Rift

What are the implications of this shift for Christian mission? If we want to present the saving message of the gospel in meaningful terms we need to keep adapting our mission strategies to the constantly shifting cultural context of modern Ireland, where traditional, church-based initiatives often prove insufficient to bring people to the Lord. An independent, cross-denominational, and international ministry appears to be best equipped to close the rift between living faith and secular worldview. We believe that personal evangelism is the bridge connecting these two dimensions. *An Tobar Nua* wants to play its part in this mission to bring the good news that the lost meaning can be restored to our lives and communities through a personal encounter with the living and life-giving God.

An Tobar Nua

We now move on to present a case study of *An Tobar Nua*, an outreach of Foundation in Christ Ministries to the people of Ireland. We are an ecumenical, charismatic, and international mission that is not associated with any particular church. Our main objective is to kindle in the hearts of the young people of Ireland a desire for a personal relationship with God. Since its humble beginnings in 1998, the ministry has expanded along an uncommon trajectory. Our founders, Kelly and Susan, "strongly believed that they were not called to convert people from one Christian denomination to another, but to encourage a deep and growing faith in Christ."[9] This unusual approach marks the new era of Spirit-empowered mission in the nation historically torn by conflict between Catholics and Reformed Christians. In recent decades, Ireland has seen many failed attempts to reinvigorate the Christian faith through aggressive proselytism and "sheep-stealing." Against such a backdrop, *An Tobar Nua* established a new paradigm of mission where believers are encouraged to deepen their commitment to Christ in their respective faith communities. One of our friends who witnessed the growth of the ministry over the years aptly described its distinctive character:

> Respect, tolerance, common orthodoxy, healing, joy, delight—these are some of the words that describe the heart of *An Tobar Nua*. Jesus told us to be one. *An Tobar Nua* strives to obey this command. It is a safe place for the children of God as well as a place to experience God's love even if you do not believe in God.[10]

Foundations

"For no one can lay any foundation other than the one already laid, which is Jesus Christ" (1 Cor 3:11, NIV). This verse is programmatic for the community that is "built on the foundation of the apostles and prophets, Christ Jesus himself being the cornerstone in whom, the whole structure, being joined together, grows into a holy temple in the Lord. In Him, you also are being built together into a dwelling place for God by the Spirit" (Eph 2:20–22, ESV). The same Spirit who is the primary agent of God's indwelling in the community is also instrumental in drawing those who are far off into the single family of God, breaking down the dividing walls of hostility and making us able to reach beyond the racial, social, and denominational boundaries (cf. Eph 2:12–17). All of us have open access to the Father in one Spirit, and no one needs to be estranged from this family any longer since God was pleased to reconcile to himself all things through the blood of the cross (cf. Eph 2:18; Col 1:20–21).

Consequently, our ministry is one of reconciliation and solidarity with "sinners for whom Christ gave and continues to give himself.... The truly holy life is a life lived in radical solidarity with sinners just because it is a life consumed by intimacy with the holy God."[11] An ongoing relationship with the living God is the driving force of our missionary engagement with the people around us. "In Christ God was reconciling the world to himself, not counting our trespasses against them, and entrusting to us the message of reconciliation" (2 Cor 5:19, ESV). We can deliver that divine message of reconciliation to the fractured world only inasmuch as we rediscover the relational nature of our Christian vocation. Most Christians would agree that having a personal relationship with God is crucial for our salvation. Likewise, engaging in personal evangelism is pivotal for the salvation of others. "The fullness of the Spirit-baptized life is revealed in solidarity with the sinning and the sinned-against for whom Christ died and has been raised as saving Lord. Holiness does not so much make us sinless as it impels us to care for those who have been broken by sin."[12]

The Continuing and Enabling Ministry of the Holy Spirit

At *An Tobar Nua*, we believe in the "continuing ministry of the Holy Spirit as the deposit guaranteeing our redemption, and enabling the believer to live a victorious and Godly life."[13] It is not incidental that "continuing ministry of the Holy Spirit" and "enabling" appear in our mission statement. The belief that the Spirit is very much alive today and enables Christians to carry out the remaining task of the Great Commission is central to our missional spirituality. We realize this commission through different forms of outreach.

Ministry work in *An Tobar Nua Café* is based on a consistent effort made by the staff to build personal relationships with people visiting the café with a view to creating an opportunity to share the good news with them. The students from local secondary schools are our focal point. They come to *An Tobar Nua* because they feel accepted and understood. We are determined to create a friendly and welcoming environment in our café. Teens find here a safe haven where they can hang out, study, play, and talk about all things life and faith without fear of being judged. This indirect approach to evangelization has proven quite effective in the secularized environment that remains predominantly suspicious of, and even hostile to, open manifestations of the Christian faith.

Another form of outreach aims to realize the commission to teach all nations through Scripture-based courses and discipleship groups in the Emmaus Scripture School. The students coming from diverse ethnic, cultural, and denominational backgrounds appreciate the community-building aspect of the classes taught in an ecumenical paradigm.

Facilitating one-day religious retreats for secondary schools across Ireland constitutes the wide field of *An Tobar Nua* outreach. This form of direct evangelism started almost two decades ago, from engaging the local schools of Galway to gradually embracing the whole nation. Through an original and ever-expanding retreat program, students receive a unique opportunity to hear about the Father's love revealed through the life, death, and resurrection of his Son and the outpouring of his Spirit.

Mike Shortt, our Director of Outreach, summarized our missional agenda in these words: "We know that without the Holy Spirit, we will not be able to present the gospel. We try to remain teachable and obedient to the promptings of the Holy Spirit. We want to accept people lovingly and meet them where they are at."[14] In recent years, our ministry has been revitalized by missionaries coming from other European countries, Africa, and both Americas. We perceive the increasingly international profile of *An Tobar Nua* as yet another mark of the Spirit's empowerment for mission.

The Source of Inspiration and Validation

The Great Commission is a dynamic reality, lived out in the Spirit who calls to the community and sends out from within the community. Just as with biblical leaders, so also today, "it is the presence of the Spirit that validates the leader's appointment for ministry work."[15] Obviously, that engenders the need for spiritual discernment lest we chase our phantoms rather than God's will. The crucial biblical term for discernment—*diakrisis*—can be understood as "a critical capacity to discern the genuine transcendent activity of the Spirit from merely human attempts to replicate it."[16] We are intentional about making time to allow the Holy Spirit to guide and refine us. We have seen him speak through concrete events and circumstances, orchestrating our efforts to follow his lead. To better equip ourselves for the demands of mission, we devote considerable community time to studying and interpreting the divine truths revealed in the Bible. We want to be well prepared to give the reason for the unfailing hope that has been poured into our hearts by the Spirit. We present it with gentleness and respect (cf. 1 Pet 3:14–15; Rom 5:5). We constantly draw inspiration and spiritual wisdom from the Spirit-inspired scriptures so as to be able to bring the living word of God to all those who hunger for it without even realizing it. The Holy Spirit will direct our steps only insofar as we employ sound discernment and critical evaluation of biblical data and circumstantial signs in ever-changing existential and cultural contexts. This continuous work of Spirit-led discernment shapes, in turn, our missional "ability to show forth relational signs of God's grace in an increasingly graceless world."[17]

Gifts of Relationality and Community

Relationality is the backbone of every ministry undertaken by *An Tobar Nua* in this secular age of Irish history. On many occasions, we have experienced that evangelism happens in the relational context or it does not happen at all. Investing in ongoing relationships with the people we meet lays the groundwork for fruitful outreach. "The Spirit as 'power' or 'giver of life' opens up our existence to become relational, so that he may at the same time be 'communion' (*koinonia*, cf. II Cor 13:13)."[18] Relational God created relational man in his image and likeness. The Spirit enables us to expand the horizons of divine *koinonia* to embrace those who are thirsty for meaningful relationships but do not yet know the triune God who is the source of relationality and community:

> Relationality and community are engendered through the gift of the Spirit. In this way, the Spirit's gift, which is nothing less than the mutual love of Father and Son, finds economic expression. The Spirit of life enables reconciliation and healing among human creatures. The divine breath renews life through reestablishing relationality, fellowship, and community.[19]

Spirit-enabled reconciliation and renewal through reestablished relationality are manifested primarily in unity and self-giving love:

> This unity is demonstrated in the love that members of this body have for each other, in the same way, that the Father loves the Son and vice versa. It is, therefore, appropriate to consider this love as "the unity of the Spirit in the

bond of peace" (Eph. 4:3), eschatologically inaugurated at Pentecost.[20]

A practical consequence of this theological truth is that "every division and strife opposes the Spirit's very nature as the Spirit of unity."[21] Conversely, our unity manifested in diversity, rather than despite it, can be a convincing sign of God's faithful presence in this world torn by divisive pride and hostilities, not least pride and hostility among the followers of Christ. "The eternal God who is characterized by diversity within unity has decreed the same for the people who are to bear God's likeness, the church."[22] There is an essential connection between the diversified unity within the Trinity and the unity in diversity that the community of believers is called to display. "We are to inspire the world to believe by our dynamic unity in the Spirit, the substance of which is the righteous and dynamic *koinonia*, or fellowship (John 17:20–21)."[23] This realization is pregnant with practical implications.

Unity in Diversity

Unity in diversity is a clear manifestation of the relational nature of a Spirit-led mission. We are committed to realizing this unity on a practical level by the community members representing the plethora of Christian denominations:

> Christ crucified, risen, exalted to the Father's right hand, and coming again for a whole church without spot or wrinkle—that should be the unifying focus for my life and yours as disciples of a Lord who has that kind of focus. Yes, we have our distinctive practices and emphases within our various communions and traditions. But which of those distinctive practices should overshadow the work of Christ or of the Holy Spirit who makes us one in Christ?[24]

We are deeply aware that the Spirit-driven unity among Christians is the most credible witness to the gospel message of peace and reconciliation. That is the reason why we want to reflect God's love through how we treat each other as a team. "Keep the main thing the main thing"— that is the message Susan and Kelly Curry received from the Lord when they came to Ireland in 1996 in obedient response to his call.[25] Every day we make a conscious effort to cultivate our witness to God's faithful and sacrificial love toward lost humankind which remains "the main thing" in our cross-denominational ministry. As Kelly Curry often repeats, "We will close the door of our ministry the day it stops being all about Jesus."

Unity in diversity is the bedrock of a Spirit-empowered ministry.[26] The Holy Spirit is displayed in the Pauline writings as the binding agent of a Christian community. He is instrumental in the creation of the single, multi-ethnic family of God, where everyone belongs to the same table and is allowed to drink of the same Spirit, having been baptized into one body by one Spirit (cf. 1 Cor 12:13). The transformative outworking of the gospel is manifested primarily in love—the first fruit of the Spirit—that has a unifying effect on the community. Divisive pride, rivalry, jealousy, and strife do not befit those who are called to walk according to the Spirit who dwells within them.

Conversely, the attitude of humility and readiness to serve one another is indicative of the indwelling Spirit. It is evident that for Paul, the Spirit-driven unity of a Christian community remains crucial in fostering its harmonious growth. We desire to realize this great biblical ideal on a daily basis. We want to build a community where:

> Members touch and 'symphonize' with one another. Should we regard the 'ligaments' that tie all bodily joints together as the bonds of Holy Spirit love that bind one to all the others (cf. Col 2:19 with Rom 5:5)? To express such love is one's covenanted life commitment to all other Christians and must be displayed to the world (John 13:34–35)[27].

Many Gifts of One and the Same Spirit

In 1 Corinthians 12, Paul depicts the Spirit as the only source of all spiritual gifts. We exercise diverse charismata for the glory of the same God who empowers them all in everyone (cf. 1 Cor 12:6). The Spirit bestows his many gifts to deepen unity among those who exercise them. An important lesson we can take from the Corinthian church is that a disordered use of spiritual gifts shatters unity instead of strengthening it:

> We can manipulate the very manifestations of the Spirit that are intended to produce the united functioning body of Christ and thus make them instruments of harm rather than of healing balm. And perhaps unless we see clearly the goal of the Spirit—maturation in the form of conformity to Christ, as Christ's united body—we may unwarily ourselves re-tread Corinthian paths.[28]

We believe that the Spirit has endowed all the community members with his gifts to equip them for specific ministries. At the same time, we remain conscious that all the manifestations of the Spirit's empowering presence are granted not for personal enhancement but for the common good (cf. 1 Cor 12:7).

What is that common good? "Love defines which gifts are the 'best': those that build up the body."[29] As an edifying factor, love constitutes the ultimate guideline for the pursuit and use of spiritual gifts. All the manifestations of the Spirit, spectacular or not, are subject to this single guiding principle of the church's growth. Moreover, no member of the same body can be considered more spiritual or charismatic than others. All those who were given the same Spirit to drink (12:13) are equally charismatic and empowered for service.[30]

Koinonia means *Diakonia*

Following Paul's exhortation, we prioritize the gifts for service:

> The bottom line is that spiritual gifts are not intended as a measure of spirituality. Nor are they intended for the well-being of the gifted. The criterion of how well a spiritual gift has been received is how well others have been served—because a spiritual gift is a *diakonia*.[31]

Self-giving love drives the inner dynamism of the fellowship of the Spirit (*koinonia pneumatos*: Phil 2:1) that cannot be contained within its walls. Unless spiritual fellowship spreads out to include the lost and the seeking it inevitably withers away. Driven by the Spirit, "the very principle of the self-giving,"[32] we share the love of God by giving our best selves to others:

> Holy Spirit infuses in us not only "the gift of God," but also the ability and the need to give ourselves. From the Spirit, we "catch," so to say, the very qualities of what he is in himself. The Spirit is "self-giving," and in whomever he touches, the Spirit creates a dynamism that leads that one, in turn, to be a self-giving gift to others.[33]

We try to serve first and then preach the good news should a favorable opportunity arise. In words attributed to Francis of Assisi, "Preach the gospel, and if necessary, use words." We can attest to the wisdom of this adage. More often than not, our attitude of loving care is the only possible means of gospel proclamation. Kelly Curry still remembers the early days of *An Tobar Nua* when he and his wife Susan played board games with a couple of local kids. Twenty years later, our café is brimming with the youth coming to the gaming clubs and student parties we organize on a regular basis.

Young people are hardly interested in exploring the Bible, which presents a real challenge. We reach out to the local youths through the weekly discipleship group that combines Scriptural teaching with games and worship music. Summer camps provide an outstanding opportunity to invest in relationships with them and delve deeper into faith-related topics.

The social distancing restrictions introduced in 2020 due to the global pandemic had a significant impact on our operations. Yet, "we were perplexed but not driven to despair" (2 Cor 4:8) as we adapted to these turbulent times, e.g., by producing online camps, festivals, social media content, and video channels dedicated to the younger audience.

Lessons from *An Tobar Nua*

As Christians, we are called to make disciples of all nations. Not that we have already achieved this goal, but we press on to carry out the remaining task of the Great Commission (cf. Phil 3:12; Matt 28:19). What can we learn from the case study of *An Tobar Nua* that is relevant to this task?

Only Love is Convincing

At *An Tobar Nua*, we create a safe space for young people to share their thoughts with us. We look for opportunities to weave our testimony into a conversation but never shove the gospel message down people's throats. We are convinced that the truth of the gospel can be shared without belittling or judging others. Love remains the ordering principle of Christian mission. Youths can unerringly sense whether we are genuine in love we show them (cf. Rom 12:9). As *An Tobar Nua Café Evangelism Guide* states:

> Teenagers especially will be watching closely to see if we live up to what we profess to be, so in this instance, it is important that we always ask the Holy Spirit to bear witness and use us when we engage in discussion or carry out our regular Café duties.... In this respect, a "friendly and warm environment" is displayed by showing Holy Spirit inspired love and compassion to all who come into the Café through the way we serve them.[34]

We strive to remain faithful to the friendships forged through our ministry engagement, even if our friends are not ready to embrace the gospel at this particular stage of their lives. We offer them up to God in prayer, often feeling acute helplessness and yet convinced that the Spirit always comes to help us in our weakness and intercedes for us when we are lost for words (cf. Rom 8:26).

We rely on the Spirit for his fruit to become manifested in our ministry work, just as we rely on the Spirit to bring the lasting fruit of transformation in our own lives. We try to follow in the footsteps of Paul who "believed that God's Holy Spirit had been poured out upon those who believed the gospel, transforming their lives from within both with spiritual gifts and with the more slow-growing but long-lasting 'fruit' of which he speaks in Galatians 5."[35] We are deeply aware that we will fail to show people kindness and patience unless we stay connected to the Lord through prayer. We are able to reveal God's gentle and faithful love as long as we draw our sense of worth from him. If we are dependent on the validation of others, we are setting ourselves up for disappointment. We are also conscious that the encounter with us might be but a small step in someone's journey of faith. We plant seeds, someone else will water them, but it is God who gives the growth (cf. 1 Cor 3:6).

By Your Perseverance, You will Win Souls for Christ

One of our ministry leaders detected an insidious obstacle to accepting God's commission:

> We often disqualify ourselves for youth work because we do not think we fit into a typical mold of a youth worker. That is the main obstacle to engaging in youth evangelism in the first place. You may not find much common ground with the youths. But you decide to step out despite feeling inadequate. If you wait for a prophetic vision or some extraordinary events to confirm your calling, these might never happen.[36]

Confirmation of the call comes through the continuous empowerment for the ministry work, regardless of the intensity of our emotional experience of the Spirit's presence. We make the most of the Spirit's endowment of power when we show consistency in reaching out to the young people who are usually fickle and inconsistent themselves. The ministry leader continues:

> The experience of Spirit-empowerment might be charged emotionally or not, but it does not change the validity of Spirit's commission. There are moments when we feel passionate and moments when elation gives way to feelings of discouragement and burn-out. The decisive moment in our ministry work comes when we realize that it is a matter of remaining faithful to what God revealed to us as his will.[37]

Following in the footsteps of the Lord's Servant from Isaiah 42, we perceive Spirit empowerment "as a capacity, a persevering or persistence in fulfilling God's mission, especially in the face of adversaries, difficulties and even persecution. . . .The crux of the empowerment is located in tenacity and resolution to accomplish a God-given task."[38] The quality of our service in the newness of the Spirit (cf. Rom 7:6) is not dependent on some fluctuating emotional states but instead characterized by our unwavering obedience to his guidance. "Empowerment carries with it an obligation: that we commit ourselves"[39] and make ourselves available to the Lord, who is always available for us. We keep showing up, often despite feelings of discouragement and pointlessness, "being confident of this, that he who began a good work in us will bring it to completion until the day of Christ Jesus" (Phil 1:6).

Empowered in Weakness

This brings us to the most countercultural aspect of our Spirit-empowered ministry. Against the grain of the culture of success that runs rampant in many strands of the prosperity gospel, we believe "that empowerment is to minister in weakness to the weak."[40] Like Paul the Apostle, to the weak, we become weak, that we might win the weak. We have become all things to all people, that by all means, we might bring some to salvation (1 Cor 9:22, paraphrased). We agree to become vulnerable to create an intimate space for meaningful encounters that can lead people to Christ, who assumed the condition of a servant to restore the realm of our intimacy with the Father (Phil 2):

"Stewardship is the willingness to work on ourselves first, to stay in intimate contact with those around us, to own our doubts and limitations, and make them part of our dialogue with others. Our humanness is defined more by our vulnerability than by our strengths."[41]

If we want to bring the divine word of salvation into people's lives, we must first learn to embrace our fragile human condition as the chosen vessel of God's power that is perfected in our weakness (2 Cor 4:7, 12:9).

At the Mercy of the Spirit's Guidance

We are aware that some students coming to our café or a school retreat would never set foot in a church. At the same time, we encourage youth to delve deeper into the Bible and engage with their own faith communities.

We try to make our retreat program enjoyable and relevant. We include talks on wellness-related topics such as resilience or unlocking one's potential. At the same time, we focus on the scriptural *kerygma* presented in a gospel talk that is the highlight of our retreat program. We would never compromise the truth of the gospel for the sake of ill-conceived "soul-winning." One of the students participating in our retreat shared the following testimony: "I am not a religious person, but this retreat made me want to have faith and let me know that God is there as a support system whenever I need to talk to him."[42]

As simple as it may sound, the primary objective of our one-day retreat is to present a relational, caring God and encourage the students to try and get to know him personally. As one of our retreat leaders testifies:

> Being dependent on the Holy Spirit is something we are all very aware of. There have been countless moments, while on retreat, that we find ourselves at the mercy of His guidance to know what to say and when to say it. We proclaim the gospel at the end of every retreat, knowing that it's only God who can speak to a student's heart.[43]

The Holy Spirit also directed our footsteps through the precarious times of the Covid-19 pandemic. In January 2020, we first learned about the possibility of contributing our retreat program to the secondary school curriculum. The Spirit led us through every step of the complicated application process that resulted in recognizing our retreat team as contributors to the curriculum. That development turned out to be providential: a few months later, the whole country went into another lockdown. Having been recognized as essential education workers, we were able to continue to reach out to the schools across the country despite the travel restrictions. Carrying out the Great Commission is indeed an essential work, and it is the role of the Spirit to arrange the circumstances for it to be continued.

An Irresistible Call to Action

One of our team members remembers her first encounter with the ministry:

> As a teenager, I went to a healing service hosted by *An Tobar Nua*. I felt loved for who I was, as if I was the only person in the world. I received so much loving attention. *An Tobar Nua* became for me the place to go to when things got difficult. It also helped me get engaged in my home church. What mattered most was that I knew I was developing meaningful relationships with other

> Christians. I did not even need any words, for kindness and acceptance were convincing enough. If it was not for *An Tobar Nua*, I would never have drawn closer to God.[44]

It was the beginning of a life journey. Over a decade later, she is a Spirit-empowered retreat leader sharing the gospel and her personal testimony of that life-changing encounter with God on a daily basis. The experience of unconditional love and meaningful relationships developed in *An Tobar Nua* in the days of her youth yielded the hundredfold fruit of the Spirit, manifested in her dedication to evangelism and passionate love shown to the thousands of students around Ireland:

> Years later I felt the sense of irresistible calling: 'You need to go back to *An Tobar Nua* and share your story.' God was speaking even in my dreams and, despite my reluctance and against my own plans, the Spirit was insistent and gave me the desire to accept this ministry opportunity. That was the experience of encountering the Holy Spirit I could not deny. God could not have been any clearer that he wants me here.[45]

The Spirit blows where he wishes and calls whomever he chooses to complete the remaining task of the Great Commission. There is no point in trying to resist his call.

In lieu of Conclusion: Spirit-Empowered Life and Mission

Having analyzed the example of *An Tobar Nua*, we need to "raise theological and practical questions about the relationship between and consistency of Spirit-empowered mission and Spirit-empowered life"[46] and its significance for the remaining task of the Great Commission. The Spirit can empower us for the work of ministry insofar as he transforms our hearts, enabling us to walk in the newness of life (cf. Rom 6:5). "Inner transformation affects a change of lifestyle that also transforms the social environment."[47] Such a transformation is capable of restoring the eroded meaning of existence.

Rooted in the trinitarian reality of divine life, the Great Commission is a missional task focused on fostering relational, service-oriented discipleship. "The Great Commission involves the making of disciples according to the relational life of the triune God. . . . Discipleship inherently involves interface with, ministry amid, and service to the world in all of its dimensions."[48] Only those who display the attitude of a disciple are prepared to go and make disciples of all nations. Due to its relational nature, evangelism is ultimately a matter of credible witness. Through our compassionate and worshipful witness, we can participate in the work of new creation initiated on the cross and carried out by the Spirit in the age of the church. "Compassionate witness is cruciform and Spirit-empowered, directed to the glory of the Father. Worshipful witness participates perseveringly and steadfastly in the Spirit's work of renewing the creation in anticipation of the eschatological lordship of Christ."[49] The Spirit-empowered leaders of the future will be those countercultural servants of the Lord "who dare to claim their irrelevance in the contemporary world as a divine vocation that allows them to enter into a deep solidarity with the anguish underlying all the glitter of success and to bring the light of Jesus there."[50] Servanthood lies at the heart of a mission-driven by the individual and corporate witness to the compassionate love of the Father reflected in the Spirit-led life of Christ's disciples.

Notes

1 Shawn Small, *An Tobar Nua—The New Well: The Unlikely Story of An Uncommon Community* (Addison, TX: HIS Publishing Group, 2017), 55.

2 All interviews were conducted by author and remain confidential unless otherwise stated.

3 Lalsangkima Pachuau, *World Christianity: A Historical and Theological Introduction* (Nashville: Abingdon Press, 2018), 29, 35. The West is no longer Christianity's center of gravity which has shifted to the Majority World. See Todd Johnson and Sun Young Chung, "Christianity's Centre of Gravity, A. D. 33–2100," in Todd Johnson and Kenneth Ross, eds, *Atlas of Global Christianity* (Edinburgh: Edinburgh University Press, 2010), 50–51.

4 Charles Taylor, *A Secular Age* (Cambridge, MA: Harvard University Press, 2007), 716–717, 552.

5 Taylor, *A Secular Age*, 552.

6 Karol Tarnowski, *Tropy Myślenia Religijnego* [Tropes of Religious Thinking] (Kraków: Instytut Myśli Józefa Tischnera, 2009), 292.

7 Paul Tillich, *Dynamics of Faith* (New York: Harper & Row, 1958), 4.

8 "Not only is traditional Christianity weakening in Europe, but it is indeed being reinforced and reinvigorated by Southern churches by means of

immigration and evangelization," Philip Jenkins, *The Next Christendom: The Coming of Global Christianity* (Oxford: Oxford University Press, 2011), 238.

9   Small, *An Tobar Nua—The New Well*, 81.

10 Small, *An Tobar Nua—The New Well*, 149.

11 Chris E. W. Green, *Sanctifying Interpretation: Vocation, Holiness, and Scripture*, 2nd ed. (Cleveland, TN: CPT Press, 2020), 25.

12 Green, *Sanctifying Interpretation*, 104.

13 Taken from the mission statement of *An Tobar Nua*, an outreach of Foundation in Christ Ministries. https://foundationinchrist.org/about/mission-statement, accessed November 1, 2021.

14 Interview with Mike Shortt, Galway, April 5, 2021.

15 David G. Firth, "The Spirit and Leadership: Testimony, Empowerment, and Purpose," in David G. Firth and Paul D. Wegner,eds., *Presence, Power, and Promise: The Role of the Spirit of God in the Old Testament* (Downers Grove, IL: IVP Academic, 2011), 264.

16 Anthony C. Thiselton, *New International Greek Testament Commentary: The First Epistle to the Corinthians* (Grand Rapids: Eerdmans, 2000), 976. The noun *diakrisis* appears in 1 Cor 12:10 and Heb 5:14, while the verb form *diakrino* is used by Paul in 1 Cor 6:5, 11:31, 14:29.

17 Frank D. Macchia, "Signs of Grace in a Graceless World," in Vinson Synan, ed., *Sprit-Empowered Christianity in the 21st Century* (Lake Mary, FL: Charisma House, 2011), 146.

18 John D. Zizioulas, *Being and Communion: Studies in Personhood and the Church* (Crestwood, NY: St Vladimir's Seminary Press, 1997), 112.

19 Amos Yong, *Spirit—Word—Community: Theological Hermeneutics in Trinitarian Perspective* (Eugene, OR: Wipf & Stock Publishers, 2006), 130.

20 Veli-Matti, *Pneumatology: The Holy Spirit in Ecumenical, International, and Contextual Perspective* (Grand Rapids: Baker Academic, 2002), 121. The author perceives the Holy Spirit as the gift of God giving his very self to us. "The Holy Spirit is always in his essence the gift of God, God as the self-giving God… God giving himself to the world," Ibid., 45.

21 Kärkkäinen, *Pneumatology*, 45.

22 Gordon D. Fee, *New International Commentary on the New Testament: The First Epistle to the Corinthians*, rev. ed. (Grand Rapids, MI: Eerdmans, 2014), 820.

23 Frank D. Macchia, "Justification and the Spirit: An Appreciative Interaction with N. T. Wright," in Janet Meyer Everts and Jeffrey S. Lamp, eds., *Pentecostal Theology and the Theological Vision of N. T. Wright: A Conversation* (Cleveland, TN: CPT Press, 2015), 268–269.

24 Arden C. Autry, "A Response to Dr. Craig Keener's Presentation 'The Spirit and Biblical Interpretation,'" *Spiritus: ORU Journal of Theology* 4:1 (Spring 2019): 46.

25 For a detailed account of the Spirit-guided journey of discernment that led Currys to the West of Ireland, see Small, *An Tobar Nua—The New Well*, 47–73.

26 "If, as Augustine said, the sign of the presence of the Holy Spirit is 'love of the unity,' we need to say that the Holy Spirit is at work today above all where we find lively enthusiasm for Christian unity, where people work for it, and where they are willing to suffer to achieve it. In the beginning, in Cornelius's house, God gave his Spirit to pagans, and the outward signs were exactly the same as they had been for the apostles at Pentecost. God did this to persuade Peter, and the whole church with him, to accept pagan Gentiles too into the communion of the one and only church. In our own day, God is giving the Holy Spirit to believers belonging to the different churches in the same way, and often with exactly the same outward manifestations, for the very same purpose: to persuade us to accept one another in the love of the Spirit and to set out together on the road to full unity." Raniero Cantalamessa, *Come, Creator Spirit: Meditations on the Veni Creator*, trans. Denis and Marlene Barrett (Collegeville, MI: Liturgical Press, 2008), 143–144.

27 Arthur F. Glasser, *Announcing the Kingdom: The Story of God's Mission in the Bible* (Grand Rapids: Baker Academic, 2008), 310.

28 Max Turner, "Spiritual Gifts and Spiritual Formation in 1 Corinthians and Ephesians," *Journal of Pentecostal Theology* 22 (2013), 197.

29 Craig S. Keener, *New Cambridge Bible Commentary: 1—2 Corinthians*, (Cambridge: Cambridge University Press, 2005), 107.

30 As we know, some Corinthians presumptuously believed to be more spiritually gifted than others. "They each possess at least one charism, but no one has all the charismata. With this principle, Paul counters any claim to the exclusive possession of the Spirit." Raymond F. Collins, *First Corinthians*, 7 (Collegeville, MN: The Liturgical Press, 1999), 451.

31 Jack Levison, "The Holy Spirit in I Corinthians," *Interpretation: A Journal of Bible and Theology* 72:1 (2018), 37.

32 Cantalamessa, *Come, Creator Spirit*, 84.

33 Cantalamessa, *Come, Creator Spirit*, 84.

34 Foundation in Christ Ministries, *An Tobar Nua Café Evangelism Guide* (Galway, 2021), 2.

35 Nicholas Thomas Wright, *Paul and the Faithfulness of God* (London: SPCK, 2013), 758–759.

36 Interview with a ministry leader, Galway, February 23, 2021.

37 Interview with a ministry leader, Galway, February 23, 2021.

38 Wonsuk Ma, "Isaiah," in.Trevor J. Burke and Keith Warrington, eds., *Biblical Theology of the Holy Spirit* (London: SPCK, 2014), 37.

39 Peter Block, *Stewardship: Choosing Service Over Self-Interest* (San Francisco: Berrett-Koehler Publishers, 2013), 46.

40 Ma, "Isaiah," 37.

41 Block, *Stewardship*, 53.

42 Feedback left by a participant of *An Tobar Nua* school retreat, Galway, November 10, 2020.

43 Interview with a retreat leader, Galway, March 1, 2021.

44 Interview with a retreat leader, Galway, March 26, 2021.

45 Interview with a retreat leader, Galway, March 26, 2021.

46 Wonsuk Ma and Julie C. Ma, "Missiology: Evangelization, Holistic Ministry, and Social Justice," in Wolfgang Vonday, ed., *Routledge Handbook of Pentecostal Theology* (London: Routledge, 2020), 282.

47 Ma and Ma, "Missiology," 285.

48 Amos Yong and Jonathan A. Anderson, *Renewing Christian Theology: Systematics for a Global Christianity* (Waco, TX: Baylor University Press, 2014), 242.

49 Yong and Anderson, *Renewing Christian Theology*, 242.

50 Henri Nouwen, *In the Name of Jesus: Reflections on Christian Leadership* (New York: Crossroad Publishing, 2002), 22.

18 Mass Healing Evangelism: The Unique Contribution of the Spirit-Empowered Movement to Evangelism

Daniel C. King

Abstract

This article explores mass healing evangelism by Spirit-empowered evangelists as a unique methodology for reaching people for Christ. It examines the origins of this model in the ministry of T. L. Osborn and its implementation through the ministry of Reinhard Bonnke, perhaps the greatest Pentecostal evangelists of the twentieth century. It looks at the reasons why this model is effective in the Global South. Finally, the article highlights a case study of the effectiveness of this unique approach, with research from a crusade conducted by the author in the nation of Brazil that tested how healing and evangelism were wedded together as an effective ministry strategy.

Introduction

Empowered21 exists as a global network of Spirit-empowered ministers with the mission to reach the world with the gospel of Jesus Christ. In the quest to "Finish the task," Empowered21 scholars are wrestling with theological issues related to the great commission. This study seeks to enter this discussion by exploring a unique methodology of evangelism: the healing crusade or healing "en mass."[1] In the context of developing nations where medical resources are limited, the Spirit-empowered practice of emphasizing the healing power of God has proved to be an effective way to attract people to evangelistic events.[2] As Candy Gunther Brown has pointed out, outside of North America, 80–90 percent of first-generation Christians attribute their conversions primarily to divine healing.[3] Advertising miracles is a different kind of "attractional" model used to reach people, particularly in the Global South. This model of evangelism has contributed significantly to Pentecostalism becoming the fastest-growing segment of Christianity in the Majority World.

This article will explore mass healing evangelism by Spirit-empowered evangelists as a unique methodology for reaching people for Christ. It will explore the origins of this model and its implementation through the ministry of Reinhard Bonnke, perhaps the greatest Pentecostal evangelist of the twentieth century. It will also explore the reasons why this model is effective in the Global South. Finally, as a case study of the effectiveness of this unique approach, research from a crusade conducted by the author in the nation of Brazil will test how healing and evangelism were wedded together as an effective ministry strategy.

Spirit-Empowered Healing Evangelism

The gospel of healing has always been an essential part of the ethos of Pentecostal spirituality. Inherited from the nineteenth-century healing movements, Pentecostals proclaimed the "Four-fold" gospel of Jesus as Savior, Healer, Spirit-baptizer, and soon coming King.[4] Early Pentecostal healing evangelists such as Marie Woodworth-Etter (1844–1924), John G. Lake (1870–1935), F. F. Bosworth (1877–1958), Aimee Semple McPherson (1890–1944), and Smith Wigglesworth (1859–1947) implemented the practice of praying for the sick during evangelistic campaigns. Some of their meetings boasted several hundred to over ten thousand believers in attendance.

While most Pentecostals preached divine healing, perhaps the most significant early Pentecostal healing evangelist was F. F. Bosworth (1877–1958). Bosworth's classic book, *Christ the Healer,* originally published in 1924, has seen multiple reprints over the years.[5] In Ottawa, Canada, in the 1930s, he conducted a campaign that filled an 11,000-seat auditorium. Many miracles were reported during this campaign, and people brought the sick in cars, ambulances, and even hearses.[6] The success of his large-scale crusades propelled Bosworth to become the prototype for the explosion of evangelists during the healing revival in the 1950s.[7]

Bosworth is an important figure in the development of mass healing evangelism because of his mentorship of many of the evangelists associated with Gordon Lindsey's *Voice of Healing* magazine in the 1950s–1960s, including William Branham (1909–1965), A. A. Allen (1911–1970), Oral Roberts (1918–2009), and T. L. Osborn (1923–2013).[8] Each of these noted healing evangelists began as Pentecostal missionaries or evangelists. They became convinced that by preaching the "full gospel" of salvation and healing, they could attract people to their revivals and demonstrate the reality of Jesus Christ in a tangible way. Gordon Lindsey, the architect behind the healing movement, wrote, "[h]ealing the sick is a Christ ordained method for evangelization around the world."[9]

At first, *Voice of Healing* evangelists followed the traditional Pentecostal methodology of laying hands on each individual who needed healing, either in a healing line or a healing tent. However, the increasing popularity and the growing crowds filling ever-larger revival tents created a new dilemma. How does a preacher lay hands on everyone when the crowds consist of thousands of people at a time? William Branham and Oral Roberts, perhaps the exemplars of mass healing evangelism, both used this method of praying for crowds one person at a time.[10] This model, while effective for those who received prayer, was not sustainable for the evangelists and could not accommodate the large numbers of people who needed prayer.

Healing en Masse

The challenge of praying for the healing of large crowds led to innovation by Tommy Lee (1923–2013) and Daisy Osborn (1924–1995), missionary evangelists who primarily conducted healing crusades internationally, particularly in Africa. T. L. and Daisy went to India as missionaries in 1945 at the ages of twenty and twenty-one, but quickly faced disappointment over the lack of Hindu and Muslim converts and returned home disappointed after only ten months.[11] In their desperation, T. L. Osborn discovered the key to effective evangelism: "people must have proof of the gospel and evidence that Jesus is alive."[12] This led Osborn to question his methodology. Osborn describes in his questions in his book *Healing En Masse*:

> Is it necessary to lay hands on the sick as a point of contact for setting a time to believe? Was it God's plan that sick people form long lines to be healed? What is the solution to the problem of ministering healing to large audiences of suffering people without the system of numbered prayer cards and prayer lines?[13]

In addition to these questions, Osborn had a conversation with F. F. Bosworth about the need for a methodology that would meet the needs of the masses.[14] Bosworth asked Osborn, "If I give an altar call and fifty people respond, and I lead them in a prayer of salvation, how many of them are saved?" Osborn replied, "All of them." Bosworth continued, "So if I give a call for healing and fifty people respond, and I lead them in a prayer for healing, how many of them can God heal?" Osborn asked, "Why not all of them?" Because of this conversation, the idea to pray a single mass prayer for healing was born.[15]

At his next crusade in Flint, Michigan, in June 1949, Osborn tried his new methodology.[16] He wrote, "God seemed to say to me, 'Why do you limit my power? I can heal ten thousand as easily as one.'"[17] Osborn explained his reasoning:

> If one sufferer stands before me in a prayer line, I lay my hands on that one and pray to God. I believe he hears my prayer [and] the sufferer is made whole. That is proof that God has heard my prayer. . . . Since I can pray and God hears and answers my prayer, why do I not ask God to perform a thousand miracles at the same time? If he is God, his power is unlimited! If he can do one miracle, he can do a thousand miracles at the same time![18]

Osborn reasoned that if salvation can be accepted by the masses, why can't healing?[19] And it worked: as he prayed a mass prayer for the deaf, he reported, "All of those present received their hearing immediately, except three. By the next day, they too had recovered."[20] Osborn concluded:

> I knew that Mass Evangelism was the only way to reach the world for Jesus. I knew we must demonstrate the power of Christ on a mass scale if the millions of heathen souls are to witness Christ's power. I knew that no person could pray for the masses individually. HEALING EN MASSE is the only answer.[21]

Over the next few years, Osborn developed his very simple methodology for healing en masse. Osborn found that through testimonies of people who were healed and a simple message about the power of Jesus, sick people would be healed. Over his seven decades of ministry, Osborn's method of praying a mass prayer for the sick at evangelistic campaigns was adopted by many other healing evangelists, including Aril Edvardsen (1938–2008) from Norway, Benson Idahosa (1938–1998) from Nigeria, Robert Kayanja (1962–present) from Uganda, D. G. S. Dhinakaran (1935–2008) from India, and Peter Youngren (1954–present) from Canada. But no one has more successfully utilized Osborn's "healing en mass" concept than Reinhard Bonnke (1940–2019).

Reinhard Bonnke and Mass Healing Evangelism

Today, there is no one more recognized for mass healing evangelism than Reinhard Bonnke. He is an exemplar of Spirit-empowered evangelism. Since the 1980s, Bonnke has demonstrated the effectiveness of healing evangelism as a model, particularly in Africa, where his crusades often draw crowds of over one million. For example, in Lagos, Nigeria, on November 12, 2000, 1.6 million people came to a single crusade meeting that Bonnke held.[22] In this six-day crusade, over 6 million people heard the gospel message, and 1.1 million made faith commitments to Jesus.[23] The effectiveness of merging healing and evangelism as a tool for bringing people to Christ in Africa can be seen in the over 78 million documented decisions for Christ in the ministry of Bonnke.[24]

Reinhard Bonnke and his wife Anni accepted the call to be missionaries in Africa in 1967. After being assigned to the country of Lesotho, Bonnke quickly became frustrated at the low number of salvations produced by traditional missionary methods. A critical moment came when Bonnke was exposed to T. L. Osborn's method of healing "en mass" and realized it was the key to reaching Africa with the gospel.[25] God showed him a vision of a "blood-washed Africa," and he began to proclaim, "All of Africa shall be saved, from Cape Town to Cairo."[26]

An Effective Model of Evangelism

Over the past four decades, Bonnke has refined and improved upon Osborn's methodology of mass evangelism to become perhaps the greatest Pentecostal evangelist of the twentieth century. Yet, despite Bonnke's incredible impact on Spirit-empowered evangelism and the continent of Africa, few academic studies have evaluated his impact. We would like to suggest several reasons why Bonnke's implementation of this uniquely Spirit-empowered model of evangelism has been so successful.

First, Bonnke uses miracles as an attractional method to introduce people to the gospel of Jesus Christ. Miracles are the primary "attractional" draw for people who attend his meetings to hear the gospel. As Paul Gifford has observed, this is seen primarily in Bonnke's advertising strategy which is focused more on God's power to heal than on the salvation message.[27] Miracles take center stage in Bonnke's crusades, not only in his preaching, but through the countless testimonies of people who have been healed that are given in the crusades and fill his advertising literature. The "en mass" phenomenon is only possible because of the possibility of miracles.

A second factor that makes Bonnke's method particularly effective is the "bigness" of his popularity itself, which perpetuates a sense of legitimacy and facilitates the ability to pull a large group of people.[28] Because he focuses on felt needs, i.e., healing in a country plagued by poverty and diseases, his appeal is broadly recognized. There is a strong draw in African culture to see the spectacle of signs and wonders from the "powerful man of God," a key factor in the growth of some of the largest ministers in Africa.[29] Although some criticize the method of "come and receive your miracle," the "bigness" factor is directly a result of the unique Pentecostal spirituality on display in his meetings.[30] But this phenomenon is not necessarily unique to Africa, as Bonnke's model of doing evangelistic campaigns has worked in other contexts such as India,[31] Brazil,[32] Jamaica,[33] Argentina,[34] Singapore,[35] Australia,[36] Germany,[37] and the United States. Vinson Synan notes, Bonnke is largely effective because "Everyone goes to Bonnke crusades—Catholic, Muslims, people from all religions, and those with no religion."[38] In this way, it is not so much Bonnke himself; rather, it is the model he has implemented, focused on uniquely Pentecostal aesthetics, that has been successful. This is seen in the growing number of indigenous itinerate mass healing crusades within African contexts.[39]

A third factor is Bonnke's effectiveness is his ability to mobilize his campaigns. Peter Vandenberg, the Executive Vice President of Christ for All Nations, says, "To be effective [in doing crusades], you need to have systems, you need to have structure. You need to have integrity. You need to have money, and you need to have opportunity."[40] As Ezekiel O. Ajani notes, "None of Bonnke's crusades is an accident of history."[41] Each location and date is meticulously planned and organized by the "Central Working Committee" that works according to specific organizational manuals. Each detail of the crusade is planned carefully to ensuring the success of the event, even down to the "expert" who mounts the large banners around the city in such a way as for it not to be easily stolen. The team has a detailed advertising strategy that includes full-color posters, hundreds of thousands of handbills, and hired taxis with PA systems announcing the meeting all precede any campaign.[42] Each crusade costs an average of $900,000.[43] All this is possible because of Bonnke's well-funded ministry from outside the crusading context, primarily by other Spirit-empowered ministries and pastors.[44]

A Truly Spirit-Empowered Model of Evangelism?

In what sense does Bonnke's ministry stand as an example of Spirit-empowered evangelism? Two important points come to mind. First, Bonnke is deeply dependent upon the Holy Spirit in his ministry. Bonnke was marked by his upbringing as the son of a Pentecostal pastor in Krempe, Germany. Bonnke was baptized in the Holy Spirit and spoke in tongues for the first time at a revival meeting at the age of eleven.[45] As a boy, Bonnke was teased by his Lutheran classmates for being a "tongue talker." He writes, "Pentecostals were seen as primitive people, religious Neanderthals, a knuckle-dragging sect that only existed because of its ignorance."[46] He attended an Evangelical Bible school in Wales, where speaking in tongues was forbidden.[47] The persecution he received there helped develop in him a resilience to criticism and the boldness to do what God told him to do, despite what others thought of him. His crusade preaching stayed centered in the full gospel message of salvation, the invitation to receive baptism in the Holy Spirit, and an emphasis on miracles.[48] Rather than hiding his Pentecostal identity for the sake of drawing crowds, as is so often the case in seeker-oriented evangelism in the United States, it was the strength of his Spirit-empowered identity that made his ministry uniquely effective around the world.

Beyond simply having a Pentecostal identity, Bonnke's relationship to the Holy Spirit was real and dynamic. Without the Holy Spirit, he knew he could not be an effective evangelist at all. He says: "The Holy Spirit makes evangelism possible. Without the Holy Spirit, the Great Commission is only an impossible dream."[49] The method of using miracles as an attraction for evangelism wasn't a gimmick. He truly believed that miracles were a byproduct of the real presence of Jesus in the believer. This was his goal, whether for personal evangelism or large crusades: put Jesus on display through the power of the Holy Spirit inside you. He says, "No preaching of our own, however brilliant, brings miracles...the divine purpose in Holy Ghost preaching is nothing less than the miraculous."[50]

Second, the Spirit-empowered aspects of Bonnke's mass evangelism model extended beyond miracles to other aspects of non-Western spirituality, including confrontation with the spirit realm. Bonnke's crusades were filled with confrontational rhetoric, from deliverance from the demons of disease to the power over witch doctors.[51] This emphasis was to such a degree that Pentecostal historian, Grant Wacker, labeled Bonnke's portrayal of God as more of a "God of terror" than most Westerners are comfortable with.[52] However, for African spirituality, the reality of evil spirits is embedded in the worldview. Thus, Spirit-empowered Christianity offers both eternal salvation and power over the works of Satan on earth. As Clifton Clark points out, "Salvation includes redemption from the powers of the devil and his demons since these powers are, ultimately, the cause of sickness (both physical and psychological), poverty, and other material and socioeconomic ills that keep human beings from experiencing the abundant life promised by God."[53] This means there is no artificial bifurcation of salvation and miracles; rather, they are two sides of the same coin. This, too, is a unique contribution of Spirit-empowered Christianity.

Of course, some may raise the objection that mass healing evangelism is simply Western Christianity exported to the global South. Concerns over the prosperity gospel and other Western ideas have drawn criticism of Bonnke and other Spirit-empowered evangelists. However, we would argue that the Spirit-empowered healing evangelism model is effective precisely because it is by nature non-Western in orientation. As Gifford points out, while Evangelical evangelists focus primarily on spiritual needs—such as the need for peace with God or forgiveness of sin—Spirit-empowered evangelists have a more holistic approach, appealing to the physical and emotional needs of their audiences. Second, the Spirit-Empowered model of evangelism is effective in Majority World contexts because the supernatural and natural are perceived to be much closer together. Healing of the body, exorcism of evil spirits, the presence of invisible angels, and spiritual blessings are very real concepts because of the spiritual characteristics that already exist in these cultures.[54] Finally, mass healing evangelism closely mirrors Jesus' method of evangelism. While Jesus' miracle ministry was not on the scale of modern evangelists, the emphasis on proclaiming the good news with healing as a sign of the kingdom of God that Christ proclaimed.[55] In this way, the narrative nature of African spirituality has much in common with the Pentecostal worldview. As Clifton Clarke notes, African Christianity is often oral in nature, and scripture is "re-oralized through preaching."[56] The emphasis on testimonies in mass healing evangelism relates well with pre-modern imagination, bringing the miracle stories of the scripture to life before the participant's eyes. Bonnke's example had a big impact on African Pentecostals. For example, Emmanuel Array Gewe, the pastor of World Harvest Church Assemblies of God in Kahama, Tanzania, considers Reinhard Bonnke to be his spiritual father even though he never met him. Gewe regularly preaches on miracles and prays for the sick in his church because of what he has learned from Bonnke's books.[57]

Case Study: A Healing Crusade in Brazil

In order to evaluate the true effectiveness of mass healing evangelism as an effective model of evangelism, one must question whether it is a universal model or simply effective in Africa? To test this, we want to offer a case study of one of my own crusades to demonstrate how the Spirit-empowered practice of praying for healing enhances an evangelistic event. As an evangelist, I have traveled to over seventy nations and done over one hundred healing crusades. I want to focus on a recent meeting I conducted in Caicò, Brazil, in 2018, that emphasized the Spirit-empowered practice of praying a mass prayer for the sick.[58]

Caicó is a city located in Northeast Brazil in the state of Rio Grande do Norte. There are 67,554 people who live in the city.[59] The city has the highest rate of suicide in the state and the third-highest rate of suicide in Brazil. Local pastors identified idolatry and depression as major issues in the region.[60] All nine of the Evangelical churches in the city were invited and participated in the crusade. The total membership of these nine churches equals 1,357, which is about 2 percent of the population of the city of Caicó. A three-day training event for local believers was held in order to train them in how to pray for the sick. To advertise the crusade, we emphasized in our promotions that attendees could "Come and Receive a Miracle."

On Saturday night, an estimated 4,300 people attended the crusade, of which 48.7 percent of those surveyed before the crusade reported that they arrived with some sort of pain or ailment in their bodies. Like the Spirit-empowered evangelists presented in this study, I preached the gospel message that God can forgive sins and heal the physical body.

I prayed a mass prayer for healing for the whole crowd. A total of 641 people filled out decision cards at the crusade indicating they had decided to follow Jesus. According to the post-crusade survey, 78.5 percent of those who came with pain in their bodies felt better after the healing prayer. In a post-crusade survey of 182 people who answered they came with a need for physical healing, 176 (96.7 percent) "strongly agreed" or "agreed" that they had received a miracle.[61] While this does not account for the experience of the whole crowd, the remarkably high number of those surveyed who felt they experienced healing confirms that healing was a felt need for a large number of attendees.

Advertising the possibility of healing through the power of God played an enormous role in convincing people to come to the crusade. On the question, "Why did you come to this meeting?" 55 out of 169 (32.54 percent) respondents on Friday night and 116 out of 460 (25.22 percent) on Saturday night said they came because they needed a miracle. Another 46 out of 169 (27.22 percent) on Friday and 106 out of 460 (23 percent) on Saturday said they came because they wanted to witness miracles.[62] The fact that healing was a major factor for over half of the attendees of the crusade demonstrates that advertising healing is an effective attractional element or "bait" in the evangelist's efforts of "fishing for men."

Healing also played a significant role in the responsiveness of the people to the call for salvation. A total of 641 (14.9 percent) people at the crusade filled out decision cards indicating they had decided to follow Jesus. On the open-ended question, "Why did you pray the salvation prayer?" the need for healing was primary for 98 percent of respondents. Examples of what they wrote include: "Because I needed a miracle," "I needed to be healed," "Because my daughter needed to be healed."[63] This suggests that healing provides a space for people to believe and respond to the call for salvation.

Further Research

Mass healing evangelism has contributed to the growth of global Pentecostalism. As the Pentecostal movement continues to mature, additional theological questions should be examined, such as: Is healing for everyone? What should be done about those who are not healed? If a sick person at a crusade is not healed, does this hinder him or her from getting saved? Will mass evangelism continue to be effective in the future, or will evangelism take a different form? What is the best way to follow up on new believers after a mass evangelism event?

Conclusion

This study set out to explore the development of the methodology of mass healing evangelism and how this method continues to be effective in reaching people with the gospel of Jesus Christ. The case study of the Brazil crusade confirms that the merging of healing and evangelism in the Spirit-empowered movement over the past century continues to be vital to its success. First, healing evangelism is effective because it is attractional. The major reason people came to the Caicó crusade was that they either needed a miracle or they wanted to see a miracle with their own eyes. Other Evangelical methods have worked well for people in the United States, but for those in other countries, Spirit-empowered evangelists emphasize a holistic approach that appeals to more basic needs. Second, healing was not only effective for drawing people; it was a real benefit to those who came. Many of the people who came to the crusade came in search of a miracle and reported that they were healed by God. Not only does healing give people hope in a God who loves them, but it also inspires them to put their faith in Jesus Christ for salvation. Third, the testimonies of healing were effective in convincing others that they should also come to the meeting. This sense of knowing that God is real helps local believers stay committed to sharing their faith with others and can lead to both spiritual and numerical church growth. In the years to come, I believe healing will continue to play a role in the growth of the Spirit-empowered movement around the world.

Notes

1 Daniel D. Isgrigg (Ph.D.), Director of the Holy Spirit Research Center at Oral Roberts University, aided in the development of this study with his insightful questions and helpful feedback.

2 For information on the rise of healing evangelism, see David Edwin Harrell, Jr., *All Things Are Possible: The Healing and Charismatic Revivals in Modern America* (Bloomington, IN: Indiana Univ. Press, 1975).

3 Candy Gunther Brown, ed., *Global Pentecostal and Charismatic Healing* (Oxford: Oxford University Press, 2011), 3.

4 Bernie A. Van De Walle, *The Heart of the Gospel: A.B. Simpson, the Fourfold Gospel, and Late Nineteenth-Century Evangelical Theology* (Eugene: Pickwick Publications, 2009).

5 F. F. Bosworth, *Christ the Healer* (Forest River, IL: F. F. Bosworth, 1924).

6 David J. du Plessis, "A Faithful Pioneer Passes," *Worldwide Revival Magazine*, April 10, 1958, 10.

7 Douglas Jacobsen, *Thinking in the Spirit* (Bloomington: Indiana University Press, 2003), 294.

8 Roscoe Barnes, *F. F. Bosworth: The Man Behind "Christ the Healer"* (Newcastle upon Tyne, UK: Cambridge Scholars, 2009), 5; Jacobsen, Thinking in the Spirit, 294.

9 Gordon Lindsay, *Worldwide Evangelism Through Healing and Miracles* (Dallas: Christ for the Nations, 2015), 7; Dennis Gordon Lindsey, "The History and Global Impact of Christ for the Nations Institute," (D.Min. proj., Oral Roberts University, 2014), 12.

10 Oral Roberts personally laid hands on more than one million people during his healing ministry. See Vinson Synan, "The Pentecostal Roots of Oral Robert's Healing Ministry," *Spiritus: ORU Journal of Theology* 3:2 (2018), 296.

11 Vinson Synan, *The Century of the Holy Spirit* (Nashville: Thomas Nelson, 2001), 332.

12 T. L. Osborn, *Soul Winning* (Tulsa, OK: OSFO, 1963), 403.

13 Osborn, *Healing en Masse*, 11.

14 Barnes, *F.F. Bosworth*, 65, points out that although Osborn was the first to implement healing en mass, it was Bosworth who first talked about the need in 1949.

15 T. L. Osborn, interview by author, Tulsa, April 23, 2010.

16 Osborn, *Healing en Masse*, 11.

17 Osborn, *Healing en Masse*, 11.

18 Osborn, *Healing en Masse*, 12.

19 Osborn, *Healing en Masse*, 13, argues, "I knew that if a thousand people wanted to accept Christ and be saved, I would not pray for each one individually; I would teach them all to call on the Lord and to believe at one time. All who believed would be saved. I knew the same method should be followed in ministering to the sick."

20 Osborn, *Healing en Masse*, 15.

21 Osborn, *Healing en Masse*, 13.

22 Reinhard Bonnke, *Living a Life of Fire*, (Orlando: E-R Productions, 2011), 568.

23 John W. Kennedy, "The Crusader," *Christianity Today* 57:9 (2013), 52.

24 Kennedy, "The Crusader," 50–54. Bonnke keeps a running total of "decisions for Christ" on his website, now totaling over 78 million. See Christ for All Nations, "Reinhard Bonnke: Biography," n.d., n.p., shttps://cfan.org/reinhard-bonnke, accessed July 29, 2019.

25 At the age of fourteen, Bonnke watched Osborn's movie *Black Gold* shown in German churches by Eric Pleuger, and he sought Osborn out for advice in the early stages of his evangelistic ministry (Bonnke, *Living a Life of Fire*, 339).

26 Bonnke, *Living a Life of Fire*, 259.

27 Paul Gifford, "'Africa Shall be Saved:' An Appraisal of Reinhard Bonnke's Pan-African Crusade," *Journal of Religion in Africa* 16 (1987), 68, notes that in the list of benefits in his advertisement, "forgiveness" is mentioned last behind a least a dozen other physical benefits of healing.

28 Ezekiel O. Ajani, "Reinhard Bonnke's Crusades in Nigeria: An Analysis," in David O. Ogungbile and Akintude E. Akinade, eds., *Creativity and Change in Nigerian Christianity* (Lagos, Malthouse Press Limited: 2010), 110.

29 Sylvia Owusu-Ansah and J. Kwabena Asamoah-Gyadu, "Mass Evangelistic Crusades and the Gospel: A Comparative Study of American and African Healing Evangelists," *Ogbomoso Journal of Theology* 18:3 (2013), 72.

30 Kennedy, "The Crusader," 54.

31 Bonnke, *Living a Life of Fire*, 355, 513.

32 Bonnke, *Living a Life of Fire*, 485.

33 Bonnke, *Living a Life of Fire*, 384.

34 Bonnke, *Living a Life of Fire*, 481.

35 Bonnke, *Living a Life of Fire*, 354, 382.

36 Bonnke, *Living a Life of Fire*, 340.

37 Bonnke, *Living a Life of Fire*, 410.

38 Kennedy, "The Crusader," 54.

39 Owusu-Ansah and Asamoah-Gyadu, "Mass Evangelistic Crusades and the Gospel," 55–73.

314 The Remaining Task of the Great Commission

40 Peter Vandenberg, interview by author, Kahama, Tanzania, November 13, 2020.
41 Ajani, "Reinhard Bonnke's Crusades in Nigeria," 114.
42 Ajani, "Reinhard Bonnke's Crusades in Nigeria," 115.
43 Kennedy, "The Crusader," 53.
44 Kennedy, "The Crusader," 53, notes that many American Charismatic ministers have partnered to the sum of hundreds of thousands of dollars to sponsor events.
45 Bonnke, *Living a Life of Fire*, 93.
46 Bonkke, *Living a Life of Fire*, 68.
47 Bonnke, *Living a Life of Fire*, 135.
48 Gifford, "'Africa Shall be Saved,'" 65–92.
49 Reinhard Bonnke, *Holy Spirit: Are We Flammable or Flame Proof* (Orlando: Christ for All Nations, 2017), 34.
50 Reinhard Bonnke, *Evangelism by Fire* (Lake Mary, FL: Charisma House, 2011), 296.
51 Gifford, "'Africa Shall be Saved,'" 74.
52 Kennedy, "The Crusader," 53.
53 Clifton R. Clarke, *Pentecostalism: Insights from Africa and the African Diaspora* (Eugene, OR: Wipf and Stock, 2018), 152.
54 Brown, *Global Pentecostal and Charismatic Healing*, 18.
55 Howard M. Ervin, *Healing: A Sign of the Kingdom* (Peabody: Hendrickson, 2002).
56 Clarke, *Pentecostalism*, 3.
57 Emmanuel Array Gewe, interview by author, Kahama, Tanzania, November 12, 2020.
58 The crusade took place on the evenings of June 1–2, 2018.
59 "Data of the Municipality," n.d., n.p., https://caico.rn.gov.br/omunicipio.php, accessed July 16, 2019.
60 Interview with local pastors, by author, May 28, 2018, Caicó, Brazil.
61 Daniel King, "Appraising the Impact of an Evangelistic Campaign in Caicó, Brazil," (D.Min. proj., Oral Roberts University, 2019), 153–155.
62 King, "Appraising the Impact," 158–160.
63 King, "Appraising the Impact," 152–154.

19 The Impact of Evangelism and Prayer: Pentecostals in Central America, with Emphasis on Guatemala and Honduras

Mireya Alvarez

Abstract

The purpose of this chapter is to review the representations of evangelism and prayer prevailing in Latino churches within the Pentecostal milieu of the Latin American continent. Pentecostal scholars concede that the new center of Christianity is Africa, Asia, and Latin America. This study will focus particularly on the emerging characteristics of evangelism and the role of prayer in Central America within the context of Guatemala and Honduras.

Introduction

Andrew Walls stated:

> ...there has been a massive southward shift of the center of gravity of the Christian world so that the representative Christian lands now appear to be in Latin America, Sub-Saharan Africa, and other parts of the southern continents. This means that Third World theology is now likely to be the representative Christian theology...[1]

It is estimated that at least three-quarters of Pentecostals and Charismatics are found in the global South. The number of Pentecostals-Charismatics worldwide was estimated at 669 million in 2017, which is over one-fourth of the world's Christian population.[2] In a period of one hundred years, Latin America transitioned from being a neglected continent, excluded from the 1910 Edinburgh mission conference[3] to a continent where diverse Evangelical churches and organizations implemented evangelism and mission strategies contributing to phenomenal church growth. It is undeniable that in one hundred years, the development of Evangelical/Pentecostal churches has transformed the religious landscape of Latin America.

Numerical Growth

Latin America has experienced explosive numerical growth within the Pentecostal communities. One Central American nation in particular, Guatemala, holds one of the highest growth rates of Evangelical churches in Latin America. Guatemala has a population of about 16 million. The percentage of Evangelicals was 25.4 percent in 2003. By 2013, 40 percent of the population was considered evangelical. There are about 40,000 churches in the nation.[4] Besides engaging in evangelism, Evangelicals promote educational efforts, and medical and community outreaches.

Allan H. Anderson discusses the "multiple origins" of the Pentecostal revival in the early twentieth century.[5] Precisely such a revival occurred in 1932 in Totonicapán, a village in the Western mountainous region of Guatemala. Humble believers in a Methodist church received the baptism in the Holy Spirit with the evidence of speaking in tongues. Those who were baptized in the Spirit left the Methodist church and became associated with the work of missionaries of a Pentecostal denomination based in Cleveland, Tennessee. The fire of revival remained strong in the area, and indigenous workers went by foot and empty-handed throughout the mountain villages preaching the gospel. Many signs and wonders occurred in the Totonicapán church and in the places where they preached and established churches. The indigenous workers evangelized in their mother tongue, K'iche' Maya. Evangelism and church planting were mainly carried out in unsophisticated forms and in a Pentecostal fashion. Despite the presence of North American missionaries in Guatemala, the local workers gave impetus to many congregations where the local Mayan languages were spoken. The Totonicapán church recently celebrated its eighty-eighth anniversary on April 13, 2020. The church is part of the "Iglesia de Dios Evangelio Completo" (Church of God, Cleveland, TN).

From 1960 to 1996, a brutal civil war targeted relations between the Guatemalan army and a rural-based guerrilla uprising. The oppression of the population increased and there were cases where pastors also lost their lives to attacks from either the military or the guerilla forces. It is estimated that the army destroyed 441 villages over a two-year period, and the violence moved into urban areas, including the capital. The repression grew worse during the 1980s. In spite of the circumstances, church workers continued to evangelize, and Guatemala experienced church growth.

The following tables show the numerical growth of churches and members in Central America of the "Iglesia de Dios Evangelio Completo."

Table 1: Churches and Church Members in Central America, 2019[6]

COUNTRY	CHURCHES	MEMBERS
Guatemala	3,055	331,783
Honduras	1,454	94,826
El Salvador	410	40,483
Nicaragua	834	75,600
Costa Rica	493	46,065
Panama	324	22,307
Belize	21	1,584
TOTAL	6,591	612,648

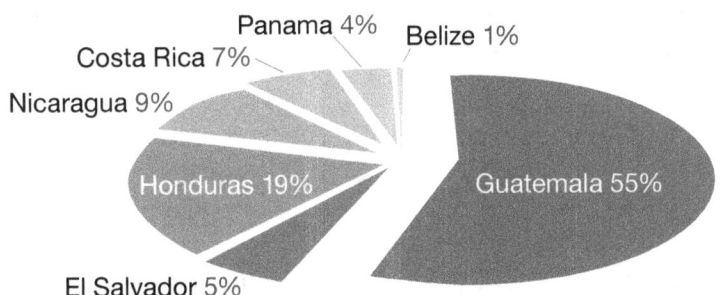

Table 2. Comparative Church Growth 2019[7]

Honduran Pastors and Evangelism

Honduran society is plagued with political instability. Organized crime has increased dramatically and there is a high murder rate that has escalated since the 1990s. In 2018, thousands of Hondurans traveled north in "caravans" that attracted worldwide attention. Men and women begin to look North as a way to find labor and send money back home to their families. The social and political circumstances seem hopeless for thousands of unemployed Hondurans. Sadly, corruption prevails in Honduran government operations, as seen in bribery scandals in the national health and education agencies. Meanwhile, the poor get poorer and desperate. All these pressures are a push factor for many people to seek migration. People want a better future for their children, although it may mean working sacrificially and facing discrimination in the North.

In Tegucigalpa, Honduras, a city of one million people, there are several growing congregations and pastors who have become public figures. There are pastoral organizations; the main one is known as Confraternidad Evangélica de Honduras (Evangelical Fellowship of Honduras) was founded in 1990. This organization has been sought by several Honduran presidents over the past twenty years as an advisory board to the anti-corruption agency of Honduras.

Growing churches have strong evangelism outreaches and are present in the media, radio, television, and social media. Prayer is emphasized in church meetings. In public meetings, prayers abound for the peace, prosperity, and stability of the nation. One local pastor, who is also a medical doctor, began preaching in a small building in the capital city. In 2015, the church constructed a large building on the outskirts of South Tegucigalpa. The church is called "Iglesia Unción, Poder, y Avivamiento" (Anointing, Power and Revival Church). His congregation now reports over 5,000 members. It is known as a praying church with bible studies in home cell groups.[8]

There are Pentecostal churches in Honduras pastored by women ministers. One denomination in Tegucigalpa has ten female pastors with congregations between 200 to 4,000 members.[9] There are also several outstanding Honduran female pastors who are highly esteemed and considered role models due to their loyal commitment to the church. Their preaching is carried out with authority and in a classical Pentecostal way. Through preaching and teaching, they emphasize a personal encounter with God, healing, speaking in tongues, prayer, the gifts of the Spirit, and deliverance.

Women in the church usually make up more than 50 percent of the members. They are given the opportunity to preach, pray, and evangelize in home groups. Through these events, women are trained in practical skills, including public speaking, which increases a sense of confidence in being a leader. It is common and acceptable for women to participate in leadership roles in this context. Women seem to become more independent in the home and in the public domain. Males shift away from drinking, gambling, and adulterous relationships.[10] Pentecostalism is considered a main social force against machismo.[11]

Pentecostals and Prayer

The one common element for early Pentecostals was their emphasis on prayer. For example, the Latin American Bible Institutes founded in California and Texas in 1926 included the discipline of prayer: "Every student must maintain communion with God."[12] For them, prayer was essential to maintain a Pentecostal worldview. Miller and Yamamori concur:

> There is something personal and primitive about the prayers of Pentecostals. They tend to flow from the heart, expressing spontaneous feelings of praise as well as the deepest anguish of the heart. Sometimes these prayers are focused on an individual's needs, other times on those of loved ones, the congregation, the community, or the world. And, not infrequently, prayer is a potpourri of needs and thanksgiving, personal and public.[13]

For Pentecostals in Latin America, prayer becomes a collective experience, and the needs of others are raised in prayer before the entire community. Prayer has an empowering quality since shared burdens are no longer individual struggles. The results are left to God. The believer is liberated to continue with the daily tasks of life.[14]

Latino Pentecostals believe in healing and in deliverance or casting out demons as Jesus did.[15] For a Western mindset or for people who operate on assumptions of empirical evidence, the tendency is to dismiss the reality of demons. That is not the case with Latin American Pentecostals. Generally, Pentecostals believe they are in a spiritual battle and acknowledge that there are struggles to be fought on different fronts, for different reasons, and with varying degrees of intensity. In Latin America, Pentecostals take spiritual battles seriously, even though they cannot physically see the attacker. They wrestle evil powers in the strength of the Spirit.

Latin American Pentecostals follow the Spirit's leading in their church services. Instead of a structured liturgical service, a typical Latin American service includes singing, shouting, clapping, and dancing. "As the service begins, the congregants become deeply immersed, their eyes closed, some crying, others singing at the top of their voice or 'speaking in tongues,' and still others lifting faces and hands toward heaven."[16] Shouts of praise and clapping abound as the pastor preaches or as responses to testimonies and answered prayers. There is no clear beginning of the service, and usually no clear end.

Latinos have incorporated native traditions into their liturgical practices. Their music includes local and popular rhythms and less of the traditional Western hymnology. It is common to incorporate native music and their own instruments. Several forms of dance are incorporated during worship which includes tambourines and colorful banners. Among Latin American Pentecostals, there is an open attitude toward the public expression of emotions. The church becomes the place where they are free to laugh and cry and shout and sing. These emotional expressions become evident at many points during a Pentecostal service. Tears often accompany the spontaneous prayers of congregants. People share their testimonies of being saved by God from drugs, alcohol, or depression. Their services are more fluid as most participants anticipate listening to God's voice and to be "led by the Spirit."

Prayer and fasting are common spiritual disciplines in the ethos of Pentecostal churches in Latin America. Pentecostals are aware of the significance of prayer in the life of Christ and in the early church, as described in the book of Acts. Pentecostals are satisfied and comforted in prayer for their personal needs and for those in their communities. Prayer emboldens Christians to witness to their families and in the workplace.

Pentecostals and Social Justice

Overall, Pentecostals have taken a limited prophetic stand on the role of the church and social responsibility. It can be said that Latino Pentecostals have remained within the four walls of their churches and remain cautious about expressing their opinions on political matters. They might have social outreaches to help the poor, such as distribution of food or medical missions, but they do not denounce injustice. Pentecostals in Latin America prefer to emphasize personal evangelism and piety. They have steered away from political activism or political participation. In response to this attitude, Eldin Villafañe argues that Pentecostals must see themselves not just called to engage in personal liberation but to position themselves as agents of social liberation.[17] Beyond the *culto* (service) there are structures and institutions that must be confronted in the power of the Spirit to break the chains of hate, hostility, and injustice.[18]

Sin leads people to abuse, engage in corrupt acts, and misuse resources in a way that is hurtful to themselves, their families, and their communities. Racism, sexism, and economic oppression are affronts to God. Pentecostal churches do not exist in a vacuum, and although Pentecostals have excelled in evangelism and missionary outreaches, they also need to reach out to the social problems in their context. The role of the Spirit is understood in terms of spiritual disciplines and moral life.

Pentecostals must discern and critically examine social and political issues and engage in a clear proclamation of the gospel to their community.[19] "Christianity is eschatology, is hope, forward-looking, and forward moving, and therefore also revolutionizing and transforming the present."[20] Scripture commands Christians to pray, and as they do, they have a responsibility to discern the pulse of the times:

> The church must dare to assume responsibility for the prayer:"Thy Kingdom come," without reservation. This courage before him who hears prayer is essential to the doxology that begins already in this life and will someday change into a new song.[21]

It is undeniable that prayer can empower Pentecostals to have greater compassion for the needs of those who suffer conditions of injustice. Pentecostals are now coming to the realization that "the Lord calls the church to speak prophetically to society and work for the renewal and reform of its structures."[22] In our era of increasing globalization, Pentecostals can join efforts for peacemaking in regions of widespread corruption and violence. Isolation from the sinful world is no longer a possibility. "The illusion of a Christian life in a convent or hermitage is no longer an option."[23]

Despite the lack of involvement in the transformation of social structures, there is a rising generation of Pentecostal scholars who critically analyze the harsh reality of the Latin American nations. For instance, Nestor Medina, in his book, *Pentecostals and Charismatics in Latin America and Latino Communities*, discusses the concerns and challenges faced among believers in Latin America.²⁴ Hence, the writings of young academicians and practitioners reveal the difficulties and suffering of people in Latin American societies.

Violence in Latin America

Latin America is considered one of the most murder-prone, violent regions of the world, with the highest rate of armed violence and 42 percent of global homicides occurring here. Gang and drug-related brutality have emerged in Guatemala, El Salvador, and Honduras at an alarming rate. Young people are the most visible culprits and are also the victims.²⁵ As churches become involved in prayer, they can become sensitive to unjust social structures and seek the transformation of their social milieu. Although Latin America is deemed the heartland of the Christian world today, social exclusion and violence have created conditions of a very hostile environment for the majority of citizens. *Maras* (gangs) have sprung up mostly in the poor barrios of major urban centers. Thousands of *mareros* (gang members) across Latin America employ violence to acquire justice, control, and economic benefits. The *maras* practice extortion by collecting *impuesto de guerra* (war tax) from shop owners and, in some cases, from local residents. Refusal to comply has resulted in the assassination of innocent victims.

Paul Freston made an accurate observation on the presence of the church amidst the shanty towns of Latin America: "The state is virtually absent. The Catholic Church is virtually absent. There are really only two things that function. One is organized crime. The other is the Evangelical churches."²⁶ A pastor in Tegucigalpa relates how her church deals with gang members and addicts in the community of *Las Torres* (The Towers). Her church is generating an impact in a community that is very crime-ridden.²⁷ There are cases of families asking the church to celebrate funeral services for their sons who were involved in gangs. Church members also drive their vehicles to pray around the vicinity of Las Torres. During special holidays, the church prepares meals and distributes them door-to-door. The church engages in weekly prayer meetings as they minister to people involved in illicit activities.

In Puerto Rico, there is a prayer effort called *Bayamón Postrado en Ayuno y Oración* (Bayamón Bows Down in Prayer and Fasting).²⁸ Pastors, church leaders, and church members meet from five to seven in the morning at the local stadium, Estadio Juan Ramón Loubriel. They plan prayer meetings for forty consecutive days and intercede for different requests each day. The prayer topics include the church, the city, the government, families, education, social issues, and the economy. This prayer emphasis is also carried out in other cities throughout Puerto Rico.

Prayer holds the possibility for increased involvement of churches in the areas where violence predominates. Some churches remain isolated from ministering to those that suffer social injustice. However, praying churches yearn to see peace, justice, security, accountable leaders, and egalitarian governments.

Prayer in Difficult Times

Latin American Pentecostals find refuge in the Lord through prayer. When any critical time arrives, they pray both individually and collectively. Usually, churches are open for prayer vigils or all-out prayer meetings called by local leaders. Churches admonish believers to hold on to prayer in times of sickness, danger, or pestilence. They appeal to biblical passages that encourage the faithful to remain steadfast to prayer even in critical circumstances. For some, this is one reason the church has grown strong in the region.[29] Hence, in recent years, calamity and other sources of suffering caused people to turn to Christ. Churches open their doors, and intensive prayer bring people to an encounter with the Almighty. These kinds of circumstances uplift prayer in the lives of Christians.

As might be expected, the momentum is thus set for the church to experience revival.[30] In such times of revival, there have been supernatural manifestations. Believers have been baptized with the Holy Spirit and empowered with charismatic gifts to operate efficiently. Manifestations of evil and sickness are expelled, thus setting the environment for the reigning of peace and joy in the community. These and other events have paved the way for a major spiritual breakthrough in Latin America. In spite of countless limitations, churches have grown, particularly among the poor. People in the margins have had the opportunity to meet Christ in congregations that made those encounters possible.

The battle against the forces of evil in the region is still underway. Social injustice, drug trafficking, gangs, political corruption, and other evils are being shaken by the power of the gospel. Spiritually empowered believers are taking the initiative to neutralize evil that hinders evangelism and missions. The presence of the Holy Spirit is a gift to the Christian community and to the larger social strata in each country. For this environment to take place, prayer is indispensable. Faithful believers continue to pray, and the Holy Spirit continues empowering them in their prayers with the goal of making Christ known in the region.

The Spirit of God guides his people: "This is what we speak, not in words taught us by human wisdom but in words taught by the Spirit, explaining spiritual realities with Spirit-taught words" (I Cor 2:10, NIV). "Prayer is the lifeline of theology . . . God is the subject matter of theology and prayer is our way of being in the world with God."[31] Prayer is multifaceted, and it is a way of being in the world for people and for Christian communities.

The Christian Diaspora to the United States

Christianity is increasingly becoming associated with immigrants. Christian Evangelicals in North America are divided over the issue of undocumented immigrants.[32] Some Evangelicals believe immigrants do not belong in the United States. However, the influx of immigrants, which may be God-ordained, have provided "spiritual reinforcement" to a Christian community in the United States that had been in noticeable decline."[33]

Generally, the Catholic church has taken a stand that favors immigrants.[34] During his visit to the United States, Pope Francis made reference to his immigrant experience and encouraged a Latino audience in Philadelphia to keep a sense of pride and dignity in their traditions.[35] The Pope's statements about immigrants took place during a time when condescending remarks about Latino immigrants had pervaded the national dialogue. Generally, North American Evangelical and Pentecostal churches permit immigrants to use their church buildings for Spanish-speaking services, although the Anglo constituency is politically conservative and generally favors tougher immigration laws.

Christianity is now mainly associated with the underprivileged and with some of the poorest nations of the world. People from the non-Western world are becoming the principal agents of Christian mission across the world. Migrant churches are beginning to have an impact on the

Western population in North American and European cities. Immigrants from Latin America are evangelizing European residents who have been unreached by traditional Western Christianity.[36]

There is an international Christian diaspora migrating to the United States.[37] For instance, Hispanic, Asian, and African congregations are proliferating in New York. The United States, more than any other country in the world, is likely to remain the principal recipient of new migration, a new Christian diaspora of multicultural and multi-ethnic composition. The rich diversity of the diaspora, generally unfamiliar to traditional, mono-cultural Anglo congregations, has the capacity to advance the Christian mission in both the Western and the non-Western worlds.

Brown-skinned missionaries continue to move across the globe. The Center for the Study of Global Christianity (CSGC) at Gordon-Conwell Theological Seminary estimated that approximately 400,000 international missionaries were sent out in 2010. At least five of the top missionary-sending countries are in the global South, including Brazil, South Korea, India, South Africa, and the Philippines.[38] On October 24, 2015, the Asian Center for Missions (ACM) held a missionary conference with more than 900 in attendance. The ACM has trained 1,692 Filipino missionaries in the last twenty years. Other significant missionary senders include Mexico, Guatemala, Colombia, China, and Nigeria. Such a movement opens the possibility for the body of Christ to be built up as people of diverse ethnicities and cultures integrate Christian communities (Ephesians 4:12).

The new diaspora differs from the great European migration in considerable respects. In the old migration, ties with the origin homeland faded and were often broken completely. The new diaspora seems to keep its ties with its places of origin. These growing congregations maintain international networks and plant new churches across the world. For example, Central Americans are involved in church planting in Spain, France, Italy, Alaska, and across the continental United States.

Mission is being carried out not just by Western missionaries but by Christians from the global South. Latin Americans are advancing in the leadership of world missions. The context of the mission includes the legacies of the great European migration and the elements of the new Christian diaspora. Indigenous leadership in the global South has variations with Western leadership. For example, the assertiveness of North American culture may clash with servant-oriented cultures.[39] Paul Borthwick asks, "Are we ready to serve and let them lead?"[40] There may be paradigm shifts in which the North no longer tells the South how to do their mission, but instead, those in the North listen and build relationships.

According to Allan H. Anderson, "We must listen to the 'margins' by allowing . . . the voiceless and often nameless to speak."[41] This is a way to recognize the contribution of unsung Pentecostal workers in the majority world. The new blending can be a powerful means to evangelize and bring about social justice and reform in places of the world where it is most needed. For example, in the United States, Latino Evangelicals are rising to make a stand in favor of immigration reform. Some of these Latinos are Wilfredo de Jesus (Pastor New Life Covenant Church); Luis Cortés (CEO of Esperanza); and Gabriel Salguero (National Latino Evangelical Coalition).

[A hed] Conclusion

As we have seen, Latin America has undergone a significant religious transformation since the mid twentieth-century. In this study, we have discussed the importance of prayer in evangelism. Prayer has enabled believers to witness effectively across many cultures of the region. Through prayer, Pentecostals have been anointed to evangelize and plant churches, especially among people of the margins. At the same time, a transition into indigenous, contextual evangelism and discipleship has occurred.

Church leaders in Latin America have become less dependent on the support of foreign denominations. This should be taken as a positive indication of maturity among the national churches. Evangelicals and Pentecostals are moving toward more authentic discipleship in spite of the social and political difficulties of the region.

Churches are becoming aware of the need to carry out integral mission for a balance in the preaching of the gospel. There is a greater expression of contextual forms of worship and liturgical practices. Indigenous voices are making an impact in their communities. These voices represent a new expression of theological impetus. We can clearly assert that all these developments are taking place thanks to powerful prayer initiatives.

Pastors and churches continue to be intentionally involved in church planting and mission efforts. Believers equate prayer and evangelism as an obedient response to the mandates of Jesus Christ: "'What a huge harvest!' he said to his disciples. 'How few workers! On your knees and pray for harvest hands!'" (Matthew 9:37, MSG).

Notes

1 Andrew F. Walls, *The Missionary Movement in Christian History: Studies in the Transmission of Faith* (Maryknoll, NY: Orbis, 1996), 9–10.
2 Allan H. Anderson, *Spirit-Filled World: Religious Dis/Continuity in African Pentecostalism* (London: Palgrave Macmillan, 2018), 3.
3 Miguel Alvarez, "Latin American Mission, Then and Now," in Miguel Alvarez, ed., *The Reshaping of Mission in Latin America* (Oxford, UK: Regnum Books, 2015), 1.
4 Israel Ortiz, "Más Allá del Crecimiento Numérico: El Desafío de la Transformación en Guatemala," in Miguel Alvarez, ed., *The Reshaping of Missions in Latin America*, (Oxford: Regnum Books, 2015), 205–225. In Central America, the term "Evangelical" is used to refer to the Reformed, Pentecostal, or Neo-Pentecostal churches and their adherents.
5 Allan H. Anderson, Michael Bergunder, Andre F. Droogers, Cornelis van der Laan, eds., *Studying Global Pentecostalism: Theories and Methods* (Berkley: University of California Press, 2010), 100–150.
6 Data provided by the Latin American Office of the "Iglesia de Dios Evangelio Completo."
7 Data provided by the Latin America Office of the "Iglesia de Dios Evangelio Completo."
8 Carlos Alvarez was appointed as pastor to the church, previously called Iglesia de Dios del Manchén.
9 Data provided by the National Office of the Church of God in Honduras.
10 Stephen Offutt, "The Transnational Locations of Two Leading Evangelical Churches in the Global South," *Pneuma: The Journal of the Society for Pentecostal Studies* 32 (2010): 390–411.
11 Elizabeth Brusco, *The Reformation of Machismo: Evangelical Conversion and Gender in Colombia* (Austin: University of Texas Press, 1995), 28–29, 61–64.

12 Arlene Sanchez-Walsh, *Latino Pentecostal Identity: Evangelical Faith, Self, and Society* (New York: Columbia University Press, 2003), 59.

13 Donald Miller and Tetsunao Yamamori, *Global Pentecostalism: The New Face of Christian Social Engagement* (Berkley: University of California Press, 2007), 145.

14 Miller and Yamamori, *Global Pentecostalism*, 145.

15 Miller and Yamamori, *Global Pentecostalism*, 154.

16 Pedro C. Moreno, "Rapture and Renewal in Latin America," *First Things* (June/July 1997), 31–32.

17 Eldin Villafañe, *Seek the Peace of the City: Reflections on Urban Ministry* (Grand Rapids: Eerdmans, 1995), 50–51.

18 Villafañe, *Seek the Peace of the City*, 27.

19 Douglas Petersen, "Towards a Latin American Pentecostal Political Praxis," *Transformation* 14:1 (1997), 30–33.

20 Andre van Oudtshoorn, "Prayer and Practical Theology," *International Journal of Practical Theology* 16:2 (2012), 296.

21 G. C. Berkouwer, *The Return of Christ* (Grand Rapids: Eerdmans, 1972), 453.

22 Robert Davis, "What About Justice?: Toward an Evangelical Perspective on Advocacy in Development," *Transformation* 26:2 (2009), 91.

23 Davis, "What About Justice?" 92.

24 See, Néstor Medina and Sammy Alfaro, *Pentecostals and Charismatics in Latin America and Latino Communities* (London, UK: Palgrave McMillan, 2015).

25 UNICEF, "Searching for Safe Harbour," February 14, 2019, https://www.unicef.org/stories/searching-safe-harbour, accessed February 20, 2020.

26 Paul Freston, "Christianity and Conflict in Latin America," *Pew Research Center* April 2006, http://www.pewforum.org/2006/04/06/christianity-and-conflict-in-latin-america/, accessed May 4, 2022.

27 Interview with Daisy Villatoro,Tegucigalpa, Honduras, December 16, 2018.

28 Interview with Pedro Marrero, Bayamón, Puerto Rico, January 20, 2016.

29 See for instance, Walter J. Hollenweger, *The Pentecostals: The Charismatic Movement in the Churches* (Minneapolis: Augsburg Publishing House, 1972), 24–32.

30 See, Andrew Chesnut, "Latin American Charisma: The Pentecostalization of Christianity in the Region," in Martin Lindhardt, ed., *Ways of Being Pentecostal in Latin America* (Lanham, MD: Lexington Books, 2016), 1–14.

31 Marilyn McCord Adams, "Prayer as the Lifeline of Theology," *Anglican Theological Review* 98:2 (2016), 390–411.

32 Soon-Chan Rah, *The Next Evangelicalism: Freeing the Church from Western Cultural Captivity* (Downers Grove, IL: Intervarsity Press, 2009), 74–75.

33 Rah, *The Next Evangelicalism*, 191.

34 David A. Badillo, *Latinos and the New Immigrant Church* (Baltimore: Johns Hopkins University Press, 2006), 180; see also, Paul Ehrlich and Anne Ehrlich, *One with Nineveh: Politics, Consumption, and the Human Future* (Washington DC: Island Press, 2004), 107.

35 Manuel Roig-Franzia, Arelis Hernandez, and Pamela Constable, "Pope Francis to Immigrants: Do Not Be Ashamed of Your Traditions," *Washington Post*, September 26, 2015, https://www.washingtonpost.com/lifestyle/style/2015/09/26/8e1faa4c-6488-11e5-b38e-06883aacba64_story.html?utm_term=.e406e57568f1, accessed May 4, 2022.

36 Elena Vilaca, Enzo Pace, Inger Furseth, and Per Pettersson, *The Changing Soul of Europe: Religions and Migrations in Northern and Southern Europe* (Burlington, VT: Ashgate, 2014), 55.

37 Andrew Walls, "Mission and Migration: The Diaspora Factor in Christian History," *Journal of African Christian Thought* 5:2 (December 2002), 30.

38 Melissa Steffan, "The Surprising Countries Most Missionaries Are Sent From and Go To," *Christianity Today*, July 25, 2013, http://www.christianitytoday.com/gleanings/2013/july/missionaries-countries-sent-received-csgc-gordon-conwell.html, accessed May 4, 2022.

39 Paul Borthwick, *Western Christians in Global Missions* (Downers Grove, IL: Intervarsity, 2012), 120.

40 Borthwick, *Western Christians*, 120.

41 Allan H. Anderson, *An Introduction to Pentecostalism: Global Charismatic Christianity* (Cambridge: Cambridge University Press, 2004), 183.

20 Missional Spirituality of the Global G12 Network

Richard Harding and Manuela Castellanos Harding

Abstract

The discipleship movement has been through many different transformations over the last century. One of the pioneers of this movement, Cesar Castellanos, Pastor of International Charismatic Mission (ICM) Church, Bogota, Colombia, and founder of the worldwide G12 movement, has remained true to his call and focus of discipleship. Through the growth of this movement, the nature of the important relationship between discipleship and evangelism has been key to its permanence and continuing influence around the globe. This study will look at the development of this important movement, its success in continuing discipleship, and its global expansion.

Forming Disciples who Form Disciples

Without a doubt, God is shaking the earth in these times. He is clearly waking up the church so that it may take seriously the mission he has commanded her to do. Consequently, there is great expectation. Like never before, there must be a clear strategy and stamina to fulfill the Great Commission. In Matthew 9:37, Jesus gives a statement that is very relevant for the church: "The harvest is plentiful, but the workers are few. Ask the Lord of the harvest, therefore, to send out workers into his harvest field." Derek Prince comments on this passage, "What is the harvest? In the spiritual sense, it is the last, great ingathering of people from all nations, all over the world, into God's kingdom at the close of this age."[1]

Everyone as a Minister

What is interesting about this passage is the focus and direction Jesus gives for effective ingathering. Jesus does not pray for the harvest; his intercession is lifted high specifically for the workers that will go out and gather the harvest. The word apostle in its original language means "sent out"; the harvest will not happen if the disciples of Jesus Christ remain "inside" the four walls of the church. Furthermore:

> The Great Commission is not a special calling or a gift of the Spirit; it is a command—an obligation incumbent upon the whole community of faith. There are no exceptions. Bank presidents and automobile mechanics, physicians and schoolteachers, theologians and homemakers—everyone who believes in Christ has a part in His work (John 14:12).[2]

This has been a lived principle among the members of the International Charismatic Mission (ICM) in Bogota, Colombia. Discipleship is not a "special program" reserved for a few members of the church. It is a lifestyle, and every member is encouraged, trained, and invited to do their part in discipleship. The result of this is that members are not mere spectators in the church; they are protagonists of the Great Commission.

Forming Missional Teams

In the beginning of ICM, it was not like this. Most of the evangelistic and discipleship tasks of the church relied on the Senior Pastor, Cesar Castellanos. Following a more traditional way of doing church, Castellanos came to a point in his life and ministry where he felt completely disappointed with the results. After thirteen years in full-time ministry, he cried out to God: "Lord, if doing ministry means I have to beg people to come to church and stay, I don't want to do this anymore."[3] However, the Holy Spirit led Castellanos to visit *Yoido Full Gospel Church* in Seoul, South Korea. During this trip, God began to change his mind concerning all the traditional schemes of church growth. Being in the midst of thousands of people truly revived the promise God had given to his life and his church at its first beginnings in 1983. A spark of faith was ignited during the two minutes that were spent with Pastor Cho in Korea. "It was worth seeing this man of faith who dared to believe God and set out to conquer. His ministry has been very innovative and has underscored the fundamental concept that the cell church is God's purpose for these end times."[4]

Immediately after this trip, Castellanos began to implement cell groups in his church. People received salvation, leaders were encouraged, and a new move of the Spirit began to take place. However, the church was not multiplying. Seven years passed, and in a quest for answers, Castellanos began to seek God in prayer. As a result of fervently crying out to God, God opened his understanding, and it was as if a veil was removed from Castellanos' eyes. This revelation was an understanding of the strategy Jesus used while on earth to make disciples. It was clear:

When God brought this revelation into my life, I felt in the deepest part of my heart that he was telling me: "If you train twelve people and you are able to reproduce in them the same Christlike character that is found in you, and if these, in turn, are able to do the same with another twelve and so on, then the church will experience unprecedented growth."[5]

Matthew 10:1 states: "Jesus called his *twelve disciples* to him and gave them authority to drive out impure spirits and to heal every disease and sickness" (emphasis added).[6] It is clear that even though he did ministry for only three and half years, it was focused, strategic, and certainly effective. History reveals how in a matter of just a few years, Christianity spread around the world. Jesus, while on earth, was able to influence a few men who were so committed to his work and his vision, that as a result, these men went out and did the same with other men and women. These few who were sent out were able to turn the world upside down (Acts 17:6).

Having this understanding of the way Jesus did ministry completely shifted the focus of Castellanos' effort and ministry. He began to study and analyze the way Jesus did it. It was clear: focus on a few people and build them up so that they, in turn, can go out and do the same with others. Building up men and women, as stated, is hard work. How did Jesus do it in just three and half years? First, he invested the best in his team:

> Jesus' contact with the multitudes was sporadic. One day he was with one group, and the next day he was with another. The only group that Jesus never changed nor rotated was the one made up of his twelve apostles. For three and a half years, he poured out his life into each one of them. He spoke to them with his example, with parables, and with teachings from daily life. During that time, he formed their character; each one of his teachings left an imprint on their hearts. Jesus understood that with those twelve individuals, he would provide continuity to his vision.[7]

Second, he was very intentional. He knew his time on earth was very limited; therefore, he made sure his disciples understood it was their responsibility to continue spreading the gospel. Furthermore, "Jesus knew that a solid church must be built out of solid rocks in order to stand the test of time. For this reason, he changed Simon's name to Peter, which means 'rock.'"[8]

The ministry of Jesus was very strategic, and therefore, the question one must ask is how to replicate this model that Jesus demonstrated? The Apostle Paul, in one of his last writings to his faithful disciple

Timothy, encouraged him to put into practice the heart behind effective discipleship: "The things which you have heard from me in the presence of many witnesses, entrust these to faithful men who will be able to teach others also" (2 Tim 2:2). In this single verse, Paul mentions four spiritual generations. Furthermore, he portrays the idea that effective discipleship happens when faithful people do their part by receiving the teaching in their hearts, living it out, and then training other people who, in turn, will do the same. "If a leader or pastor decides to form a group of twelve people and trains them in the word, they will dedicate themselves to doing the same. As a result, they will produce 144 disciples. Now, if each of the 144 disciples makes an effort to build up the lives of twelve men, they will multiply into 1,728 people."[9] Through this principle of forming twelve, in only six generations, entire nations could be reached for Christ.

Discipleship and Mission

At this point, it would be good to mention Jesus' words in Matthew 28:18–19. This passage has been used to promote both evangelism and discipleship movements and is seen as the essence of the missional call upon the church. This study is not trying to perform an exegetical look at the passage but rather to examine a practical approach to both evangelism and discipleship as found in the G12 Global movement, inspired by this passage. Within the G12 framework of cell groups, this understanding of the relationship between evangelism and discipleship has been fundamental to Castellanos' development of the ministry in forming disciples with a missional focus.

Understanding missions within the church comes from understanding the meaning and connection of these two important parts of the church's focus. This relationship can be described in the following way: evangelism plus discipleship equals missions, whereas if either of these is missing, we cannot arrive at the completion of "missions" through the efforts of the church. We will either focus on the evangelism or "winning" side, adding numbers of those who make the decision to follow Christ in great crusades, but who are left as a number within a crusade context. On the other hand, if the focus is on discipleship alone, there is no outward orientation of the church. The church becomes an inward institution that focuses primarily on itself, concentrating largely on the development of its own members. The need for a holistic approach to missions has been clear to Castellanos and the G12 movement from the very beginning of founding the church.

Evangelism within the G12 Vision

At the beginning of his ministry, Castellanos would describe himself as an evangelist: "After my personal encounter with Jesus, when my life was completely transformed, there awakened in me a great desire to reach those who were far from God."[10] There were some weeks when Castellanos would reach up to 200 new souls for Christ. This drive to tell others about Jesus Christ has formed the backbone of the ICM church and the G12 movement. Compassion for the lost is key to the success and growth of a church. This passion led Castellanos to form the beginning of his missional process within ICM church and the G12 concept of church growth, called "The Ladder of Success," the first stage of which is "Win."[11]

This, however, was only the beginning. Before long, Castellanos realized that his efforts were not being converted into disciples within the church and that each week, after winning so many new people, the church attendance did not increase at all. The answer was simple and formed the next steps on "The Ladder of Success."[12]

Discipleship within the G12 Vision

At the foundation of ICM church, emphasis on church growth was stressed, with Castellanos encouraging his small and new congregation to dream of the next step. The goal was to see 200 new souls won in six months. They achieved this within just four months.[13] Once the cell vision was established, Castellanos quickly saw the need for training new leaders. This is where he implemented the next stage of "The Ladder of Success." The next stage is called "Disciple." The focus was not on forming mature Christians just for the sake of it, but for a purpose: to form and train every member as a leader to then be able to be sent out, the final step of this ladder. This completes the missional focus of the discipleship process.

Since that time, Castellanos has developed a second stage, as he found there was something missing between winning the lost and forming them into true disciples and leaders, a gap where many would disappear before being fully established in their faith. For this reason, a second stage was added, "Consolidate." In this stage, the new believer is confirmed and encouraged in their faith and given the opportunity to experience a life-changing encounter with Christ.[14] In some ways, this consolidation stage is the beginning of the discipleship process whereby the new believer is encouraged and taught to connect with the Word of God for themselves. This takes the form of a daily devotional through a seven to a nine-week course called "Lifeclass."[15] These three stages, however, are not a means in themselves but look forward to the fourth and final stage, "Send."

The Missional Focus of Discipleship in the G12 Vision

This final stage, "Send," is the culmination of the missional work. For ICM and the G12 network, missions are not necessarily "cross-cultural" or "international." Being missional does not have to involve training and sending out missionaries to other nations en-masse, although we will look at this aspect of missions in the second half of this chapter. Rather, for ICM, "Send" focuses on the training and sending of leaders to begin the process within their local context. This is where mission is expressed. At this stage, the disciple is sent to begin their own cell group to start the four stages with new believers, to win them, consolidate them, disciple them and then, in turn, send them out to do the same.

In the G12 model, true missional work can be fulfilled locally through the winning and discipling of every member. Without this, missions are often left to the "Evangelist," and there is no real focus on the holistic missional work of the church to fulfill the Great Commission. We will now spend the second part of this study looking out how this concept is outworked on a global scale. After all, through the Great Commission, we are called to "Make disciples of all the nations" (Matt 28:19).

Global Missions

Since an assassination attempt on his life in 1997, Cesar Castellanos has looked to fulfill the Great Commission in the nations through the G12 movement, drawing inspiration from Matthew 28:19. At first, his focus was primarily on Colombia as a nation, but after an attempt was made on his life, where he was shot five times and spent ten days in a coma at the point of death, his view was drawn away from local missional development, and he felt an urgency to form a more globally impacting movement.[16]

Global G12 Expansion

Castellanos states that Matthew 28:19 is clear in using the plural for "nations" and not just "nation." This, he argues, leads the reader of the Gospel to conclude that the Great Commission is for entire nations; that we are called to make disciples of "nations" and not just a collection of disciples in each nation.[17]

However, it was actually very early on in his ministry that Castellanos determined a strategy for missions based on these concepts. In 1995, he was attending a conference for missions when he had the opportunity to ask a group of around 300 international missionaries about their experiences. The response came almost unanimously that the majority were tired, weary, and over-stretched. Seeing this group, he immediately thought, "I never want to put my people through the same."[18] He decided from that moment to work through strategic pastors within the nations and form a global network of local churches to carry out local missions through the strategy outlined in the previous section.

Today, that network includes over 8,000 churches with annual conferences in over forty nations and over 150,000 global attendees.[19] The Philippines, the area of greatest growth within the G12 network, has experienced such a revival that each year over 300,000 members gather for a great church evangelistic open-air meeting. The amazing thing is that these are not all different church groups but rather an organized, nationally coordinated effort to both win and disciple the nation of the Philippines.

This expansion could be attributed to the focused multiplication concept of the vision that every member should be taken through the four steps of the ladder of success in order to become leaders and win others to Christ. If this work is taken seriously, then whole nations can potentially be won for Christ in a short space of time.

Bill Hull points out that these strategies are not wrong in themselves but do lack a biblical foundation of true discipleship as found when the three streams of discipleship come together, "Classic Discipleship" "Spiritual Formation," and "Environmental Discipleship."[20] Hull posits that a reproductional discipleship model does not conclude that we can win the world through this style of multiplication, arguing that this simply has not happened.[21] We disagree with this, having seen the results in both Latin

America and Asia. The skepticism Hull presents born out of his North American experience could be a completely different study in itself. There is, however, faith and belief within the G12 movement that this work can be successful and see dramatic change, growth, and influence across the globe. This effort has led to a global focus by Castellanos and the G12 movement.

Establishing National Teams and Conferences

Instead of trying to form missionaries to travel out to these nations, Castellanos opted to connect with and form local pastors and leaders in those regions. Through the discipleship model of twelve, groups of twelve have been established with great success on a national level. This has produced both a community of like-minded pastors with the same vision as well as a sense of focus and strategy. It has placed the focus not on inter-cultural or inter-national missions but rather on local missions, with the local pastor trained in how to "Win," "Consolidate," "Disciple," and "Send" to fulfill the Great Commission within the local church.

The focus is on training leaders to win twelve people and then training each of the twelve to do the same. The network began to spread by word of mouth, with the first international conference held in Bogota in January 1996, going on to grow to over 20,000 leaders with over 37 nations represented by 2020.[22] This representation includes both pastors and local leaders from each nation who are working and being trained to train and disciple others.

This focus has allowed the G12 network to reach across national, cultural, linguistic, and denominational barriers and has facilitated a flexible and agile movement that has not been hindered by the normal barriers of traditional missions. With the expansion of the G12 Vision across the globe, Castellanos has formed an international team, with coordinators heading up the work in each region. In some of these regions, a single pastoral couple from his primary team of leaders has been sent out from Colombia to coordinate that national effort, but only after proving themselves as pastors and ministers on a local level at the main church in Bogota. A great example of this has been the missional work in Mexico. We will look at this work in more detail in this next section as a case study of how the G12 network has worked through the local church without having to train and send out large numbers of missional pastors to another nation. Instead, on occasion, a single couple are sent out as missionaries to a nation to coordinate the work on a national level as well as start a local work often in the capital city. This saves the need for large numbers of missionary workers, and in many cases, the pastors sent have often been working with the national pastors for some years. As stated, an example of this is in Mexico, where Pastor Saul and Gloria Salamanca, Colombian nationals who were pastors in Bogota, Colombia, moved to Mexico to continue the national G12 work they were already involved in and start a local MCI church in Mexico City.

Case Study: G12 Mexico

Pastors Saul and Gloria Salamanca have been actively doing missions for more than eight years in Mexico. Their experiences in missional discipleship have enriched the G12 movement and pastors around the world. Before moving to Mexico City, pastors Saul and Gloria visited the nation for more than seven years alongside their ministerial work as pastors at ICM, Bogota. Their desire was to really grasp the cultural context, connect with local leaders and missionaries, and understand God's vision for this nation. When they began their missionary work in Mexico, there were more than seventy churches that were part of this discipleship movement. Today, there are more than 350 churches and more than 9,000 leaders that join them yearly at their discipleship conference.[23] They have not only accomplished work on a national level by uniting pastors from different denominations, but at the same time, they started a brand-new church when they arrived in Mexico City in 2012.

Leading other pastors, and at the same time, starting a new church has opened their perspective on missional discipleship. On a national level, they have been able to organize the country into four regions. Each region has a coordinating pastor, and each coordinating pastor has several pastors under them. They have become spiritual "pillars" for this extraordinary work that is taking place in this nation. Saul Salamanca states: "Something that the G12 model offers, once a church implements it, is special freedom and respect for its own identity. This is one thing that is greatly valued with each church that joins this movement."[24]

A pastor joins the G12 movement through relationships. The G12 Vision is more than a method or a strategy; it begins by connecting with a pastor and showing care and support for that pastor as a person. Pastor Gloria shares one of many testimonies they have witnessed:

> We had a pastor's daughter from a different city visit our church. However, when she arrived, she got very ill. This created in us a sense of urgency to really look after her. We would call her every day, we were able to find medical help, and in this short amount of time, we were able to become her spiritual mentors. Because of this, a special bond was formed with the entire family, and this has been a principle in our leadership. Serving is the way to spiritual authority. When one serves, and one is willing to go the extra mile to care for those God brings in one's path, this creates a special bond. It's the way Jesus formed his twelve, by serving them.[25]

Jesus left a clear model of discipleship, and in a sense, the G12 model simply follows his model. Jesus called people to be near him. He taught them, and he worked day and night with a clear focus. It went beyond gathering people for special events and meetings. The processes of winning and subsequently discipling a person cannot be detached; they are completely interdependent. For Saul and Gloria, having this mindset and hard work ethic has led to the following results.

First, it helps in consolidating local leadership teams across Mexico. "Doing the G12 Vision demands hard work. Following the four steps of the "Ladder of Success" demands excellence and strong teams to make it work. This raises the need to form trustworthy leaders and let others join the work. This missional approach does not simply fall on the pastor."[26]

Second, they are reaching over 1,000 faithful members in a brand-new church in less than eight years. Most of the members of this church plant are actively involved in small cell groups, they serve in the church, and they have all been through different processes and training to help them strengthen their relationship with Christ. Mexico City has more than 21 million inhabitants, and the local church has encountered people that are willing to travel for more than three hours to be at the Sunday service. This is because they receive solid spiritual food, and as a result, their lives have changed, their families have been restored, and they are sharing with others a living gospel.

Third, strengthening a G12 church network (nationally). The emphasis in this network has been on character more than method. Raising solid churches comes as a result of people that grasp the work of the cross and surrender their lives completely to follow Jesus. The G12 Vision is not just a strategy; it is a lifestyle. Every pastor is encouraged to be an open book, a blameless person of integrity, starting with their family, marriage, good spiritual habits (prayer, Bible study), and financial stewardship. This wholesome discipleship approach has been modeled by the main pastors and leaders in the G12 movement, where most of them have been able to raise families who love, serve, and fear the Lord, and it has been this example that has encouraged most of the pastors that join the Vision: "I truly admire Pastor Cesar and his wife. They have been able to exemplify a priesthood family, it's something that we've been able to transmit to our children, and it's what G12 pastors are first encouraged to do: put their family in order."[27]

The foundation to make this missional discipleship work relies on four aspects: Complete reliance on the Holy Spirit, strong biblical doctrine in the leaders, emphasis on character more than an emphasis on results or service, and a clear strategy:

> We are modeling the leadership of Jesus through making disciples. We are raising leaders who truly understand what Jesus has done for them on the cross, who are passionate for evangelizing others, and who are willing to persevere. Jesus spoke to the multitudes through parables, but he was very careful in sharing the secrets of his father. He chose, trained, and tested twelve men for three and half years. Why? Because he knew that one disciple who was willing to surrender it all for him would do more than ten thousand sympathizers, that is effective discipleship.[28]

Pastors Saul and Gloria conclude by affirming that discipleship is not for the weak or faint-hearted. It is not an easy road to popularity, and not everyone will respond with gratitude. Making disciples demands time, effort, and much perseverance. Raising effective leaders demands everything, and that is what the Salamanca's have been giving. That is why they left their country, sold their house, gave it all: because they love the Lord, and more than anything, they long for people to encounter the person of Jesus Christ, not mere religion. This has led them to pastorally care for people with tenderness and love for the "sheep" God has entrusted to them. "It is not enough with once-a-week, hour-long training to form disciples. Pastors and leaders need to understand that in the same way that natural children demand effort and time when they are little, young believers will demand prayer, counseling sessions, and genuine love."[29] It is this selfless heart that has stirred them, and it is stirring up a nation to be awakened for Christ.

Conclusion

The G12 Vision has reached across continents and touched many nations. Its focus on local missional work through a clear discipleship strategy has led to explosive growth in both Latin America and Asia and has seen thousands commit to Christ as disciples. The need for discipleship is the same today as it was during the establishment of the Church in the early years. As Coleman points out, there are more "unevangelized people" on the earth now than there were when the horseless carriage was invented.[30] How then should we clearly rise up to meet this great need and take responsibility as a church? Should we have more "seeker" friendly services and meetings? Should we hold more massive evangelistic crusades like those we have seen sweep across the continent of Africa? Or is there another much simpler way?

As previously mentioned, there are some such as Hull, who are incredibly skeptical of this "simpler way," having yet to see the results originally believed for. The fact that this has not necessarily happened right away does not mean, however, that it never will or that the faith-filled theory is misguided. Indeed, we can conclude several things regarding the G12 Vision when examining the effect of discipleship on missional work across the globe.

1. The Bible is clear, even if we are not, that all are called to be disciples and that this requires a price to be paid by all believers to work in order to fulfill the Great Commission.
2. The work should not fall upon a few trained missionaries who are sent out to plant churches either in their own nation or in other nations.
3. Everyone can fulfill the Great Commission when they are helped through a simple process to be won, consolidated, discipled, and then, in turn, sent out to do the same.
4. Global missions are supremely important to the evangelical work of the gospel and the Great Commission and can most effectively be carried out locally.
5. Discipleship is not and should not be the end goal but rather the means through which the world can be won for Christ, where evangelism plus discipleship equals missions.

All this leads to the understanding that discipleship is essential to missions and can be the most effective way to truly fulfill the Great Commission alongside a healthy strategy for evangelism. The G12 Vision has embodied these concepts and has sought to implement them across the globe on a local and national level.

Notes

1 Derek Prince, *The Harvest Just Ahead* (Northampton, UK: Derek Prince Ministries, 2011), 46.
2 Robert E. Coleman, *The Master Plan of Discipleship* (Grand Rapids: Revell, 1987), 10.
3 Cesar Castellanos, *Dream and You Will Win the World* (Miami: G12 Editors, 2006), 150.
4 Castellanos, *Dream*, 160.
5 Castellanos, *Dream*, 160.
6 Unless otherwise stated, all Bible references in this study are to the New American Standard Version (La Habra, CA: Lockman Foundation, 1971).
7 Castellanos, *Dream*, 158.
8 Cesar Castellanos, *Pass the Torch to Reach New Generations* (Miami: G12 Editors, 2010), 33.
9 Castellanos, *Pass the Torch*, 53.
10 Cesar Castellanos, *Win Through the G12 Vision* (Miami: G12 Editors, 2006), 191.
11 Cesar Castellanos, *The ABC's of the G12 Vision* (Miami: G12 Editors, 2019), 57.
12 Castellanos, *The ABC's*, 113-143.
13 Castellanos, *Dream*, 35.
14 Castellanos, *The ABC's*, 131-141.
15 Castellanos, *The ABC's*, 141.
16 Castellanos, *Dream*, 51-56.
17 Cesar Castellanos, *Visión Integral Para un Liderazgo Eficaz* (Bogotá, Colombia: G21 Editors, 2020), 12.

18 Interview with Cesar Castellanos, Senior Pastor of International Charismatic Mission, Bogota, Colombia, Sept 27, 2019.

19 Information provided by G12 Global Office, Bogota, Colombia.

20 Bill Hull, *The Complete Book of Discipleship: On Being and Making Followers of Christ* (Colorado Springs, CO: NavPress, 2006), 20.

21 Hull, *The Complete Book*, 28.

22 Statistics provided from G12 registrations office, Bogota, Colombia Calle 22c #31-01.

23 Statistics provided by G12 Office Mexico.

24 Saul Salamanca, Senior Pastor of International Charismatic Mission in Mexico City, Mexico, interview by author via Zoom, Oct 15, 2020. The author was in Bogota, Colombia and Saul Salamanca was in Mexico City.

25 Gloria Salamanca, Senior Pastor of International Charismatic Mission in Mexico City, Mexico, interview by author via Zoom, Oct 15, 2020. The author was in Bogota, Colombia and Gloria Salamanca was in Mexico City.

26 Interview with Gloria Salamanca.

27 Interview with Gloria Salamanca.

28 Interview with Gloria Salamanca.

29 Interview with Gloria Salamanca.

30 Coleman, *The Master Plan*, 31.

21 The Stubbornness of the Spirit: A Reflection on the Mission of God in Brazil

Elizabeth Salazar-Sanzana

Abstract

This study seeks to identify the work of the Spirit in Brazil, with special attention given to the plurality of charismatic expressions within this vast country. While Brazil is home to a variety of Spirit-empowered expressions, including some economically and politically privileged Evangelical figures, it is among the most vulnerable on the margins of society where the Spirit stubbornly resides. Indeed, the Spirit displays his stubbornness in Brazil, through tenacious, ongoing, and creative outpourings of his love and presence among communities of the most humble populations.

Introduction

I have been asked to write about the mission of God in the midst of the movement of the Holy Spirit in Pentecostalism in Brazil, a country in which I lived part of my life. In my undergraduate studies, I did a student exchange between the Evangelical Faculty of Theology of Chile and the Graduate School of Theology of the IECLB Lutheran Church in southern Brazil. I also completed Postgraduate studies at the Methodist University of Sao Paulo, UMESP. My husband and I then collaborated with a Chilean Evangelical Pentecostal mission in the City of Sao Paulo, where my two oldest daughters were born. It is from this Chilean-Brazilian perspective that I reflect on the Brazilian experience.[1]

Brazilian Pentecostalism

Brazil, Chile, and other places in Latin America were countries where a native Pentecostal movement was formed, imposing itself on foreign Pentecostalism.[2] The spiritual sensitivity of Brazilian society to embrace the Pentecostal faith has been widely recognized. The Pentecostal movement infiltrated society and culture and became involved in the country's public affairs. The growth of the Pentecostal movement exerted a decisive influence on how the historic Evangelical churches functioned, which in turn reduced the membership of the historic churches. As the decades passed, the Protestant Evangelical churches began accommodating a revivalist emphasis in their liturgy, with the result that these churches' praxis and worship bore a much closer resemblance to the Pentecostal movement. The decline of some traditional Protestant agendas started becoming noticeable in the face of the independent, Pentecostal, and neo-Pentecostal churches that were multiplying, especially the Christian Congregation Churches and the various Assemblies of God Churches. In some cases, there was a modification of the liturgical aesthetic[3] itself, incorporating elements such as dance, specific evangelization for age groups, and a growing fascination with being in the media and mass evangelization. According to researcher Magali Cunha:

> The influence took place in a special way in the reinforcement of groups called "revivalists" or "charismatic renewal." These groups, based on the similarity of proposals and postures with Pentecostalism, began to conquer important spaces in the religious practice of historical churches and to open space for them to achieve some numerical growth.[4]

Notwithstanding these general observations, it must be recognized that there is a heterogeneity of Pentecostalism in Brazil, though all emphasize corporeal spiritual manifestations.[5] In most Latin American and Caribbean countries, this reality is shown as part of the process of the various Evangelical expressions.[6] The plurality of expressions and the constant fragmentation do not allow us to define a single position of Brazilian Pentecostalism.[7] In reality, it is not possible to define a single position in any religious expression, yet it is part of our dogmatic arrogance to want to encompass this diversity in a uniform way.

God's Mission Among the Vulnerable

It is because of God's mercy that we observe the most humble, fervent, and persevering missionary movements. We are witnesses of a constant renewal of God's mission in Brazil and it is these independent movements that cling to spiritual action, which have remained despite the difficulties inherent to their inexperience. In the country's current circumstances, including great polarization, there are faithful remnants that renew hope. Diakonic youth ministries are seen amid the signs of pain from the COVID-19 pandemic health and social crisis. The sovereign work of

God continues and cannot be dismissed. Based on the media portrayal of Pentecostal, neo-Pentecostal, and Charismatic churches and ministries, the movement of the Spirit is stigmatized, but God acts with or without an audience. Brazil has been a fertile land in the action of God in the midst of the most vulnerable population. The congregations offer community character, solidarity among members, and a loving welcome to all kinds of people affected both physically and emotionally by multiple experiences of precariousness, abandonment, and loneliness. Since their inception, the Pentecostal churches and ministries renewed by Pentecostalism in Brazil have been a response to a large population abandoned by society, which is displaced from one state to another, come to these fervent, loving, and welcoming communities. There they are embraced by networks of love, and prevention of violence, drugs, and multiple afflictions.[8]

Lived Experience

Seen from below, it would seem that from the viewpoint of people, there is a perception that the world is bad, and that it is getting worse every day. While the media, in the service of economic power, portrays a society where everyone satisfies their desires, has their comforts and comfortable private spaces, in reality, there are millions of people who are impoverished and daily dehumanized and are seeking to survive their misery. These are people marginalized by the system, who have become the ones who bother the large real estate projects that are seeking greater surplus value. They are the marginalized who are not part of the development project and are only considered as cheap labor for work. However, it is from this perspective of "below" that we see the action of God in the world because these are the ones who respond to the call of faith, of the mission of God empowered by the Spirit of Life. This population: displaced people, migrants, homeless people, and those without land to cultivate, respond to the offer of God's goodness, preached through living testimonies of those who have already come out of that desolation.

In the face of the metaphorical deafening thunder of big capital, the song of the saved can be heard. This song affirms both their rights to life and their aspirations in a reality where they are looked at by God and called children (John 1:12). They fill their mouths with songs of joy and manage to dream of conditions where everyone fits. In each neighborhood or city, there is a space that opens every day, especially on Sundays, and that manages to establish itself as a place for socializing the community of faith. These meetings are not only to celebrate the harmony of faith that calls them, in many cases, it is also the only space for peace. These congregations rise up from their surroundings as oases of identity and belonging. These spiritual communities of indigenous Bolivians, Peruvians, or the same Chilean mission in which I served, were created to serve God in the same way that Italian migrants of the last century formed Evangelical congregations in Sao Paulo.[9] Today the pandemic has not managed to quench the Spirit. Indeed, the determination to meet as groups in order to resist times of pain and deprivation is a distinguishing feature of these congregations. Despite ethical criticisms that could be made, these congregations have continued to meet in domestic spaces, rented commercial premises, or rooms in the *favelas* (suburbs) to share the daily bread and the basic resources to survive spiritual and material poverty.

Brazil is home to religions of various origins due to the numerous groups of European and Asian migrants. There is also the reality of historical slavery in this country. A large part of the Brazilian population are descendants of those who survived this scourge and thus keep various ancestral African religious expressions in their memory. For centuries, Catholicism has held the adherence of a great majority of the congregation. Despite this, Protestantism timidly established itself and thus opened space to the various Evangelical expressions. Then Pentecostalism was born and established itself as a recognized force of faith in the national territory.[10] The action of the Spirit of God has surprised many by multiplying groups of diverse spiritual ministries, which are established in more affluent neighborhoods and follow the same dynamic of pastoral and spiritual care as in the poorer neighborhoods. This is a service to the middle-class population, which require spaces for social insertion and belonging, in which they are offered spiritual accompaniment according to the standards of current times.[11] That is to say, this revivalist dynamic that generated a missionary awakening in the margins of society was later also located in the middle- and upper-class sectors. The great contribution of the congregations, which were sown with determination over the course of a century, speaks to the confidence of the Evangelical and Pentecostal people in the prophetic promises of the Holy Spirit. It is both these experiences of survival as recounted by the first generations and the current struggle against a dehumanized society that move Pentecostals to continue in the missionary work of the Spirit.

Today social and environmental crisis leads the church to consider these times as the last before our Lord comes. This leads to intensifying evangelization. In this evangelism, the Spirit of God manifests in the sense of living hope. We see without our own eyes that God does not stop renewing his action in the midst of the people, consoling a large, abandoned population and victims of the economic system through his Spirit. The Spirit works to help networks of cooperation that challenge economic and spiritual poverty, state abandonment, and family abandonment. Small and large physical spaces are transformed into unique spaces of healing and welcome and become spiritual spaces of the power of God that defy the logic of our current individualistic societies. That is why today, in the midst of social decline, the powerful move of the Spirit continues to save and heal, continuing to grow in Brazil. God's mission does not stop because there is much spiritual need.

A few years ago, I visited the United University of Victoria, which has a group dedicated to ecumenical academic life. Among its teachers and students, a broad vision of the Pentecostals both in the local state (called Espírito Santo) and in Brazil. I had the same experience when I returned to the Methodist University, where not only the postgraduate students harbored the presence of Pentecostal researchers like me, but the faculty was also comprised of a vast majority percentage of Pentecostals who sought to be trained to serve in the mission of God. This awakening to the deepening of the scriptures and of the Christian faith in spaces like these shows us the meeting of the experience of the Spirit and the academy and also the great strength of the Brazilian Pentecostal families in their diversity and the impulse of leaders who work in a serious and recognized realm.[12]

From this perspective, I want to share the movement of the Spirit in the corner of the enormous country of Brazil. This perspective is not necessarily according to the great and Evangelical expressions of the country or the perception of the media. In this chapter, we are not talking about the majority churches, nor those that are promoted with large sums of money, but the congregations who carry out their missionary work in a labor of love and affection, in creative ways, with a prophetic voice, in which it is always possible to see beyond the noise and the lights.

Some Relevant Percentages

In the 2010 census, 24,500,000 people were recognized as Protestants or Evangelicals in Brazil; that is, 22.2 percent of the total population. Specifically, Pentecostals number more than 17 million and are recognized as a consistently increasing group. Brazil has approximately 210 million inhabitants, and the majority declare themselves Catholic; however, there has been a significant decrease in Catholicism's adherents. According to the 1980 census, Catholics represented 89 percent, and Evangelicals only 6.6 percent. In 2010, the percentage of Catholics in Brazil fell to 64.6 percent, and Evangelicals rose to 22.2 percent. This is very surprising. The surprise is compounded when we understand that this large Evangelical percentage refers to the Pentecostal churches of Brazil, who have only been present in Brazil for one century.

These are congregations empowered by the Holy Spirit (not all of them self-identify as Pentecostals), which have been spaces for youth, minorities, women, and many illiterate people who found in these spaces their place of dignity. When the end of slavery and other stigmas were not yet fully socially accepted, the Evangelical congregations provided spaces for not only religion but for social belonging for those who were still socially marginalized and stigmatized. These are spaces of affection and belonging for a group of people, especially those from the suburbs of the big cities, who found in the congregational militancy and perseverance of faith their space of refuge.[13]

The growth of these congregations shows that they are not only places of refuge but also act as stages on which God's mission is enacted. The churches establish rapport with people, providing daily meeting spaces, spiritual counseling, emotional, and financial support, including financial or work support networks. The pastors are generally very accessible. The spiritual leaders are no longer missionaries who do not speak Portuguese well. Today's pastors belong to the people and manage to be very close because they join them and live in the same neighborhood. The churches are governed independently, with a certain decentralization as opposed to being controlled or administered by a larger institution. They end up being self-sustaining, local enterprises with a simple economy. This can be very harmful when there are problems of abuse and dishonesty. However, most of the time, there is a filter of those who adhere to practices of scrupulous honesty and therefore legitimize the space, group, or ministry. Faith is lived with freedom and with the lightness of being moved by the Holy Spirit.

Today ostentatious Evangelical congregations can be found in Brazil, for example, "The Temple of Solomon" of the Universal Church of the Kingdom of God (UCKG) and others that follow this path. But these do not represent the majority of Brazilian Evangelicals, since there are, for the most part, simpler congregations with reduced spaces or temples built with limited local resources. We must consider that these churches respond to the logic of the market and the success of the mission, which is measured by the acquisition of (or power to) goods and services. However, God's mission in the middle of Brazil is conducted along different paths and according to its people. As Néstor Míguez notes:

> From the worship of the golden calf in the book of Exodus to the fall of the opulent Babylon in the apocalypse, the desire for money and its accumulation, its destructive power when it is elevated to the category of deity, appears marked as idolatry: the clumsiness of the human being who ends up worshiping and submitting to what he has created, instead of making his work a service to others (Isa 44:13–20).[14]

Since 1985, Evangelical churches have ventured into active politics with scattered political inclinations, from the left to the extreme right. The analyses in this regard are varied, but it is important to recognize that the majority alliance arises from a common "moral agenda" (Christian, Catholic, Evangelical, Pentecostal). This reality is common in several countries but is intensified in Brazil by the presence of the *bancada evangélica* (Evangelical caucus) in the Chamber of Deputies. Since the 1988 Constitution, participation has been increasing. Although there is not a proposal from just one political party, there is a slogan "brother votes for brother," and that is why the candidates are tempted to show a religious conversion, in the style of Constantine the Great, with the desire to gain adherents.

The Spirit and the Church say Come!

Many ministries and Evangelical and Pentecostal churches currently carry out the task of giving freely what they have freely received. In this way, the Spirit of God finds expression without being closed to the demands of a pluralistic society. This is the vocation of the gospel empowered by the Spirit of Jesus Christ, who calls whoever he chooses to fulfill the multifaceted mission of God. Most of the faithful in the neighborhoods identify with their local congregations, where relationships are more direct and face-to-face. People who live on the same block don't know each other, but then they discover their neighbors at Sunday worship. Entering the community of faith, they connect to their social networks as a new way of connecting spiritually.[15] The churches within the Pentecostal movement create a sense of belonging and of community, including the social reintegration of inmates and drug addicts, who form a family based on the faith that unites them.[16]

In March 2019, the Faith and Order Commission[17] of the World Council of Churches, in conjunction with the Unity College of Victoria, held a public consultation entitled, "For a Global Vision of the Church." The consultation was the opening of the dialogue of the World Council of Churches with Evangelical, Pentecostal, and neo-Pentecostal leaders from Latin America. They reflected on the issues that divide churches and shared reflective theological materials that include the action of the Spirit in the midst of independent communities.[18] In this consultation, a group of theologians and researchers participated in sharing about the current situation of the Evangelical-Pentecostal world, as well as in spaces of renewal that encourage hope. As part of this consultation, we visited a ministry called Missão (The Mission), whose proximity to the university enabled students to be part of its pastoral leadership.[19] This mission has similarities in many Brazilian states and is a hybrid work in the midst of seemingly hopeless times.

The pandemic has not only given human losses that have been much stronger in Brazil than in many places in Latin America, but has also disappointed the Evangelicals who have seen themselves completely abandoned by public policies. It has revealed human misery, the lack of solidarity, and the unconsciousness of those who are in power to establish the minimum care for the population. However, the work of the Spirit is also perceived as giving a powerful, creative mission, which manifests itself in the midst of the turbulence of everyday life.

Mission in Transformation

There is great perversity in the way that groups in economic power manipulate Christians. As Magali Cunha tells us: "The food of hope is knowing that against an ethical blackout, the prophets remain, despite being the minority and persecuted. They do not cease to exist. They are in communities throughout Brazil."[20] For this reason, I believe it is essential to recognize that we cannot understand God's mission in Brazil without considering the great religious plurality present in its territory.[21] This is why we should not judge Evangelical churches so drastically. Pentecostal movements lack credibility and civic training that leads people to recognize speeches violating the principles of love and mercy of the gospel. We must make Evangelical "good practices" that follow Christ and his gospel visible and not settle only for what the media shows. The Evangelicals who have an exclusive space in the communication networks throughout the country are not representative of the majority of Evangelicals nor of Pentecostals. We know that it is the hegemony of one of the many existing groups. As is the case in many countries, there is a common agenda between Catholics and Evangelicals, active in open politics regarding the "moral" agenda" that they present to public opinion. These are the most controversial issues to which the Evangelical movements, in general, feel called to support, when it is understood that the family is in danger, the freedom to preach, religious education, it is accepted to fight on the side of whoever raises that flag, and it is precisely this fragility caused by the fear that has led to a situation of great pain. It is a very notorious manipulation. But there is also an ecumenical agenda of celebration, respect, and prayer.

The expression commonly attributed to Karl Barth, "Ecclesia semper reformanda est" (the church must always be reformed) gives a clear invitation to think that God does not want the church to be static, but to engage in the renewal of understanding. The movement of the Spirit in all corners of the world is constantly renewed and dynamic. It is difficult to precisely define the Spirit's logic, because it moves according to the rhythm of God rather than the rhythm of purely human strategies. As previously mentioned, Pentecostal churches have been linked to the poorest population. We then considered the great incursion of the millionaire ministries, which are precisely the ones who have led Evangelicals to be the center (even privileged center) of the media. However, the greatest dimension of Pentecostalism in Brazil continues to be an expression of the most disadvantaged people. Christ continues calling the peasant, the worker, and the migrant to himself through his Spirit. Those who thirst for God and answer his call find belonging of dignity and space of security in Pentecostalism.

Brazil currently faces great political polarization, due to the handling of the pandemic and the accompanying violations of health and human rights. The work of the Spirit advances and is notorious in prisons, caring for street children, in peasant settlements, and ministries providing dignified education through small Sunday schools. In these diakonic actions, the presence of the Spirit becomes a daily, visible work; in the name of faith, bread is distributed with joy, and charity is shared in dignity. In many of these spaces where mission unfolds, daily life is worked out, and differing feelings, ideas, intellectual capacities, desires, projections, and ideologies of a better society interact. Faith challenges each person to make their way in the midst of various levels of precariousness, overcoming the psychosocial damage caused by economic and/or social marginalization. Faith gives the power to overcome isolation, improve the well-being of families, and to resist a destiny almost established by neoliberalism in these corners of Brazil. Fragility becomes strength, and from this, there are many local works that establish the strength of the mission of Spirit in our society.[22] God has glorified himself among the humblest, and his work is magnificent.

Looking at Spirit-driven groups in different cities that are responding to spiritual and social needs puts us in a position to know that there is hope because God is with us. Looking at the mission of God in Brazil sheds light on the action of the Spirit in our times. There are always prophets announcing the gospel. Despite the manipulation that makes the population vulnerable, God's Spirit acts in the midst of his people.

The prophetic and life-transforming voice of the Spirit of God must be recognized and encouraged. There is no other hope in life, only Christ, our Lord and Savior.

Notes

1 I thank Dr. Gedeón Freire de Alencar and David Mesquiatti for their comments on this chapter. Both are theologians, researchers, and members of the Assembly of God Church.
2 These are understood as congregations of their own Brazilian specificity, which include the Assemblies of God in Brazil. Cf. Gedeón F. de Alencar, *Matriz Pentecostal Brasileira* (Rio de Janeiro: Novos Diálogos, 2013), 17–26.
3 I am referring to liturgical aesthetics, such as symbols, music, decoration, and architecture.
4 Magali Cunha, "Vinho Novo Em Odres Velhos. Um Olhar Comunicacional Sobre a Explosão Gospel No Cenário Religioso Evangélico No Brasil" (Ph.D. Diss., University of São Paulo, São Paulo, 2004), 29.
5 I must clarify that in many cases there are groups that do not call themselves or identify themselves as Pentecostals, but have all the traits, fundamental characteristics.
6 See, for example, Relep Brasil, which works from historical, sociological, and theological frameworks on the subject, https://www.relep.org.br/.
7 Alencar, *Matriz Pentecostal Brasileira*, 171–184.
8 Ari Pedro and Marcelo Tadvald, "Consideraciones Sobre el Campo Evangélico Brasileño," *Revista Nueva Sociedad* 280 (2019), 55–67.
9 See, Yara Monteiro, "Congregação Cristã no Brasil: A Trajetória de Uma Igreja Brasileira," *Estudos de Religião* 24:39 (2010), 122–163.
10 Philip Jenkins, *The Next Christendom: The Coming of Global Christianity* (Oxford: Oxford University Press, 2002), 101–133.
11 Ricardo Mariano, "Análise Sociológica do Crescimento Pentecostal no Brasil," (Ph.D. Diss., Universidade de São Paulo, São Paulo, 2001), 253
12 Jung Mo Sung, "El Espíritu y la Educación Teológica," in Jung Mo Sung, Néstor Míguez, and Lauri Wirth, eds., *Misión y Educación Teológica* (La Paz, Cetela, 2012), 93–120.
13 Christian Lalive D'Epinay, *O Refúgio das Massas* (Río de Janeiro, Paz y Tierra, 1970).
14 Néstor Míguez, "El Capitalismo como Religión" (paper presented at the International Seminar for Theology, Politics and Culture, São Bernardo do Campo, October, 2013) .
15 See, Alexandre Fonseca, *Evangélicos e Mídia no Brasil*, vol 1 (Bragança Paulista, Brazil: Editora Universitária São Francisco, 2003).

16 One of the greatest Evangelical strengths in Rio de Janeiro is its presence in the favelas as a recognized ethical reserve.

17 The Faith and Order Commission is a multilateral forum for ecumenical dialogue in which the various expressions of Christian work in the world are present, including the young Pentecostal and independent churches.

18 These tables for dialogue and theological production are spaces that help the World Christian Forum, World Forum of Theological Educators and Commission of Christian Unity, and other fraternal spaces.

19 The Mission is an Evangelical Church located in Vila Velha, on Praia da Costa. It was started in January 1997, with Pastors Simonton, Mirna Araújo and their three children. The story of the Mission merges with the journey of Pastor Simonton. At the age of seventeen he was already attending seminary and he began to evangelize in the countryside of Rio de Janeiro. For more information see, https://www.missaopraiadacosta.com.br/.

20 Magali Cunha, "Superar o Apagão ético e Fortalecer a Profecia," *Carta Capital*, June 30, 2021, www.cartacapital.com.br/blogs/dialogos-da-fe/superar-o-apagao-etico-e-fortalecer-a-profecia, accessed May 31, 2022.

21 Claudio Ribeiro, *Espiritualidades Contemporâneas*, Pluralidade Religiosa e Diálogo (São Paulo: Fonte Editorial, 2016).

22 In 2014, I was invited to work on missiological keys with theology students at the Methodist University (FATEO-UMESP) where most of them were Pentecostal. In that context I was blessed by the stories of diaconic actions from the various communities and ministries represented by the students.

22 Let the River Flow: A Study on the Cross-Cultural Church Planting Ministry of a Chinese Spirit-Empowered Church in the United States

Stephen Yeem

Abstract

The following is a study on the cross-cultural church planting ministry of River of Life Christian Church (ROLCC), the largest Mandarin-speaking church in the United States. It starts with a brief narration of ROLCC's cross-cultural church planting ministry, from its beginning in 1996 and tracing its growth to 268 churches in thirty-one nations as of Dec 2020. Then, this essay proceeds to analyze ROLCC success factors, focusing on ROLCC's vision, strategy, and culture. Last, this study critically evaluates ROLCC's missiological convictions and sustainability. It asserts that ROLCC has four core missiological convictions and offers two criticisms before concluding that ROLCC's cross-cultural church planting ministry is both scalable and replicable.

Introduction

River of Life Christian Church (ROLCC) is considered a flagship church by many due to its rapid growth to become the largest Chinese church in the United States, with many influential parachurch ministries both locally and globally. Among others, its commitment to cross-cultural mission via church planting has garnered significant attention throughout Chinese Christianity in the past decade, evidenced by the countless invitations for Rev. Tong Liu, the founder and senior pastor of ROLCC, to share the journey of planting 268 churches in thirty-one nations within twenty-five years.[1] The following is a study on ROLCC's cross-cultural church planting ministry. It will begin with a brief narration of the ministry's growth before analyzing its success factors and assessing its missiological convictions and sustainability. This study contends that ROLCC's vision of a glorious church participating in *Missio Dei*, strategies of prayer and partnership, and culture of audacity and generosity resulting from its charismatic and mission-centered spirituality are the critical success factors of its ministry. It also proposes that its missiological convictions include viewing church planting as the most effective way for local churches to participate in mission, Chinese churches are uniquely positioned to conduct cross-cultural missions, empowering others, and the necessity of holistic mission. It concludes that the ministry is scalable and replicable.

River Of Life Christian Church's Cross-Cultural Church Planting Ministry

In October 1996, ROLCC held its first mission conference and received faith pledges totaling 310k despite being a newfound church of 130 members. With this, they decided to support Every Home for Christ (EHC)'s ministry in Mongolia. In 1999, Reverend Tong Liu attended a small prayer meeting led by Pastor Batbold Lkhamsuren while visiting Mongolia and invited him to become affiliated with ROLCC upon discovering that the young church planter and ROLCC share the same vision and ministry philosophies. In November 1999, Amid Ug Christian Church became ROLCC's first cross-cultural church plant, and in due time this church of six members would become the only megachurch in Mongolia, with 2000 active members, while planting 51 Mongolian churches in Mongolia, Korea, Switzerland, and the United States.

In 2000, because of the pleasant and effective partnership with EHC in Mongolia, ROLCC began supporting EHC's ministry in Togo and planted the first African church plant there in February 2001, and then eight months later planted another church in Benin. Between March 2004 and April 2005, ROLCC welcomed three churches into the network, thereby expanding to Ghana, Nigeria, and Cameroon. In 2009, ROLCC commissioned a pastor of ROLCC Benin to plant in Burkina Faso, which marked the beginning of a new model of church planting, where ROLCC's church plants became active partners in ROLCC's church planting ministry by supplying the planters. This enabled ROLCC to plant in Senegal (2012), South Africa (2013), Ivory Coast (2016), Niger (2018), Eswatini (2018), Mozambique (2019), and Congo (2020). Together with a Guinea-Bissau church that joined the network in 2014, these constitute the vibrant ROLCC's African ministry that consists of eighty-six churches in fourteen nations.

Besides beginning a new model of church planting, 2008–2009 also marks two other milestones. First, in 2008, ROLCC planted its first church in Europe by welcoming an African church in Italy into the network. Second, in 2009, ROLCC planted a church in Kazakhstan, which is among the most significant breakthroughs of the ministry, for efforts since the early 2000s to establish a Central Asia church had proved unavailing. Through the help of Russian-speaking Pastor Batbold of Mongolia, ROLCC recruited Pastor N. to plant in Kazakhstan and later became connected with Pastor D. of Turkey (2014) and Pastor S. of Uzbekistan (2017).[2]

In 2010, Pastor Bill Baldwin, an itinerant speaker who frequently spoke at ROLCC, held revival meetings in the Philippines and asked ROLCC to consider planting a church to pastor the new converts, which led to ROLCC planting its first church in Southeast and South Asia. In 2013 and 2015, ROLCC planted in India and Myanmar by recruiting fresh graduates of partner seminaries. Then in 2019, ROLCC welcomed a Guatemalan church and thirty-five Cambodian churches into its network through South East Asia Prayer Center (SEAPC), which marked two records. While the Guatemalan church marked ROLCC's expansion into Latin America, the Cambodian churches marked the largest number of churches joining the ROLCC network.

By Dec 2020, ROLCC had planted forty churches in the United States and Canada, all of whom were mandarin speaking, with the exception of three Mongolian churches. In Latin America, there is a Guatemalan church and three Chinese churches in Brazil and Mexico. In Asia, ROLCC has planted 134 churches in ten Asian countries, with members exceeding 10,000. Africa has a cumulative congregation of 22,000 people, scattered among eighty-six church plants in fourteen nations. As for Europe, there are three African churches in Italy and a Mongolian church in Switzerland. All together, ROLCC has planted 268 churches in thirty-one nations, with an estimated 40,000 members over the past 24 years.

Success Factors Analysis: Vision, Strategy, and Culture

This section seeks to examine ROLCC's vision, strategy, and culture to uncover its motivation, methodology, and value toward cross-cultural church planting ministry.

Vision: Building A Glorious Church that Participates in *Missio Dei*

When Liu was preparing to launch a new church in 1994, he happened to read Revelations 22:1–5 and conceived the idea of naming the new church "River of Life." Upon further study of the passage, he drew from the imageries of the throne, river, leaves, and servants in the passage and developed them into the four "strategies" of River of Life Christian Church, namely "Praise and Worship," "Holy Spirit Renewal," "Cell Church," and "World Mission." Among the four, World Mission was the first that came to Liu with the phrase "the river of life shall flow to all nations and all people." This, along with his encounter with the Lord where the Lord challenged him, "did your Bible says 'Go and make disciples of all Chinese,' or 'all people?'" and commissioned ROLCC, "then you go," position mission right at the center of ROLCC's understanding of its identity and purpose.

It is crucial to note that ROLCC's commitment to mission also stems from Liu's personal commitment to *Missio Dei*.[3] When Liu attended Bread of Life Christian Church (BOLCC) Taipei as a teenager, the founder Timothy Dzao's dedication to mission left Liu with an enduring impression that mission is essential and worthy of lifelong commitment.[4] Then when Liu, a seminarian at Westminster Theological Seminary, participated in the preparation and follow-up of the first Chinese Mission Convention (CMC) in 1983, his interactions with the speakers convinced him that every Christian ought to participate in *Missio Dei*. In Liu's first pastorate in a Christian Mission and Alliance (CM&A) church from 1985 to 1995, his interactions with CM&A missionaries broadened his exposure to God's work outside of the Chinese diaspora. Eventually, while attending the first All Nations Worship and Praise Celebration in 1991,[5] Liu conceived that God's heart is for the nations to return to Him and thus dedicated his life to mission. He attributed this conference as a watershed moment that made him "a goner for mission." As the founder and senior pastor of ROLCC, Liu's personal commitment to the Great Commission inevitably became a crucial factor in making the church mission-minded.

ROLCC's affiliation with Bread of Life Christian Church Taipei has further enhanced its connection to *Missio Dei*. Bread of Life Christian Church Taipei, following the footstep of Dzao,[6] sees mission and church planting as what the Lord has entrusted to the largest Chinese church in Taiwan, therefore making church planting its ministry focus while encouraging all its daughter churches to participate in church planting. As a daughter church of Bread of Life Christian Church Taipei, ROLCC sees itself as part of a Chinese movement of world mission and church planting, first began by Dzao himself and carried on by Bread of Life Christian Church and ROLCC. This connection provides a profound sense of calling and destiny, which further fueled ROLCC's vision of a glorious church participating in *Missio Dei*.

Strategy: Prayer and Partnership

Prayer, which ROLCC views as "the beginning of cross-cultural mission," is a core strategy for its church planting ministry as the key to discerning God's leading and discovering God's guidance in the field. ROLCC often sends key stakeholders to prayer walk in the land it plans to enter. For example, when ROLCC was considering whether to plant in Benin, it sent a team from the United States to a prayer walk in Benin with the planter, Pastor Corneille, before finalizing the decision. As the churches in Togo, Benin, and Ghana began to plant cross-culturally in the last decade, part of the decision process was a prayer walk in the prospective locations. Prayer plays a dominant role in discerning God's call and experiencing God's divine guidance.

Besides its indispensable role in the field, prayer plays a crucial role at ROLCC in raising mission awareness. ROLCC designates times in every Sunday service and weekly prayer meeting to pray for a country, people group, daughter church, or mission organization, and this has become a subtle yet effective way to cultivate a passion for mission. On top of that, ROLCC's assignment of an organization or daughter church to every cell group and asking all cell groups to pray regularly for them has allowed individuals to learn about mission via prayer letters. Prayer plays an irreplaceable role in the ministry of mission at ROLCC, to the point that ROLCC has a motto of "mission begins with prayer."

Besides prayer, ROLCC has been taking the initiative to form strategic partnerships with sending agencies, evangelistic ministries, media ministries, and seminaries (collectively "organizations" here onwards), believing that partnering with organizations in the field is the key to overcoming cross-cultural challenges. It is critical to note that these partnerships go beyond the usual sponsor-beneficiary model to a relational model that this researcher dubs as "friendship partnership,"[7] where intimate relationships are intentionally cultivated and maintained through prayer initiatives and mutual visitations. While prayer garners genuine care for the organizations, the regular visitations to and from the field provide incredible opportunities to bond. In some cases, ROLCC's partnership with organizations is structured as full sponsorships of particular projects ("adoption" in ROLCC's glossary), which allows for ongoing collaborations.[8] Such cultivation of intimate relationships and unwavering support is so effective that multiple partners have publicly claimed that ROLCC is a comrade that joins them in their quest to accomplish their calling, not merely a financial sponsor.

Besides partnering with organizations, ROLCC adamantly insists on recruiting seminary-trained local ministers, viewing supporting them as an efficient way of conducting cross-cultural mission. Whereas cross-cultural missionaries often face tremendous linguistic and cultural barriers, the local ministers can effectively minister as they are familiar with the context. Moreover, in critical fields such as the Arab world and Communist regimes, where visas remain an insurmountable challenge for foreign missionaries, the local ministers are often the only relatively safe and effective way to conduct ministry.[9] While evading the sending model's weaknesses, the local minister model faces its greatest challenge in communication, especially when the local ministers only speak the local languages.[10] When it comes to recruiting local ministers, though trustworthy candidates are indeed hard to come by, ROLCC navigates this particular challenge with relative ease by soliciting referrals from the organizations. Being close friends of ROLCC, organizations are usually enthusiastic about referring ideal candidates who can work with ROLCC and them to ROLCC. As a result, ROLCC almost never finds itself in the dire circumstances of recruiting problematic candidates.

Prayer and partnership are essential strategies for ROLCC's church planting ministry, as there would not be a cross-cultural ministry without them. Prayers are regarded as the most critical key to discerning God's call and experiencing divine guidance in the field, as well as the most natural way to cultivate mission awareness and provide mission education at ROLCC, while partnerships with organizations and local ministers successfully navigate the challenge of crossing cultural barriers to expand quickly.

Culture: Audacity and Generosity

While ROLCC's culture may be a neglected factor in the observation and discussion of ROLCC's church planting ministry, an analysis of ROLCC culture is crucial as it explores the necessary underlying conditions that enabled the flourishing of its cross-cultural ministry. This subsection will first explore how ROLCC's culture of audacity and generosity mobilizes and sustains ROLCC's cross-cultural ministry before analyzing how ROLCC's charismatic and mission-centered spirituality contributes to such a culture.

More commonly expressed as "courageously following God's leading by faith," ROLCC's culture of audacity enables it to pursue cross-cultural ministry despite uncertainties and adversities. The fact that ROLCC had neither directions nor strategies when it first began cross-cultural ministry, coupled with ROLCC's innovative ways to do mission, such as recruiting local ministers and "adoption" style sponsorship, reveals a high-risk tolerance amid uncertainties. Such culture is also expressed via its tenacity when a ministry faces great adversities. The first five years of the Benin church were extraordinarily challenging, but ROLCC chose to unwaveringly stand with and support the planter, even when he wondered if he should continue. Likewise, after Central Asia's initial setback in 2003, ROLCC did not give up but was determined to keep striving until a breakthrough happened, conducting prayer walks in Central Asia every year until it found Pastor N. to plant in Kazakhstan six years later. Without such risk tolerance and tenacity resulting from a culture of audacity, ROLCC would have a much smaller ministry in Africa and no ministry in Central Asia.

As expressed in the motto "the anointing of River of Life is the anointing of giving," generosity is another crucial element of ROLCC's culture, having resolved that financial commitment is the most basic that ROLCC can do to advance the kingdom of God. Even though the regular support for church plants has exceeded one million dollars annually, ROLCC remains committed to supporting them and planting new churches. Besides daughter churches, ROLCC also gives generously to the partner organizations, allocating $375,000 in 2020 to support eighteen organizations and five missionaries.[11] Note that these financial commitments are stable and sacrificial in nature, as ROLCC has long determined to never decrease financial support due to its financial challenges. As a result of such priority given to mission, some daughter churches had completed their building projects at the time when ROLCC was still renting. Along with audacity, generosity forms the backbone of ROLCC's cross-cultural church planting ministry. Audacity enables ROLCC to step out in faith and persevere when things do not happen in the ways ROLCC wished, while generosity releases resources necessary for ROLCC to expand rapidly.

Such a culture of audacity and generosity arises from its charismatic spirituality of viewing ministry as the ultimate purpose of charisma and believing it has received a missional anointing. When teaching on the purpose of charisma, Liu often claims that ROLCC is not charismatic but "practical charismatic," using the qualifier to denounce the tendency of self-indulgence resulting from charismatic experiences, stressing the ministerial aspect instead. This researcher observes that three factors may have contributed to such insistence. The first is Liu's interpretation of passages that spoke of the Spirit's works, the second was him receiving glossolalia while praying for a sister in a coma, and the third is his observation that many in the Renewal movement have become self-serving. Such an insistence on ministry naturally creates a tendency to view God's blessing-at-large, such as earning power and technology, as having the ultimate purpose of contributing to God's kingdom. ROLCC's conviction of having received a special anointing for cross-cultural mission stems from countless inspiring testimonies of God's wondrous works, such as opening doors in impossible circumstances and granting breakthroughs beyond expectations.[12] As a result, setbacks in the fields are never viewed as dreadful failures but only as temporal obstacles that will be conquered, thereby generating fervent prayers and expectations of God's breakthrough rather than fears and discouragements, which Liu views as top killers for mission. While the idea of ministry as the ultimate purpose of charisma gives rise to ROLCC's culture of generosity, its conviction of being anointed for mission contributes to ROLCC's culture of audacity.

Apart from its charismatic spirituality, mission-centered spirituality is another factor that contributes to ROLCC's culture of audacity and generosity. Besides the "adoption" style sponsorships and prayer initiatives that generate mission awareness, the designation of October as mission month has provided opportunities for mission education, as Liu would preach on ROLCC's vision and strategies of mission while also having organizations and daughter churches give their updates. On top of the campaign, the smaller fundraising campaigns and send-off prayers that ROLCC does for each mission team serve as an excellent way for the congregants to participate in mission.[13] Through these intentional designs, along with the constant sharings of testimonies and updates through sermons and media productions, a ROLCC congregant will have multiple exposures of mission on any given service, which minimizes the sense of distance between the congregation and the fields while raising mission awareness, providing mission education, and paving ways for mission participation. Such mission-centeredness is the key to formulating a culture of audacity and generosity at ROLCC, as it creates an atmosphere where everyone understands that ROLCC is serious about mission.

This section has examined how ROLCC's vision, strategy, and culture contribute to its thriving cross-cultural church planting ministry. ROLCC's vision of a glorious church participating in *Missio Dei* comes from its interpretation of Rev 22:1–5, Liu's personal commitment to *Missio Dei*, and its affiliations with BOLCC Taipei, provides the ultimate motivation that fuels its commitment to church planting. ROLCC's thoughtful devising of prayer and partnerships as core mission strategies have helped ROLCC bypass many bottlenecks to expand rapidly. At the same time, its culture of audacity and generosity, which bases upon its charismatic and mission-centered spirituality, provides the settings that allow ROLCC's vision and strategy to take root, which enable such committed missional engagement.

Critical Assessments: Missiological Convictions and Sustainability

The most apparent missiological conviction of ROLCC is that church planting is an effective strategy for local churches to participate in the Great Commission. This is based on three observations. First, while evangelistic efforts such as massive gospel rallies have brought hundreds of thousands to Christ, most new converts do not join a local church, as evidenced by the growth of church attendance far below the number of decision cards. Second, while many churches have sent mission teams to a mission field to conduct outreach, the dynamics of being an outsider often limit the ministry's effectiveness. By establishing a local-led church plant, the churches and organizations from the outside world would have a reliable partner trusted by the locals for long-term evangelism and societal transformation efforts. Third, since local churches have developed expertise in pastoral ministry and conducting services, church planting would be playing to their strengths while relieving organizations from the pastoral demands so they can focus on evangelism. From these observations, ROLCC has come to view church planting as the most effective way for local churches to participate in mission.

Also at the heart of ROLCC mission engagements is the conviction that the Chinese churches are uniquely positioned to conduct cross-cultural mission. Given the vibrance of Christianity among the Chinese diaspora, many Chinese ministers have advocated the idea that "the twenty-first century is a century of Chinese mission" and encourage Chinese Christianity to "take up the baton of mission" to "repay the gospel debt."[14] As ROLCC experiences firsthand that the Chinese are viewed more favorably than Caucasians in many critical mission fields, ROLCC believes that the time has come for Chinese churches to reach the world with the gospel.[15] Furthermore, as a megachurch located in the prosperous and innovative Silicon Valley of the United States, where most ROLCC congregants are open to innovative ideas, willing to support worthy causes, and conversant in English, ROLCC believes that it has been uniquely positioned to contribute to *Missio Dei*.

Realizing that the task of completing the Great Commission is beyond what any organization can achieve by itself and requires the whole Church to participate, empowering others in their missions becomes another of ROLCC's core missiological convictions. Liu often stresses that the ultimate reason for committing significant financial resources to support organizations is not to expand ROLCC but to help to advance what the Lord is doing through them. Therefore, ROLCC is careful to ensure the relationship with organizations is one of frontline and back-support where both are fighting together for the long haul. Similarly, the pastors of ROLCC's church plants have complete ownership of their ministries; even the regional directors that oversee national directors are the local ministers and not someone from ROLCC. Besides partnering with organizations and local ministers, ROLCC is also prone to accept invitations from others to share ROLCC's journey of cross-cultural ministry, hoping that such sharing will help others to engage in *Missio Dei*.

Holistic mission is also another core missiological conviction of ROLCC. Triggered by an African minister's cry that his deepest desire is for his fellow countryman to be saved before they die of AIDS, Liu began to reflect on the implication of the gospel on the present life and concluded that God's concern over his image-bearers is not limited to just personal salvation but includes the wellbeing of the present life. Therefore, missional engagement has to go beyond saving the souls to other facets of life, such as lack of access to medical resources and education. This broadened comprehension of mission has resulted in ROLCC changing its fourth strategy from "World Mission" to "Glocal Impact" in 2007 to make such an expanded view of mission explicit.[16] It has since established multiple parachurch ministries to seek societal transformations, including a charitable foundation that establishes four orphanages housing 250 children, two career training centers that have trained 400 adults with a 95 percent job placement rate, and a medical clinic that serves thousands throughout COVID-19. It is noteworthy that these parachurch ministries are tied closely with the church plants, examples being them carrying "River of Life" in their name and are often located on the church's premises. Such arrangement helps the church in gaining a good reputation, making it easier for the churches to expand.

At the same time, missiologically, two issues may be of concern. First is the tendency of triumphalism. While ROLCC does not subscribe to the prosperity gospel, the mentionings of the ministry sometimes carry a tone of triumphalism. Though ROLCC mentions challenges and setbacks during prayer times, other mentionings sometimes carry a triumphalistic tone. When inquired about his view on this, Liu felt that he has been restrained in sharing these breakthroughs as there are much more that he has not shared. And he sees these sharings as illustrative of God's nature while being accountable to the church. While Liu's points are valid, some observers have pointed out that an overtly triumphalistic narrative could lead to some version of the prosperity gospel.

The second potential issue is the diversity of theological viewpoints. While ROLCC only recruits ministers who agree with its vision and strategies, one may question if this alone is enough to sustain the ministry in the long run. For example, while all pastors are Spirit-filled, some hold classical Pentecostal theology while others lean close to the prosperity gospel; both differ from ROLCC's third-wave orientation. In an interview with Liu, he contends that unity should be based on vision and not theology, seeing theologies as matters of personal convictions that he needs not interfere with.[17] While such an inclusive approach is respectable, this researcher opines that overtly diverse theological viewpoints have a high potential of developing into disunity and splits, especially when patriarch-like figures like Liu are no longer at the helm.

The most significant uncertain element in the long-term sustainability of this ministry would be the impact of the post-Tong Liu era, specifically whether ROLCC can continue to be successful in carrying the vision of planting churches and raising adequate funds. Liu feels that the chances for the abovementioned concerns to materialize are tiny, as long as the next senior pastor and his/her pastoral team have the passion, exposure, and anointing in cross-cultural ministry, which he believes they are and will remain so.[18] While agreeing with Liu's sentiment, this researcher feels less certain about fundraising, as it may be hard to preserve ROLCC's congregation size (and subsequently mission offerings), given that Liu is the number-one factor in many choosing to become ROLCC's congregants.

Apart from this, it seems that ROLCC's church planting ministry is highly scalable, as illustrated by the impressive prospects in Central Asia and Africa. ROLCC Mongolia, having grown from a tiny church of six members in 1999 to the only Mongolian megachurch and planted fifty Mongolian churches throughout Mongolia, South Korea, Switzerland, and the United States, is now conducting mission cross-culturally throughout Central Asia. Besides connecting trustworthy ministers in Kazakhstan, Turkey, and Uzbekistan to ROLCC which resulted in around a dozen churches, ROLCC Mongolia has sent missionaries to Kyrgyzstan and Afghanistan while seeking opportunities to enter Tajikistan and Turkmenistan. Likewise, with ROLCC's current footprint in more than a quarter of African nations and its various influential parachurch ministries, it is within its purview to project ROLCC will plant in every African nation. With these prospects, it seems that ROLCC will continue to plant cross-culturally.

Besides being scalable, it also seems that some of ROLCC's practices in conducting cross-cultural church planting are replicable, such as recruiting local ministers and adoption style partnerships. The Lutheran denomination in Taiwan is now working on recruiting African ministers to plant cross-cultural churches in Africa after some explorations of

ROLCC's model. EHC, which has witnessed firsthand how the "adoption" style sponsorship benefits both ROLCC and itself, has developed ROLCC's model into its "adopt-a-nation" campaign. While most churches would neither be able to commit two million dollars per year for mission nor send their senior pastor to travel intensively, ROLCC is confident that its approaches to empowering locals and deep partnership with organizations are game-changing to most churches that want to participate in *Missio Dei*.

Conclusion

This study begins with a narration of how God has led ROLCC from a tiny congregation in 1996 to 268 church plants in over thirty-one nations of all major continents, with an estimated 40,000 people gathering every Sunday. Next, this study analyzes how ROLCC's vision, strategy, and culture contribute to such growth. It proposes that the vision of a glorious church participating in *Missio Dei* is the ultimate motivation for cross-cultural mission, while the strategies of prayer and partnerships paint a roadmap to turn the vision into a reality, with a culture of generosity and courage resulting from its charismatic and mission-centered spirituality, provided the basis of the ministry. Last, in assessing ROLCC missiology and sustainability, this study identified four core missiological convictions: viewing church planting as an effective mission strategy, believing that the Chinese churches are uniquely positioned to contribute to *Missio Dei*, empowering others, and holistic mission. While there are some minor concerns with triumphalism, theological diversity, and potential challenges in the post-Liu era, ROLCC's cross-cultural church planting ministry is scalable and replicable.

Notes

1. In ROLCC's glossary, "church planting" includes accepting existing churches to join the network, not necessarily starting a new church from scratch. The numbers in this study are current as of December 2020.
2. Names redacted for the pastors' safety.
3. Most information from this paragraph is from an interview with Tong Liu, November 27, 2020. Interview conducted in Santa Clara, California.

4   Dzao was a prominent Chinese evangelist in the twentieth century, having held countless gospel rallies in Greater China, East, and Southeast Asia, Germany, Greece, Switzerland, Sweden, Holland, and North America. He was the most widely traveled Chinese evangelist of his time.

5   The organizer of this event, Korean missionary Stephen Ha (Ha Yong-Inn) and All Nations Worship and Praise Ministries has been widely credited as the most important influence that stimulated the Chinese Praise & Worship movement and fostered the Taiwanese church's commitment towards *Missio Dei*.

6   Dzao was the earliest Chinese involved in cross-cultural mission. Besides advocating for cross-cultural mission, including as a speaker on the Berlin Congress of World Evangelism, he founded the first Chinese mission agency that conducted cross-cultural mission intensively.

7   The term derives from Liu's often referring of these partners as "our good friends."

8   ROLCC has adopted Every Home for Christ ministry in Mongolia since 1997, Togo since 2000, and Iraq since 2007.

9   ROLCC once sent a congregant to Kyrgyzstan as cross-cultural missionary in 2002, but due to language, visa, and lack of reliable local connections, it had to exit the field in 2003. For ROLCC, this incident illustrates the difficulty for a foreigner to establish a ministry in restricted area, particularly when there is no local connections.

10 This occurs most frequently in Central Asia and Africa, where some ministers speak neither English nor any major languages like Russian or French. As a result, communications sometimes have to go through three or even four layers of translations: from English to French (Africa) or Russian (Central Asia), then to one or two local language(s).

11 A full list of all organizations and individuals that ROLCC supports may be found at: https://www.rolcc.net/rolcc/glocal-impact/map.

12 These, along with the often-repeated narrative of "ROLCC began its mission ministry with neither direction nor strategy, yet God has led us to accomplish this much," paint a narrative that God has specifically called ROLCC and is working through ROLCC.

13 For every overseas mission trip, one third of the expenses are raised via a small church-wide fundraising campaign.

14 "Take up the baton of mission" was an analogy of a relay race, where the Chinese are thought of as the receiver of the baton that is being passed down from the western missionaries, while "repaying the gospel debt" is a term borrowed from Romans 1:14. Note that this represents a significant

paradigm shift; for as recent as forty years ago, most Chinese churches would argue that mission should focus on the vast majority of Chinese who are non-Christians.

15 Partly due to China's rising prominence and Chinese economic power, the Chinese have relatively more opportunities to engage in critical mission fields like the Arab world and communist regimes.

16 The term "Glocal" comes from global+local, reflecting the understanding that mission has to be done both locally and globally.

17 Interview with Tong Liu, November 27, 2020.

18 Interview with Tong Liu, November 27, 2020.

23 Spirit-Empowered Internet Evangelism in an Age of Global Individuality

Mark Flattery

Abstract

This chapter presents internet evangelism as a contextual strategy for twenty-first century ministry. In order to fulfill the remaining task of Great Commission, Spirit-empowered believers can leverage the internet as an evangelistic tool and interact with individuals on a global scale. This necessitates the understanding of the opportunities in the virtual world and requires a strategy to journey online with individuals and connect them with communities of faith in the physical world. This study explores both the challenges and opportunities for evangelism presented by the virtual world.

Introduction

As followers of Jesus Christ, we take The Great Commission as our marching orders. It is our desire to "go make disciples of all nations" (Matt 28:18–20) and to "Go into all the world and preach the gospel to all creation" (Mark 16:15). As internet usage has exploded and is now woven into the fabric of societies worldwide, the church has an unprecedented opportunity go to all nations to speak truth into the lives of individuals in every nation, tribe, people, and language (Rev 7:9). An outcome of the global expansion of the internet is the creation of a new persona that I call "global individuality." Global individuality is a mindset that empowers the individual in the global marketplace. Individuals are equipped to express opinions, join groups that were previously unreachable, participate in the global economy, and interact with anyone, anywhere. It enables individuals to develop a personal sense of "self" and empowers them to exist far beyond the limitations of the physical world. Spirit-empowered believers can leverage the internet as an evangelistic tool and interact with individuals on a global scale. This necessitates the understanding of the opportunities in the virtual world and requires a strategy to journey online with individuals and connect them with communities of faith in the physical world.

The Impact and Usage of the Internet

We can begin our journey by considering the internet and its impact on individuals and nations. First, Internet World Stats reported that as of March 31, 2021, there are an estimated 5.1 billion internet users in our world, whose total estimated population is 7.8 billion people.[1] This means that 65.6 percent of the world's population uses the internet. Second, the impact and reach of the internet are immense and growing. It is reported that China has the highest amount of internet users in the world, with 854 million individuals. It is estimated the internet has over 1.8 billion websites, 354.7 million domain name registrations, and that revenues from e-commerce retail reaching $4.2 trillion in 2020.[2] Third, it is estimated that of the world's 7.75 billion people, over 5.19 billion use a mobile phone, 4.54 billion people are internet users, and 3.8 billion individuals are "active social media users."[3] Fourth, the United Nations (UN) saw the importance of the internet on a global scale and acted. The UN's draft resolution entitled, "The Promotion, Protection, and Enjoyment of Human Rights on the Internet," condemned internet access disruption as a human rights violation.[4] In the United States, life, liberty, and the pursuit of happiness are valued as unalienable rights. Now, internet access is valued as a human right.

The fact is that the internet is impacting the lives of individuals in both the physical and the virtual world. It is so significant that the lines between the physical and virtual worlds are increasingly blurred and becoming ever more indistinguishable. This gives Spirit-filled believers an open door to fulfilling the Great Commission within the virtual world. It provides opportunities to engage people in almost every nation in the world, as well as those who are not reachable in the physical world due to their beliefs or living in a location where Christianity is discouraged or persecuted.

The Internet as a Mission Field

The internet is becoming so woven into the fabric of society that a new phrase has been created: "the internet of things." This is when almost anything electronic can be operated in an existing internet structure. Televisions, refrigerators, vehicles, and lights can all intersect via the internet. People around the world are embracing the internet and discovering ways to embed it into their lifestyles. Soon, the internet will be available for everyone on the planet. Some companies are working diligently to get power wirelessly to every location on the globe. Others are lowering the cost so that hand-held devices will be affordable even to the poorest of the poor. Competitors are attempting to be the first to bring artificial intelligence to everyone, everywhere, and will take internet usage to a whole new level. The internet is not a passing fad but is becoming a necessity of life.

As technology advances, people around the world are gaining increasingly more access. The internet goes beyond being a one-way communication medium. It goes to the next level because it creates a community in which people live, interact, and have a choice as to what content they will consume. Online people can find their identity, persona, and brand so much so that they can be a completely different person than they are in physical reality.

Individuals from every continent, nation, economic status, religious belief, gender, political viewpoint, language group, marital status, parental status, and ethnicity go online for the same reasons: business, news, entertainment, social networking, and education. But they are also searching for answers to the dilemmas of life that trouble them. Like the marketplace of old, the *agora* of antiquity, the internet is a place of commerce, interaction, and exchanging of ideas. Most are ready and willing to voice their opinions and interact with others. Many people of different religions, political views, and various motives are willing to provide answers. We, as the church, must be online to tell the searching about Jesus. The church has an unprecedented opportunity to present the gospel, interact with individuals at their point of need, offer discipleship, and direct people to local churches around the world. The harvest fields of the internet are plentiful (Matt 9:35–38). Thus, the internet is a mission field.

"Internet Users" as a People Group

Since the internet is a mission field, it follows that "internet users" is a people group. The 1982 Lausanne Committee Chicago meeting statement defines a people group as:

> A significantly large sociological grouping of individuals who perceive themselves to have a common affinity with one another. For evangelization purposes, a people group is the largest group within which the gospel can

spread as a church-planting movement without encountering barriers of understanding or acceptance.⁵

Of course, when this statement was written, we were unaware in the general public of the concept of the internet and of its ability to empower individuals. Internet users comprises a group of individuals who gather online and have a "common affinity with one another." The common affinities include using the internet for many reasons such as business, news, entertainment, social networking, education, and even church services. On the internet, you can find like-minded people, do business, find and build relationships, download and upload news and opinions, find entertainment, and learn from others about life, love, and languages. These reasons are needs-based as individuals find online what they are seeking.

Another common factor for internet users is that they go online as individuals who have a choice as to what content they will consume. They may or may not allow that which defines them in their physical life to impact their online activity. For example, a Muslim seeking an understanding of who Jesus is may not feel safe asking people within his immediate social context but will do so online with the anonymity and security it affords. A devout Christian man would never visit a brothel and yet is tempted to delve into the depths of pornography online. Regardless of what they do, they have a choice, and the presence of this choice is a "common affinity."

In one sense, the concept of "people group" has directed mission agencies and missionaries to focus on reaching people as groups, losing the fact that we can minister to individuals. Ministry opportunities online offer believers ministry on an individual basis rather than projecting their evangelistic message to crowds or training others to minister. As people migrate to other nations and are forced to adapt, the concept of defining them by their languages, tribal affiliation, and geography becomes increasingly difficult. Also, when they become believers in Christ, their identity in the family of God trumps all other designations. However, an increasing number of these same people go online to join the internet culture and are empowered to express their voice, engage others, and find solutions to their life issues. Thus, we must add to the conversation about people groups, the mission field of the internet, and internet users as a people group.

Globalism as a World System

As people around the world join together online, "globalism" as a world system has developed, forcing us not to be limited by geography or language but to consider how people can interact on a global scale. Globalism is a world system that influences everyone. Our world is becoming increasingly smaller as people move from one nation to another and economics have brought nations together in working relationships. For example, some people in the United States want to buy vehicles that are "made in America." However, the fact is that most cars have parts that were created in other nations and shipped to the United States to be assembled. In fact, there are a significant number of vehicles assembled in the United States, with none of the parts being manufactured in the States. It may be that to buy a new car made entirely in the United States or any other single country is impossible. The world comes together to manufacture, assemble, and ship vehicles in the global marketplace.

Internet users are now enabled to engage others around the world as global citizens. Online, you are in the cyber world and can communicate with anyone on the globe. You can play video games with someone in Russia. You can facetime family in Argentina. You can watch a video placed on Facebook by the missionary you support who is in a sensitive nation. You can receive emails from friends in Japan just as easily as you can from your friends in Florida. You can order online from China, South Africa, or Los Angeles and have it delivered to your front door within days. You can watch videos of church services from the International English Church in Jakarta, Indonesia, or from James River in Ozark, MO. You can follow your favorite sports team, be they a professional football team in the United States or a professional soccer team in the English Premier League. The world is just a click away. Access to everyone everywhere is easy as using your handheld device. We are limited by time, space, and finances in the physical world. In the virtual world, we are global citizens interacting with others in our internet users people group.

Globalism and Evangelism

Globalism as a world system presents the church with an opportunity to present the gospel. God's anointing is on believers around the world, and thus, ministry can be networked on a global scale and is not limited to only one people group, denomination, or nation. The church can engage the internet to learn more about individuals and their beliefs as they migrate from their country of origin to a new nation. Globalism should cause the church to no longer be limited by geographic boundaries but instead should seek to impact individuals no matter their location, economic status, or religion.

With the common use of the internet, ministers of the gospel have the opportunity to proclaim truth to the people in the global marketplace. A worship leader in Australia, a pastor in Kenya, an evangelist from Brazil, or a teacher from France can all have a powerfully effective ministry to the nations via the internet. People are no longer limited to receiving truth from only what is available in their local town or media market. Globalism is uniting the world and bringing people together.

"Global Individuality" as a Mindset

I submit that members of the internet users people group have developed a new mindset, a new manner of looking at themselves and how they fit into society. I call this new identity "global individuality." While individuals participating in the mission field of the internet will not recognize this label, once they learn of it, they will have to admit that it applies to them on some level. Individuals worldwide, like you and me, engage the internet to meet their needs, become global citizens, and experience empowerment as individuals. Global individuality is the mindset that empowers the individual in the global marketplace. Individuals worldwide can now declare, "I am in control of my life. I can do anything, with anyone, and be anyone I want to be in a virtual, on-demand world. I am not limited by geography, nationality, religion, economic status, culture, gender, or language. I am looking for communities to join so that I can grow in my areas of interest, interact with like-minded people, and have a sense of belonging."

Individuals around the world are using the internet daily for many of the same reasons, and that is to fulfill a need, including searching the internet to discover answers to life's issues that trouble them. The issues range from the practical, like how to change a light bulb, to the profound, such as how to discover true meaning in life. Some use the internet for personal improvements, such as how to learn to play a musical instrument or to learn another language, while others will feed the desires of their flesh which leads to their spiritual demise.

When internet users participate in the virtual world, they are acting as global citizens of the internet mission field. One can buy and sell goods online from those who are on the other side of the world and have those items delivered to their front door in days. Online, you can read current events from news agencies from the world nations and upload your video, podcast, or article and create news for other global citizens to consume. Social media provides access to people not only from other nations at the click of a mouse, but also provides a bridge to unite friends from decades past. In that sense, we are no longer limited by geography or accessibility.

I use the word "individuality" because it emphasizes the individual, the person. To me, "individualism" implies that I can stand out among others and be unique in the context of my group. "Individuality" means that I can be whomever I want regardless of my context. In fact, I choose the contexts where I want to be. No longer am I limited by the realities of my physical life, such as nationality, language, social status, or economic status. If I choose, I can present my identity online in one community vastly different than my identity in a different community.

Global individuality empowers individuals to express their views in the global marketplace. Blogs, chat rooms, and comment sections on websites are examples of how the internet provides anyone the opportunity to voice their opinions. Previously, only those with appropriate credentials, name recognition, or status of some nature had their comments made public. Today, everyone has a voice to the extent that those who consume the opinion no longer care about the qualifications of the one presenting the views but take the comments at face value. A benign example of empowering the individual is seen when someone has a negative experience at a hotel, restaurant, or place of business. Previously, a disgruntled customer would proclaim, "I will sue!" or "I am contacting the Better Business Bureau!" The contemporary response is "I'm writing a terrible review on your website!" or "I'm telling my friends on social media and warning them about you!" Grave and tragic examples include the man in Egypt who was photographed after being beaten to death[6] and the man in Tunisia whose self-immolation sparked uprisings that went viral and led to the Arab Spring.[7] The internet empowers individuals to deliver their message to their nation and to challenge the people of the world to respond.

Global individuality empowers the individual to seek answers and address their quest for learning. People might be afraid to investigate issues of life that interest them or cause them to question their friends. In doing so, they risk shame, rejection, or reprisal. So, they go online looking to interact on subjects such as religious views, health issues, or relationship matters. Online, there is a sense of anonymity and security that empowers individuals to delve into issues that matter to them and connects them to those who are in the same situation.

It should be noted that not everyone who is active online as an internet user will create a new persona or be someone in the virtual world that they are not in the physical world. It seems that most people will be the same person online that they are in physical reality. However, their participation as internet users activates the global individuality mindset. They are empowered with the opportunity to open go their hearts and minds online and find answers. While a Muslim woman in Algeria, an atheist man in France, and a Kenyan teenager in Nairobi contemplating suicide may not seek answers from a religious person, go to a church, or seek spiritual answers, they will go online looking for help, hope, and even a reason to live. The global individuality mindset empowers them to look beyond their physical world and limitations of their personal reality and engage in conversation with people they could encounter in no other manner. For this reason, we must be online to tell them about Jesus.

Implications of Global Individuality

We will now consider three specific outcomes of global individuality. First, an outcome of global individuality is that individuals are so active online, and it captures so much of their time that their presence in the virtual world has become their reality. A significant number of adults in first-world nations are constantly online. The stereotype for younger people is that they spend multiple hours daily playing video games. Others are very active on social media such as Facebook, Instagram, and Twitter. While some may not consider the virtual world to be their reality, they use the internet regularly to the point that they would not want to live life without it. Imagine if you went through today without internet access, without using your computer, handheld device, or cell phone. How would you feel, and how productive would you be? What if businesses were forced to operate without technology? Your experiences in the grocery store, at your bank, and the airport would be vastly different; frustratingly and painstakingly so. Without internet access, your involvement as a global citizen and empowerment to control aspects of your life in an on-demand world would be altered severely.

The second outcome of global individuality is that many are empowered now to be self-focused in both the real and virtual worlds. Individuals are enabled to be whomever he or she desires to be without regard to others or the rules of society. Thus, the focus shifts from the community to the individual. "Individualism" means that I could be all that I can be within the context of the group, and ultimately, it will benefit the community. Global individuality means that I can be whomever I want regardless of my external communities and thus mandates that either my community changes to accommodate me or I will find like-minded people, and we will form our own community.

Third, in spiritual matters, the huge positive implication of global individuality is that people are searching online for answers to the dilemmas of life. As previously mentioned, this presents an amazing open door into their hearts and lives so that we can help them "discover and grow in their journey with God."[8] The negative aspect of global individuality is that people have such an overabundance of information that they can pick and choose biblical teaching and curate their own personal theology. Global individuality presents an opportunity for the church to proclaim Jesus Christ to all the world on a one-to-one basis. Individuals are empowered online to go beyond the physical world that defines them to seek answers to issues that concern them and heart-felt needs that matter most to them. They are encouraged online to interact with others, to listen to alternative views, and to state their personal opinions. While the internet is a tool and neutral in and of itself, when evaluated in the light of morality, the users of the internet are empowered to utilize it as a community in which they can interact with others.

The internet is a mission field, internet users are a people group, globalism is a world system, and global individuality is the mindset that empowers individuals in the global marketplace. Over five billion people are online. Internet Users are enabled to participate online as individuals and participate without the limitations of the physical world.

The global individuality mindset presents an open door for the church with them on a personal level, presents the love of Christ, and fulfills the Great Commission. We must seek continually to understand better the opportunities in the virtual world while simultaneously utilizing an effective strategy to journey online with individuals and connect them with communities of faith in the physical world.

The Network211 Strategy

An impactful strategy to reach individuals through the virtual world can be exemplified by an online ministry called Network211.[9] Network211 was founded by Dr. George M. Flattery and became incorporated in December 1996. The original intent was to use twenty-first-century technology to communicate the first-century gospel. Dr. Flattery's goal was to make gospel presentations to ten million individuals in ten years. The plan became a reality when Network211 launched Project 10Million on October 15, 2008. Project 10Million was completed in five years and then expanded to become Project 100Million.

The vision of Network211 is to proclaim Christ to all people, build a global community of believers, and work with our partners in ministry. The mission is still to use twenty-first-century technology to communicate the first-century gospel by helping people discover and grow in their journey with God. The strategy is to join individuals in their journey as together they search, they view a Network211 gospel presentation online, they connect to Network211 by writing, they grow as they receive further Network211 content online, and they are directed to belong to a local church; in summary, search, present, connect, grow, and belong. The Network211 motto is that they journey with individuals, "from searches to churches." As of January 1, 2022, Network211 has made over 46.7 million gospel presentations to individuals from 242 countries and territories. Over 2.2 million individuals have made an evangelism response, and over 390,000 have written to Network211 to begin a discipleship connection. Network211 offers JourneyOnline.org: an online interactive community that includes "JourneyAnswers" and "WhoJesusIs" websites and provides discipleship content called "The Jesus Path." It also offers "JourneyPrayer," "JourneyWorship," and "JourneyTalks" as well as over 4,000 articles that help individuals apply God's truth to daily life.

The key reason that Network211 has been able to connect individuals online to their content is that it focused on the "commonality of human nature."[10] Many missiologists believe that every culture and people group are different; thus, they must be addressed specifically. However, Dr. Flattery not only agreed but took another step. He believed that people share a commonality of human nature with life issues that are relevant in most cultures. For example, while people may laugh and cry for different reasons, they all laugh and cry.

As the global individuality persona empowered individuals to express themselves on a virtual platform and participate in a global system, the commonalities of human nature brought people into a common affinity. Network211's primary online interactive evangelism feature is called "JourneyAnswers." This identifies thirteen life issues that are relevant in most cultures. They are anxiety, brokenness, confusion, death, depression, emptiness, fear, guilt, hopelessness, insignificance, illness, love, and shame. Whether individuals are in Japan, Nigeria, Brazil, the United States, or any other country, they encounter depression on some level. The answer to this common affinity is Jesus Christ, as he will journey with them to discover freedom, wholeness, and transformation. Network211 offers JourneyAnswers in sixteen languages and is found on JourneyOnline.org. Network211 presents Jesus as the answer and directs individuals to write to them for further conversation. Network211 has teams located in many nations of the world who answer these individuals with a personalized response, direct them to further online content at JourneyOnline.org, and connect them to a local church. This connection brings individuals from the anonymity of an online search in the virtual world into a community of faith in the physical world. A second main online interactive community is Network211's WhoJesusIs.com. People worldwide search "Who is Jesus?" or "Who Jesus Is?" in an effort to find an answer to a question that they may hesitate to ask in person or one that they are unsure of who could provide an adequate answer.

Focal Points for an Effective Strategy

As we seek to create an effective online strategy, we must remember that we are ministering to individuals. While the internet is global, we are interacting with an individual with a specific need. This necessitates that our endeavors are focused on the opportunities that the venue provides. Here are ten focal points for an effective strategy that can be considered for online evangelism. First, the persona of those we are attempting to reach is that of global individuality. Individuals are being empowered online in the global marketplace. They are moving beyond their physical realities and are empowered to interact online as a global citizen.

Second, our presentations must speak to the individual. As most internet access is viewed on a hand-held device, we are presenting the good news to individuals who have searched online for an answer to a life dilemma. Thus, our content and approach must go beyond uploading a church service but be designed to speak into the life of one person and encourage interaction.

Third, we meet individuals at their point of need. Individuals go online searching for answers to life's dilemmas. They will engage anyone online who presents what they consider a viable answer. While these seekers may not darken the door of a church, they are open online to hear alternative views. We avoid a cold call mentality where we attempt to convince them to buy what we are selling, and instead, we meet them at their point of need and allow the Holy Spirit to take the truth of the gospel to penetrate their hearts and transform their lives.

Fourth, as we engage the internet, we must be clear as to what is our desired outcome. The Great Commission reveals that our goal is to make disciples. We journey with individuals from discovering who Jesus is to developing them into followers of Christ who walk in Christian maturity (Matt 28:18–20 and Eph 4:11–13).

Fifth, we must be prepared to journey with individuals. We want to go with them from where they are to where they need to be in Christ. The start of our journey with people often begins at their point of need. Once we engage them online and then with a personal response, we direct them to develop their relationship with Jesus and to apply God's truth to their daily lives. Content for the various aspects of their life journey must be available online so as to continually empower and exhort them to become disciples and to mature in their faith.

Sixth, we must define our terms. Network211 defines a "visit" as individuals who actually visit their page. They do not count "impressions" or visit by bots. An "evangelism response" for Network211 is when a visitor responds to the evangelism presentation by clicking a button such as "I prayed the prayer," "I still have questions," or "prayer request." Network211 terms someone who writes to them as a "discipleship connection." We must be clear as to our terminology and true to what the analytics reveal.

Seventh, we must determine what a win is. Once our terms are defined, we must state what we value in the effort to obtain our desired outcome. Is a visit a win? Are evangelism responses or discipleship connections wins? Is there a combination of responses that formulate a win? Network211 views each aspect of ministry as a win, and yet the ultimate goal is to see people go from "searches to churches."

Eighth, we must be kingdom minded rather than locally fixated. A local church that offers interactive communities online cannot assume that all who view their content will attend their specific church. The goal for fulfilling the Great Commission must be to see people come to Christ and be a disciple. We are not to limit the goal by wanting only for people to attend a specific local church.

Ninth, partnerships must be formed to fulfill the Great Commission. Network211 partners with Spirit-filled believers who serve as "1–2–1 Connectors" (response teams), content providers (written, audio, and video), prayer and financial partners, and local churches around the world. We can do more together than if we attempt to fulfill the Great Commission alone.

Tenth, we must view the internet as its own ministry opportunity for evangelism and discipleship. As mentioned earlier, it is a new wine that must not be forced into old wineskins (Luke 5:36–38). Online activity is a venue in its own right, offering new opportunities to journey with individuals to a transformed life.

Conclusion

The fields of the internet are white unto harvest. Individuals are empowered with a global individuality mindset to participate in the global marketplace. This necessitates the understanding of the opportunities in the virtual world and requires a strategy to journey online with individuals and connect them with communities of faith in the physical world. May the Lord give us wisdom as Spirit-empowered believers to use the internet as a tool of evangelism in an age of global individuality for the purpose of fulfilling the Great Commission and for the glory of God.

Notes

1. "Usage and Population Statistics," Internet World Stats, https://www.internetworldstats.com, accessed January 3, 2022.
2. Ying Lin, "10 Internet Statistics Any Marketer Should Know in 2021," *Oberlo*, May 9, 2021, https://www.oberlo.com/blog/internet-statistics, accessed June 1, 2022.
3. Simon Kemp, "Digital Trends 2020: Every Single Stat You Need to Know About the Internet," *The Next Web*, January 30, 2020, https://thenextweb.com/news/digital-trends-2020-every-single-stat-you-need-to-know-about-the-internet, accessed June 1, 2022.
4. United Nations, "The Promotion, Protection, and Enjoyment of Human Rights on the Internet: Draft Resolution," June 27, 2016, https://digitallibrary.un.org/record/845728?ln=en, accessed June 1, 2022.
5. Dan Scribner, "A Simple Guide to People Group Lists for World Mission," *Lausanne World Pulse* (Sept 2010), https://lausanneworldpulse.com/perspectives-php/1320/09-2010, accessed June 3, 2022.
6. Lara Logan, "The Deadly Beating that Sparked Egypt Revolution," *CBS Evening News*, February 2, 2011, https://www.cbsnews.com/news/the-deadly-beating-that-sparked-egypt-revolution/, accessed June 8, 2022.
7. Thessa Lageman, "Remembering Mohamed Bouazzi: The man who Sparked the Arab Spring," *Al Jazeera*, December 17, 2020, https://www.aljazeera.com/features/2020/12/17/remembering-mohamed-bouazizi-his-death-triggered-the-arab, accessed June 8, 2022.
8. This is the tag phrase for Network211's JourneyOnline.org.
9. See, www.Network211.com.
10. George M. Flattery, "Cooperative Multinationalism: An Emerging Philosophy of Missions" (Unpublished paper, 1969).

Almost, Not Yet, Already: Postscript

Rebekah Bled

"After this I looked, and there was a great multitude that no one could count, from every nation, from all tribes and peoples and languages, standing before the throne and before the Lamb, robed in white, with palm branches in their hands. They cried out in a loud voice, saying, 'Salvation belongs to our God who is seated on the throne and to the Lamb!'" (Revelation 7:9).[1]

Introduction

Jesus gave his disciples the Great Commission, instructing them to make disciples of every nation, baptizing those disciples in the name of the trinity, and teaching them obedience to his commands (Matt 28:19–20). Christ then promised his continual presence, which moments before he had endued with "all authority in heaven and on earth" (28:18) until the end of the age; that is, until the fulfillment of the Great Commission (28:20; Matt 24:14). Thus began the era of the church; an age which stretches from the early disciples until Christ's return, and the one in which we find ourselves today.

The mandate set forth in Matthew 28 is not yet complete, and the era of the church continues. However, though it has not yet arrived in fullness, the mandate's fulfillment is assured. In between the bookends of the Great Commission in Matthew 28 and the great consummation described in Revelation 7:9, we, the church, are called into a process of obedience and faithfulness that spans culture, language, geography, and generation. We are called into full participation in a mandate whose outcome we do not control, but whose promised fulfillment we anticipate. It is in between these poles that this book takes place. Through theological reflection, geographically focused studies, and the examination of new strategies, this book gives insights and encouragement into the Spirit-empowered movement's unique contributions and contextualized approaches for engagement with the remaining tasks of the Great Commission.

Take Heart

In one sense, the future is unknown. That is, we do not know "the day or hour" (Matt 24:36) when "the end will come" (Matt 24:14, 44). That knowledge belongs to the father alone (Matt 24:36). However, we are not left without a guide or instructions. We have been given the presence of the Spirit as advocate and guide (John 16:7, 13–15). There are also specific things we know and are responsible to. While we do not know the day or the hour of Christ's return, we are promised that he is indeed returning. We do not know how many generations the era of the church will include, but we do know that it is the church's calling to preach, baptize, and teach all nations in concert with the Spirit in every generation. We know too that every nation will be present before Christ's throne in glory, where the "multi-ethnic, multi-racial, multi-lingual, multi-cultural" family of God, "united in being his" will worship together (Rev 7:9).[2] The Great Commission is not isolated calling, but rather a mandate sweeping across human history, encompassing every tribe, tongue, nation (Isa 25:6–7; Phil 2:10–11; Rev 5:9–10) and generation (Psalm 78:6–7; Psalm 102:18; Dan 4:3; Luke 1:50). Indeed, the participation in the Great Commission mirrors its fulfillment.

Julie Ma describes Jesus' disciples as "vigorously tak[ing] part in the actualization of Old Testament scriptures" such as Isaiah 49:6 through their reception of and subsequent engagement with the Great Commission.[3] We know that Christ expects to find the church, his bride, eagerly anticipating his arrival (Matt 24:42) and making herself ready (Rev 19:7). Thus, as the global Church, we now follow in the disciple's path of vigorous actualization of both the Old and New Testament, with full assurance of the Great Commission's success (Rev 7:9). God's good creation, begun in a garden, finds joyful fulfillment in an urban banquet in which "a great multitude which no one could count" (Rev 7:9) lifts unified voices "with the sound of many waters . . . and the sound of mighty thunder peals" (Rev 19:6) crying out the consummation of the Great Commission (Rev 19:6–8). Let us take heart: the Great Commission will be realized, the task will be fulfilled, and our unique participation as individuals and communities is called for. As Christopher Foster states: "When gifts of the Spirit are exercised properly and communally, unbelievers and outsiders will declare, 'God is really among you' (1 Cor 14:25)."[4]

Spirit-Empowered Witness

Pentecostal and charismatic faith communities can be microcosms foreshadowing the incredible diversity depicted in Revelation. Regarding the urban Asian context, for example, Connie Au notes, "Urban Asian Pentecostal churches embrace a diverse ethnoscape characterized by multi-cultural, multi-ethnic, and multi-racial congregations constituted by a significant component of migrants."[5] Au describes a parallel dynamic unfolding in the rural Asian context where the revival in the jungle: "transform[ed] this tribal area into a multi-ethnic, multi-national, and multi-denominational carnival."[6]

Each community and culture of believers offers unique giftings and witness, which becomes interwoven into the tapestry of God's grand redemption of the world. Spirit-empowered communities hold among their missiological distinctives: power encounters,[7] healing evangelism,[8] vibrant and expressive prayer and worship,[9] and grassroots church planting and discipleship movements.[10]

Prayer and Worship

Thang San Mung describes the extroversion of prayer and worship that we see taking place in Revelation 19 as a present-day missional strategy that Spirit-empowered worshipping communities are well-poised to embrace.[11] Mung locates this strategy in part in the Lord's Prayer, noting that this liturgy "has a global perspective in view, action steps in the project, and inclusive tones in practice."[12] Indeed, according to Miguel Alvarez, "Pentecostals have learned to depend on prayer and fasting for most of their actions."[13] Emphasizing the communal nature of prayer, Mireya Alvarez describes community prayer as "foundational to the Pentecostal worldview"[14] and, by extension, a primary "engine" of courageous missiological engagement that Julie Ma states is the "key to the crucial elements for revival."[15] Beyond prayer as a missional strategy, prayer has urgent, personal implications as well. Harvey Kwiyani notes that Pentecostals in Southern Africa "pray like their lives depend on it—and usually, their lives actually do depend on it."[16]

Power Encounters and Healing Evangelism

Daniel King notes, "The gospel of healing has always been an essential part of the ethos of Pentecostal spirituality. . . .there is no artificial bifurcation of salvation and miracles; rather, they are two sides of the same coin."[17] It is perhaps no surprise then that power encounters, another distinctive element of Pentecostal spirituality and healing evangelism frequently go hand-in-hand as people seek spiritual protection from what Harvey Kwiyani describes as "contrary spirits."[18]

Au describes power encounters in geographically specific places that were known to "belong" to evil or contrary spirits. These places thus become potential spiritual battlegrounds. Au makes the significant observation that it is charismatic experiences that empower believers to engage in power encounters with contrary spirits, confronting them "in a way consistent with their culture."[19] Power encounters provide evidence in the physical world that demonstrates the authority of the Holy Spirit over forces and powers both seen and unseen, systemic and personal. Emboldened and empowered by the Spirit, Pentecostals "intentionally increase and intensify their prayer," practicing fidelity with their actions to their fervent belief that the Spirit is at work winning the battle.[20]

Grassroots Discipleship Movements

Raphaël Anzenberger, Harvey Kwiyani, Stephen Yeem, Richard Harding and Manuela Castellanos Harding, Victor John and David Coles, and Evan Liu all note the role of grassroots discipleship movements. That is, discipleship and/or church planting strategy that is accessible to and reproducible among laypeople.[21] As Harding and Harding observe, "evangelism plus discipleship equals missions."[22] Scholars, pastors, and other traditional experts have significant, even potentially prophetic roles to play in discernment; however, the authors here, emphasize their role is to offer insight, encouragement, and support rather than to be the head of the funnel through which discipleship efforts flow. Indeed, in discipleship movements across the globe, what we see is the democratization of "experts." Kwiyani reminds us that as members of the priesthood or "evangelisthood" of all believers, "it is every Pentecostal Christian's duty to witness and evangelize."[23] Glenn Balfour echoes this, anchoring this evangelical duty in the power and creativity of the Spirit: ". . .the "creative" characteristics of the Holy Spirit need to be seen in all of us." Balfour continues, noting that through breathing his life into us, the Spirit gives us the ability to ". . .take on ourselves the creativity of the Spirit.

Our spiritual DNA, our spiritual identity has creativity, innovation, even inventiveness, already built into it."[24]

Writing from secular contexts, Arto Hämäläinen and Tomasz Białokurec, stress the importance of ecumenical unity through bonds of fraternal love. In secular contexts where faith has already been dismissed as superstition and efforts to evangelize perceived as manipulative and self-serving, it is the unified and self-sacrificial church who presents a winsome invitation of discipleship as "belonging before believing." Both Hämäläinen and Białokurec agree that it is the consistently respectful and gentle[25] undercurrent of the Spirit in secular contexts that allows for "open and sincere mutual dialogue."[26]

In contexts where the spiritual realm is considered part of everyday life, there is a focus on the particular uniqueness of Christ's commands and the Spirit's authoritative power. In these contexts, one might argue for "believing before belonging" as a path to discipleship where the specifics of Christ as a unique savior and his specific salvation are worked out in the believing community of the Spirit-empowered church.

Where these converge, such as in the migration taking place in Western Europe for example, the delineation between discipleship classifications lessens. Consider, for example, Samson Fatokun's description of missionaries from a highly spiritual worldview bringing this worldview into a secular society:

> The 1980s and 1990s witnessed a new form of Spirit-empowered evangelism in Europe and North America with the emergence of neo-Pentecostal churches in Nigeria whose members carried a new Evangelical zeal to European nations in their quest for fulfilling the mandate of the Great Commission... today several Nigerian pioneered Pentecostal church denominations are found in virtually every city in Europe, North America, Australia, and the Caribbean.[27]

Stavros Ignatiou shares testimonies that describe a process of what may be a potential third way of conceptualizing belonging and believing.[28] That is, believing as belonging. Ignatiou contends that Spirit-empowered witnessing among people coming from a Muslim background is made possible, in part, by migration. New communities are thus formed of clusters of believers coming out of Islam via charismatic experiences, often as their physical geography shifts. Here, believing and belonging are intertwined as people in liminal spaces with both their geography and spirituality undergoing a process of redefinition.

Spirit-Empowered Courage

The Pentecostal worldview, encompassing a present spiritual reality whose good end is assured, gives tenacious courage and hope in participating in the Great Commission in the face of grim material and spiritual circumstances. A recent conversation with a non-Pentecostal pastor speaks to the witness of this bold tenacity: ". . . Pentecostals will go where no one else has the courage to go. The universities, the desperately poor, places that are just a mess. Pentecostals are already there ministering. If the people in these situations had to wait for the mainline denominations to have enough courage to go . . ." Here the pastor trailed off with a shrug of the shoulders indicating the wait would be long indeed.[29]

Invitation to Humility in Mission

In my youth, I prayed for a close friend's salvation for what seemed like a lifetime. In reality, it was probably closer to a year. The season of prayer for this friend's salvation ended one night at a Christian youth camp. We stood next to each other in the back of the tabernacle, while I wrestled with the tension of my internal longing to participate in worship by lifting my hands and the knowledge that if I did so, my friend would laugh at me. I compromised by raising one hand and keeping the other in my pocket. My friend laughed and rolled her eyes. A moment later, she said, "I'm going," and walked straight down the long aisle to the altar. I was taken aback by her sudden declaration. Here, finally, was the long-awaited outcome to my prayers! We were going to the altar to pray together and, for the rest of our lives, would share the moment and the memory of salvation. My thoughts raced along these lines as I followed my friend to the altar. My surprise was complete, then, when she knelt and prayed, yes, for salvation, but with someone else. Though the answer to my long-requested prayer was unfolding in front of me, my narrative at that time was one of bewildered betrayal that my friend's salvation was happening in the "wrong" way.

As believers, we are called into full participation in a process which is beyond our control, and this can sometimes feel like betrayal. In fact, it is often our sense of control that has been betrayed. These emotions when expectations go awry can be appropriate for an adolescent like the young teenager I once was feeling betrayed rather than elated at the altar. But we are called to put childhood behind us as we mature in faith (1 Cor 13:11; Eph 4:13–15). Maturity requires taking full responsibility for oneself, including our reactions, emotions, responses, and expectations. By necessity, then, maturity also requires relinquishing reaching for power over that which is inappropriate for us to control, such as another's response to the Spirit.

Many years later, I visited another country at the invitation of a relative stranger who said that the Spirit had prompted him to invite me to be part of a group traveling to a pastor's conference in a rural area, many thousands of miles away. The pastors would all be male, he explained, but there were women who could and perhaps even would take on significant leadership roles in the faith community if only that community was able to visualize the possibility. So off we went, each in our small team using the flights to prepare our teachings for the conference. As the only woman in the group, my preparation extended further. I sat with the local women on the floor with my head covered like the other women the first day, then, as the days progressed, moved to the couch at the front of the room and sat down next to the men on my team in the place of honor. This was a walk not often taken and observed by both the pastors and their wives. When it was my night to preach, the women in my host family set about making me beautiful by local standards: loaning me their clothes, shoes, and headscarves, applying their own makeup on my face. I danced with the pastor's wives and children and the women in my host family for the first hour of worship that night. When it was time, I was introduced and walked on stage while people took photographs on their phones. Meanwhile, cheers and "Hallelujahs" rang out in answer to the question shouted through the mic by the local host, "Can God use a woman?!"

I was sure that God was honoring my obedience to travel halfway around the world at his mysterious call, that I was witnessing and participating in a culture-and-paradigm-shifting miracle. I opened my mouth and began to preach. Immediately, the pastors and their families stood and began leaving the room. I edited my sermon quickly but not fast enough for people to stay in the building. By the time a note was passed to me on stage to wrap it up, half the participants of the conference were gone. I rode home afterward with the women in my host family, and we all went to bed, none of us saying a word.

The next day someone reported my group's presence to the anti-Christian authorities, and we stayed far away from that night's meeting for the safety of everyone. I moved from the host family's home to the hotel in a different village where the others in my group were staying. My group waited at the hotel long into the small hours of the morning for a report of the conference, which was going ahead, without our presence but with the watchful presence of the local authorities. When the local host arrived at the hotel, it was in a state of exuberance. It had been a night of revival and miracles. A local young woman, about my same age, had taken the stage and testified while the crowd sat, enraptured. She even captured the attention of the authorities, whose respect she won. The altars were full afterwards as an extended time of prayer and healing broke out. Not one person had turned to leave when the local young woman spoke. Again, my emotions of disorientation and disappointment rose to the surface.

Indeed, twin temptations are ever-present. The first is that of controlling the Spirit's activity according to our own definitions and expectations. The second is to filter God's unfolding fulfillment of his promises through the lens of what we think we deserve as participants in that promise. Indulging in either of these temptations, however, puts us in the posture of the older son whose prodigal brother has returned in Luke 15. Instead of enjoying the feast, the older son "refuses to go in" (15:28). Yes, the fatted calf had been raised for a feast. It is feasible that the older son had participated in the care and feeding of the calf, anticipating the taste of the meat and the ambiance of celebration that was to come. Yet, when the calf is actually killed, the older brother is disoriented and angry (15:26–28). He has lost his perception of control and will not participate in the results of his own thwarted expectations. "It wasn't supposed to happen this way," we can imagine the older son thinking, in line with the Pharisees "grumbling" (15:2 NRSV) or "muttering" (15:2, NIV) about Jesus' eating habits and companions at the beginning of this parable (Luke 15:2).

As the father ran to the younger son (15:20), he now comes to the older son to "plead" for his presence (15:28). In a caricature of missing the point, the older son responds in complaint that his father has "never given [him] even a young goat" (15:29). This complaint minimizes the father's gifts in the past (15:31), the promised future inheritance, and the invitation of nearness to the father and the father's family (cf. 15:30–32) currently extended. Both sons have access to the father. The older son's embarrassment of the father's embrace of his brother causes him to miss the father's embrace extended to him as well. The joke of the story is that in preserving his own sense of dignity and rights, the older son becomes absurd, missing the presence and joy of both the father and his brother.

Brainerd Prince states, "There is a strong critique against treating those we missionize or research upon as objects for whom we have an agenda. . . .Hence, there is no other way to meet with the other but as a person, in friendship, without agenda."[30] Elizabeth Salazar-Sanzana adds her voice, saying, "The action of the Spirit of God has surprised many. . ."[31] There is a warning and an invitation here. Another feast is promised (Isa 25:6; Rev 19:9). Will we accept the father's invitation to the party by both participating in the Great Commission and releasing attempts to control, letting the Spirit to blow where and how it pleases (John 3:8)? May we joyfully embrace a willingness to be surprised.

Julie Ma states that Spirit-empowerment is "Pentecostalism's treasured experience"[32] which leads directly to mission. Yet, we hold this treasure in tension. Spirit-empowerment invites us into the paradox of weakness and powerlessness. We are invited into the tension of bearing witness to the one who spoke the galaxies into being and who gives and sustains all life, yet remaining grounded in full humility, accepting that without the Spirit's enlivening, witness alone cannot bring transformation. Indeed, as Białokurec describes: "The belief that the Spirit is very much alive today and enables Christians to carry out the remaining task of the Great Commission is central to our missional spirituality."[33] The Spirit's centrality is a gift, requiring our ongoing dependence and submission to the Spirit for the sake of our own ongoing transformation and for the transformation of the world.

Areas of Further Research

Daniel Isgrigg poses the question, "What if the goal of reaching the whole world is not a prediction but rather a challenge to every generation to take responsibility for reaching the world they have inherited?"[34] This challenge invites us into an ongoing process of creative and courageous discovery in order for our faith communities to continually ask the question, "how might the next group of people (culture, generation) best hear the gospel so that they have a fair chance of responding?"[35]

Areas of further research within these perimeters include but are not limited to: mission preparation, debrief, and re-entry for both long and short-term missionaries; authentic sharing of authority and influence between generations and cultures; and winsome witnessing in settings of intra-religious dialogue, including universalism, secularism, and "nones."

Conclusion

The song "Mary Consoles Eve" by Rain for Roots describes Mary reaching back through history to a "blushing" Eve, inviting her to lift her head because "the Promised One is finally on his way." The chorus simply sings, "Almost, not yet, already!"[36] We sing this song in concert with the Spirit and with the church across history and geography, anticipating the day when the task will be consummated in its fullness, and we will sing a new song together (Rev 5:9). That day is almost here. We feel the anticipation growing as we groan along with creation "while we wait" (Rom 8:22–23). It is not yet here. We know both that the tears will be wiped from all faces (Isa 25:8) and that in the present, we still weep. It is already here in part. We taste the sweetness of the coming kingdom in worship and in fellowship. Almost, not yet, already. To God be the glory!

Notes

1. Unless otherwise noted all scripture is taken from the New Revised Standard Updated Edition (Chester Heights, PA: Friendship press, 2021).
2. John Odom, "God's Multiracial Vision," (a sermon delivered on May 8, 2022, at Cornerstone Church, Tulsa, OK).
3. See chapter 3.
4. See chapter 2.
5. See chapter 6.
6. See chapter 6.
7. See chapters 3 and 13.
8. See chapters 6, 13, 15, and 18.

9   See chapters 14 and 19.

10 See chapters 11, 12, 20, and 22.

11 See chapter 14.

12 See chapter 14.

13 See chapter 8.

14 See chapter 19.

15 See chapter 3.

16 See chapter 5.

17 See chapter 18.

18 See chapter 5.

19 See chapter 6.

20 See chapter 8.

21 See chapters 16, 5, 22, 20, 13 and 12 respectively.

22 See chapter 20.

23 See chapter 5.

24 See chapter 1.

25 See chapter 17.

26 See chapter 7.

27 See chapter 10.

28 See chapter 15.

29 Interview with John Hamilton, August 24, 2021. Hamilton was located in Montevideo, Uruguay and the author was in Tulsa, OK. The interview took place via Zoom.

30 See chapter 4.

31 See chapter 21.

32 See chapter 3.

33 See chapter 17.

34 See chapter 9.

35 Michael Rynkiewich, *Soul, Self, and Society: A Postmodern Anthropology for Mission in a Postcolonial World* (Eugene, OR: Cascade Books, 2011), 44.

36 "Mary Consoles Eve," by Rain for Roots. Track Six on *Waiting Songs* album, 2015.

Contributors

Miguel Alvarez, a missionary from Honduras, is President of the Seminario Bíblico Pentecostal Centroamericano (SEBIPCA) of the Church of God in Guatemala. His publications include *Integral Mission: A New Paradigm for Latin American Pentecostals* (2016) and (co)-edits two journals, *Pentecostal Education and HECHOS: Una Perspectiva Pneumatológica*.

Mireya Alvarez, a missionary from Honduras, has been Professor of Christian Education and Practical Theology at the Asian Seminary of Christian Ministries in Manila, Philippines, the Pentecostal Theological Seminary in Cleveland, Tennessee, and currently at Biblical Pentecostal Seminary of Central America, located in Quetzaltenango, Guatemala. Her research interest is women's ministries in Latin America and the Northeastern United States. Mireya is an ordained minister with the Church of God, Cleveland, Tennessee, USA.

Raphaël Anzenberger is Assistant Professor of Intercultural Studies at Columbia International University in the United States and also teaches at the Evangelical Theological Faculty of Vaux-sur-Seine in France. He also serves as a resident scholar for the Lausanne Church Planting Issue Group.

Connie Au is a theologian in Hong Kong who publishes on Asian Pentecostalism, Chinese church history, and ecumenism. She also works as a translator of theological books on liturgy and spirituality. Her publications include *Grassroots Unity in the Charismatic Renewal* (2011).

Glenn Balfour serves as Principal and Lecturer of New Testament at Missio Dei (formerly Mattersey Hall), UK Assemblies of God college, in Manchester, England. Previously he pastored several congregations and served various administrative posts at the college. His publications include *A Step-by-Step Introduction to New Statement Greek (2005) and A Step-by-Step Introduction to Bibical Heberew* (2009).

Tomasz Białokurec is an ecumenically oriented Catholic from Poland, currently pursuing his Ph.D. in Theology at Oral Roberts University in Tulsa, OK. Since 2012, he has been working with *An Tobar Nua/ Foundation in Christ Ministries* in Ireland.

Rebekah Bled is an ordained minister currently pursuing a Ph.D. in Contextual Theology at Oral Roberts University. Her publications include chapters in *Proclaiming Christ in the Power of the Holy Spirit: Opportunities and Challenges* (2020), *Good News to the Poor: Spirit Empowered Responses to Poverty* (2022), and *The Remaining Task of the Great Commission* (2022). She also served as Assistant Editor for all these titles.

Manuela Castellanos Harding serves as a pastor at Mision Carismatica International (MCI), Bogota, Colombia, leading the children's ministry. Her work includes the production of materials for churches and families through the Little Big Heroes (Pequeños Heroes) and leadership over Hero Moms, a global community of Christian mothers, providing a Christian homeschool curriculum.

Dave Coles is an encourager and resourcer of Church Planting Movements among unreached groups, serving with Beyond. He has served in the United States for ten years and among Muslims in Southeast Asia for twenty-four years. His research interests are in church planting movements, contextualization, reaching Muslims, and the nature of the church. He co-authored *Bhojpuri Breakthrough: A Movement that Keeps Multiplying* (2019) and co-edited *24:14—A Testimony to All Peoples* (2019).

Samson Adetunji Fatokun is Professor of Church History, Doctrinal Theology and Pentecostal Studies in University of Ibadan, Nigeria. He was the pioneer Dean of Postgraduate School of Samuel Adegboyega University (of The Apostolic Church Nigeria), Ogwa. He is the Pioneer National President of the Nigerian Association of Church History and Missiological Studies, and the current Editor-in-Chief of NJOCHAMS.

Mark Flattery, a (US) Assemblies of God missionary, serves as President of Network211, Springfield, Missouri, USA. Growing up in Belgium as a missionary kid, he later ministered in Tanzania and Pacific Oceania. He authored *Stand Firm: What to Do When Live Knocks You Down* (2019).

Christopher G. Foster is Chair of the Department of Undergraduate Theology and Associate Professor of Biblical and Theological Studies at Oral Roberts University, Tulsa, Oklahoma, USA. He authored *Communal Participation in the Spirit* (Mohr Siebeck, 2022). Previously, he was a visiting lecturer at Nazarene Theological College, UK, and a full-time church minister.

Makonen Getu, originally from Ethiopia, is Vice President of Transformation and Training with Edify. He has forty years of experience working as an international development practitioner. He has also taught at the University of Stockholm and the Oxford Centre for Mission Studies, Oxford, UK. He has published and spoken widely on topics related to development, foreign aid, microfinance, HIV/AIDS, human trafficking, faith, and development.

Arto Hämäläinen served as Director of Fida International, the Finnish Pentecostal mission organization, and served several continental and global Pentecostal networks, including Pentecostal World Fellowship, Empowered21, and World Alliance of Evangelicals. He is the author of several missiological books and articles.

Richard Harding, from the United Kingdom, currently serves as one of the Lead Pastors at MCI Church, Bogota, Colombia, while leading Pequeños Heroes TV, a Christian animation content project of the church. Previously, he led the global leadership training program for G12 and MCI churches worldwide.

Stavros Ignatiou, a native of Nicosia, Cyprus, began a pastoral ministry in Athens, Greece. His first-hand encounter with the refugee crisis in the region led him to start a distribution center helping the poor and refugees, today, serving thousands of refugees and migrants from the Balkan and Middle East regions.

Daniel D. Isgrigg is Assistant Professor and Director of the Holy Spirit Research Center at Oral Roberts University. His recent books include *Imagining the Future: The Origin, Development, and Future of Assemblies of God Eschatology* (2021) and *Pentecost in Tulsa: The Revivals and Race Massacre that Shaped the Pentecostal Movement in Tulsa* (2021).

Victor John, an Indian national, has led from the early 1990s a ministry among the Bhojpuri Movement through holistic evangelism and church planting. He is the primary author of *Bhojpuri Breakthrough: A Movement that Keeps Multiplying* (2019).

Daniel King is a missionary evangelist and a graduate of the Doctor of Ministry program at Oral Roberts University, Tulsa, Oklahoma, USA.

Harvey Kwiyani is a Malawian mission theologian currently based in Liverpool, England, where he serves as CEO of Global Connections, while providing executive leadership at Missio Africanus. His publications include *Sent Forth: African Missionary Work in the West* (2014) and *Multicultural Kingdom: Ethnic Diversity, Mission, and the Church* (2020).

Evan Liu, a Chinese New Testament scholar, is the founder of China Servant Leadership Center in the United States and leading a global Chinese mission beyond China. His publications are in Pauline theology, commentaries on the Pauline books, and the Chinese Christian movement.

Julie C. Ma serves as Professor of Missiology and Intercultural Studies, Oral Roberts University, Tulsa, OK. Previously served as a Korean missionary in the Philippines and Research Tutor of Missiology at Oxford Centre for Mission Studies, Oxford, UK. Publications include *When the Spirit Meets the Spirits: Pentecostal Ministry Among the Kankana-ey Tribe in the Philippines* (2000), *Mission Possible* (2015), and *Mission in the Spirit* (2011).

Wonsuk Ma, a Korean Pentecostal, serves as Dean and Distinguished Professor of Global Christianity at Oral Roberts University, Tulsa, Oklahoma. He previously served as Executive Director of the Oxford Centre for Mission Studies, Oxford, UK. He serves as Co-chair of Scholars Consultation, Empowered21.

Thang San Mung is a Myanmar Assemblies of God pastor and Bible teacher, currently pursuing his Ph.D. at Oral Roberts University, Tulsa, Oklahoma. He is the founder of Tyrannus Gospel Ministry and is the curriculum developer of the Master of Arts in Pentecostal Studies program of Bethel College, Myanmar.

Opoku Onyinah is the immediate past president of Ghana Pentecostal and Charismatic Council and the immediate past chairman of the Church of Pentecost, Ghana, with branches in 135 countries. Currently, he lectures at Pentecostal University, Accra, Ghana, and is the president of the Bible Society of Ghana. He also serves as Co-Chair of Scholars Consultation, Empowered21.

Brainerd Prince, an Indian Christian, teaches and tutors students and researchers both in academic skills as well as in research skills and methodology. He specializes in providing learning support to students. He also consults for higher education institutions in the field of research and academic skill training. He is presently working on the book *Rethinking Christian Engagement with Hindus* (Routledge, Forthcoming).

Elizabeth Salazar-Sanzana, a Chilean Pentecostal, serves as Professor of Systematic Theology at the Evangelical Faculty of Theology-CTE of Chile. She widely publishes in Spanish, English, and Portuguese, and serves in various theological commissions including ecumenical commissions.

Stephen Yeem, a Chinese-American, is an ordained minister of River of Life Christian Church, Santa Clara, California, the largest Mandarin-speaking church in the United States, serving as the Academic Dean of River of Life Pastoral Leadership Institute. He is currently pursuing a Ph.D. in Contextual Theology at Oral Roberts University, Tulsa, Oklahoma. His research interest includes charismatic ecclesiology, Chinese Christianity, theology of transformation, and mission studies.

Select Bibliography

Adedibu, Babatunde. "Prospects and Challenges: Migration, Identity in Christ, and Integration of Britain's Black Majority Churches." *Spectrum: Journal of Contemporary Christianity and Society* 2:1 (April 2017): 94–104.

Altes, Edy Korthals. *Heart and Soul for Europe: An Essay on Spiritual Renewal.* Assen, Netherlands: Van Gorcum, 1999.

Alvarez, Miguel. *Beyond Borders: New Contexts of Mission in Latin America.* Cleveland, TN: CPT Press, 2017.

Amster, Matthew H. "New Sacred Lands: The Making of a Christian Prayer Mountain in Highland Borneo." In Ronald A. Lukens-Bull, ed. *Sacred Places and Modern Landscapes: Sacred Geography and Social-Religious Transformations in South and Southeast Asia.* Tempe, AZ: Arizona State University Program for Southeast Asia Studies, 2003: 131–160.

Anderson, Allan H. *African Reformation: African Initiated Christianity in the 20th Century.* Trenton, NJ: Africa World Press, 2001.

_____. *An Introduction to Pentecostalism.* Cambridge: Cambridge University Press, 2004.

Appadurai, Arjun. "Disjuncture and Difference in the Global Cultural Economy." *Theory, Culture and Society* 7:2–3 (June 1990): 295–310.

Barrett, David and James W. Reapsome. *Seven Hundred Plans to Evangelize the World.* Birmingham, AL: New Hope, 1988.

Bevans, Stephen B. and Katalina Tahaafe-Williams, eds. *Contextual Theology for the Twenty-First Century.* Cambridge: James Clarke, 2012.

Bhabha, Homi. *The Location of Culture.* London: Routledge, 1994.

Block, Peter. *Stewardship: Choosing Service Over Self-Interest.* San Francisco: Berrett-Koehler Publishers, 2013.

Bonnke, Reinhard. *Living a Life of Fire: An Autobiography.* Orlando: E-R Productions, 2011.

Borthwick, Paul. *Western Christians in Global Missions.* Downers Grove, IL: Intervarsity, 2012.

Brown, Candy Gunther, ed. *Global Pentecostal and Charismatic Healing.* Oxford: Oxford University Press, 2011.

Brusco, Elizabeth. *The Reformation of Machismo: Evangelical Conversion and Gender in Colombia.* Austin: University of Texas Press, 1995.

Buber, Martin. *I and Thou*. Ronald Gregor Smith, trans. New York: Scribner Classics, 2000.

Campos, Bernardo. "In the Power of the Spirit: Pentecostalism, Theology, and Social Ethics." In Dennis A. Smith and Benjamin F. Gutiérrez, eds. *In the Power of the Spirit: The Pentecostal Challenge to Historic Churches in Latin America*. Guatemala City, Guatemala: CELEP, 1996: 41–50.

Cantalamessa, Raniero. *Come, Creator Spirit: Meditations on the Veni Creator*. Denis Barrett and Marlene Barrett, trans. Collegeville, MI: Liturgical Press, 2008.

Castellanos, Cesar. *ABC's of the Vision*. Bogota, Colombia: G12 Editors, 2019.

_____. *Crecimiento Explosivo*. Bogota, Colombia: G12 Editores, 2020.

Chandomba, Lyton. *The History of Apostolic Faith Mission and Other Pentecostal Missions in South Africa*. Milton Keynes: AuthorHouse, 2007.

Cho, David Yonggi. *Successful Home Cell Groups*. South Plainfield, NJ: Bridge Publishing, 1981.

Chong, Terence, ed. *Pentecostal Megachurches in Southeast Asia: Negotiating Class, Consumption, and the Nation*. Singapore: ISEAS-Yusof Ishak Institute, 2018.

Christerson, Brad and Richard Flory. *The Rise of Network Christianity: How Independent Leaders are Changing the Religious Landscape*. Oxford: Oxford University Press, 2017.

Clarke, Clifton R. *Pentecostalism: Insights from Africa and the African Diaspora*. Eugene, OR: Wipf and Stock, 2018.

Coleman, Robert E. *The Master Plan of Evangelism*. Grand Rapids, MI: Revell, 1993.

Duncan, Ligon, Dan Kimbell, Michael Lawrence, Mark Denver, Timothy Quill, Dan Wilt, and J. Matthew Pinson, eds. *Perspectives on Christian Worship: 5 Views*. Nashville: Broadman & Holman, 2009.

Ervin, Howard M. *Healing: A Sign of the Kingdom*. Peabody, MA: Hendrickson, 2002.

Escobar, Samuel. *The New Global Mission: The Gospel from Everywhere to Everyone*. Downers Grove, IL: InterVarsity, 2003.

Fanon, Frantz. *The Wretched of the Earth*. Constance Farrington, trans. New York: Grove, 1963.

Fatokun, Samson A., ed. *Christianity and African Society*. Ibadan: BookWright Publishers, 2013.

_____. "Pentecostalism in Cameroon and Nigeria's Cross-Border Influence." In Vinson Synan, Amos Yong and J. Kwabena Asamoah-Gyadu, eds. *Global Renewal Christianity: Africa Spirit-Empowered Movements—Past, Present, and Future*. Lake Mary, FL: Charisma House, 2015.

Fee, Gordon. *God's Empowering Presence: The Holy Spirit in the Letters of Paul.* Grand Rapids, MI: Baker Academic, 2012.

Firth, David, and Paul Wegner, eds. *Presence, Power, and Promise: The Role of the Spirit of God in the Old Testament.* Westmont, IL: Intervarsity Press, 2011.

Freeman, David. *Diamonds Lost in the Sand: Gems of Wisdom for Educating Our Children.* Truenorthpublish.com, 2015.

Freire de Alencar, Gedeon. *Matriz Pentecostal Brasileira: Assembléias de Deus – 1911 a 2011.* Rio de Janeiro: Novos Diálogos, 2013.

Garrison, David. *Church Planting Movements: How God is Redeeming a Lost World.* Monument, CO: WIGTake Resources, 2007.

Glasser, Arthur F. *Announcing the Kingdom: The Story of God's Mission in the Bible.* Grand Rapids, MI: Baker Academic, 2003.

Goldingay, John. *Isaiah for Everyone.* Louisville, KY: Westminster John Knox, 2015.

Guthrie, Stan. *Missions in the Third Millennium: 21 Key Trends for the 21st Century.* Milton Keynes, UK: Paternoster, 2000.

Hattaway, Paul. "A Captivating Vision: Why Chinese House Churches May Just End Up Fulfilling the Great Commission," ChristianityToday.com, April 1, 2004, https://www.christianitytoday.com/ct/2004/april/5.84.html.

_____. *Back to Jerusalem: Three Chinese House Church Leaders Share Their Vision to Complete the Great Commission.* Downers Grove: Intervarsity Press, 2003.

Hayford, Jack W. *Prayer is Invading the Impossible.* Orlando: Bridge-Logos, 1977.

Herms, Ronald, John. R. Levinson, and Archie T. Wright, eds. *The Spirit Says: Inspiration and Interpretation in Israelite, Jewish, and Early Christian Texts.* Boston: De Gruyter, 2021.

Hirsh, Alan. *The Forgotten Ways: Reactivating the Missional Church.* Grand Rapids, MI: Brazos Press, 2006.

Homer, Lauren B. "Registration of Chinese Protestant House Churches Under China's 2005 Regulation on Religious Affairs: Resolving the Implementation Impasse." *Journal of Church and State* 52:1 (Winter 2010): 50–73.

Jenkins, Philip. *The Next Christendom: The Coming of Global Christianity.* Oxford: Oxford University Press, 2011.

John, Victor and Dave Coles. *Bhojpuri Breakthrough: A Movement that Keeps Multiplying.* Monument, CO: WigTake Resources, 2019.

Johnson, Todd M., and Gina A. Zurlo. *Introducing Spirit-Empowered Christianity – The Global Pentecostal and Charismatic Movement in the 21st Century.* Tulsa: ORU Press, 2020.

Jorgensen, Knud, ed. *The Lausanne Movement: A Range of Perspectives.* Oxford: Regnum Books, 2014.

Kärkkäinen, Veli-Matti. *Pneumatology: The Holy Spirit in Ecumenical, International, and Contextual Perspective.* Grand Rapids, MI: Baker Academic, 2002.

Keener, Craig S. *Spirit Hermeneutics: Reading Scripture in Light of Pentecost.* Grand Rapids, MI: Eerdmans, 2016.

Kennedy, Jeff. *Father, Son, and the Other One: Experiencing the Holy Spirit as a Transforming, Empowering Reality in Your Life.* Lake Mary, FL: Charisma House, 2014.

Levinson, John R. *The Holy Spirit Before Christianity.* Waco, TX: Baylor, 2019.

López, Darío. *Pentecostalimo y Transformación Social.* Buenos Aires, Argentina: Ediciones Kairos/FTL, 2000.

Ma, Wonsuk and Julie C. "Missiology: Evangelization, Holistic Ministry, and Social Justice." In Wolfgang Vondey, ed. *The Routledge Handbook of Pentecostal Theology.* Abingdon: Routledge, 2020: 279–289.

Ma, Julie C. and Wonsuk. *Mission in the Spirit: Towards a Pentecostal/Charismatic Missiology.* Oxford: Regnum Books, 2010.

Mandryk, Jason. *Operation World.* Colorado Springs, CO: Biblica, 2010.

Mariano, Ricardo. "Crescimento Pentecostal no Brasil: Factores Internos." *Revista Estudos da Religião* (December 2008): 68–95.

Martin, Lee Roy, ed. *Toward a Pentecostal Theology of Worship.* Cleveland, TN: CPT Press, 2016.

Medina, Nèstor and Sammy Alfaro. *Pentecostals and Charismatics in Latin America and Latino Communities.* London: Palgrave McMillan, 2015.

Menzies, Robert. *Empowered for Witness: The Spirit in Luke-Acts.* Sheffield: Sheffield Academic Press, 1994.

Moerman, Murray. *Mobilizing Movements: Leadership Insights for Discipling Whole Nations.* Littleton, CO: William Carey Publishing, 2021.

Monteiro, Yaira. "Congregación Cristiana en Brasil, de la Fundación Centenario: La Trayectoria de una Iglesia Brasileña." In Daniel Chiquete and Luis Orellana, eds. *Voces del Pentecostalismo Latinoamericano.* Concepción, Chilé: RELEP, 2011: 77–140.

Montgomery, James H. DAWN 2000: *7 Million Churches to Go.* Pasadena, CA: William Carey Library, 1989.

_____ and Donald A. McGavran. *The Discipling of a Nation.* Milpitas, CA: Global Church Growth, 1980.

Moreau A. Scott, and Beth Snodderly eds. *Evangelical and Frontier Mission: Perspectives on the Global Progress of the Gospel.* Oxford: Regnum Books, 2011.

Núñez, Emilio and William Taylor. *Crisis and Hope in Latin America: An Evangelical Perspective.* Pasadena, CA: William Carey Library, 2012.

Newbigin, Lesslie. *The Pen Secret: An Introduction to the Theology of Mission.* Grand Rapids, MI: Eerdmans, 1995.

Olofinjana, Israel. *Reverse in Ministry and Missions: Africans in the Dark Continent of Europe.* Milton Keynes: AuthorHouse, 2010.

Paas, Stefan. *Church Planting in the Secular West: Learning from the European Experience.* Grand Rapids, MI: Eerdmans, 2016.

Pedro Oro, Ari and Marcelo Tadvald. "Consideraciones Sobre el Campo Evangélico Brasileño." *Revista Nueva Sociedad* 280 (March–April 2019): 55–67.

Ross, Kenneth R., J. Kwabena Asamoah-Gyadu, and Todd M. Johnson, eds. *Christianity in Sub-Saharan Africa.* Edinburgh: Edinburgh University Press, 2017.

Sanchez-Walsh, Arlene. *Latino Pentecostal Identity: Evangelical Faith, Self, and Society.* New York: Columbia University Press, 2003.

Saphier, Jon, Mary Ann Haley-Speca, and Robert Gower. *The Skillful Teacher.* Acton: Research for Better Teaching, 2008.

Small, Shawn. *An Tobar Nua—The New Well: The Unlikely Story of An Uncommon Community.* Addison, TX: HIS Publishing, 2017.

Smith, David W. *Against the Stream: Christianity in the Age of Globalization.* Leicester: Inter-Varsity, 2003.

Stiller, Brian C., Todd M. Johnson, Karen Stiller, and Mark Hutchinson, eds. *Evangelicals Around the World: A Global Handbook.* Nashville: Thomas Nelson, 2015.

Strohbehn, Ulf. Pentecostalism in *Malawi: A History of the Apostolic Faith Mission in Malawi, 1931–1994.* Zomba, Malawi: Kachere Series, 2005.

Sung, Jung Mo. "El Espíritu y la Educación Teológica." In Jung Mo Sung, Néstor Míguez Lauri Emilio Wirth, eds. *Misión y Educación Teológica.* La Paz, Bolivia: Cetela, 2012.

Synan, Vinson. *The Century of the Holy Spirit.* Nashville: Thomas Nelson, 2001.

_____ and Billy Wilson. *As the Waters Cover the Sea: The Story of Empowered21 and the Moment it Serves.* Tulsa, OK: Empowered Books, 2021.

Taylor, Mark. *1 Corinthians.* Nashville: B & H, 2014.

Thiselton, Anthony C. *The First Epistle to the Corinthians: A Commentary on the Greek Text.* Grand Rapids, MI: Eerdmans, 2000.

Turaki, Yusufu. *Ethno-Religious Crises and Conflicts in Northern Nigeria.* Jos: Yusuf Turaki Foundation, 2017.

Twelftree, Graham. "Paul's Ministry and the Miraculous." *Evangelical Quarterly* 88:3 (2016/17): 223–236.

Van Brummelen, Harro. *Walking with God in the Classroom: Christian Approaches to Teaching and Learning.* Colorado Springs: ACSI Purposeful Design Publications, 2009.

Van der Veer, Peter. *The Modern Spirit of Asia: The Spiritual and the Secular in China and India.* Princeton, NJ: Princeton University Press, 2014.

Villafañe, Eldin. *Seek the Peace of the City: Reflections on Urban Ministry.* Grand Rapids, MI: Eerdmans, 1995.

Vondey, Wolfgang, ed. *The Routledge Handbook of Pentecostal Theology.* London: Routledge, 2020.

Walls, Andrew. "Mission and Migration: The Diaspora Factor in Christian History." *Journal of African Christian Thought* 5:2 (December 2002): 3–11.

Yiwu, Liao. *God Is Red: The Secret Story of How Christianity Survived and Flourished in Communist China.* New York: HarperCollins, 2011.

Yong, Amos. *Hospitality and the Other: Pentecost, Christian Practices and the Neighbor.* NY: New York University, 2008.

_____ and Jonathan A. Anderson. *Renewing Christian Theology: Systematics for a Global Christianity.* Waco, TX: Baylor University Press, 2014.

_____ and Vinson Synan, eds. *Global Renewal Christianity: Asia and Oceania Spirit-Empowered Movements—Past, Present, and Future.* Lake Mary, FL: Charisma House, 2016.

Name and Subject Index

A
Abiola, Olu, 186
Abraham, 1
Adedibu, Babatunde, 189
Adegboyega, S. G., 189
Adenauer, Konrad, 127
adversity, Holy Spirit provision through, 46–47
Africa. *See also specific locations*
 migrant workers from, 101
 Reinhard Bonnke within, 304–309
 River of Life Christian Church (ROLCC) within, 368–369
 spirit-world belief within, 82
 statistics regarding, 156
African Christianity, 79–80, 89, 308–309. *See also* Christianity; specific locations
African Diaspora, 87
African Independent Churches (AICs), 79, 80–83
Ajani, Ezekiel O., 306
Aladura International Church, 186
Allen, A. A., 302
Allen, Leonard, 46
All Nations Church (China), 214
Alva, Reginald, 103
Alvarez, Miguel, 389
Alvarez, Mireya, 389
Amid Ug Christian Church (Mongolia), 358
Amster, Matthew, 111–112
Anderson, Allan H., 80, 157, 166, 316, 326
Angley, Ernest, 84
anointing, 18
Antioch church, concept of, 270–271, 278–279n26
An Tobar Nua (Ireland)
 call to action within, 294–295
 community within, 287–288
 COVID-19 restrictions to, 291, 294
 discipleship within, 295–296
 empowerment within, 293
 foundations of, 284–285
 Holy Spirit's guidance within, 293–294
 Holy Spirit's ministry within, 285–286
 lessons from, 291–295
 mission of, 283
 overview of, 281, 282, 284–291, 295–296
 perseverance within, 292–293
 relationality within, 287–288
 self-giving love within, 291–292
 servanthood within, 296
 spiritual gifts within, 289–290
 unity in diversity within, 288–289
Apostolic Church Nigeria (TACN) (Nigeria), 184, 188
Apostolic Faith, The (Seymour), 49
Apostolic Faith Mission, 81, 87
apostolic signs, 32
Appadurai, Arjun, 97, 99
apprenticeship, for leadership development, 231
Area of Darkness, An (Naipaul), 222
Aristotle, 73
Arnold, Clinton, 29–30
Asia. *See also specific locations*
 global networking within, 102–103
 international churches within, 100
 introduction to, 97–98
 meditation practices within, 110–111
 Pentecostalism within, 109–114
 prayer mountains within, 106
 prosperity gospel within, 102
 religion within, 98
 River of Life Christian Church

(ROLCC) within, 359
rural mission within, 106–109
seminaries within, 103–104
spirituality within, 109–114
statistics regarding, 98, 156
urban missions within, 99–106, 115
Asia for Jesus, 104
Asian Center for Missions (ACM), 325
Asian Christianity, 98–99. *See also* Christianity; *specific locations*
Asian Pacific Theological Association, 104
Asia Pacific Theological Seminary (Philippines), 104
Assemblies of God, 81, 86, 104, 157–158, 159, 161–162
astrology, 67–69
Au, Connie, 389, 390
Ayorinde, Samson, 187
Azusa Centennial, 160
Azusa Street revival movement, 45, 48–49, 157

B

Back to Jerusalem (BTJ) (China), 210–213
Baguio City, Philippines, 52
Bahamas, 50
Baker, H. A., 50
Bako, Abubakar, 187
Balaam, 20
Baldwin, Bill, 359
Balfour, Glenn, 390
baptism of the Holy Spirit, 47–48, 55, 56, 165–168, 258–259. *See also* Holy Spirit
Barrett, David, 156, 158, 159
Barth, Karl, 353
Bauman, Chad M., 112
Bayamón Postrado en Ayuno y Oración (Bayamón Bows Down in Prayer and Fasting) (Puerto Rico), 322–323

Beijing Zion Church (China), 213
Belgium, 125
Belize, 317
belonging, believing and, 391–392
Benin Republic, 188
Beougher, Timothy K., 123
Berg, Daniel, 50
Beruldsen, John, 50
Bethany Church (Indonesia), 103
Bethel Bible College (India), 104
Bezalel, 17
Bhabha, Homi, 65–66
Bhakti community, 67–69
Bhojpuri people
  church planting challenges regarding, 225–227
  church planting development regarding, 231–232
  Community Learning Centers (CLCs) for, 227–228
  deliverance among, 233–234
  discipleship work and development regarding, 228–229
  evangelism challenges regarding, 225–227
  evangelism work and development regarding, 227–228
  God's work through, 234
  healing among, 233
  Holy Spirit's work among, 232–234
  leadership development among, 230–231
  movement within, 223–224
  multiplication strategies for, 231–232
  socio-religious setting of, 221–223
Białokurec, Tomasz, 391, 395
Bismarks, Tudor, 87
bi-vocational leadership, 230
Bjork, David E., 125
Black Skin, White Masks (Fanon), 64
Blumhofer, Edith, 161–162

bodily resurrection, Holy Spirit's role within, 13
"Bold Mission Thrust" (Southern Baptist Convention), 159
Bonnke, Reinhard, 54, 83–84, 304–309
Boomer Generations, 167, 170
Borthwick, Paul, 326
Bosch, David, 277n4
Bosworth, F. F., 302, 303–304
Branham, William, 54, 302
Brazil
  Catholicism within, 348
  COVID-19 pandemic within, 346–347, 352
  economic power within, 353
  evangelism within, 349, 352–353
  healing within, 309–311
  lived experience within, 347–350
  marginalization within, 347
  missionaries within, 50
  mission in transformation within, 353–354
  mission to vulnerable within, 346–347
  Pentecostalism within, 141, 345–346
  politics within, 351, 354
  religions within, 348
  River of Life Christian Church (ROLCC) within, 359
  statistics regarding, 350
  Universal Church of the Kingdom of God (UCKG), 351
Bread of Life Christian Church Taipei, 360–361
Bread of Life Church (Taiwan), 103
Bright, Bill, 159
British East Africa, 50
Brown, Candy Gunther, 301
Buber, Martin, 67, 69–72, 74
Buchman, Frank, 127
Buddhism, 98

Burkina Faso, 358
Bush, Luis, 158

C

Caiaphas, 20
Caicó, Brazil, 309–311
Caleb, 17
Calvary Life Ministries, 101
Cambodia, 359
Cameroon, 358
Canada, 162, 359
Carey, William, 222
Carson, D. A., 243
Castellanos, Cesar, 332–334, 335, 336–339
Catholic Apostolic Holy Spirit Church in Zion, 81
Catholicism, 103, 159, 348, 350
Celestial Church of Christ, 186
Cerullo, Morris, 84
Chakwera, Lazarus, 86, 88
Charismatic movement, 132–133, 315. *See also* Pentecostalism
Chemin Neuf Community (France), 132–133
Cherubim and Seraphim Church, 186
Chile, 141
Chiluba, Frederick, 87
China
  All Nations Church, 214
  Back to Jerusalem (BTJ), 210–213
  Beijing Zion Church, 213
  charismatic conferences and, 216
  Chinese house of prayer (CHOP), 216–217
  Christian farmers within, 209
  Christian growth within, 207–209
  Christianity's history within, 207
  Christian restrictions within, 113–114
  church effectiveness from, 366
  eschatology and, 217–218
  family churches within, 208–209

Great Cultural Revolution within, 207
healing within, 212
Holy Spirit's role within, 212–213
house churches within, 208, 211, 215
internet usage within, 374
miracles within, 212
missionaries within, 50
Mission China 2030 (MC2030), 210–211, 213–215
mission within, 209–215
nationalism within, 112–113
Northwest Spiritual Fellowship (NSF), 210
persecution within, 114, 208, 209–215, 214
prayer houses within, 216
religion within, 109–110, 112–114
revival within, 209–215
social media use within, 216
Spirit-empowered ecclesiastic signs within, 215–217
statistics regarding, 207–208
temple community within, 217–218
underground churches within, 209–210
Zion Church, 214–215
Chinese house of prayer (CHOP) (China), 216–217
Chiquete, Daniel, 147
Cho, David Yonggi, 51, 102–103, 332
Choi, Jasil, 51–52, 108
Chow, Ewen, 104
Chow, Jonathan, 104
Chow, Nathaniel, 104
Christ Apostolic Church of Great Britain, 186
Christerson, Brad, 163
Christ for All Nations (CfAN), 83–84
Christianity
  African, 79–80, 89, 308–309
  Asian, 98–99
  in China, 207
  in Southern Africa, 79
  statistics regarding, 98, 155–156
  Western decline of, 2
Christian Mission and Alliance (CM&A), 360
Christian schools, 131, 195–206, 196
Christ the Healer (Bosworth), 302
Christ Together, 271–272
Chrysostom, 29, 32
Church. *See also specific churches; specific locations*
  Great Commission approach of, 1
  as missional, 255
  scriptural prophecy regarding, 46
  technology within, 105–106
Church Missionary Society, 182
Church of Christ in Nations (Nigeria), 183
Church of God (Cleveland, TN), 159–160
Church of Pentecost (Ghana), 129
Church of the Brethren (Nigeria), 182–183
Church of the Lord (Aladura), 186
church planting. *See also* Saturation Church Planting (SCP)
  among Bhojpuri people, 225–227, 231–232
  cross-cultural, 358–359, 361
  effectiveness of, 365–366
  God's work through, 234
  process of, 235–236
  of River of Life Christian Church (ROLCC), 358–359
"Church Target 2000," 160
Ciampa, Roy, 30
Clark, Clifton, 308–309
Clowney, Edmund P., 255
cohabitation, 35–36
Coker, J. B., 185
collaboration, 274–276
colonialism, 63–64

Columbia, 332
communal evangelism, 85. *See also* evangelism
Communist Party (China), 112–113
community
  within *An Tobar Nua* (Ireland), 287–288
  communal Holy Spirit participation within, 37, 38
  miracles within, 38
  within Pentecostalism, 145–146
  Spirit-empowered witness to, 34–38
Community Learning Centers (CLCs), 227–228
Confraternidad Evangélica de Honduras (Evangelical Fellowship of Honduras), 318
contextualization, 62
Continuation Committee, 2
conversion, 32, 84–85, 125–126, 128, 258
Conzelmann, Hans, 40n23
Cook, William, 244
Corinth/Corinthian Church, 28, 31, 34, 35–36, 244–246
Cornelius, 259
Cortés, Luis, 326
Costa Rica, 317
Cote d'Ivoire, 188
courage, Spirit-empowered, 392
covenant, 1
COVID-19 pandemic
  An Tobar Nua (Ireland) and, 291, 294
  in Brazil, 346–347, 352
  in Europe, 131–132
  Holy Spirit's role following, 14
  mission following, 23
  River of Life Christian Church (ROLCC) and, 367
Cox, Harvey, 106, 124
creation, 12–14
cross-cultural church planting, 358–359, 361. *See also* church planting

Crowther, Samuel Ajayi, 182
Cunha, Magali, 346, 353
"Curriculum for New Disciples," 229
Curry, Kelly, 288, 290
Curry, Susan, 290

D

Dam Suan Mung, 238–239
dancing religion (Myanmar/Burma), 239–240
Daniel, 17
Daniel, Yvan, 125
David, 15, 18, 20
Dawkins, Richard, 198
DAWN 2000 (Montgomery), 268–269
"Decade of Destiny" (Church of God (Cleveland, TN)), 159–160
"Decade of Harvest" (Assemblies of God), 159
Deeper Life Bible Church (Nigeria), 185
Deeper Life Bible Church (United Kingdom), 187
deliverance, 233–234
Delors, Jacques, 127
Democratic Republic of Congo, 80, 81
Democratic Republic of the Congo, 358
Dhinakaran, D. G. S., 304
discernment, 286
Disciple a Whole Nation (DAWN), 265–266, 267–272
disciples, 19, 45–47, 388
discipleship. *See also* G12 Vision
  among Bhojpuri people, 228–229
  within An Tobar Nua (Ireland), 295–296
  challenges of, 341
  effectiveness of, 334
  by example, 200–202
  within G12 Vision, 335–336
  grassroots, 390–392
  Great Commission and, 179
  importance of, 260–261

ministers within, 331–332
missional team formation within, 332–334
mission and, 334–336
overview of, 331–334
within Pentecostalism, 145–146
of poor/poverty, 203–204
Discipleship Clubs (DCs), 199
Discipling of a Nation, The (Montgomery), 267
Discovery Bible Studies, 229
dispensationalism, 164
diversity, unity in, 288–289
divorce, 35
Duhm, Bernhard, 18
Dutch Reformed Church Mission (Nigeria), 182
dynamis (power), 29–30
Dzao, Timothy, 360, 370n4, 370n6

E

Ecclesia Theological Seminary (Hong Kong), 103–104
edification, 245
Edify, 193, 194, 195–196, 206. *See also* low-fee independent Christian schools
education, 131. *See also* Christian schools; low-fee independent Christian schools
Edvardsen, Aril, 304
Elijah, 20, 205
Elisha, 21
El Salvador, 317, 322
El Shaddai, 103
Emmaus Scripture School (Ireland), 286
Empowered21, 160–161
Empowered 21 Scholars Consultation, 3–5
empowerment
holiness and, 22–23
Holy Spirit's role within, 17–23, 45–47, 55–56
for leadership development, 231
obligation within, 293
prophecy and, 20–22
in weakness, 293
En-Chieh Chao, 101
engagement, philosophy of, 68–69
Erola, Walter, 239
eschatological mandate, 164–165
eschatological urgency, 55
eschatology, 84, 217–218
Escobar, Samuel, 253, 254–255
Eswatini, 82, 358
ethnoscapes, 99, 100–102
Eu Choong Chong, 102
Europe. *See also specific locations*
barriers within, 135
believers within, 125
Charismatic movement role within, 132–133
Christian history of, 121–124
Christian schools within, 131
Constantine era within, 123
converts within, 125–126
COVID-19 pandemic within, 131–132
demographics of, 128
dualistic thinking within, 124–125
generational gaps within, 131
independent churches within, 132–133
migration to, 128
Nigerian churches within, 186
overview of, 121
Pentecostal European Mission (PEM), 133–134
Pentecostal statistics within, 130, 133
pilgrims within, 125
postmodern worldview within, 127
River of Life Christian Church (ROLCC) within, 359
scientific beliefs within, 126–127
spiritual awakenings within, 123–124

spiritual changes within, 128–132
spiritual heritage of, 127
unreached people groups (UPG) within, 134, 136
European Pentecostal Charismatic Research Association (EPCRA), 132–133
evaluation, for leadership development, 231
Evangelical Church of Winning All (ECWA), 187–188
Evangelical Church Winning All (Nigeria), 183
Evangelicalism, statistics regarding, 122
evangelism
within African Christianity, 79–80
among Bhojpuri people, 225–228
as Assemblies of God priority, 157–158
Boomer Generation viewpoint regarding, 167
in Brazil, 349, 352–353
as communal, 85
efforts regarding, 158–161
function of, 156
G12 Vision and, 335
Gen Z viewpoint regarding, 167
globalism and, 377–378
in Guatemala, 316
healing and, 389–390
in Honduras, 317–319
Lord's Prayer and, 242–244
mass healing, 301–311
Millennial viewpoint regarding, 167
missional living and, 167
in Nigeria, 180–186
in North America, 156, 163–170
obedience-based discipleship within, 223–224
perseverance within, 292–293
personal, 285
politics and, 87–90

power encounters and, 389–390
in secular culture, 282–283
in Southern Africa, 83–87
Spirit-empowered healing, 302–303
through education, 204–205
youth, 281–283
"Evangelism 2000," 159
Evangelism in Depth (EID), 268–269
evangelists, healing impact through, 54–55
Evangelization of the World in this Generation (Mott), 157
Every Home for Christ (EHC), 358
exorcism, 111–112
Ezekiel, 21

F

Faith and Order Commission of the World Council of Churches, 352
Faith Tabernacle (Nigeria), 184
family churches, 208–209
Fanon, Frantz, 63–64, 66
Farrow, Lucy, 50
fasting, 145, 320
Fatokun, Samson, 391
Fee, Gordon, 30, 245
Fengshui, 110
field training, for leadership development, 231
Filipino Catholic Charismatic networks, 103
filled with the Spirit, 46–47. *See also* Holy Spirit
finanscapes, 99
Finland, 124, 134
Flattery, George M., 382
Flood narrative, 13
Flory, Richard, 163
"For a Global Vision of the Church," 352
forgiveness, 243
Forrest, Tom, 159
fortune-telling, 110

Foster, Christopher, 388
Four-Square Movement, 266–267
France, 125, 128, 130, 132–133
Francis of Assisi, 290
Franklin, Jentzen, 168
Freeman, T. B., 181
Freston, Paul, 322
friendship, 73
Full Gospel Assembly (FGA), 238–239

G

G12 Vision
  discipleship within, 335–336
  evangelism within, 335
  expansion of, 337–338
  global missions and, 336–339
  in Mexico, 339–341
  missional focus of discipleship within, 336
  national teams and conferences within, 338–339
  overview of, 342–343
Gandhi, Mohandas Karamchand, 112
Gangetic Plain (India), 222
gangs, 143, 144, 322
Garr, Alfred and Lillian, 50
Gary, Jay, 158
generosity, 363–365
Gentiles, 33
Gen Z, 167, 169
Germany, 128
Gewe, Emmanuel Array, 309
Ghana, 129, 188, 358
Gideon, 18
Gideon Monastery (South Korea), 108
Gideon Theological Seminary (South Korea), 108
Gifford, Paul, 305
Gillis, Jerry, 271
Glaser, Arthur F., 252
global individuality, 373, 378–382
globalism, 377–378

globalization, 99, 101–102
global missions, 336–339
global networking, 102–103
Global South, statistics regarding, 315. *See also specific locations*
glory, defined, 241
God, 1, 12–14
God Delusion, 198
Godin, Henri, 125
Gold Coast, 188
gospel, politicizing of, 168–170
Gospel Faith Mission International, 187
gospel saturation, 271–272
grace, defined, 142
Graham, Billy, 158
Graham, Donovan, 196
Great Britain, 128, 222
Great Commission
  Holy Spirit and, 252–255
  meaning of, 86
  overview of, 1, 193–194, 251–252, 331–332, 387
  taking heart regarding, 388
Guatemala, 316–317, 322, 359
GuQuan Zhang, 210
Guthrie, Stan, 259–260
Guti, Ezekiel, 87
Gypsies (Roma), 134

H

Ha, Stephen (Ha Yong-Inn), 370n5
Hämäläinen, Arto, 391
Hammerling, Roy, 242
Hayford, Jack, 242
Head, Peter, 42n49
healing
  across the world, 45
  among Bhojpuri people, 233
  in Brazil, 309–311
  in China, 212
  evangelism and, 389–390

impact on global growth through
    evangelists, 54–55
  mass, 301–311
  in the Philippines, 52–53
  Spirit-empowered, 302–303
  on Yoido Island, 51
Healing en Masse (Osborn), 303–304
heart revolution, 194
Henry, Carl F. H., 158
Hervieu-Lèger, Danièle, 125
Hezmalhalch, Thomas, 50
Hicks, Tommy, 54
Hiebert, Paul G., 110
Hinduism, 98, 225
Hindu nationalist ideology, 112
Hindus, 53–54
Hindutva, 112
Hinn, Benny, 54
Hirsh, Alan, 252–253, 255, 260
Hlimsang revival (Myanmar/Burma),
    239–240
holiness, 22–23, 34, 145
holistic mission, 367
Holy Spirit
  anointing role of, 18
  baptism of, 47–48, 55, 56, 165–168,
    258–259
  benefits of, 142, 147–148
  as Christian community agent, 289
  communal participation within, 37, 38
  conversion role of, 32
  creation role of, 12–14
  demonstration of, 28–33
  dynamism of, 255
  empowerment role of, 17–23,
    45–47, 55–56
  filling by, 46–47
  God's provision of, 46–47
  Great Commission and, 252–255
  guidance of, 293–294
  identity through, 16
  indwelling of, 14, 22
  intercession by, 18
  Jesus and, 254
  life-producing role of, 14–17
  making time for, 286–287
  methodology regarding, 11–12
  missional role of, 253–254
  outpouring of, 45
  personal benefits versus missional
    benefits of, 165–168
  in post-COVID-19 world, 14
  pouring out of, 13
  power of, 28–33
  re-creation role of, 13
  restoration through, 13
  spiritual gifts from, 21–22
  teaching on, 260
  terminology regarding, 12
'Home Mission Department'
    (Nigeria), 185
Honduras
  challenges within, 143–144
  Confraternidad Evangélica
    de Honduras (Evangelical
    Fellowship of Honduras), 318
  corruption within, 318
  evangelism within, 317–319
  female leadership within, 318–319
  gangs within, 143, 144
  Iglesia Unción, Poder, y
    Avivamiento (Anointing, Power,
    and Revival Church), 318
  Las Torres (The Towers), 322
  migration from, 144, 317–318
  pastors within, 317–319
  Pentecostalism within, 145
  political challenges within, 146–147
  poverty within, 144
  prayer within, 318
  social and spiritual realms within, 146
  statistics regarding, 317
  violence within, 322
Hong Kong, 101, 103–104

Hosea, 21
house churches, 208, 211, 215–218
Hull, Bill, 337–338, 342
humility, 289, 392–395
Hunter, H. D., 260
Hutchinson, Mark, 130
hybridity, 66

I

I and Thou (Buber), 70–72
Idahosa, Benson, 187, 304
ideoscapes, 99, 102–104
Iglesia Unción, Poder, y Avivamiento (Anointing, Power, and Revival Church) (Honduras), 318
Ignatiou, Stavros, 391
Illich, Ivan, 260–261
Imakando, Joseph, 88
I'm Gonna Let it Shine (Montgomery), 278n20
immigration, 128–129, 144, 324–326
inculturation, 62
independent churches, 132–133
India
  Bhojpuri people within, 221–223
  British within, 222
  Community Learning Centers (CLCs) within, 227–228
  Gangetic Plain within, 222
  Hinduism within, 225
  missionaries within, 50, 53–54
  spirituality within, 112, 232
  westernization within, 223
India (Bethel Bible College), 104
Indonesia, 101, 103
intercession, by the Holy Spirit, 18
intermarriage, 35
International Charismatic Mission (ICM) (Columbia), 332
International Christian Assembly (ICA), 100
International Missionary Council, 2
International Pentecostal Holiness Church, 160, 162
International Review of Missions, 2
internet
  effective strategy for, 383–385
  global individuality within, 378–382
  globalism and, 377–378
  impact and usage of, 374
  as mission field, 374–376
  Network211 strategy regarding, 382–383
  users as people group within, 375–376
Introducing Spirit-Empowered Christianity (Johnson and Zurlo), 81
Ireland, 281, 283. See also An Tobar Nua (Ireland)
Irish, Kerry, 242
Isaiah for Everyone (Goldingay), 241
Isgrigg, Daniel, 395
Islam, 179–186
Israel, 46
Italy, 128
"I-Thou" relationship, 67, 70–72
Ivory Coast, 358

J

Jabula New Life Community Church, 87
James, Lucy, 50
Japan, 103, 134
Jenkins, Philip, 128
Jephthah, 18
Jeshua, 13
Jesus, Wilfredo de, 326
Jesus Christ
  fulfillment by, 253
  Holy Spirit and, 19, 254
  interaction with unclean people by, 42n52
  life-producing role of, 16–17
  mind and heart revolutions through, 194

ministry of, 333
mission of, 1
Jesus Film, 159
Jesus People movement, 237
Jin, Ezra, 213, 214
Jinadu, Paul, 187
Joel, 21
Johanson, B. C., 245
John, 22
John Paul II, 62, 159
Johnson, Todd, 81, 155
John the Baptist, 21
Joseph, 17
Joshua, 17
Joshua Band, 104
Joyful Witness in the Muslim World (Reisacher), 254
Judaism, 216

K

Kaunda, Chammah, 88–89
Kay, William, 168
Kayanja, Robert, 304
Kazakhstan, 359, 368
Keener, Craig, 243
Kelabit people, 107
Kenya, 90, 188
Ketcham, Maynard, 104
Kimbangu, Simon, 82
King, Daniel, 389–390
Kogon, Eugene, 69
Kuala Lumpur, 101
Kuhlman, Kathryn, 54
Kumkang Mountain (South Korea), 108
Kumuyi, W. F., 187
Kunga, Van, 239
Kwiyani, Harvey, 389, 390

L

"Ladder of Success, The," 335–336
La France Pays de Mission (France, a country of mission) (Godin and Yvan), 125
Lake, John G., 50, 54, 81, 82, 302
Lambrecht, Jan, 33
Lange, John, 244
Las Torres (The Towers) (Honduras), 322
Latin America. *See also specific locations*
  church response within, 147–148
  community and discipleship within, 145–146
  migration from, 144, 149
  missionaries from, 325–326
  mission within, 143–144, 326–327
  native traditions within, 320
  Pentecostalism within, 141–143, 319–320
  political challenges within, 146–147
  poverty within, 142, 144
  prayer within, 323–324
  River of Life Christian Church (ROLCC) within, 359
  service structure within, 319–320
  social evils challenge within, 148–149
  social justice within, 320–322
  spiritual warfare within, 323–324
  statistics regarding, 156, 315, 316, 317
  underdevelopment within, 143
  violence within, 322–323
Latin American Bible Institutes, 319
Latter Rain, 163–164
Lausanne Congress on Evangelism, 158
Le, Vince, 101
leadership skills, 17, 18, 230–231
Lee, Sang Yun, 108
Lee, Tommy, 303
Lee, Yongdo, 108
Lekganyane, Engenas, 81
lepers, Jesus' interaction with, 42n52
Lesotho, 80, 188
Li, Daniel, 213, 214
Lian, Thang D., 238
Liao, Ian, 104

liberalization, 169–170
Liberia, 50
life, Holy Spirit's role in producing, 14–17
Lindsey, Gordon, 302, 303
Living Waters Church of Malawi, 87
Lkhamsuren, Batbold, 358, 359
Location of Culture, The (Bhabha), 65–66
Lord's Prayer, 242–244
Loubriel, Juan Ramón, 323
love, self-giving, 287–288, 290, 291–292
love, within I-Thou relationship, 71
low-fee independent Christian schools
  discipleship within, 195–196, 199, 200–202
  evangelism within, 204–205
  salvation participation within, 200
  school proprietors and leaders within, 196–197
  School Transformation Committees, 199
  students within, 202–203
  teachers within, 197–202
  youth leadership training camps within, 199
Lun Bawang people, 107, 111
Lutheran Mission (Nigeria), 182

M

Ma, Julie, 388, 389, 395
Macau, 103
MacDonald, Margaret, 35
macro-institutional leadership, 276
Malawi, 81, 85, 87, 88, 90
Malaysia, 101, 102, 107–108
Mancini, Will, 255
Mantofa, Philip, 104
marriage, 35
"Mary Consoles Eve" (Rain for Roots), 396
mass healing evangelism, 301–311

Mayowa, Banji, 185
McAlister, Stuart, 124–125
McGavran, Donald, 267–268
McLeod, John, 64
McPherson, Aimee Semple, 54, 302
media, role of, 105
mediascapes, 99, 104–105
Medina, Nestor, 321–322
meditation, 110–111
megachurches, 101–102
mentorship, 261
meso-apostolic leadership, 276
Methodists, 141, 183, 316
Mexico, 338–341, 359
Micah, 21
micro-institutional leadership, 276
Middle East, 101
migration, 144, 149, 251–252, 317–318
Míguez, Néstor, 351
Millennials, 167, 169
Miller, Darrow, 203
Miller, Kathleen, 50
"Million Souls Crusade," 158
mind revolution, 194
ministers, everyone as, 331–332
miracles. *See also* healing
  advertising, 301
  among Bhojpuri people, 233–234
  in China, 212
  within community experience, 38
  Holy Spirit within, 28–33
  in Southern Africa, 84, 90–91
Missão (The Mission) (Brazil), 352
Missio Dei, 357–358, 360, 366
mission
  activities regarding, 1–2
  baptism of the Holy Spirit within, 258–259
  call to, 56
  in China, 209–215
  of the church, 1, 255

as collaboration, 73
discipleship and, 334–336
Holy Spirit's role within, 253–254
humility in, 392–395
in Latin America, 143–144
in Nigeria, 186–189
North America and, 165–168
from position of power, 64–65
in post-COVID-19 world, 23
in Southern Africa, 83–87
worship as goal of, 240
"Mission 2000," 160
missional living, 167
missional teams, 332–334
missionaries. *See also specific people*
agenda of, 66
history of, 50
hybridity of, 66
mission researcher versus, 62
one-way, 55
postcolonial critique regarding, 63–67
relationships of, 73–74
statistics regarding, 325
missionary effect, of Spirit-inspired revelation, 38
Mission China 2030 (MC2030) (China), 210–211, 213–215
mission research, on Bhakti community, 67–69
mission researcher, missionary versus, 62
Mondal, Anindita, 64
Mong, Ra Woon, 108
Mongolia, 358, 368
Montgomery, Jim, 265–267, 268–269, 278n20
Moreno, Salixto Salvatierra, 142
Morrison, Elmor, 104
Moses, 17, 20
Mott, John R., 157
Mount Mao sect (China), 110
Mount Murud (Malaysia), 107–108

Movement for Multiparty Democracy (MMD), 95n29
Mozambique, 87, 358
Mumba, Nevers, 88, 90, 95n29
Muslims, 128, 255–257, 258, 376
Myanmar/Burma, 101, 238–240

N

Naipaul, V. S., 222
Namibia, 80, 87
National Christian Coalition (NCC), 95n29
National Church Planting Processes (NC2P), 272
National Citizens Coalition (NCC), 95n29
nationalist spirituality, 112
Network211, 382–383, 383–385
New Apostolic Reformation (NAR), 163
Newbigin, Lesslie, 252, 253
New Covenant Church (United Kingdom), 187
"New Life 2000," 159
Next Christendom, The (Jenkins), 62
Nicaragua, 317
Nicomachean Ethics (Aristotle), 73
Niger, 358
Nigeria
challenges within, 189
evangelism within, 180–186
'Home Mission Department' within, 185
international missions and, 186–190
Islam within, 179–186
overview of, 179–180, 189–190
River of Life Christian Church (ROLCC), 358
Spirit-empowered Christianity within, 180–186
1910 Edinburgh Conference, 2
Nissen, Johannes, 253, 259
Njotorahardjo, Niko, 100–101, 103

nonfaith, 283
North America. *See also specific locations*
  Apostolic Church Nigeria (TACN) within, 188
  baptism of the Holy Spirit and, 165–168
  evangelism challenges within, 156
  evangelism factors within, 163–170
  liberalization within, 169–170
  mission and, 165–168
  overview of, 155–156
  politicizing the gospel within, 168–170
  premillennial eschatology within, 163–166
  statistics regarding, 161
  unfinished task within, 161–163
North American Renewal Service Committee (NARSC), 160
Northwest Spiritual Fellowship (NSF) (China), 210
Norway, 124
Nyanni, Caleb Opoku, 129

O

obedience-based discipleship, 223–224, 228–229
Oke, Wale, 187
Okonkwo, Mike, 187
Ola, Joseph, 133
Olofinjana, Israel, 186
Only Way Movement (Philippines), 268–269
Osanri Choi-Jasil Fasting Prayer Mountain, 51, 108–109
Osborn, Daisy, 303
Osborn, T. L., 54, 302, 303–304
"other," 63–64, 65, 66, 71–72
Othniel, 18
Our Lady of Fatima Church (Macau), 103

outsiders, unbelievers versus, 36
Owens, Eschel, 31
Oyedepo, David, 187

P

Panama, 317
Parks, Keith, 158
Paul. *See also specific Scriptures*
  anti-sophistic approach of, 28
  apostleship of, 32
  boasting by, 33
  call of, 28, 32, 42n49
  conversion writings of, 245
  discipleship writings of, 333–334
  evangelization by, 33
  holiness of, 34
  Jewish worldview of, 30
  marriage viewpoint of, 35
  signs and wonders of, 29, 30, 33
  Spirit-empowered preaching by, 27–28, 31, 33, 42n49
  worship writings of, 245
Payne, Leah, 168
Pentecostal Assemblies of Canada, 160, 162
Pentecostal European Mission (PEM), 133–134
Pentecostalism. *See also specific locations*
  African Independent Churches (AICs) and, 80–82
  baptism of the Holy Spirit within, 47–48
  challenges regarding, 259–260
  eschatology within, 92n4
  indicators of, 89–90
  mass healing evangelism and, 310–311
  as missionary movement, 157
  mission of, 49
  opposition to, 142–143
  prayer emphasis within, 319–320

social justice and, 320–322
socially disregarded within, 56
in Southern Africa, 84, 89–90
spiritual realm awareness within, 56
statistics regarding, 130, 315
witness for Christ within, 56–57
Pentecostal pneumatology, 11
Pentecostals and Charismatics in Latin America and Latino Communities (Medina), 321–322
Pentecostal theology, 11
people group, 375–376
persecution, 19, 114, 208, 209–215, 214, 235
perseverance, within evangelism, 292–293
personal evangelism, 285
Peter, 21, 259, 333
Pharaoh, 17
Philip, 20–21
Philippines, 52–53, 99, 104, 266–267, 268–269
Pierson, A. T., 156–157
pilgrims, in Europe, 125
Piper, John, 240
"Plan to evangelize the world" (Pierson), 156–157
Plessis, Amanda du, 242
Plüss, Jean-Daniel, 132
politics, 87–90, 146–147, 168–170, 351, 354
poor/poverty, 142, 144, 148, 203–204
postcolonial critique, 63–67
postmodernism, 127
power encounters, 389–390
prayer
   Bayamón Postrado en Ayuno y Oración (Bayamón Bows Down in Prayer and Fasting) (Puerto Rico), 323
   in difficult times, 323–324
   for forgiveness, 243
in Honduras, 318
importance of, 145, 389
Lord's Prayer, 242–244
within Pentecostalism, 319–320
as revival element, 53–54
River of Life Christian Church (ROLCC) and, 361–362
in Southern Africa, 83, 85–86
prayer houses, 216
prayer mountains, 106
preaching, Holy Spirit's power within, 32
premillennial eschatology, 163–166
Priest, Robert, 166
Prince, Brainerd, 395
Prince, Derek, 331
"Principle for Promoting Chinese Christianity in China for the Next Five Years" (China), 113
Project 10Million, 382
prophecy, 20–22
proselytism, 126
prosperity gospel, 102
Prosser, Peter, 164
Puerto Rico, 322–323
Pule, Danny, 88
Puteri Rimba (female spirit), 111

Q
Quan Cui, 213, 214

R
Rad, Gerhard von, 12–14
Ramabai, Pandita, 53–54, 58–59n32, 58n30
Ramirez, Erica, 168
re-creation, Holy Spirit's role within, 13
Redeemed Christian Church of God (RCCG) (United Kingdom), 133, 187
Reed, David, 101
Reformed Party, 95n29
refugees, in Europe, 128–129
Reisacher, Evelyn A., 254

relationality, 287–288
renewal movements, 260
repentance, of David, 15
Republic of Togo, 188
restoration, 13
reverse mission, 187
revival, spiritual
  in China, 209–215
  defined, 123
  in Europe, 123–124
  in Guatemala, 316
  Holy Spirit's role within, 15
  in Kelabit Highlands (Malaysia), 107
  as latter rain, 55
  locations of, 49
  in Malaysia, 107
  in Myanmar/Burma, 239–240
  prayer as element for, 53–54
River of Life Christian Church (ROLCC)
  adopt a nation campaign of, 369
  audacity of, 363–365
  COVID-19 pandemic response by, 367
  critical assessments of, 365–369
  cross-cultural church planting ministry of, 358–359, 361
  culture of, 363–365
  generosity of, 363–365
  holistic mission vision of, 367
  missiological convictions of, 365–369
  overview of, 357–358, 369
  partnerships of, 361–362
  prayer strategy of, 361–362
  strategy of, 361–362
  success factors analysis of, 359–365
  sustainability of, 365–369
  vision of, 360–361
Roberts, Oral, 45, 54–55, 158, 302
Roman Catholic Mission (Nigeria), 182
Romania, 134
Rosner, Brian, 30
Runyon, Daniel V., 260
rural mission, 106–109, 226

S

Saidi, Afaf Al-, 65
Salamanca, Saul and Gloria, 339–341
Salguero, Gabriel, 326
salvation, 310. *See also* conversion
Samson, 18
Samuel, 20
Sanchez-Walsh, Arlene, 169
Satan, strategy of, 225
Saturation Church Planting (SCP), 265, 266–272, 273–276
Saturation Church Planting Global (SCPG), 270–271
Saul, King, 20
School Transformation Committees, 199
Schuman, Robert, 127
science, European viewpoints regarding, 126–127
Scripture, 14, 21, 197–199. *See also the Scripture Index*
secularism/secular culture, evangelism within, 125, 282–283
self-giving love, 287–288, 290, 291–292
seminaries, 103–104
Senegal, 358
servanthood, 296
service, 289
Seymour, William J., 45, 48–49
ShaoTang Yang, 210
Shembe, Isaiah, 82
Shortt, Mike, 286
Sidang Injil Borneo (SIB), 107
Sierra-Leone, 188
signs and wonders, 28–33. *See also* healing; miracles
Simpson, William, 50
Sinicization of Religion (China), 113
slaves, 35–36
Smith, Chad, 276

Smith, David W., 123
Smith, Dwight, 276
Snyder, Howard A., 260
social evils, 148–149
social justice, 320–322
social media, 216
Society for International Mission (Nigeria), 183
South Africa, 50, 81–82, 188, 358
Southern Africa. *See also specific locations*
  Assemblies of God within, 86
  challenges within, 90–91
  Christianity within, 79
  countries within, 92n1
  eschatology within, 92n4
  miracle corruption within, 90–91
  Pentecostal mission and evangelism within, 83–87
  politics within, 87–90
  prayer within, 83, 85–86
Southern Baptist Convention, 159
South Korea, 101, 108–109, 332, 368
spiritual gifts, 21–22, 28, 36, 38, 245–246, 289–290
spiritual utterances, 36
spiritual warfare, 323–324
Spring, Craig, 167
Stafford, Glen, 239
stewardship, 293
Strang, Stephen, 168
Sudan United Mission (Nigeria), 182
Suffering Servant, 18
Sweden, 124
Switzerland, 368
Synan, Vinson, 160

T

Tadem, Pudun, 108
Taiwan, 50, 101, 103, 360–361
Tanzania, 188
Taylor, Mark, 245

teachers, within low-fee independent Christian schools, 197–202
Teaching Redemptively (Graham), 196
technoscapes, 99, 105–106
Tegucigalpa, Honduras, 318
Thailand, 134
Thang San Mung, 389
Then the End Will Come (Montgomery), 269–270
"Theology of Blessings" (Cho), 102
Thieme, Karl, 69
third space, 66–67
Thiselton, Anthony, 29
Three-Self Patriotic (TSP), 208
Tibet, 50
Tinlin, Paul, 161–162
Tong Liu, 357, 358, 360, 364, 365, 367–368
tongues speaking, 37, 38, 90. *See also* baptism of the Holy Spirit
Trump, Donald, 168
Turkey, 134, 368
Twelftree, Graham, 30

U

Uganda, 188
Ukpai, Uma, 187
unbelievers, 35, 36, 38
unclean people, Jesus' interaction with, 42n52
underground churches, 209–210
United Kingdom
  Apostolic Church Nigeria (TACN) within, 188
  immigrants/refugees within, 128
  Nigerian churches within, 186, 187
  Redeemed Christian Church of God (RCCG), 133
  Zimbabwean churches within, 87
United Missionary Society (Nigeria), 182
United States, 144, 324–326, 359, 368
United University of Victoria, 349

unity, 287–289
Unity College of Victoria, 352
Universal Church of the Kingdom of God (UCKG) (Brazil), 351
unreached people groups (UPG), 134, 136, 273–274
urban missions, 99–106, 115, 225–226, 273–274
U. S. Center for World Mission, 159
Uzbekistan, 368

V

Vaage, Leif, 35
Vandenberg, Peter, 306
Vanderbout, Elva, 52–53
Veer, Peter van der, 112
Vermander, Benoît, 113, 114
Vietnam, 101
Villafañe, Eldin, 321
Vingren, Gunnar, 50
Voice of Healing (magazine), 302–303

W

Wacker, Grant, 308
Wagner, C. Peter, 265
Wallnau, Lance, 168
Walls, Andrew, 315
Wang, Enoch, 210
Wang, Thomas, 158
Warri Kingdom (Nigeria), 180
weakness, empowerment in, 293
White, Paula, 168
Whiteman, Darrell L., 62
Wigglesworth, Smith, 302
Wilker, Karl, 69
Wilkinson, Michael, 162
Wilson, Billy, 160
Winter, Ralph, 159, 265
wisdom, 17
Witherington, Ben, 245
witnessing, theological incentive for Pentecostal, 55–56. *See also* evangelism
women, 50–54, 318–319
Woodworth-Etter, Maria, 54, 302
World Consultation on Frontier Mission, 159
World Evangelical Alliance (WEA), 276–277
world evangelism, 2, 4, 49, 50. *See also* evangelism
World Missionary Conference, 2
world of spirits, 111–112
worship
  criticism of, 238
  importance of, 389
  introversion *versus* extroversion of, 238–240, 246–247
  Isaiah's vision regarding, 240–242
  as mission goal, 240
  in Myanmar/Burma, 238–240
  in the Old Testament, 240–242
  overview of, 237–238
  purpose of, 246
  technology within, 105–106

X

Xi Jinping, 112–113
Xu, Peter, 210, 211, 212

Y

Yen, Timothy, 104
yoga, 110, 225
Yoido Full Gospel Church, 51
Yoido Island, 51
Yong, Amos, 74
Yonggi Cho, David, 51, 102–103, 332
Yongmun Mountain (South Korea), 108
Youngren, Peter, 304
youth evangelism, 281–283
youth leadership training camps, 199
Yun, Brother, 210, 212
Yunnan, 50

Z

Zambia, 81, 88, 89, 95n29
Zaozhuang Research Center on Sinicization of Christianity (China), 113
Zechariah, 21
Zerubbabel, 13, 17
Zhao, Simon, 210, 212
Zimbabwe, 81, 82
Zimbabwe Assemblies of God (ZAOGA), 87
Zion Apostolic Faith Mission, 81
Zion Christian Church, 81
Zion Church (China), 214–215
Zurlo, Gina, 81, 155

Scripture Index

Old Testament

Genesis
1:1-2	12, 13
1:2	12, 13, 24n9
1:28	204
2:7	14
2:7 LXX	25n12
2:15	204
6-8	13
6:3	13
6:17	13, 14
7:15, 22	13, 14
7:22	25n14
8:1	13
12:1-3	1
41:38	17

Exodus
7:3	39n13
10:13, 19	13
14:21	13
15:8, 10	13
24:15-16	35
28:3	17
31:3	17
35:31	17

Leviticus
18	35

Numbers
11:17	17
11:25-29	20
14:24	17
16:22	14
24:2	20
27:16	14
27:18	17

Deuteronomy
2:30	25n18
4:34	39n13
7:3-4	35
28:46	39n13
31:16	35
32:11	24n4
34:9	17
34:11	39n13

Judges
3:10	18
6:34	18
11:29	18
13:25	18
14:6, 19	18
15:14	18

1 Samuel
10:5-12	20
16:13	18
19:20-24	20

2 Samuel
22:16	25n14
23:2	20

1 Kings
18:8-15	205–206
18:12	20
22:22-23	24n6, 26n34

2 Kings
2:1-16	20
2:9, 15	21

1 Chronicles
12:18	18

2 Chronicles
15:1	18
18:21-22	26n34
20:14	18
24:20	18

Nehemiah
9:20	22
9:30	21

Job
4:9	25n14
12:10	14
26:13	12
27:3	14
27:3-4	25n14
32:8	17, 25n14
32:18	21
33:4	14, 25n14
34:14	14
34:14-15	25n14

Psalm
18:15	25n14
27:13	110
33:6	12
51	15
51:10	194
51:10 (12)	26n34
51:10, 11, 12, 17	15
51:11	15, 22
78:6-7	388
102:18	388
104:29	14
104:30	12
135:9	39n13
135:17	14
139:7	15
143:10	22
146:4	14

Proverbs
9:10	197
11:30	85
23:7	194

Ecclesiastes
8:11	194
11:5	14
12:7	14

Isaiah
6	240
7:11	29
8:18	39n13
11:2	18, 25n16, 26n32
12	240
25:6	395
25:6-7	388
25:8	396
28:6	18
28:10	43n61
28:11-12	36

32:15	13	33	85	9:35-38	375
38:16	14	36:26	194	9:37	327, 331
40-55	241	36:26-27	15	10:1	333
42:1	18	36:27, 35	13	10:11	227
42:5	12, 25n14	37:1	15	10:20	19
43:1-7	240	37:5-10	14	12:29	222
44:3	13, 15	37:14	14	12:38	39n13
44:6-8	240	39:21-29	15	16:18	1
44:13-20	351	39:29	15	17:2	26n38
45:14	43n67	43:5	15	19:3-12	42n50
49:6	46, 388	**Daniel**		22:37-39	230
52:7	85	2:4b-7:28	25n17	22:43	21
53	240	4:3	388	24:14	156, 164, 244, 387
56-66	240	4:8, 9, 18	17	24:14, 44	388
57:16	25n14	5:11, 12, 14	17	24:36	388
59:21	15	6:3	17	24:42	388
59:21-60:22	240	6:28	33	28:16-20	244
60	240–241	9:27	217	28:18	1, 387
60:1	241	**Hosea**		28:18-19	193, 334
60:1-3	237, 238	9:7	21	28:18-20	373, 384
60:3	241	**Joel**		28:19	16, 186, 265, 291, 336, 337
61:1	18	2:28-29	21	28:19-20	387
61:1-3	240	2:30-31	29	28:20	387
61:1-62:12	240	**Micah**		**Mark**	
63:10-11	22	3:8	21	1:40-44	42n52
Jeremiah		**Habakkuk**		3:27	86
4:19-26	15	2:14	164	5:25-34, 39-42	42n52
4:23	13	**Haggai**		8:11	39n13
4:25-26	15	2:5	13	9:2	26n38
5:13	24n6	**Zechariah**		10:2-12	42n50
10:12-13	12	4:6	17, 135	12:36	21
14:13-15	24n6	6:8	13	13:11	19
23:9-40	24n6	8:23	26n32, 43n67	14:36	16
51:15-16	12	12:10	13	16:15	1, 373
Ezekiel		**New Testament**		**Luke**	
1:12, 20, 21	15	**Matthew**		1:15	26n26
2:2	15, 21	1:21	23	1:17	21
3	85	3:2	193	1:35	23
3:12, 14, 24	15	6	237	1:50	388
8:3	15	6:9-13	238	2:32	46
10:17	15	8:2-3	42n52	3:22	25n21
11:1	15	8:10-13	244	4:16-21	25n21
11:1, 5, 24	15			4:18	141
18:31	15			5:12-14	42n52
31:31, 33	15				

Scripture Index 433

5:36-38	385	14:15-17, 25-26	16	15:12	33
9:1-2	232	14:15-23	19	16:16-18	33
10:5	227	14:16	14	17:6	333
10:17-20	231	14:17	25n24	18	34
11:16, 29	39n13	14:23, 25-26	14	19:6, 11-12	33
12:12	19	14:25-26	254	20:7-12	33
15	394	15:26	25n24	26:23	46
15:2	394	15:26-27	16	28:3-8	33
15:20	394	16:1-4	19	28:25	21
15:26-28	394	16:5-16	16		
15:28	394	16:7	260	**Romans**	
15:29	394	16:7, 13-15	388	1:4	40n19
15:30-32	395	16:12-13	254	1:11	21
15:31	394	16:12-15	19	5:5	15, 287, 289
16:16	21	16:13	25n24	8:2, 4-6	16
16:18	42n50	17:20-21	288	8:6	292
24:44	46	18:14	20	8:9	16, 26n30
24:44-45	46	20:21-22	1	8:10	15
24:44-49	45	20:22	14, 16	8:11	15
24:46	46	20:22-23	19	8:11, 19, 23	13
24:46-49	1	20:31	14, 19	8:13	22
24:47	46			8:15-16	16
24:47-49	45	**Acts**		8:22-23	396
		1-7	251	8:26-27	18
John		1:2-3	46	11:25-26	215
1:1-4	14	1:4	47	12:2	26n38, 194
1:12	347	1:4-8	46	12:9	291
1:14	19	1:6	46	15:13	18
1:17, 41	19	1:8	1, 46, 47, 52, 55	15:16	18
1:32-34	19		56, 132, 165, 207, 251	15:18-19	30, 33
3:6-8	14	1:16	21	15:19	18, 40n19
3:8	395	2	258, 260	15:29	40n29
3:16	14	2:4	47	15:30	18
3:24	16	2:17-18	21, 56		
3:34	19, 252	4:25	21	**1 Corinthians**	
4:4, 13	16	8-12	251	1:1	32
4:14-16	241	8:26-40	253	1:10	32
4:23-24	26n25, 241	8:29, 39	21	1:12	32
6:44	200	9:10-19	253	1:17b	28
6:63	16	10:1-20	253	1:18	28
7:37-39	14	10:44	26n26	1:22	29
7:39	16, 19	13-28	251	2:1	39n4
11:49-53	20	13:1-3	218	2:3	28
13:34-35	289	13:4-12	33	2:4	27, 28
14:2	24n10	13:47	46	2:4-5	18, 28, 32
14:12	19, 252, 253, 332	14:3, 8-10	33	2:10	324
				2:10-16	23

2:12	23, 31	12:4-6	17	9:7	91	
2:12-15	16	12:6	289	10:5	194	
2:13	31	12:7	290	12:9	32, 293	
3:1	23	12:8-10	258	12:12	27, 29, 30, 32	
3:1-12, 11	34	12:8-11	38	13:13	287	
3:6	292	12:13	289, 290	13:14	17	
3:11	284	12:28-29	38			
3:16	35	13	37	**Galatians**		
3:16-17	23	13:11	393	3:1-5	30	
3:21	34	13:31	37	3:2-3, 14	15	
4:19	39n2	14	27, 32, 35, 36	3:5	33	
4:20	31, 40n19	14:1	36	3:8	1	
5	35	14:1-3, 12-17	22	4:6	16	
5:1-13	34	14:12, 25-26	36	5	292	
5:3-5	16	14:12b	32	5:16-18, 22-25	22	
5:6	34	14:16	34, 36	6:1	22	
5:9	35	14:20	37	6:8	22	
5:10	34	14:21-25	245	6:10	227	
5:11-13	35	14:23	36, 37, 245			
5:12	34	14:23-25	237, 238, 245	**Ephesians**		
6	35	14:24	34	1:13	25n15	
6:1-6	34	14:24-25	3, 7	2:12-17	284	
6:6	34	14:25	22, 28, 245, 388	2:18	285	
6:9	34	14:26	37	2:18, 22	25n15	
6:11	16, 34	14:26-40	36	2:19	14	
6:13-20	34	15:45	16	2:20	22	
6:17	16			2:20-22	284	
6:19	23, 35	**2 Corinthians**		3:5	22	
7	27, 35, 36	1:5-7	32	3:16	18, 47	
7:12	34, 35	1:10	32	3:24	203	
7:19	34	1:22	13	4:3	288	
8:1-13	34	3:1-3	32	4:3-4	18	
8:10	34	3:3	15, 31	4:11	215	
9:2	32	3:16	37	4:11-13	384	
9:22	293	3:17-18	23, 26n30	4:12	325	
10:8	34	3:18	38	4:13-15	393	
10:31	34	4:4	37	4:30	25n15	
10:32	34	4:5	38	5:18	18	
11:1	34, 200, 254	4:7	32, 293	6:17-18	18	
12	37, 289	4:8	291	6:18	25n22	
12-14	32, 36	4:26	38	**Philippians**		
12:1	36	5:5	13	1:6	293	
12:2	22	5:17	13	1:19	46	
12:3	16	5:18-20	38	2	293	
12:4, 7-11, 13	22	5:19	285	2:1	290	
12:4, 9, 28, 30, 31	36	8:2	132	2:3-11	230	

2:10-11	388	**1 John**		*T. Levi*	
3:3	18	4:6	25n24	9:9-10	42n51
3:12	291	**Jude**			
Colossians		1:18-19	16		
1:20-21	285	1:20	16, 25n22		
2:2	40n29	**Revelation**			
2:5	16	1:4	25n20, 26n31		
2:19	289	1:10	22		
3:23	197	2:7	22		
1 Thessalonians		2:7, 11, 17, 29	22		
1:5	31, 40n19	3:1	25n20, 26n31		
1:5-6	15	3:6, 13, 22	22		
4:8	15	4:2	22		
		4:5	25n20, 26n31		
2 Thessalonians		5:6	25n20, 26n31		
2:9	33, 40n19	5:9	396		
1 Timothy		5:9-10	388		
3:16	15	7:9	373, 387, 388		
2 Timothy		13:18	217		
1:14	25n15	17:3	22		
2:2	334	19:6	388		
3:16	21, 202	19:6-8	388		
		19:7	388		
Titus		19:9	395		
3:5-6	25n15	19:10	22		
Hebrews		21:3-4	204		
2:4	18	21:10	22		
3:7	21	22:1-5	360, 365		
6:11	40n29	22:17	22		
9:8	21				
10:15	15, 21	**Ancient Sources**			
10:22	40n29	**1 Clement**			
James		42:3	40n29		
5:19	85	**Dead Sea Scrolls**			
1 Peter		1QS			
1:2	23	3.18-4.26	25n24		
1:12	18	4QMMT			
2:10	203	CD 4:12-18	42n51		
3:14-15	287	*Jubilees*			
4:14	16	25:1	42n51		
2 Peter		41:26	35		
1:19-21	21	**Spec**			
1:21	21	3.5.29	42n51		
3:11-12	204				

www.ingramcontent.com/pod-product-compliance
Lightning Source LLC
Chambersburg PA
CBHW071950110526
44592CB00012B/1044